Reading the Bible in an Age of Crisis

Reading the Bible in an Age of Crisis

Political Exegesis for a New Day

Bruce Worthington

Fortress Press
Minneapolis

READING THE BIBLE IN AN AGE OF CRISIS

Political Exegesis for a New Day

Cover image: USA. New York City. 17 November 2011. Police arrest demonstrators of the Occupy Wall Street movement. © Christopher Anderson/ Magnum Photos

Cover design: Tory Herman

Library of Congress Cataloging-in-Publication Data

Print ISBN: 978-1-4514-8286-7

eBook ISBN: 978-1-5064-0039-6

The paper used in this publication meets the minimum requirements of American National Standard for Information Sciences — Permanence of Paper for Printed Library Materials, ANSI Z329.48-1984.

Manufactured in the U.S.A.

This book was produced using PressBooks.com, and PDF rendering was done by PrinceXML.

Contents

Contributors vii

Abbreviations ix

Part I. Global Crisis and the Practice of Biblical Studies

1. Introduction *3*
Political Exegesis for a New Day
Bruce Worthington

2. Reading the Bible with the Poor *21*
Building a Social Movement, Led by the Poor, as a United Social Force
Liz Theoharis and Willie Baptist

3. Occupying My Desk *53*
Neil Elliott

4. Solidarity! Conditions Apply *85*
Christina Petterson

Part II. Global Crisis and the First Testament

5. On the Feasibility of Subsistence Economics *109*
Roland Boer

6. Occupying the Temple in Ancient Judah — *131*
Resisting Debt Abuses, from Jerusalem to Wall Street
Matthew J. M. Coomber

7. The Global Crisis of Debt in Context — *163*
Biblical and Postcolonial Reflections on the Ideology of Empire
Robert Wafawanaka

8. Food, Power, and Ecological Hermeneutics — *191*
Reading Joseph with Monsanto
Gregory P. Fewster

Part III. Global Crisis and the Second Testament

9. Homelessness, Neoliberalism, and Jesus' "Decision" to Go Rogue — *217*
An Analysis of Matthew 4:12-25
Robert J. Myles

10. Romans 13:1-7 — *245*
With an Eye to Global Capital
Bruce Worthington

11. Occupy Solomon's Portico — *265*
On the Community of Goods in the *Longue Durée*
Jonathan Bernier

12. On Trying to Praise the Mutilated World — *285*
Reading Revelation in the Midst of Ecological Crisis
Ryan L. Hansen

13. Why Bother with Biblical Studies? — *313*
Richard Horsley

Index — *357*

Contributors

Willie Baptist	The Poverty Initiative, Union Theological Seminary
Jonathan Bernier	McMaster University
Roland Boer	University of Newcastle
Matthew J. M. Coomber	St Ambrose University
Gregory P. Fewster	University of Toronto
Ryan L. Hansen	Blakemore Church of the Nazarene
Richard Horsely	University of Massachusetts Boston
Robert J. Myles	University of Aukland
Christina Petterson	University of Newcastle
Liz Theoharis	The Poverty Initiative, Union Theological Seminary
Robert Wafawanaka	Virginia Union University
Bruce Worthington	Wycliffe College, University of Toronto

Abbreviations

BDAG	Frederick William Bauer, *A Greek English Lexicon of the New Testament*, 3rd ed., revised and edited by F.W. Danker
BI	*Biblical Interpretation: A Journal of Contemporary Approaches*
BTB	*Biblical Theology Bulletin*
CBQ	*Catholic Biblical Quarterly*
ETL	*Ephemerides theologicae louvanienses*
ICC	The International Critical Commentary
JBL	*Journal of Biblical Literature*
JNES	*Journal of Near Eastern Studies*
JSNT	*Journal for the Study of the New Testament*
JSOTSup	Journal for the Study of the Old Testament, Supplementary Series
LNTS	Library of New Testament Studies
NICOT	New International Commentary on the Old Testament
NovT	*Novum Testamentum*
NTS	*New Testament Studies*
RBL	*Review of Biblical Literature*
SBL	Society of Biblical Literature
VetTest	*Vetus Testamentum*
WBC	Word Biblical Commentary

PART I

Global Crisis and the Practice of Biblical Studies

1

Introduction

Political Exegesis for a New Day

Bruce Worthington

Political exegesis, as it is currently practiced, has been characterized by hermeneutics that were defined during the end of the Cold War, a period recognized by its clash between the "free world" and, to use Ronald Reagan's phrase, "the evil empire."[1] Now, however, in

1. Significant examples of political exegesis include the work of Warren Carter, *Matthew and Empire: Initial Explorations* (New York: T&T Clark, 2001); Brian Walsh and Sylvia Keesmaat, *Colossians Remixed: Subverting the Empire* (Downers Grove: InterVarsity, 2004); and J. D. Crossan, *God and Empire: Jesus against Rome, Then and Now* (San Francisco: HarperOne, 2006). Previous political exegesis includes the excellent work of Richard Horsley, for example, *Jesus and Empire: The Kingdom of God and the New World Disorder* (Minneapolis: Fortress Press, 2005), and of Norman K. Gottwald, *The Tribes of Yahweh: A Sociology of Religion of Liberated Israel 1250 to 1050 B.C.E.* (Maryknoll, NY: Orbis Books, 1979). In many ways, the work represented in this volume is merely an extension of their quality scholarship. Other recent pieces that deserve attention include Jörg Reiger and Kwok Pui-lan, *Occupy Religion: Theology of the Multitude* (Lanham, MD: Rowman and Littlefield, 2012) and Susan Brooks Thistlethwaite, *Occupy the Bible: What Jesus Really Said (and Did) About Money and Power* (New York: Astor and Blue Editions, 2013).

many ways, the structural antagonism of communism versus liberal democracy is a political paradigm that has been replaced by the ubiquitous universality of global capitalism, and the rise of populist movements of protest and resistance in Europe and the United States. However, as the symbolic system of global capitalism is perfected, we are beginning to see it decompose and dissolve under its own pressure, revealed in the form of various crises that have begun (unfortunately) to mark our time as an era of global crisis. Thus, the immediate task of political exegesis is the construction of a new paradigm that incorporates a deep, profound critique of our existing structural conditions, an exercise in engaged biblical interpretation that questions the unsolicited dominance of market ideology, and values the non-representable excess created by this fantasy.[2]

A more modest claim, made by Naomi Klein in her popular book *The Shock Doctrine: The Rise of Disaster Capitalism*, is that the exploitation of crisis and disaster has been the modus operandi of disaster capitalism since the Milton Friedman movement usurped Keynesian approaches to macroeconomic theory in the late sixties global marketplace.[3] Klein argues, rightfully, that catastrophic events and global disasters are an exciting market opportunity, a necessary pretext to overrule the expressed wishes of voters in the interest of economic technocrats.[4] For Klein, the emerging corporatist-state model functions on the necessary precondition of increased state surveillance, mass incarceration, shrinking civil liberties, and coercive interrogation.[5] Undergirding the disaster capitalist approach is the reified notion that if the market is not functioning properly, it is

2. Slavoj Žižek, *The Year of Dreaming Dangerously* (London: Verso, 2012), 21.
3. Naomi Klein, *The Shock Doctrine: The Rise of Disaster Capitalism* (Toronto: Vintage Canada, 2009), 9.
4. Ibid., 10.
5. Ibid., 15.

because human interference has created a market disturbance, and perturbed the delicate balance of unbridled capital exchange.

While we should appreciate the accessibility and popularity of Klein's work in the public consciousness of the North American Left, her analysis fails to identify global capital as, in some manner, the *root cause* of our contemporary global crisis, and thus instead the corporatist state model looks more like a greedy raven picking up unfortunate scraps from the wake of a roadside disaster. Such an approach deflects attention from the systemic irrationality of the capitalist system itself, and encourages sympathetic, liberal approaches to change with a view to "saving the system."[6] The cynical distance of the North American Left, with all its ironic detachment and neo-Keynesian sentimentalities, leaves untouched the fundamental structure of our current capitalist fantasy.[7] The value of a more theoretical approach to understanding our contemporary crisis can be quickly found when we begin to identify the structural necessity of crisis endemic to the global capitalist schema itself.

It has become clear that the structural crisis of capitalism is a system geared not toward the maximization of material wealth in general (held in public commons), but toward the maximization of wealth in the socially antagonistic form of private profit--specifically in the hands of those who own the means of production, distribution, and capital exchange.[8] Thus, in this present economic crisis, the poor and working classes have been instructed to "maintain effective demand" by plunging further and further into debt via credit expenditures, cheap loans, and sub-prime mortgages.[9] Between the fourth quarter of 1981 and that of 2008, credit market debt in the United States

6. Murray E. G. Smith, *Global Capitalism in Crisis: Karl Marx and the Decay of the Profit System* (Winnipeg: Fernwood, 2010), 7.
7. Slavoj Žižek, *The Sublime Object of Ideology* (London: Verso, 1989), 30.
8. Smith, *Global Capitalism in Crisis*, 6.
9. Ibid., 9.

mushroomed from 164 percent to 370 percent of total American GDP, while at roughly the same time the average real income of the bottom 90 percent of American taxpayers declined by more than 7 percent.[10] Global capital continues to prey on the crisis of poor and working peoples through more simple credit arrangements, which reveal the structural imbalance necessary for capitalist control: predatory lending rates, increased rates for automobile and home insurance, rent-to-own furniture, and roll-over loans through credit companies like Check 2 Cash, Fast Cash, or H&R Block.[11]

On a macroeconomic level, the structural condition of crisis continues to be noticed in the escalation of international debt and the growing reality of financial precarity worldwide. Through the expansion of the credit system, it is estimated that the United States owes in excess of $11 trillion dollars to global finance conglomerates, while at the same time the US government gladly took over the liabilities of the giant mortgage companies Fannie Mae and Freddy Mac—to the tune of $5.4 trillion dollars.[12] Globally, the size of the "real economy" in which goods and services are produced is estimated at $48.1 trillion dollars, while the size of the "global financial economy" (the total amount of stocks, securities, and deposits) adds up to more than $151.8 trillion dollars.[13] This means that the global financial economy (the speculative economy) has swollen to more than three times the size of the real economy (or actual monies).[14] Perhaps figures like this help to augment our definition of global capitalism as a "fantasy" that produces non-

10. Ibid.
11. Brett Williams, "Body and Soul: Profits from Poverty," in *The Insecure American: How We Got Here and What We Should Do about It*, ed. Hugh Gusterson and Catherine Besteman (Berkeley: University of California Press, 2010), 227.
12. Istvan Meszaros, *The Structural Crisis of Capital* (New York: New York University Press, 2014), 29.
13. Ibid., 28.
14. Ibid.

recognizable excesses, often in the form of what appear as contradictions to free market ideology: poverty, homelessness, and environmental destruction.

Recent shifts in the relationship between state and market indicate the predominance of the multinational corporation, at the expense of democratically elected regulatory state bodies. In their work entitled *System in Crisis: The Dynamics of Free Market Capitalism*, authors James Petras and Henry Veltmeyer highlight the growing predominance of "transnational corporations" to usurp the power of the state in times of economic uncertainty:

> International financial institutions such as the World Bank and the International Monetary Fund, through their structural adjustment policies, free trade doctrines and privatization directives, had so drained the wealth of local economies that client states were weakened and rife with corruption, as private sector elites and politicians pillaged the treasuries.[15]

Global capital, and specifically the transnational corporation, has replaced (or is replacing) the state as the dominant mode of political-economic power at the international level, and this phenomenon should change the manner in which we approach the problem of global instability.

Thus, when we begin to search for answers regarding the nature and scope of our global crises, we must bear in mind the general impotence of the state against the ubiquitous power of the global marketplace. It is the structural crisis of global capital that has provided us with a consistent narrative of instability from which we interpret our world—a perpetual "state of exception" that perversely defines economic, social, and ecological instability as *normal.* In this new state of exception provided by global capital, the proper

15. James F. Petras and Henry Veltmeyer, *System in Crisis: The Dynamics of Free Market Capitalism* (Winnipeg: Fernwood, 2003), 26.

functioning of the law is thus "unformulatable," as power exists outside of the scope of democratic control and legal order.[16] The exception proves what was there all along—that true sovereignty exists in the hands of those who control capital and define reality in terms of an embedded crisis. That global capital defines reality as a constant state of exception means that the vast majority of people are deprived of any meaningful cognitive orientation, and thus lack the means (administrative, democratic, or economic) by which to change their circumstances in any significant fashion.[17]

In recent theoretical engagements with this issue, what has become increasingly clear is that the incessant development of global capital relies on a constitutive imbalance within the system; that crises (ecological, financial, social) are far from constrictions on the global market, instead they are the "very impetus of its development."[18] Slavoj Žižek notes that in global capitalism, the structural crisis of capital is contained within the system itself, and this internal contradiction compels capital to extended permanent reproduction.[19] According to Žižek, global capital is a ubiquitous cultural system that relies on structural crisis or "failure" as a necessary feature of its own existence, a pathological imbalance that requires crisis to animate the libidinal structure of consumptive desire.

Žižek's notion is a useful one, for it identifies the structural necessity of global crises (ecological, economic, and social), which unfortunately appear as atomized, isolated phenomena within the "worldless constellation" of global capital.[20] The paradoxical feature of global capitalism is its ability to transform crisis (its very limit) into

16. Giorgio Agamben, *The Time that Remains: A Commentary on the Letter to the Romans* (Stanford: Stanford University Press, 2005), 106.
17. See Žižek, *Year of Dreaming Dangerously*, 54.
18. Žižek, *Sublime Object of Ideology*, 52.
19. Ibid.
20. Žižek, *Year of Dreaming Dangerously*, 53.

the source of its power. In these conditions, crisis is not an ancillary feature to the structure of commodity exchange, nor is it a strange coincidence, an aberration: rather the "normal" state of global capital is the permanent revolutionizing of its own conditions of existence, evident in any number of rotating crises or "disturbances immanent to the system."[21]

Biblical Interpretation in a Time of Crisis

Global capitalism, in many ways, represents a new, or novel ideological constellation—one that cannot be represented within the field of previous ideological constellations, one that requires a new lens of interpretative concerns. Within this ideological constellation, biblical interpretation does not remain immanent to itself, but is fashioned by the goals, expectations, concerns, and dialectical tension(s) established by global capital, in its diverse forms. It would be remiss to call global capital a hermeneutical lens in a formal manner, as it lacks one single methodological principle; however, global capital now appears to function in what Michel Foucault might call an internal regime of power, which means that it serves, among other things, to organize biblical interpretation in terms of intelligibility and coherence to its ends.[22] Within the discourse of biblical interpretation, it is specifically a question of what governs statements, and the way in which they govern each other, that constitutes a set of propositions that are methodologically, scientifically, or, even, theologically credible.[23] So, to suggest that contemporary biblical interpretation is not impacted by the logic of global capitalism is akin to suggesting, for instance, that we could

21. Frederic Jameson, "Postmodernism and the Market," *Social Register* 26 (1990): 279.
22. Michel Foucault, "Truth and Power," in *Power/Knowledge: Selected Interviews and Other Writings 1972–77* (New York: Pantheon, 1980), 112.
23. Ibid.

understand, let's say, Friedrich Schleiermacher apart from Romanticism, or that, perhaps, the apostle Paul was not influenced by the goals or expectations of the Roman Empire itself.

In order to appear as truthful biblical interpretation (as diverse as "truthful interpretation" may now appear), biblical studies is already linked in a circular manner with "systems of power which produce and sustain" the regulation, distribution, and operation of appropriate statements within global capital.[24] This is not to suggest, in a naïve manner, that global conglomerates purposely manipulate the proceedings of yearly society meetings, or that senior scholars are paid off by dishonest publishers to write in favorable, pro-capitalist terms. In this sense, the paranoid should recognize that there is no global conspiracy; instead, biblical studies proceeds within the context of global capital because it purposely avoids, or simply cannot address, ultimate questions of meaning.

Specifically, the modern historical critical method, and its approach to scholarly objectivity, leaves religious material as an isolated feature of the past, and this now functions as an apologetic for capital in the world. It is the perceived distance between the neutral, objective observer and his or her observed religious phenomena that keeps religious phenomena as isolated features of the past, usually viewed in terms of ancient primitivism, or naïve superstitions. In this context, questions of ultimate meaning are inappropriate to the task of scholarly biblical interpretation, and presuppositions—which are fashioned in an ideological manner—remain concealed in the interest of an imagined scholarly objectivity. So, modern biblical interpretation has proceeded, and continues to proceed in a distinctly apolitical fashion. Biblical history remains an ad hoc collection of random, isolated fragments, and, likewise, possible solutions and

24. Ibid., 133.

alternatives to our global plight remain buried somewhere in the historical mud.

Biblical scholarship of the modern ilk, in general, relies on a "unitary conception of rationality, one which takes for granted that any attentive and honest observer, unblended and undistracted by the prejudices of prior commitments to belief, would report the same data, the same facts."[25] It is the radical positivism of the Enlightenment period that has remained as a strange artifact, or ode to modernity in biblical interpretation, an approach that establishes a functional relationship between an unbiased, neutral observer and religious or biblical data that can be demonstrated as observable fact. It is the avowedly "unbiased" approach of modern biblical interpreters that sees scholarly objectivity as simply "the real world seen aright," and to a certain extent, these methodological assumptions still remain disguised, often as historical rigor.[26] Within this scholarly "world seen aright," the question of the impact of global capital on the practice of biblical interpretation is, quite simply, a question that cannot appropriately be asked. In this context, economic, environmental, or social crises cannot legitimately be included into the methodological assumptions of the modern critical historical approach, and therefore the practice of biblical interpretation continues to proceed as if the global crises created by capital are "unformulatable," an unrecognized, neglected element within the hermeneutical horizon of the interpreter.

With the advent of postmodern biblical interpretation, and the subsequent recognition of ideology as ideology, it was thought that, with the addition of new, advanced hermeneutical approaches and the rejection of modern object-centered rationalities, biblical

25. Alasdair MacIntyre, *Three Rival Versions of Moral Inquiry: Encyclopedia, Genealogy, and Tradition* (Notre Dame, IN: University of Notre Dame Press, 1990), 17.

26. Timothy Fitzgerald, *The Ideology of Religious Studies* (London: Oxford University Press, 2003), 15.

interpretation might be able to identify in a more clear manner its own relationship to ideology, and thus reveal latent, liberating elements overlooked by the false modern fascination with scholarly objectivity. Guided by the notion that all interpretation was, in some sense, a "false will to power," postmodern biblical interpretation was a rallying cry meant to establish a new relationship between the bible and subaltern political approaches.[27]

In many ways, now, postmodern biblical interpretation remains "within the confines of the pessimistic wisdom" of a failed encounter, one that seeks to maintain a distance between the interpreter and the impossible fullness of an idea.[28] In order to avoid the totalitarian consequences of full attachment to an idea, postmodern biblical interpretation has sought to consistently reassert difference as a feature of its existence, noted, perhaps, by the growing proliferation of alternative subsections at yearly academic conferences and scholarly gatherings.[29] Within this context, the exhausting proliferation of difference and the creation of nuanced scholarly identities occur in a manner that is consistent with the goals and

27. Postmodern biblical interpretation is best witnessed by a few key works, most noticeably George Aichele et al., *The Postmodern Bible: The Bible and Culture Collective* (Binghamton: Yale University Press, 1995); David Jobling et al., *The Postmodern Bible Reader* (New York: Wiley, 2001), and A. K. M. Adam, *What is Postmodern Biblical Criticism?* (Minneapolis: Fortress Press, 1995). Under the general rubric of postmodern biblical interpretation functioned a number of key sub-disciplines such as: deconstructionism, postmodern feminism, postcolonial criticism, ideological criticism, and queer biblical interpretation. Perhaps one of the first major attempts at postmodern re-readings of biblical material was Elizabeth Schüssler Fiorenza's landmark work, *In Memory Of Her: A Feminist Theological Reconstruction of Christian Origins* (Hertford NC: Crossroad, 1994). Other, more recent attempts at postmodern biblical interpretation include Moore, *Poststructuralism and the New Testament*, 1994; Jerry Camery-Hoggatt, *Irony in Mark's Gospel: Text and Subtext* (Cambridge: Cambridge University Press, 2005); Aichele, *Sign, Text, and Scripture: Semiotics and the Bible,* 1997.
28. Slavoj Žižek, *The Ticklish Subject* (London: Verso, 1999), 134. The death of postmodern biblical interpretation was, perhaps, first witnessed by many of us in attendance for Stephen Moore's excellent address "Past the Post: The Slight Rise and Precipitous Decline of Postmodernism in Biblical Studies" at the 2014 Society of Biblical Literature Annual Meeting, San Diego California (November 24, 2014).
29. Žižek, *Ticklish Subject*, 135.

expectations of global capital, developing a scholarly apparatus that cannot address fundamental questions of ultimate meaning. This confirms the insight of Alain Badiou, whose perspective into the dynamics of capital can be appropriately applied to the practice of postmodern biblical interpretation:

> Capital demands a permanent creation of subjective and territorial identities in order for its principle of movement to homogenize its space of action; identities, moreover, that never demand anything but the right to be exposed in the same way as others to the uniform prerogatives of the market.[30]

Here, the dynamics of global capital does not necessarily limit the proliferation of alternative scholarly voices, nor does capital necessarily produce violent scholarly hegemony or academic monoculture, or quash minority voices. Instead, global capital produces scholarly subjectivities with impressive variety, a context in which almost any interpretive approach is now valid, except for the approach that challenges the patron of all interpretation itself—global capital.

Now, global capital functions not only as a simple means of monetary exchange, but rather as a universal system of meaning, one that affects the very fibers of ourselves, and thus fashions the goals, expectations, insights, and practices of scholarly interpretation. Due to the manner in which global capital proceeds as a universal system of meaning, there is no nook or cranny within biblical interpretation that remains immanent to itself. Recognizing global capital as a universal system of meaning in a formal manner does not negate its impact within the practice of biblical scholarship, nor does raising global capital to the level of hermeneutical awareness change the cold

30. Alain Badiou, *Saint Paul: The Foundation of Universalism*, Cultural Memory in the Present (Stanford: Stanford University Press, 1994), 14.

fact that capital is, already, "in all and through all" (to borrow the language of Eph. 4:6).

In many ways, this is a perverse, yet stimulating turn in biblical scholarship itself. All of a sudden, the old fault lines of liberal Protestant interpretation versus conservative evangelical interpretation are, quite simply, irrelevant—all exist within the same machinery and apparatus. Likewise, biblical interpretation that previously sought to fashion an authentic account of one's relationship to the state, most notably in the popular "(insert biblical character here) versus empire" genre, should begin to revise this relationship, given the irrelevance of the state within the horizon of global capital. The ubiquity of global capital has established new fault lines that demand new models of interpretation—ones that include the contradictions and crises that capital creates—in order to address and provide meaning to those of us who suffer under these various, rotating crises.

The goal of this volume is not to provide voice to a particular shade of difference, we are demanding more than just another voice to add to the mix. Nor should we fall into the trap of "finding capital everywhere in the past," thus reifying the concept of capital in an anachronistic manner—as if it were always there. This volume represents a robust attempt to include capital, and the rotating crises within which the interpreter exists, formally into the field of biblical interpretation, so that biblical interpretation may become meaningful within the precarious context of global crisis. It may have been a simpler task to organize the volume around specific issues of crisis—a volume for ecology, a volume for debt, a volume for this or that other aspect of crisis—but we thought that these issues in isolation would not highlight the universal manner in which global capital proceeds. Organizing discussions of various crises together perhaps helps us to see these crises as a whole, and not as unrelated, or isolated phenomena.

The volume is organized into three main sections. In Part 1, Global Crisis and the Practice of Biblical Studies, contributors give thought to some of the implications of global capital to the task of biblical studies as a discipline itself. In the lead article, "Reading the Bible through a Hermeneutic of the Poor," the Reverend Liz Theoharis and Willie Baptist (both of the Poverty Initiative at Union Theological Seminary) discuss the implications of Jesus' statement in Matthew 26:11 that "the poor will be with you always," not only in terms of its reception history among scholars of privilege, but also with regard to how the verse functions within poor populations in America today. Such a nuanced reading is not a warm, fuzzy academic affinity with the poor; rather, each scholar has spent time suffering under the crisis of capital, in order to develop a methodology that they now call "Reading the Bible with the Poor." The goal of such a reading is to begin to see the poor as legitimate readers and interpreters of biblical material, and to include economic catastrophe into the hermeneutic lens of our contemporary situation.

Following the excellent work of Theoharis and Baptist, Fortress Press's own Neil Elliott addresses the relationship between academic publishing and global capital—not only as that relationship fashions the discourse of biblical studies, but also as it fails to address fundamental issues of materiality and economic crisis. Writing from the perspective of an insider who is knowledgeable about the apparatus of scholarly publishing, Elliott addresses the role and function of religious information as it pertains to denominations, academic presses, journals, seminaries, and university classrooms. Elliott forcefully argues that biblical scholarship itself is built to withstand, deflect, and generally contain mass social change, suggesting that, in many ways, biblical interpretation needs to question the ideological manner in which the term "religion" now functions—mostly as a means to ignore questions of materiality and deflect the communal task of economic justice.

In the third essay in Part 1, Christina Petterson (University of Newcastle) challenges the recent "turn toward the individual" in postmodern biblical interpretation. Petterson notes that in many ways (autobiographical criticism, personal criticism, etc.), the individual has become the ultimate horizon in postcolonial biblical studies, and this individualizing tendency is noticeably consistent with the logic of global capital. Here, what appear as legitimate contextual horizons in postcolonial interpretation include one's own individual feelings, existential displacement, hybrid ethnic origins, and other, exotic types of self-representation. However, due to the fragmentation of social life after the rise of global capital, neglected features within postcolonial biblical interpretation include the obvious—collective socioeconomic relations, and all that cannot be represented by the individual. Petterson's work is a strong challenge to postcolonial interpretation, which she views as a discourse that can too easily be accommodated within diverse logic of global capitalism. The answer? In returning to the difficult task of history, we might begin to re-conceptualize ancient collectivity beyond the individual, and reveal all that was negated by our current, individualist ideological constellation.

The essays in Part 2, Global Crisis and the First Testament, address various global crises through reflection on the Hebrew Bible. The section is anchored by the excellent work of Roland Boer (University of Newcastle), who (given the crisis of food shortage and the need for alternative methods of food production) proposes a detailed model of subsistence farming, based on the practices of farmers in the southern Levant (ancient Israel). Boer does not seek to prooftext the practice of subsistence farming through a cheap appeal to ancient Israelite farming practices; however, by exploring the reality of subsistence farming in the southern Levant, Boer is, likewise, able to explore the real possibility of subsistence farming in our contemporary context of global food shortage and corporate food control.

Following Boer, Matthew Coomber (St. Ambrose University) addresses the issue of debt and debt abuses in the Hebrew Bible from the context of the economic collapse in America after 2008. After a lengthy, helpful introduction to the concept of debt and the "gamble" of international capitalism, Coomber highlights a number of instances and controls over the phenomenon of debt in the Hebrew Bible (see Isa. 5:8-10 and Mic. 2:1–4, for example). Coomber carefully avoids establishing an equivocal relationship between Israelite economic practices and contemporary global capitalism; however, Coomber is able to compare the Assyrian extraction of Israelite resources to contemporary forms of global exploitation (Tunisia is his case study). In all cases, according to Coomber, debt functions a means of social exploitation and control, and requires prophetic engagement to limit its obvious abuses. Here is a great example of a biblical scholar familiar with the contemporary practice of debt exploitation carefully using this expertise to understand and highlight the mechanism of debt in ancient Assyrian-Israelite relations.

Continuing with the theme of debt and displacement in the Hebrew Bible, Robert Wafawanaka (Virginia Union University) explores the phenomenon of land exploitation and the "race for Africa" through the story of Naboth's stolen vineyard in 1 Kings 21:1-16. This essay poignantly highlights similarities between the two narratives of land exploitation and exegetes the text in a manner that fully identifies with the practice of land exploitation in both ancient Israel and modern-day Africa. Wafawanaka argues that 1 Kings offers a useful window into the unjust world of land seizure, and in this manner 1 Kings and the story of Naboth resonate with many Africans like Wafawanaka, who have suffered under similar social and financial injustices.

To end Part 2, Gregory Fewster (University of Toronto) charts the relationship between food production and political control, first in the narrative of the patriarch Joseph, and secondly through the multinational contemporary food conglomerate Monsanto. In this innovate piece, Fewster highlights similarities between control of ancient foodstuffs, political power, and corporate food production. Fewster offers a refreshing critique of contemporary ecological hermeneutics as a naïve attempt to "save the system," and suggests ways in which the practices of Monsanto are eerily similar to the dream of Joseph in Genesis 37:1–11.

In Part 3, Global Crisis and the Second Testament, scholars address key topics related to the various crises created by global capital. In the first essay, Robert Myles (University of Auckland) charts the crisis of homelessness through the homelessness of Jesus as outlined in Matthew 4:12–25. Here, Myles suggests that (false) modern neoliberal perspectives on homelessness do not allow for a proper interpretation of Jesus' own itinerant travel in the Gospel of Matthew. Popular capitalist interpretation, clouded by high Christology, cannot but see Jesus' homelessness as a personal choice, and therefore fails to understand Jesus himself as one who suffers as a homeless person, one under significant political threat due to his relationship to John the Baptist.

My own essay, "Romans 13:1–7: With an Eye to Global Capital," applies Gadamerian and Habermasian insight into the political plight of Paul in Romans 13:1–7. I suggest that here, Paul understands "ideology as ideology," yet can do nothing but continue to pay his taxes—a political deadlock many of us continue begrudgingly to reflect. Though Paul recognizes the Roman authorities "do not bear the sword for nothing," we are reminded to submit to authority on earth, as it reflects authority in heaven (a nasty, complicated political insight). I conclude by suggesting that any biblical interpretation or application of this passage that ignores the reality of global capital, now, as an "authority" is irrelevant; true authority in the world now exists in the hands of global capitalists, not the modern state apparatus. Interpretation of this passage should change in kind.

In the third essay, Jonathan Bernier (McMaster University) argues that just as Tahir Square and Zucotti Park became places for resistance in the recent Occupy movement, so too did Solomon's Portico become a place in which early Christian believers sought resistance to universalizing powers (see Acts 4:11; 5:12-13).[31] Using the methodology of Alain Badiou and the "Event," Bernier graciously charts the tale of competing universalisms—one of the Occupy movement and the other of global capital, as parallel to the competing universalisms of the early Christian movement and the Roman Empire. This saves for us, in the end, the progression of an idea that we might call communism.

Finally, Ryan L. Hansen (Blakemore Church of the Nazarene) is appropriately focused on the book of Revelation, highlighting the reality of ecological catastrophe within a world currently dominated by global capital. Here, Revelation is significant in that its author, John, presents an alternative vision where cosmic reality, known as crisis, or "an ordeal" (Revelation 1:9; 2:9, 10, 22; 7:14), is fragmented and dissolves. Thus, John's call to the seven churches should be seen as establishing local pockets of resistance to the false rhetoric of Rome, and provides a pattern of resistance for contemporary interpretation, within the context of ecological catastrophe.

31. As an aside, it should be noted that the idea for this volume was first proposed to me by Jonathan Bernier, and he is to be credited for the initial inertia behind the book.

The volume is appropriately rounded out by a postscript by preeminent political exegete Richard Horsley. Such a decision reflects our concern to tie contemporary political exegesis with the work of Richard Horsley and others, many of whom have courageously attempted to intersect biblical material with our current political situation. While the political horizon continues to change, in many ways our work is merely an extension of a project that began long ago, with the work of Norman Gottwald, Horsley, and others. One may also notice the strange inclusion of the theological voice within the vision of some of the essays. This is by design. There was a time when the theological voice remained separate from the practice of biblical interpretation. We, however, we have found it useful to include the theological perspective in the practice of political exegesis, as a possible site of resistance. So, in many ways, we are picking up the task of political biblical exegesis, but in ways that explicitly identify global capitalism as the new site of ideological control. In this manner, the Bible provides exciting opportunities for resistance and creative mechanisms to deal with rotating crises, all of which profoundly affect the manner in which we read and exegete biblical material.

2

Reading the Bible with the Poor

Building a Social Movement, Led by the Poor, as a United Social Force

Liz Theoharis and Willie Baptist

Biblical texts have long been used to justify the inevitability of poverty and inequality and to provide religious sanction for the dispossession of the majority for the benefit of the few. In particular, Jesus' saying that "the poor will be with you always" (Matt. 26:11, parallels in Mark 14:7 and John 12:8) has been interpreted either to establish that God condones poverty or that although God condemns poverty, it is an unfortunate but unalterable reality of the human condition.[1] For many people, the fact that Jesus is the one saying this

1. Regular Google searches of "the poor will be with you always" reveal the omnipresence of this biblical missive (728,000 mentions on one search) as well as a debate emerging on the role of Jesus, the Bible, and faith communities in the eradication and amelioration of poverty. Typically, the entry is a personal assertion, reflection, blog post, or series of questions on whether this statement from Matthew 26:11, John 12:11, and Mark 14:7 is saying: a) that we can never end poverty, b) that it is the role of Christians, not the government, to try

statement about the "poor" and that he uses the word "always" makes the meaning clear and unequivocal: they may not know where this line falls in the biblical story or the context of the Gospel of Matthew, but they posit that this biblical statement establishes poverty as perpetual and inevitable. Even for those more versed in the Gospel of Matthew, the use of this passage still results in a similar conclusion. For some, Jesus and the poor are juxtaposed in Matthew 26, and the point of the saying is that attending to Jesus and the spiritual realm is rendered more important than concern for the poor. For others, Jesus' discussion of the ointment and his invoking of Deuteronomy 15 (see below) suggest that money and/or charity are the biblical solution to poverty, which makes the wealthy the ones with agency in this story.

However, a more robust contextual exegesis of Matthew 26:1-16, with an emphasis on verses 6-13 in their intertextuality with Deuteronomy 15:1-11, reveals a critique of charity or euergetism and the ancient slavery-based Roman imperial economy. Insight into this intertextuality shows how Jesus, his disciples, and various writings the New Testament apply an extant biblical theology of justice taken from the Hebrew Scriptures.[2] The Roman Empire, like earlier empires, was a highly class-stratified economy. Every imperial

to care for the poor, or c) that Jesus rather than the poor should be our concern, as well as other common interpretations of this passage. There are various interpretations that support this statement including those discussed in: Ulrich Luz, *Matthew 21–28*, trans. J. E. Crouch, Hermeneia (Minneapolis: Fortress Press, 2005), 340; Craig Evans, *Matthew*, New Cambridge Bible Commentary (Cambridge: Cambridge University Press, 2012), 426; Grant R. Osbourne, *Matthew*, Zondervan Exegetical Commentary on the New Testament (Grand Rapids, MI: Zondervan, 2010), 951; Gail O'Day, "John," in *Women's Bible Commentary*, ed. Carol A. Newsom and Sharon H. Ringe (Louisville: Westminster John Knox, 1998), 387–88; Amy-Jill Levine, "Matthew," in *Women's Bible Commentary*, ed. Carol A. Newsom and Sharon H. Ringe (Louisville: Westminster John Knox, 1998), 349.

2. In order to understand the potential relationship between Deuteronomy (especially ch. 15) and Matthew 26 (especially v. 11 about the poor), one must first explore the concept of intertextuality in general. Richard Hays proposes seven criteria (availability, volume, recurrence, thematic coherence, historical plausibility, and history of interpretation, satisfaction) to determine the potentiality of echoes in Scripture (*Echoes of Scripture in the Letters of Paul* [New Haven, CT: Yale University Press, 1993]). We are confident that Deuteronomy 15 and Matthew 26 agree with Hays' criteria for intertextual echoes.

conquest of oppressed peoples added to the growing ranks of the impoverished classes and accumulated more wealth for the ruling slave-holding strata.[3] The hegemonic theology that found expression in the different religious belief systems of the time upheld a set of values and views that justified cruelly unjust societies.[4] In contrast,

3. One such example of this comes from an account of the dispossession of the Italians as told by Appian: "The rich had got possession of the greater part of the undivided land. They trusted in the conditions of the time, that these possessions would not be again taken from them, and bought, therefore, some of the pieces of land lying near theirs, and belonging to the poor, with the acquiescence of their owners, and took some by force, so that they now were cultivating widely extended domains, instead of isolated fields. Then they employed slaves in agriculture and cattle-breeding, because freemen would have been taken from labor for military service. The possession of slaves brought them great gain, inasmuch as these, on account of their immunity from military service, could freely multiply and have a multitude of children. Thus the powerful men drew all wealth to themselves, and all the land swarmed with slaves. The Italians, on the other hand, were always decreasing in number, destroyed as they were by poverty, taxes, and military service. Even when times of peace came, they were doomed to complete inactivity, because the rich were in possession of the soil, and used slaves instead of freemen in the tilling of it" (Appian, *Bell. civ. I*.7 [White, LCL]).

4. There are many expressions of the imperial theology and the system of euergetism and patronage that helped uphold that theology and justified the slave-based economy. Some come from Caesar Augustus himself who, although he was the richest person in the world and responsible for the dispossession and poverty of the majority in the empire, claimed to be a savior of the poor:
"To the Roman plebs I paid out three hundred sesterces per man in accordance with the will of my father, and in my own name in my fifth consulship I gave four hundred sesterces apiece from the spoils of war; a second time, moreover, in my tenth consulship I paid out of my own patrimony four hundred sesterces per man by way of bounty, and in my eleventh consulship I made twelve distributions of food from grain bought at my own expense, and in the twelfth year of my tribunician power I gave for the third time four hundred sesterces to each man. These largesses of mine reached a number of persons never less than two hundred and fifty thousand. In the eighteenth year of my tribunician power, as consul for the twelfth time, I gave to three hundred and twenty thousand of the city plebs sixty denarii apiece. In the colonies of my soldiers, as consul for the fifth time, I gave one thousand sesterces to each man from the spoils of war; about one hundred and twenty thousand men in the colonies received this triumphal largesse. When consul for the thirteenth time I gave sixty denarii apiece to the plebs who were then receiving public grain; these were a little more than two hundred thousand persons." (*Res gest. divi Aug.* 3.15)
Aristotle also writes philosophical justification for poverty and inequality:
"If one is a better man than the other, he thinks he has a right to more, for goodness deserves the larger share. And similarly when one is more useful than the other: if a man is of no use, they say, he ought not to have an equal share, for it becomes a charity and not a friendship at all, if what one gets out of it is not enough to repay one's trouble. For men think that it ought to be in a friendship as it is in a business partnership, where those who contribute more capital take more of the profits. On the other hand the needy or inferior person takes the opposite view: he maintains that it is the part of a good friend to assist those in need; what is the use (he argues)

as Richard A. Horsley has argued, the Hebrew Bible depicted God's will and God's justice in the context of, *and in opposition to* the unjust theology, poverty, and inhumanity of the empires of those times.[5]

Interpreting and contextualizing Matthew 26:11 within a biblical theology of justice also attributes a leading agency to the poor, and promotes the primacy of material security and prosperity for all humanity. In this verse, Jesus reacts strongly to the disciples. His words echo Deuteronomy 15:4 ("there will be no one in need among you"), so Matthew 26:11 is to be read not as a prediction, [6] but as a warning regarding the perils of disobedience to God's

of being friends with the good and great if one is to get nothing out of it?" (Aristotle, *Eth. Nic.* 1163a [Rackham, LCL])

One other quote comes from Plutarch and speaks to how the imperial theology was imposed among the people in an effort to instill inequality:

"The masses are more hostile to a rich man who does not give them a share of his private possessions than to a poor man who steals from the public funds, for they think the former's conduct is due to arrogance and contempt of them, but the latter's to necessity. First, then, let the gifts be made without bargaining for anything; for so they surprise and overcome the recipients more completely; and secondly they should be given on some occasion which offers a good and excellent pretext, one which is connected with the worship of a god and leads the people to piety; for at the same time there springs up in the minds of the masses a strong disposition to believe that the deity is great and majestic, when they see the men whom they themselves honour and regard as great so liberally and zealously vying with each other in honouring the divinity." (Plutarch, *Mor.* 279-81 [De Lacy and Einarson, LCL])

5. "At the center of the Pentateuch/Torah, both substantively and as the organizing structure, is the Mosaic Covenant. From Exodus 19 through the rest of Exodus, all of Leviticus, and up to Numbers 10, Israel is encamped at Mount Sinai receiving the Covenant and covenantal law. The whole book of Deuteronomy is then a 'second (covenantal) law' taught by Moses as the Israelites prepare to enter the land. . . . The historical books include key passages that summarize and elaborate the political-economic structure of the monarchs, including how they replicate the structure of ancient Near Eastern empires. The earliest oracles of the classical prophets pronounce God's indictment and punishment of kings and their officers for violating the principles of the Covenant and the economic rights of the people. . . . That Jesus was every bit as concerned with economic issues as the Hebrew prophets has often gone unnoticed. The biblical tradition of covenantal principles and mechanisms continued into the time of Jesus. This can be seen particularly in the covenant renewal and extensive covenantal teachings evident in some of the Dead Sea Scrolls. The renewal of the Mosaic Covenant was also central to Jesus' proclamation of the kingdom of God." Richard Horsley, *Covenant Economics: A Biblical Vision of Justice for All* (Louisville: Westminster John Knox, 2009), xix–xx.
6. The verbs used are not in the future tense. The disciples have (*echete* meaning "you have" in the present tense) the poor around—the Jesus-movement is based among them—but time is running out for Jesus (*ou pantōtē echētē* meaning "you do not always have" me).

commandments (resulting in poverty and inequality) and even as Jesus' call to the disciples to continue to take up the struggles of the poor for economic and social justice even after his death.[7] That the woman who anoints Jesus in this passage is not named, that she does not follow euergetistic patterns of benefaction, that Jesus reacts so strongly to the practice of buying and selling suggested by the disciples, and that later in the passion narrative, the potter's field donation of money for the poor (from the blood money offered to Judas by the temple elites) is treated negatively—all point to a strong critique of money, charity, and hegemonic economics on the part of the Evangelist.

Unpacking the context and implications of this consequential passage is an appropriate and important part of a larger exegetical and political project of centering the interpretation of the poor themselves. Located at the intersection of poverty and the New Testament, we seek in this essay to examine how the Bible has been used to justify and condemn poverty and how poor people are both coming up against this use of the Bible and simultaneously using the Bible in their own quest to end poverty. By gathering and analyzing the perspectives of Poverty Initiative Poverty Scholars (grassroots anti-poverty organizers and leaders who are working to build a social movement to end poverty, led by the poor as a united force), we offer these interpretations as revealing, legitimate, and important for scholars, religious leaders, and others in our communities to hear. Finally, we suggest that the messiah Jesus is a leader of a social

7. "The disciples' concern for the poor is by no means incorrect. . . . Jesus' statement 'you always have the poor among you' (v 11) must not be taken to mean that as a consequence one need not worry about them or that all attempts to ameliorate the condition of the poor are ill-founded and futile. This cannot be made clearer than by citing the full text of Deuteronomy 15:11 . . . The ongoing presence of the poor does not provide an excuse to ignore them and their plight, but, quite the contrary, it provides the ongoing opportunity and stimulus to help them" (Donald A. Hagner, *Matthew 14–28*, WBC 33 [Dallas: Word Books, 1995], 759).

movement who works to reign in God's kingdom and end slavery, debts, and poverty on earth.

This article is a partnership between two leaders of a growing movement of the poor who have worked closely together for over twenty years: the Rev. Dr. Liz Theoharis and Willie Baptist. I, Liz, am both a trained interpreter of biblical texts and a committed activist in a growing effort to end poverty. I am also a mother of two and an ordained minister in the Presbyterian Church (USA). For the past twenty years I have been organizing, educating, and uniting the poor aimed at building a movement to end poverty. I first got involved with the National Union of the Homeless and the Kensington Welfare Rights Union in the early 1990s, helping to weave a network of poor people's organizations dedicated to using a human rights framework to confront poverty in the late 1990s and early 2000s. Through this organizing work, I returned to my religious roots, consulting for the National Council of Churches and other mainline Protestant denominations that were struggling with new interpretations and questions about the Bible's message regarding poverty. I received my PhD from Union Theological Seminary in 2014, where I wrote my dissertation, "'Will the Poor Be With You Always?': Towards a Methodological Approach to Reading the Bible with the Poor."[8] In my work, I concentrate on poor people's actions and theologies in the twenty-first century, inspired by Jesus, as part of a loosened and contemporary biblical canon and in concert with prominent theologians and biblical scholars. I seek to systematically document the stories, lessons, and interpretations of poor people organizing to end poverty in order to illuminate implications for our churches and to chart the development of a liberation theology for the United States for the twenty-first century.

8. Available at http://dx.doi.org/10.7916/D85Q4T7D.

I, Willie, have been an educator and organizer amongst the poor for over forty years. I first got involved in politics as a youth participant in the 1965 Watts Rebellion. I was an organizer with the Black Student Union at Pepperdine University from 1965 to 1969 and founder of Operation Cereal Bowl in Watts in 1971. I was an organizer and shop steward with the United Steel Workers, the Texas Farmworkers, Jobs with Peace, and the National Union of the Homeless. I have lived a life of poverty, spending time on the streets of Philadelphia, homeless. I served as the education director for the Kensington Welfare Rights Union for ten years and was founder and co-coordinator of the University of the Poor. I am a father of three and have 3 grandchildren. I was raised in the Baptist Church, preached my first sermon at age twelve, and was planning to become a Baptist preacher but got pulled more deeply into freedom and anti-poverty movements.

Both of us helped found the Poverty Initiative at Union Theological Seminary and it's umbrella the Kairos Center for Religions, Rights, and Social Justice; Liz serves as the Co-Director of Kairos and Coordinator of the Poverty Initiative and Willie as the Coordinator the Poverty Scholarship and Leadership Development for the Kairos Center and Poverty Initiative. The genealogy of the Kairos Center traces back through efforts of the poor to organize themselves across racial and other dividing lines into a united, leading, new, and unsettling force,[9] including the National Union

9. Much of this genealogy and the lessons and influences from this work are documented in a series of articles written by leaders of the Kensington Welfare Rights Union and Poor People's Economic Human Rights Campaign, including: Willie Baptist and Noelle Damico, "Building the New Freedom Church of the Poor," *Cross Currents* 55, no. 3 (2005): 352–63; William Baptist and Mary Bricker Jenkins, "The Movement to End Poverty in the United States," in *Economic Rights in Canada and the United States*, eds. Rhoda E. Howard-Hassmann and Claude E. Welch, Jr. (Philadelphia: University of Pennsylvania Press, 2006), 103–20; William Baptist, Mary Bricker-Jenkins, and Monica Dillon, "Taking the Struggle on the Road: The New Freedom Bus—Freedom from Unemployment, Hunger and Homelessness," *Journal of Progressive Human Services* 10, no. 2 (1999): 7–29; Willie Baptist and Cheri Honkala, "A New

of the Homeless, the National Welfare Rights Organization, the "Redneck Army" of black and white Appalachian miners, Bonus marchers, and the Southern Tenant Farmers Union.[10] We have exchanged lessons with social movements of the poor globally including the Landless Workers Movement of Brazil, the Assembly of the Poor in Thailand, the Indian Farmers Movement, and the South African Shackdwellers Movement.[11] Our work has drawn special direction from Martin Luther King's Poor People's Campaign and its effort to bring together Native American poor, Chicano poor, sanitation workers, poor women, and poor white Appalachians on the basis of what they have in common. Since our founding in 2003-2004, we have been working to live into our mission of raising up generations of religious and community leaders dedicated to building a social movement to end poverty, led by the poor. Through three national poverty truth commissions, two leadership schools, eleven poverty immersion courses, ten faculty-sponsored semester-long courses, sixteen one-day seminars, five books and numerous written religious and theological resources, nine strategic dialogues, six intensive study programs and numerous events, symposia, and exchanges with global grassroots and religious leaders, the we have established a wide and deep network of community and religious leaders, spanning across thirty states and seventeen countries around the world. Since launching our *Pedagogy of the Poor* National Tour in 2011, based on a book written by Willie and Jan Rehmann, we have personally witnessed the breadth and depth of this network by

and Unsettling Force" *The Other Side Magazine* (2003): 38–39; David Wagner, *What's Love Got to Do with It? A Critical Look at American Charity* (New York: New Press, 2000); Guida West, *The National Welfare Rights Movement: The Social Protest of Poor Women* (Westport, CO: Praeger, 1981); David Zucchino, *Myth of the Welfare Queen* (New York: Scribner, 1997).

10. These movements are the same ones used in the contextual Bible studies we have held within the Poverty Initiative.
11. For a list of key Poverty Initiative partners see http://povertyinitiative.org/partners.

connecting with the heroes and heroines fighting on the frontlines of the struggle to end poverty in thirty states of the U.S.[12]

The Curse of Poverty

Jesus' ministry is central in the New Testament. In Luke 4:18–19, Jesus inaugurated his ministry by reading from the prophet Isaiah,

> The spirit of the Lord is upon me; therefore he has anointed me. He has sent me to bring glad tidings to the poor, to proclaim liberty to captives, recovery of sight to the blind and release to prisoners, to announce a year of favor from the Lord.

Further, in Luke 6:20–24, Jesus says,

> Blessed are you who are poor for yours is the kingdom of God.
>
> Blessed are you who hunger now, for you will be satisfied.
>
> Blessed are you who weep now, for you will laugh.
>
> Blessed are you when men hate you, when they exclude you and insult you and reject your name as evil, because of the Son of Man.
>
> Rejoice in that day and leap for joy, because great is your reward in Heaven. For that is how their fathers treated the prophets.
>
> But woe to you who are rich, for you have already received your comfort.

In 1967, the Rev. Dr. Martin Luther King Jr., said, "The curse of poverty has no justification in our age. The time has come for us to civilize ourselves by the total, direct, and immediate abolition of poverty."[13] Committing himself as Jesus did to bring about a

12. Willie Baptist and Jan Rehmann, *Pedagogy of the Poor: Building the Movement to End Poverty* (New York: Teachers College Press, 2011).
13. Martin Luther King Jr., *Where Do We Go From Here: Chaos or Community?* (New York: Harper and Row, 1967; repr. Boston: Beacon, 2010), 175. Citations refer to the Beacon edition.

revolution of values of preaching good news to the poor and in bearing the cross, Dr. King vowed,

> I choose to identify with the underprivileged. I choose to identify with the poor. I choose to give my life for the hungry. I choose to give my life for those who have been left out. . . . This is the way I'm going. If it means suffering a little bit, I'm going that way. . . . If it means dying for them, I'm going that way.[14]

While King's words are passionate and moving, poverty in the United States and across the world has deepened since they were preached nearly fifty years ago. Since the unfolding of the "Great Recession" in 2007–8, four in five Americans live in danger of falling into poverty and/or joblessness, and recent reports reveal that one in two Americans are poor or low-income (living at less than 200 percent of the poverty line).[15] Ten thousand homes are foreclosed every day in communities across the United States. Nearly 40 percent of Americans between the ages of twenty-five and sixty will experience at least one year below the official poverty line; half of all American children will at some point during their childhood reside in a household that uses food stamps for a period of time.[16]

Poverty manifests itself in myriad ways in the United States: the many poor whites, Latinos, Asians, and Blacks who suffered the most devastation and death by Hurricane Katrina in 2005; the thousands of families displaced in New York, New Jersey, and Connecticut by Hurricane Sandy in 2012; the hundreds of thousands whose water has been shut off in Detroit since the year 2000 who are now having their children taken away because of their poverty and lack of running

14. Vincent Harding, *Martin Luther King: The Inconvenient Hero* (Maryknoll, NY: Orbis Books, 1995), 58.
15. Associated Press, "4 in 5 Americans Live in Danger of Falling into Poverty, Joblessness," July 13, 2013, http://usnews.nbcnews.com/_news/2013/07/28/19738595-ap-4-in-5-americans-live-in-danger-of-falling-into-poverty-joblessness.
16. Mark Rank, "Poverty is Mainstream in America," *New York Times*, November 2, 2013.

water; the thousands of people who have to share heart attack medicine in New Jersey, do not get chemotherapy in Vermont, or are denied Medicaid in Mississippi and North Carolina and thus cannot afford medicine, their health care deductibles, or health insurance premiums even after the Affordable Care Act of 2013; and native-born and immigrants who pick tomatoes in Florida for poverty wages and sometimes in slave rings, even in the twenty-first-century United States. Poverty is made visible when children die in fires in Philadelphia because of fire station brownouts; when families in West Virginia lose their homes and family burial grounds because of mountaintop removal; when homeless citizens are buried in unidentified mass graves in potter's field in New York and many other states across the country; and when millions of workers are paid too little to be able to adequately feed, house, or clothe their families across the United States.[17]

The issue of poverty appears throughout the Bible: the Old and New Testaments are full of references to how we are to respond to poverty and injustice. Jim Wallis of *Sojourners Magazine* surveyed key biblical themes, noting,

> in the Old Testament, the suffering of the poor was the second most prominent theme. . . . In the NT we found that one out of every 16 verses was about the poor. In the Gospels, it was one out of every ten, in Luke, one of every seven, and in James, one of every five verses.[18]

17. These anecdotes come from our experience organizing and educating among the poor in the United States for the last decades. There are organizations addressing these issues including slavery and poverty wages for farm work in Florida and the American South with the Coalition of Immokalee Workers (ciw-online.org), universal healthcare and people's budgeting in Vermont with the Vermont Worker's Center (workerscenter.org), families fighting foreclosure, eviction and the privatization of water and other public utilities in Detroit with the Michigan Welfare Rights Organization (mwro.org), low-wage workers fighting for poverty's end in Maryland with the United Workers (unitedworkers.org), poor and working people's issues including cuts to public services, education, and wages with the Media Mobilizing Project in Philadelphia (mediamobilizing.org), and residents fighting against Mountaintop Removal and strip mining and its ecological impact in West Virginia with Stop Mountaintop Removal.

Common throughout the New and Old Testaments are texts addressing the redistribution of wealth and the abolition of poverty: "Is this not the fast I choose: to loose the bonds of injustice, to undo the thongs of the yoke, to let the oppressed go free, and to break every yoke? Is it not to share your bread with the hungry, and bring the homeless poor into your house; when you see the naked, to cover them?" (Isa. 58:6-7); "[God has] lifted up the lowly; he has filled the hungry with good things" (Luke 1:52-53); "For I was hungry and you gave me food, I was thirsty and you gave me something to drink . . . Truly I tell you just as you did it to one of the least of these who are members of my family, you did it to me" (Matt. 25:35, 40).

Yet, while passages like these are common, many people fixate on a small handful of passages: "The poor will always be with you" (Matthew 26:11) (as discussed above); "If you do not work, you shall not eat" (2 Thess. 3:10); "For to all those who have, more will be given, and they will have an abundance; but from those who have nothing, even what they have will be taken away" (Matt. 25:29). These verses above are regularly cited to assert that poverty cannot be ended and that if God wanted to end poverty, God would do so.[19]

18. Jim Wallis, *Faith Works: Lessons from the Life of an Activist Preacher* (New York: Random House, 2000), 71. Jim Wallis is the Founder of *Sojourners Magazine* and community in Washington, DC. He is one of the most vocal evangelical voices on poverty in the United States.

19. Following are a few examples gathered from the Internet that show how this passage is used by self-declared conservatives and liberals alike to assert the inevitability of poverty and that the poor are either charity cases or criminal cases: Poverty will never be eradicated. As Jesus said, 'The poor will be with you always. . . .' There will always be people who are physically unable to work, and people who will never work because they simply will not, and people who are too stupid to work for very much money, and people who are criminally inclined to steal from stupid or helpless people, etc. And there will always be people who want to take money away from the higher paid, smart, energetic and enterprising people who are the backbone of this country, and give it to those who are not. Those are the people who refuse to believe what God has said. Poverty CANNOT be cured or eradicated, but there will always be people who try" ("How Can Poverty Be Eradicated?" *Answers.com*, http://wiki.answers.com/Q/How_can_poverty_can_be_eradicated.). Jesus said the poor will be with you always. It has been over two thousand years and this statement still holds true. We cannot eradicate poverty but if a neighbor comes to us and asks for a loaf of bread, we should care enough to share if we can meet that need. With that in mind I propose establishing a directory with a Website

They have been used to claim that the only "good news" that poor people will hear will be in heaven, and interpreted to mean that while some lepers and hungry people in Jesus' day deserved compassion, today's poor people are at fault for their own poverty.[20]

Reading the Bible with the Poor

This essay aims to further develop and describe a biblical hermeneutic that we have termed "Reading the Bible with the Poor."[21] In many cases, starting with these difficult texts used to justify inaction in the face of growing economic insecurity, Reading the Bible with the Poor suggests a biblical theology of justice and promotes the agency of the poor. This approach is first distinguished from the prevailing approach of reading the Bible either against the poor, or toward charity for the poor. This method of contextual biblical study draws from the methods developed—and developing—in South Africa with the Academy of the Poor and Latin American liberation theology and Christian base communities.[22] What is particularly distinctive about Reading the Bible with the Poor is its US context: a large population

www.GalesburgCares.org containing all organizations offering various types of assistance. It would include churches, nonprofit organizations and government agencies to better connect the providers with recipients. The groups might be categorized by food, clothing, medical, child care, financial management, housing, etc. I would also like hard copies of the directory to be distributed to all participating organizations connecting the groups with one another for a unified approach to poverty in Galesburg. (Eric Delawder, "Mayoral Candidate Eric Delawder: Galesburg Mayoral Candidate Eric Delawder Answers Questions From The Register-Mail Editorial Board and Speaks on Video About Why Voters Should Elect Him," *The Register-Mail*, March 20, 2009, http://www.galesburg.com/archive/x1331535567/Mayoral-candidate-Eric-Delawder.)

20. Luz, *Matthew 21–28*, 340, explains that putting concern for Jesus over concern for the poor has been a central interpretation throughout the ages; he writes that Theophylactus (Theophylactus, *Ennarratio in Eug. Marci*, *PG* 123.645, 648) asserted that Jesus deserved better than the poor and that John Calvin suggested that with the approach of Jesus' death, concern for Jesus should take precedence.
21. Reading the Bible with the Poor has developed within the context of the Poverty Initiative at Union Theological Seminary including professors like Dr. Brigitte Kahl and other empire-critical and liberationist scholars committed to freedom from poverty. Therefore we use the pronouns "we," "our," and "us" to describe the communities of practice and accountability to this method and a larger liberation project with the Bible.

of impoverished Christians who are already familiar with the Bible (and its damaging interpretations), a population moving from self-blame to making a social claim in a rights-based framework, and a heterogeneous group that is growing everyday as a result of increasing sections of the middle income strata being reduced to poverty even as the poor are reduced to superfluousness.

Reading the Bible with the Poor grows out of global examples of contextual Bible study and liberation theology in Latin America, South Africa, and many other places across the globe, and has developed within the framework of the Poverty Initiative and Kairos Center for Religions, Rights, and Social Justice at Union Theological Seminary and particularly its US context. The theological and biblical battles of the nineteenth-century anti-slavery movement have been a core area of study and influence on Reading the Bible with the Poor. Abolitionists used the Bible to argue that God condemned slavery and that all Christians and people of conscience should follow. Indeed, these religious interpretations provided a crucial moral force for the abolitionist movement because the biblical legitimacy of slavery was widely assumed and thus a key prop to the institution of chattel slavery in the United States.[23]

22. Although Reading the Bible with the Poor has been influenced by a wide range of postcolonial, feminist, liberationist and other biblical scholars, particularly important have been three exemplary Bible study models, from South Africa (from Gerald West and the Academy of the Poor), Latin America (from Ernesto Cardenal and *The Gospel in Solentiname*) and the United States border (with Bob Ekblad's *Reading the Bible with the Damned*).

23. Slaveholders quoted "Slaves, obey your masters" (Col. 3:22, Eph. 6:5, 1 Pet. 2:18) and the book of Philemon about returning runaway slaves to their masters and produced a Bible without the book of Exodus or other teachings about freeing slaves to maintain and legitimate their cause. For books on the topic of slavery and the Bible see: Isaac Allen, *Is Slavery Sanctioned By The Bible?* (Ann Arbor, MI: CreateSpace Independent Publishing Platform, 2013); Hector Avalos, *Slavery, Abolitionism, and the Ethics of Biblical Scholarship* (Sheffield: Sheffield Phoenix, 2013); Stephen R. Haynes, *Noah's Curse: The Biblical Justification of American Slavery*, Religion in America Series (New York: Oxford University Press, 2002); Mark A. Noll, *The Civil War as a Theological Crisis* (Chapel Hill: University of North Carolina Press, 2006).

Reading the Bible with the Poor also draws inspiration especially from the words and work of the Rev. Dr. Martin Luther King Jr. and his launching of the Poor People's Campaign in 1967-68.[24] The strategic concept introduced by this historic campaign aimed "to lift the load of poverty" through uniting the poor across color lines into "a new and unsettling force."[25] Other influential US social movements that take up the Bible in their push for social justice include Paul Rauschenbusch and the Social Gospel Movement and the revivals and spirituals of the Southern Tenant Farmers Union. These influences and movements are integrated into our Bible studies.

Turning from the influences to the methodology of Reading the Bible with the Poor, we note that there are a set of theoretical assumptions that inform the study and use of biblical texts. First, successful social change has most often been led by those most affected by the problems they are working to resolve. Second, committed, competent, connected, and clear leaders of such a social movement need to be developed and conscientized. Third, faith and religion play a critical role in these struggles and movements; therefore the content and impact of Bible study and religious practice matter. We will explore these tenets that inform the contextual Bible study method here.

24. Robert T. Chase, "Class Resurrection: The Poor People's Campaign of 1968 and Resurrection City," *Essays in History* 40 (1998), http://www.essaysinhistory.com/articles/2012/116.
25. From Rev. Dr. Martin Luther King's "Nonviolence and Social Change" in the Massey Lectures for the Canadian Broadcast Company:
"The dispossessed of this nation—the poor, both white and Negro—live in a cruelly unjust society. They must organize a revolution against . . . the structures through which the society is refusing to take means . . . which are at hand, to lift the load of poverty. There are millions of poor people in this country who have very little, or even nothing, to lose. If they can be helped to take action together, they will do so with a freedom and power that will be a new and unsettling force in our complacent national life." (Martin Luther King Jr., *The Trumpet of Conscience* [Boston: Beacon, 1968], 53–66.)

Building a Social Movement Led by the Poor as a United Social Force

The Great Recession that started between 2007-2008 continues to impoverish increasingly more families years later.[26] Community leaders and their organizations wage innovative campaigns to demand access to affordable housing, living wage jobs, healthcare, immigrant rights, workers' rights, and education reform, but even as these grassroots organizations win unprecedented victories including labor protections,[27] higher wages,[28] universal health care,[29] and so on,

26. About rising inequality and the need to develop new models of organizing, Ann Robertson and Bill Leumer write,
"Thanks to Occupy, most working people are well aware of the growing inequalities in wealth. . . . In other words, not only are the rich getting richer, the rest of us are getting poorer. Many factors have converged to produce these trends. Good-paying manufacturing jobs have migrated overseas. Technology has replaced many other good-paying jobs. More importantly, across the country many unions have demonstrated an overwhelming willingness to accept concessions without waging a struggle, thereby contributing to the growing inequalities. This willingness to give up hard won gains in turn has resulted in the continuing decline of union membership, which now stands at 8 percent" (Ann Robertson and Bill Leumer, "Rising Poverty and Social Inequality in America," August 4, 2012, http://www.globalresearch.ca/rising-poverty-and-social-inequality-in-america).
27. Domestic Workers United won a Domestic Workers Bill of Rights in 2011 where, for the first time in history, domestic workers are guaranteed limited benefits, worker protections, and better pay under New York State law. In the fall of 2013, the National Domestic Workers Association was able to win a more universal law where domestic workers are included in the National Labor Relations Act for the first time in history. For more information on the Domestic Workers Bill of Rights, see both Domestic Workers United and the National Domestic Workers Alliance. For more information on federal labor law, see http://www.dol.gov/whd/homecare/finalrule.htm.
28. In 1999, the Coalition of Immokalee Workers (CIW) launched their Taco Bell campaign where they started pressuring companies for which Florida farmworkers picked tomatoes. Their demands were simple: pay one penny more per pound for the tomatoes (and ensure that the penny is passed on to the workers) that would double the wages of farmworkers, offer training and monitoring of the growing associations by the CIW, and broker agreements between the growers, farmworkers, and fast-food and supermarket industries. To date, Taco Bell, YUM! Brands, McDonalds, Burger King, Whole Foods, Wal-Mart, and Chipotle have all signed on. For more information on the Coalition of Immokalee Workers and the Campaign for Fair Food, see http://ciw-online.org.
29. In 2012, the Vermont Workers Center won universal healthcare for all Vermont residents after a five-year long campaign across the state. For more information on this bill and the bigger healthcare as a human right campaign that has grown to Maryland, Maine, and Pennsylvania, see http://workerscenter.org.

conditions are worsening and the victories are small and temporary compared to the erosion of rights, lowering of wages, widening of inequality, and dispossession.[30] To those engaged in community struggles, the conditions demonstrate the need for a broader social movement.[31]

Learning lessons from the Southern Christian Leadership Conference and its key role in the US civil rights movement, a modern movement requires a sophisticated core of leaders, versed in the Bible and liberative theology, capable of analyzing and developing solutions that address the complexity of poverty and injustice today.[32] Inspired by Rev. Dr. Martin Luther King Jr.'s

30. Nationwide, the count of America's poor remains stuck at a record number: 46.2 million, or 15 percent of the population, due in part to lingering high unemployment following the recession. . . . The risks of poverty also have been increasing in recent decades, particularly among people ages 35–55, coinciding with widening income inequality. For instance, people ages 35–45 had a 17 percent risk of encountering poverty during the 1969–1989 time period; that risk increased to 23 percent during the 1989–2009 period. For those ages 45–55, the risk of poverty jumped from 11.8 percent to 17.7 percent. Higher recent rates of unemployment mean the lifetime risk of experiencing economic insecurity now runs even higher: 79 percent, or 4 in 5 adults, by the time they turn 60 . . . By 2030, based on the current trend of widening income inequality, close to 85 percent of all working-age adults in the U.S. will experience bouts of economic insecurity. "'Poverty is no longer an issue of 'them,' it's an issue of 'us,'" says Mark Rank, a professor at Washington University in St. Louis who calculated the numbers. ("4 in 5 Americans live in danger of falling into poverty")

31. There are many sources for understanding the political economy of neoliberalism and the economic crisis. A few of the resources for this economic analysis include Mike Davis, *City of Quartz: Excavating the Future in Los Angeles* (London: Verso, 1990); Davis, *Planet of Slums* (London: Verso, 2006); Gérard Duménil and Dominique Lévy, *Capital Resurgent: Roots of the Neoliberal Revolution* (Cambridge, MA: Harvard University Press, 2004); David Harvey, *The Condition of Postmodernity* (Oxford: Blackwell, 1990); Harvey, *A Brief History of Neoliberalism* (Oxford: Oxford University Press, 2005); Naomi Klein, *The Shock Doctrine: The Rise of Disaster Capitalism* (New York: Metropolitan Books, 2007); Paul Krugman, *The Return of Depression Economics and the Crisis of 2008* (New York: Norton, 2009); David McNally, *Another World is Possible: Globalization & Anticapitalism* (Winnipeg: Arbeiter Ring Publishing, 2006); June Nash, *From Tank Town to High Tech: The Clash of Community and Industrial Cycles* (New York: State University of New York Press, 1989); Alejandro Portes, Manuel Castells, and Lauren A. Benton, eds., *The Informal Economy: Studies in Advanced and Less Developed Countries* (Baltimore: Johns Hopkins Press, 1989); William Robinson, *A Theory of Global Capitalism: Production, Class, and State in a Transnational World* (Baltimore: Johns Hopkins University Press, 2004).

32. For more on lessons from the civil rights movement and Black Freedom struggle, see Aldon Morris, *The Origins of the Civil Rights Movement* (New York: Free Press, 1986); Carol Anderson,

conclusions about the need for the poor in the United States to unite across color lines and issues, our work over the past two decades has focused on developing a core of highly skilled leaders in order to build a powerful multiracial, multifaith, multi-issue network of grassroots, low-income, community and religious leaders.[33] Such leaders are not just born—they rely on systematic education and training. In fact, decades of organizing experience have shown that organizations with a comprehensive education and leadership development program are more able to sustain their efforts.[34]

Historically, successful social movements have been led by those most affected by the problems they are working to resolve. Slaves and ex-slaves led the anti-slavery movement; people of color led the civil rights movement; women led the women's suffrage movement.[35] In their own time, those very people struggled for recognition that

Eyes Off the Prize: The United Nations and the African American Struggle for Human Rights, 1944–1955 (Cambridge: Cambridge University Press, 2003); John Dittmer, *Local People: The Struggle for Civil Rights in Mississippi* (Champaign: University of Illinois Press, 1995); David Garrow, *Bearing the Cross: Martin Luther King Jr and the Southern Christian Leadership Conference* (San Francisco: William Morrow, 2004); Charles Payne, *I've Got the Light of Freedom: The Organizing Tradition and the Mississippi Freedom Struggle* (Berkeley: University of California Press, 2007); The Poverty Initiative, *A New and Unsettling Force: Re-igniting Rev. Dr. Martin Luther King's Poor People's Campaign* (New York: Poverty Initiative, 2009); Jeanne Theoharis and Komozi Woodard, *Groundwork: Local Black Freedom Movements in America* (New York: New York University Press, 2005); Howard Zinn, *SNCC: The New Abolitionists* (New York: South End Press, 1964).

33. Many authors, scholars, and social justice leaders suggest that Martin Luther King Jr. left a void when he was assassinated. Books on this topic include: Michael Eric Dyson, *I May Not Get There with You: The True Martin Luther King, Jr* (New York: Free Press, 2001); Vincent Harding, *Martin Luther King: The Inconvenient Hero* (Maryknoll, NY: Orbis Books, 2008); William F. Pepper, *An Act of State: The Execution of Martin Luther King* (New York: Verso, 2008); William F. Pepper, *Orders to Kill: The Truth Behind the Murder of Martin Luther King* (New York: Carroll and Graf, 1995).
34. It has been our experience that grassroots organizations that do not have a focus on leadership development and education are not able to sustain the people who get involved in their organization. The National Union of the Homeless went into demise in the mid-1990s for lack of education and training of its leaders. Other examples from non-profits, NGOs, and other community organizations also tell the same story.
35. This understanding of the history of social movements and social change as well as an emphasis on political education and leadership development is emphasized in Baptist and Rehman, *Pedagogy of the Poor*.

the problem they were facing was immoral, that their struggle was legitimate, and that they were fit to lead it.[36] Yet today, we readily recognize the moral evil of slavery, and the right—and necessity—of slaves and ex-slaves to lead the struggle to end it.

Given popular images of the poor that dominate in US culture as lazy, crazy, addicted, ineffective, violent, or pathetic, the concept of the leadership of the poor as a united social force and as individual leaders seems remote.[37] Everyone *but* the poor is looked to for solutions to end poverty, whether it is social workers, church members, lawyers, or legislators. But as Frederick Douglass had to argue to others in the Abolitionist Movement: the leadership and unity of the slaves was the first step in ending slavery. He insisted on the moral, political, and epistemological agency of enslaved people.[38]

36. For more information about the abolitionist movement and the struggles many slaves and ex-slaves had to establish their agency and legitimacy, see especially the biographies of many of the most influential (religious) leaders: Frederick Douglass, *Narrative of the Life of Frederick Douglass: An American Slave, Written by Himself* (London: St. Martin's, 2002); W. E. B. Dubois, *Black Reconstruction in America 1860–1880* (New York: Free Press, 1999); Kate Clifford Larson, *Bound for the Promised Land: Harriet Tubman: Portrait of an American Hero* (New York: Ballantine Books, 2004); Stephen Oates, *To Purge This Land of Blood: A Biography of John Brown* (Amherst: University of Massachusetts Press, 1984).

37. Valerie Strauss, "Five Stereotypes About Poor Families and Education," *Washington Post*, October 28, 2013, http://www.washingtonpost.com/blogs/answer-sheet/wp/2013/10/28/five-stereotypes-about-poor-families-and-education.

38. In his powerful speech about West Indian Emancipation, Frederick Douglass critiques those, even within the anti-slavery movement, who diminish the role, political agency, and aptitude of the slaves and former slaves. This speech has been influential in the work of the Poverty Initiative where poor people have gotten inspiration knowing that slaves and ex-slaves had to struggle to assert their agency and dignity:
"I know, my friends, that in some quarters the efforts of colored people meet with very little encouragement. . . . This class of Abolitionists don't like colored celebrations, they don't like colored conventions, they don't like colored Anti-Slavery fairs for the support of colored newspapers. They don't like any demonstrations whatever in which colored men take a leading part. They talk of the proud Anglo-Saxon blood, as flippantly as those who profess to believe in the natural inferiority of races. Your humble speaker has been branded as an ingrate, because he has ventured to stand up on his own right, and to plead our common cause as a colored man, rather than as a Garrisonian. I hold it to be no part of gratitude to allow our white friends to do all the work, while we merely hold their coats. Opposition of the sort now referred to, is partisan opposition, and we need not mind it. The white people at large will not largely be influenced by it. They will see and appreciate all honest efforts on our part to improve our condition as a people. Let me give you a word of the philosophy of reform. The whole history

Within the Poverty Initiative network, we believe that the strategic direction of a movement is determined by uniting and placing those most affected by the problem at the forefront. The first step in building such a movement is the identification and systematic development of leaders who are highly intelligent and devoted to establishing this strategic direction. While rooted in the unity of the poor, this movement has to involve a broad cross section of people.

One of the main purposes of contextual biblical interpretation is to allow those participating in the study to view the Bible from the standpoint of the struggles of the poor and draw parallels to biblical texts, thereby challenging misconceptions of poverty, religiosity, and modes of social transformation. Since biblical interpretation has been in the hands of scholars and preachers predominantly trained in institutions of higher education, endorsed and dominated by the perspectives of the rich and the status quo—offering the space for poor people to interpret biblical stories and apply these interpretations to their life situations constitutes a considerable contribution to the field of New Testament studies.[39] Bible study is typically done in the context of a Sunday school class, oftentimes

of the progress of human liberty shows that all concessions yet made to her august claims, have been born of earnest struggle. The conflict has been exciting, agitating, all-absorbing, and for the time being, putting all other tumults to silence. It must do this or it does nothing. If there is no struggle there is no progress. Those who profess to favor freedom and yet deprecate agitation, are men who want crops without plowing up the ground, they want rain without thunder and lightning. They want the ocean without the awful roar of its many waters. This struggle may be a moral one, or it may be a physical one, and it may be both moral and physical, but it must be a struggle. Power concedes nothing without a demand. It never did and it never will. Find out just what any people will quietly submit to and you have found out the exact measure of injustice and wrong which will be imposed upon them, and these will continue till they are resisted with either words or blows, or with both. The limits of tyrants are prescribed by the endurance of those whom they oppress. In the light of these ideas, Negroes will be hunted at the North, and held and flogged at the South so long as they submit to those devilish outrages, and make no resistance, either moral or physical. Men may not get all they pay for in this world, but they must certainly pay for all they get. If we ever get free from the oppressions and wrongs heaped upon us, we must pay for their removal. We must do this by labor, by suffering, by sacrifice, and if needs be, by our lives and the lives of others." (Frederick Douglass, "West India Emancipation: Speech delivered at Canandaigua, New York, August 3, 1857," http://www.lib.rochester.edu/index.cfm?PAGE=4398)

under the direction and leadership of a pastor or other established leader, and often only addressing texts those established leaders deem relevant. Reading the Bible with the Poor provides a more far-ranging approach by putting poor people's agency, leadership, and

39. Following is an example again from South Africa of the type of interpretation of biblical texts on the part of the organized poor. The Poverty Initiative has used this speech and other writings by leaders in the South African Shackdwellers in our Poverty Scholars program and contextual Bible studies. What has been particularly influential about this quotation is the way that biblical texts are interpreted alongside the life experiences of today's poor. Rather than accepting the "interpretations" of scholars, clergy and others, poor leaders such as Mdlalose apply the stories from the Bible to their situation finding many resonances and parallels between life in the shacks of South Africa and the slums of Galilee:
"As young leaders, our elders don't forget to advise us about the 10 commandments of God which are in Exodus 20. I full [sic] engaged with this chapter, looked deeply in to it and started to compare it with the way that we are living today. I look into verse 12 which says "Respect your father and your mother, so that you may live a long time in the land that I am giving you." I don't stop asking myself if the leaders like Nigel Gumede, have even thought of reading the Bible. They don't respect elders in our presence. I fail to understand why old people are still living in shacks. How does one feel when one's elders are living in such state, while the politicians are all living in fancy houses? And our elders are treated liked naughty children when they want to discuss matters with the politicians. Building houses does take some time. But engaging people in a respectful way takes no time. All it takes is to recognise them as human beings. Verse 15 says, "Do not steal." I wonder if all the councilors who are running the communities' and government's resources as if they are running their own spaza shop where they take and give whenever they wish to—with the result that today there are lots of people who are being left homeless while according to the computers they are seen as if they have homes—have had time to read this chapter thoroughly. Verse 16 says, "Do not accuse anyone falsely." There are people from Kennedy Road who today still don't have homes after they were falsely accused and chased out. Twelve members of Kennedy served a year of imprisonment for a crime that they did not commit. Even though the police used torture to try and manufacture a case against the 12 their case was thrown out of the court. The judge found that witnesses were lying and that the police had written witnesses statements. I wonder what Nigel Gumede and Willies Mchunu will say to God for all the tears and stress and frustration they caused to people made in the images of God. Today Gumede and Mchunu are living in their homes while there are leaders from Kennedy who are still in Exile. God will answer one day. No stone will be left unturned, no tear will drop on the flow. God has a dish where all the tears are flowing to and surely he shall answer them. Soon we will be worshipping with Psalm 6:8: "Away from me, all you who do evil, for the LORD has heard my weeping. The LORD has heard my cry for mercy; the LORD accepts my prayer. All my enemies will be ashamed and dismayed; they will turn back in sudden disgrace." God made all people, rich and poor, and any oppression of any people is a sin in the eyes of God. All oppressors will have to account for their oppression. God is on the side of all struggles for justice. His spirit moves in our struggles and keeps us strong. As we struggle we are bringing his spirit into the world. Amandla! The Struggle of the poor going alongside God shall continue. Surely goodness and mercy shall follow me all the days of my life, and I will dwell in the house of the LORD forever. I am blessed to be Umlali waseMjondolo." (Bandile Mdlalose, "God in My Struggle," *Abahlali baseMjondolo*, July 3, 2012, http://abahlali.org/node/8911).

analysis at the center of the discussion. This includes a broad range of texts, including difficult biblical texts on poverty, along with the insistence that leaders of the Bible study include organizers of the poor especially from the ranks of the poor themselves.

Some assert that the theological condoning of poverty takes place because many American churches have lost a connection to the poor.[40] But mere awareness of poverty issues does not transform interpretations of "the poor are with you always" or other biblical justifications of poverty. Many poor people believe the same things about who is to blame for poverty that middle-income or wealthy people do.[41] This is why we have found it important to base new interpretations of the text not just among the poor, but among the poor who are organizing themselves against the issues of poverty, and to return to and reinterpret religious texts that have been used to justify poverty and define obedience to God in individualistic terms between a human on earth and God in heaven. Just as not having a connection to the poor can justify middle-class ideas on why people are poor, not having a connection to organized poor people more easily reinforces the predominant charity approach according to which what the fortunate, especially Christians, need to do is save the poor. So, this experience can often be transformative for poor people themselves, both intellectually and spiritually.

The form of leadership development and consciousness-raising employed in our method of Reading the Bible with the Poor combines rigorous study and applied practice. Therefore, churches and classrooms, anti-poverty campaigns and organized protests, all become locations of contextual Bible study and general political education. This variety has been effective in helping promote a

40. Jim Wallis, *God's Politics: Why the Right Gets It Wrong and the Left Doesn't Get It* (San Francisco: HarperCollins, 2005), 211.

41. Throughout our decades of anti-poverty organizing, we have found that most poor people blame themselves for their poverty and are therefore ashamed of being poor.

transformation of values, including new theoretical interpretations and new leadership practices alongside the organized poor.

The organized poor in the United States are engaged in contextual Bible study alongside their brothers and sisters in the global community through a methodology of Reading the Bible with the Poor. Reading the Bible with the Poor has an epistemological framework that encourages newly emerging leaders to examine the existing possibilities for ending all poverty and contends that organized poor people are makers and interpreters of this good news from the poor. The methodology draws from a long liberationist heritage including feminist, empire-critical, and postcolonial theories of interpretation.[42] The Bible studies combine social movement

42. Some of the theories of interpretation and books most influential for our work include: A. K. M. Adam, *What Is Postmodern Biblical Criticism?* (Minneapolis: Augsburg Fortress Press, 1995); Adam, *Postmodern Interpretations of the Bible: A Reader* (New York: Chalice, 2001); David Tuesday Adamo, *Biblical Interpretation in African Perspective* (New York: University Press of America, 2006); Joe Bageant, *Deer Hunting with Jesus: Dispatches from America's Class War* (New York: Crown, 2007); Bible & Culture Collective, *The Postmodern Bible* (New Haven, CT: Yale University Press, 1997); Walter Brueggemann, *An Introduction to the Old Testament: The Canon and Christian Imagination* (Louisville: Westminster John Knox, 2003); James Cone, *God of the Oppressed* (Maryknoll, NY: Orbis Books, 1997); Musa Dube, *Postcolonial Feminist Interpretation of the Bible* (St Louis: Christian Board of Publication, 2000); Musa Dube and Musimbi Kanyoro, *Grant Me Justice! HIV/AIDS & Gender Readings of the Bible* (Maryknoll, NY: Orbis Books, 2005); Dube, *Other Ways of Reading: African Women and the Bible* (Atlanta: Society of Biblical Literature, 2001); Ulrich Duchrow, *Global Economy: A Confessional Issue for the Churches?* (Geneva: WCC Publications, 1987); Cain Hope Felder, *Stony the Road We Trod: African American Biblical Interpretation* (Minneapolis: Augsburg Fortress Press, 1991); Norman Gottwald, *The Tribes of Yahweh: A Sociology of the Religion of Liberated Israel, 1250–1050 BCE* (Sheffield: Sheffield Academic, 1999); Joel Green, *Hearing the New Testament: Strategies for Interpretation* (Grand Rapids, MI: Eerdmans, 1995); Gustavo Gutiérrez, *On Job: God-Talk and the Suffering of the Innocent*, trans. Matthew O'Connell (Maryknoll, NY: Orbis Books, 2003); Gustavo Gutiérrez, *A Theology of Liberation: History, Politics, and Salvation*, trans. Caridad Inda and John Eagleson (Maryknoll, NY: Orbis Books, 1988); Ched Myers, *The Biblical Vision of Sabbath Economics* (Washington, DC: Church of the Saviour Publishing, 2001); Carol Newsom and Sharon H. Ringe, *Women's Bible Commentary: Expanded Edition with Apocrypha* (Louisville: Westminster John Knox, 1998); Jorge Pixley and Clodovis Boff, *The Bible, the Church and the Poor: Biblical, Theological, and Pastoral Aspects of the Option for the Poor* (Maryknoll, NY: Orbis Books, 1987); Kwok Pui-lan, *Postcolonial Imagination and Feminist Theology* (Louisville: Westminster John Knox, 2005); Christopher Rowland and Mark Comer, *Liberating Exegesis: The Challenge of Liberation Theology to Biblical Studies* (Louisville:

organization and action (people being compelled to organize to change their conditions and those around them), intellectual analysis (including an appreciation for academic scholarship), and a theological and spiritual approach. The model describes not simply a theory but an ongoing practice of foregrounding the polarization of wealth and poverty as the defining issue of our day.

Reading the Bible with the Poor is not a biblical hermeneutic for the poor, as is suggested by the old and prevalent notion of what has been called "faith-based organizing." That is, it is not a biblical hermeneutic *for* the poor, which tends to restrict religiosity to organized religious institutions and view poverty as due to the sins of the poor rather than the sins of an unjust society. Rather, it is a summary of a biblical hermeneutic developed out of struggle, living politics, and a deep spirituality that represents the program of the poor and dispossessed. The methodology itself is interested in uniting people across difference (in race, geography, religion, gender, sexual orientation, age, ability, and so on) rather than having those differences used by those in power to divide and isolate. It argues that the poor are the epistemological, political, and moral agents of change in our society and not cases of charity nor criminality. When the organized poor appropriate the Bible, a biblical program of political, economic, and social justice is brought into clear view.

Westminster John Knox, 1990); Elisabeth Schüssler Fiorenza, ed., *Searching the Scriptures: A Feminist Commentary*, 2 vols. (New York: Crossroad, 1993–1994); Schüssler Fiorenza, *Jesus and the Politics of Interpretation* (New York: Continuum, 2001); Fernando Segovia, "Methods for Studying the New Testament," in *New Testament Today*, ed. Mark Allan Powell (Louisville: Westminster John Knox, 1999), 1–9; Segovia, *Decolonizing Biblical Studies: A View from the Margins* (Maryknoll, NY: Orbis Books, 2000); Fernando Segovia and R. S. Sugirtharajah, *Postcolonial Commentary on the New Testament Writings* (New York: T&T Clark, 2007); R. S. Sugirtharajah, *Voices from the Margin: Interpreting the Bible in the Third World* (Maryknoll, NY: Orbis Books, 2006); Justin Ukpong et al., *Reading the Bible in the Global Village* (Cape Town: Society of Biblical Literature, 2002); Delores Williams, *Sisters in the Wilderness: The Challenge of Womanist God-Talk* (Maryknoll, NY: Orbis Books, 2000); Vincent Wimbush, *African Americans and the Bible: Sacred Text and Social Texture* (New York: Continuum, 2001); Vincent Winbush, *The Bible and African Americans: A Brief History* (Minneapolis: Fortress Press, 2003).

Jesus as an Organizer

When we explore Jesus' revolution of values as expressed especially in the Beatitudes in Matthew and Mary's Magnificat in Luke, as well as other practices and teachings of ministry, a condemnation of the Roman Empire and the promotion of communities of resistance and renewal across the Mediterranean comes into clear view.[43] Starting with the assertion that Jesus was poor and living under class-stratified Roman imperial rule, leaders and organizers from the ranks of the poor and Poverty Scholars generally make a series of connections and important interpretational moves. Jesus becomes recognizable as a poor person and a popular social movement leader, if we extrapolate from New Testament depictions of early Christian communities, as a budding social movement. Poverty Scholars suggest that what happens to Jesus throughout the Bible and the anointing scene in Matthew 26 specifically is not completely special or unusual, but shares similar characteristics with other poor people's experiences (including being surrounded by and finding shelter among other

43. Based on close exegetical work of Matthew, historical-critical scholarship of Galilee, Antioch, and the larger Roman Empire, and our contextual Bible study commitments as experienced through Reading the Bible with the Poor, we agree with the profile developed by Poverty Scholars and argue that Jesus was a teacher, leader, prophet, and ruler of a budding revolutionary social movement of the poor that practiced and preached about God's coming reign of abundance, dignity, and prosperity for all. This religious and political movement was accurately understood by the ruling elite of the Roman Empire to be in stark opposition to Rome, especially with respect to its economic, political, and religious structure. This Poverty Scholars' profile of Matthew's Jesus as teacher and social movement leader with a program of covenant economics connects with ideas from biblical scholars. Marcus Borg asserts that Jesus was one of four characters: a prophet, a sage, a revitalization movement founder, or a spiritual leader. John Dominic Crossan proposes that Jesus was a Cynic philosopher, a visionary teacher, and a peasant protestor. Richard Horsley depicts Jesus as a social revolutionary. E. P. Sanders suggests that Jesus is a teacher of "Jewish restoration eschatology." N. T. Wright asserts that Jesus was a messianic prophet. Geza Vermes argues that Jesus was a Galilean holy man. William Herzog writes that Jesus is a prophet in the tradition of Israel's prophetic figures, a subversive pedagogue of the oppressed, a shamanistic figure, and a reputational leader who brokers the justice of Yahweh's covenant and coming reign. Others including Stevan Davies, J. C. Becker, Joachim Gnilka, Dale Allison suggest he was seen as a healer or prophet or apocalyptic figure for the kingdom of God.

poor people, being concerned about debt and resources, valuing at times dignity over money, critiquing charity) as well as the experiences of social movement leaders in particular (including holding these leaders to high standards, emphasizing political education among movement leaders and participants, evoking movement teachings and sacred traditions, suggesting non-participation in dominant economic systems, and assuming that controversy will arise). Similarities between early Christian communities and contemporary poor people are not surprising; as social theorist James C. Scott notes, "to the degree structures of domination can be demonstrated to operate in comparable ways, they will, other things equal, elicit reactions and patterns of resistance that are also broadly comparable."[44] Such connections suggest that a depiction of Jesus as a movement leader, popular messiah, and pedagogue of the oppressed is historically possible and interpretations of biblical texts that presume this are potentially valid.[45] The social location of contemporary poor people who are engaged in the work of social transformation helps these Poverty Scholars participating in Reading the Bible with the Poor Bible studies understand and draw meaning from the words and actions in the Gospel of Matthew. These Bible studies also show that diverse people can interpret together across their differences of experience, racial and gender composition, formal education levels, and theological persuasions. Jesus is a recognizable leader of a social movement in first-century Palestine. Poverty Scholars posit that Jesus and his community of followers in Matthew and the other Gospels dealt with the politics

44. James C. Scott, *Domination and the Arts of Resistance: Hidden Transcripts* (New Haven, CT: Yale University Press, 1990), xi.
45. This assertion follows the work of Stevan Davies who relies on the presence of contemporary exorcisms in parts of Western Africa similar to the exorcisms found in the New Testament to demonstrate that Jesus' exorcisms may be historically reliable. See Davies, *Jesus the Healer: Possession, Trance, and the Origins of Christianity* (New York: Continuum, 1995).

of food and healthcare and spoke in stories. Their ministry and movement developed new forms of struggle and organization countering a class-based imperial structure, and a mission that informs us still today, two thousand years later. Following from developments in social history that posit that social transformation is fueled by the poor and dispossessed, we can observe that Jesus' teachings and actions around poverty, wealth, and power, especially in Matthew's Gospel, lend further support to a portrait of Jesus as a social movement leader. In fact, exploring the teachings and actions of Jesus in Matthew, Poverty Scholars propose six "M's" to highlight the focus on justice and movement building in the gospel: *message*, *martyrdom*, *miracles*, *media*, *mentoring*, and *missionary work*.

Message

Jesus proclaimed the "good news" that everyone was created in the image of God and has worth. Jesus and his disciples demonstrated this "good news" through shared meals, conversation, and healing. He taught stories and metaphors wherein the "least and the last" become the "greatest and the first" (Matt. 25:40; 18:1–4; 23:11); and the poor are proclaimed "blessed" (Matt. 5:1).

Martyrdom

Jesus and the disciples revealed the inequities of Roman society, which excluded the sick and the poor (Matt. 11:5). Through the turning over of the tables in the temple, Jesus disrupted commerce and drew attention to the system of economic and ritual exchange that impoverished and excluded so many poor people (Matt. 21:12). Jesus was accused of sedition and crucified by Rome as an enemy of the state and alternative "King of the Jews" (Matt. 26:63–68; 27:24–44).

Miracles

As a poor man working among the poor of his society, it follows that Jesus' miracles were about providing the survival needs of the people—care and healthcare (Matt. 8:1-34; 9:1-14; 14:34-36; 20:28-34) and other things that were denied them by the society and economic system of that time. Faced with a hungry crowd of more than five thousand (Matt. 14:13-21; 16:9) that was eager but too hungry to learn, Jesus turned to his disciples and said, "You give them something to eat."

Media

Jesus and his disciples used various means of communication. He preached sermons and handed down instruction as in the Sermon on the Mount (Matthew 5–7). He traveled throughout the area connecting up with more communities and people. Indeed theirs was a peripatetic movement; the Roman roads served as a medium through which they carried their message.

Mentoring

Political education and leadership development were at the heart of the early Christian movement. Throughout his ministry—in his responsiveness to lepers (Matt. 8:2; 10:8; 26:6), through his exposure of the temple system's regularized defrauding of the poor (Matt. 21:12), and in his teachings in parables (Matt. 13:1-53; 18:10-14, 23-34; 22:1-14; 25:1-30)—Jesus exposed the disciples to the conditions under which people were suffering and unveiled the ways in which the Roman Empire produced this misery.[46] Further, Jesus

46. There are a few parables unique to Matthew, a major form of Jesus' revolutionary teaching, that reaffirm a focus on instruction and economics, including the Parables of the Weeds (13:24-30, 13:36-43), Hidden Treasure and Pearl (13:44-46), Net (13:47-50), New and Old Treasures (13:51-52), Laborers in the Vineyard (20:1-16), Two Sons (21:28-32), and Ten

promoted leadership development by entrusting his followers to carry out healing and preaching and then to return back together to reflect on their experiences. When Jesus was doing miracles himself, he was developing other leaders. Jesus also focused on self-doubt and self-hatred, exorcising spirits and demons (Matt. 4:24; 8:23-28; 5:16)—a major hurdle that poor people must confront and conquer if they are to be successful leaders.

Missionary Work

In his own life and ministry, Jesus represented the coming together of the other five "M's" of movement building. Each of these things inseparably raised the consciousness of and built organization first among the people who were called the "least of these" (Matt. 25:40). Matthew 28:16-20, called the "Great Commission" and the finale of the Gospel of Matthew, is about charging Jesus' disciples to follow him in carrying forward their seditious mission. Focusing on this

Bridesmaids (25:1-13). The Parables of the Weeds, Net, New and Old Treasures, and Two Sons speak to the praxis of unity of words and deeds and the judgment of God for those who bear bad fruit and injustice. The Parable of the Laborers in the Vineyard (Matt. 20:1-16) is particularly important for understanding this dialectic of learning and economic practice. Workers go out to work and make an agreement with the farmer to receive one denarius, the standard rate for day laborers. When some workers start their work hours later, they are still paid the daily rate. These "undeserving" workers earn money for work they do not do. This sounds similar to an economic logic where God provides and people do not have to worry about (or work for/deserve) their daily needs. This could be an echo of the manna story in the Exodus narrative (Exod. 16:1-22) or the teaching on the lilies of the field from the Sermon on the Mount (Matt 6:25-34). Perhaps this parable shows the difference between the Roman greed-based money economy and God's need-based economy as Jesus teaches to his followers and is told (and perhaps even practiced) by the Matthean community. Also important to explore here is the Parable of the Talents/Pounds. Although contained in both Matthew 25:14-30 and Luke 19:12-30, the versions of the stories differ (in Matthew the laborers are given talents to invest while in Luke they only receive pounds—worth much less as mentioned above). Activities such as banking, trading, investing, and making outrageous profit (usury) that may have violated Torah stipulations (Lev. 25:35-38; Deut. 7–11) pervade the language of these parables, however—contributing to any analysis that a critique of these economic practices occurs throughout the Gospel. Throughout Matthew, there are economic turns and twists—places where Jesus teaches and/or demonstrates that the economy of God's kingdom is not what one would expect.

mission reminds everyone that each person is a crucial contributor to the movement's success or failure; that it is about them and their own choices, not solely focused on Jesus and his charismatic personality.

Jesus was a leader of a social, economic, political, and spiritual movement led by those at the bottom of the Roman Empire who united across nationality and other lines of division to promote dignity, prosperity, and justice for all people. Jesus' words and actions, as exemplified in the story of the "anointing at Bethany" and throughout the New Testament, can be seen as instructions for the poor to unite and organize today to transform society and end poverty for all. Therefore, the hyper-spiritualization of poverty and the call to ending poverty only in heaven does not hold.

Preacher, professor, and Poverty Initiative leader Barbara Lundblad suggests that faith is key to building a social movement to end poverty: a belief that ending poverty—especially in times of unheard-of wealth—is possible, an understanding that this is what God requires, and a conviction that this is how Christians must act out their commitment to Jesus.

> Do we need more statistics? More courage? More time to volunteer? Perhaps most of all we need more faith. Jesus' parable [on the rich man and Lazarus] ends with these ironic words: "Abraham said to the rich man, 'If they do not listen to Moses and the prophets, neither will they be convinced even if someone rises from the dead.'" Someone has risen from the dead. What more do we need?[47]

But instead of developing faith that ending poverty (existing unjustly in the midst of plenty) is possible, we ignore the controversial, revolutionary nature of a poor, resurrected Jesus as Lord and Savior who challenges the wealthy, immortalized Caesar. We forget that Jesus' kingdom is about economic and social rights in the here and

47. Barbara Lundblad, "Closing the Great Chasm: Faith & Global Hunger Part 2," *Day One*, June 20, 2010, http://day1.org/2036-closing_the_great_chasm_faith__global_hunger_part_2.

now and that the messiah Jesus came to usher in this reign. The good news of the Bible has been reduced to an individualized acceptance of Jesus Christ as a Lord and Savior, severed from his mission to the world. We deny that the poor are at the center of God's concern, ignoring that Jesus was a leader of a revolutionary movement of the poor who, rather than mitigating the unfortunate inevitability of poverty, called for a movement to transform heaven and earth.

If Matthew 26:1-16 continues to be interpreted as God willing poverty and the only solutions offered continue to be charity, if our religious institutions offer Band-Aid help and superficial solace instead of social transformation with the poor as a united social force at the helm, and if followers of Jesus Christ do not take up the call to follow Jesus and observe God's commandments, then Matthew 26:11 (and Deuteronomy 15:11) will come true. For this is what Matthew 26:11 warns: if we don't recognize Jesus, a messiah of the poor (and what Jesus asks his followers in carrying out his mission), poverty will exist forever—in disobedience to and disregard for God's will and God's justice.

3

Occupying My Desk

Neil Elliott

In 2008, presidential candidate Sarah Palin's peculiar claim to foreign policy experience, that is, that Russia is "right next to our state" (Alaska), was parodied as "I can see Russia from my house."[1] It might be as fair to characterize our credentials at Fortress Press for publishing a book premised, in part, on the significance of the 2011 Occupy movement by noting that "we could watch Occupy from

1. Palin was interviewed on the CBS Evening News in September 2008; comedian Tina Fey impersonated the governor in a spoof of the interview and a subsequent skit on Saturday Night Live: http://www.nbc.com/saturday-night-live/video/sarah-palin-and-hillary-clinton-address-the-nation/n12287. The transcript of the original interview (available online: http://www.cbsnews.com/news/exclusive-palin-on-foreign-policy) indicates that the parody was not far from its mark; Palin declared, "Our next-door neighbors are foreign countries, there in the state that I am the executive of. As Putin rears his head and comes into the air space of the United States of America, where do they go? It's Alaska. It's just right over the border. It is from Alaska that we send those out to make sure that an eye is being kept on this very powerful nation, Russia, because they are right there, they are right next to our state."

our office." Occupy Wall Street inspired a number of local manifestations of solidarity, including Occupy Minneapolis, begun in October 2011 on the Hennepin County Government Plaza (redubbed "the People's Plaza") just a few blocks from our offices. The occupation was close enough that I could, on several occasions, take a short detour on my walk to work to visit the encampment, but each time I arrived early enough that the Occupiers were still burrowed inside their sleeping bags and pup tents against a bracing cold. The Hennepin County Sheriff's Department broke up the encampment weeks later, just before the overnight freeze became potentially hazardous, but not before the Occupiers staged one last mid-morning protest march through downtown. Looking out the windows from an editorial meeting on the sixth floor, Fortress staff were able to watch a small, orderly, and apparently noisy march (we could hear muffled chants, but couldn't make out the words or read their banners) on the street below us. The police escort on either side of the march seemed superfluous: In November, downtown Minneapolis streets are largely deserted, with all pedestrian traffic routed sensibly indoors, to the second-floor Skyway system.

Bruce Worthington and Jonathan Bernier initially pitched the idea for this volume under the title *Occupy Exegesis,* on the premise that the rise in 2011 of democratic direct-action protests in city after city "changed everything" for the climate in which biblical studies now takes place. While I don't like to think of our Fortress editorial team as "staid," our early discussions of the book included questions about "just what had changed" after 2011, at least so far as biblical scholarship was concerned, and whether tying a book too closely to a particular moment in history would limit its market appeal—the same sorts of commercial considerations, I hasten to point out, that we brought to book proposal evaluations before the Occupy movement. I was gratified when Bruce welcomed a change of title to the larger topic of global crisis, and more gratified later to see that so many of the essays in this volume still show the inspiration of the Occupy movement.

I recount the episode, not to reveal dramatic insights into the inner workings of an academic publisher—there's nothing unusual about the deliberations I've just described—but to point out the momentum (others might call it inertia) of academic publishing, not least in theology, biblical studies, and related fields. (Obviously I can't speak for other publishers in these areas, nor do I intend to speak officially for Fortress Press, though the concerns I express in this essay naturally inform my work there. My purpose is nonetheless to speak as representatively of larger patterns as possible.) To varying degrees in individual cases, our work often tends to be inherently conservative, simply because it is oriented toward what many of our authors and readers understand as a stable past, available for quasi-archaeological exploration ("the ancient Near East," "the Greco-Roman world," "Medieval Europe," etc.). That hardly makes us the most obvious medium for conveying the significance of a contemporary populist resurgence, any more than biblical studies would appear a likely arena for perceiving and channeling such a movement's impulses.

The goal of this volume is to point to appropriate responses to the present situation on the part of biblical scholars. That goal leads me to reflect here on the larger enterprise of biblical scholarship, which involves a variety of institutions (universities, seminaries, academic journals, etc., as well as academic publishers) and audiences (classrooms, churches and synagogues, conferences, and subscription lists, as well as multiple "readerships") in loose congeries of industries that might be described collectively as producing knowledge about religion.[2] My thesis is that biblical scholarship as we know it today

2. See sociologist Robert Wuthnow, *Producing the Sacred: An Essay on Public Religion* (Champaign: University of Illinois Press, 1994).

is generally built to *withstand*, *contain*, and *deflect* social change, regardless of the personal predilections or commitments of individual scholars. In terms mentioned above, I think we might say that "exegesis" is *already* "occupied," and not by the likes of the activists in Zuccotti Park.

Medium and Message

In the 1960s, Black Power activists and other advocates of sweeping social change coined the slogan, "The revolution will not be televised." Like other subversive declarations made on the margins of the public transcript, that slogan conveys more than a single message. I understand it to express a certain disdain for the corporate mass media, too preoccupied with producing visually distracting ephemera to attend to currents of lasting social change, let alone help the public comprehend their importance. It is also a rallying cry for the disenfranchised to shake off the stupefaction imposed by the same media and get on with the urgent work of revolutionary change.[3]

Decades later, the rhetoric of "revolution" may sound, well, so *sixties*. It may conjure memories of the terms in which it was already mocked then, in some areas of popular culture: "Well, you know, we'd all love to see your plan. . . . We'd all love to change your head. . . . You'd better free your mind instead."[4] Whenever the corporate

3. Gil Scott-Heron composed and performed the 1970 rap poem by that title, but the phrase already had currency in the Black Power movement and beyond, notably in the speeches of activist Stokely Carmichael. Gil Scott-Heron, *Small Talk at 125th and Lenox* (Flying Dutchman Records, 1970); Stokely Carmichael and Michael Thelwell, *Ready for Revolution: The Life and Struggles of Stokely Carmichael (Kwame Ture)* (New York: Simon and Schuster, 2003), 546. On "hidden" and "public transcripts," see James C. Scott, *Domination and the Arts of Resistance: Hidden Transcripts* (New Haven, CT: Yale University Press, 1990). As Scott's work has been embraced by some biblical scholars, others have disdained it as irrelevant outside the confines of a coercive police state, surely an anachronism for the early Roman Empire. The latter might reflect on the circumstances by which a single "offstage" remark, concerning "the 47 percent," brought down Mitt Romney's 2012 campaign for the US presidency.

4. Paul McCartney and John Lennon, "Revolution," 1968; copyright © Sony/ATV Tunes LLC.

media caricature the activism of the 1960s as an isolated bubble of exuberant, irresponsible self-indulgence, they effectively marginalize the discourse of social revolution, shaping common perceptions that fundamental social change is both *impossible* and *unnecessary, anyway.* Those perceptions do not arise either spontaneously or "naturally"; they are expressions today of profound and continuing changes in the availability, selection, and dissemination of information.

In the United States in particular, the chatter of twenty-four-hour broadcast punditry assures us, for example, that after the collapse of the Soviet Union and the removal of the Berlin Wall, we live comfortably beyond "the end of history," at least as measured by the lack of any meaningful alternative to global capitalism.[5] The invisible hand of the market offers us the best of all possible worlds, we are told, if only the undeserving and irrational poor—whether in Detroit or in Athens—would cease their perverse insistence on the "socialistic" redistribution of goods and the restitution of their imagined losses. The presence of an African American in the White House demonstrates that we live in a "post-racial" age; any members of ethnic minorities who remain ungrateful need to grow out of their self-indulgent "victim" mentalities. Government has no obligation to the governed but to step out of the way of the success they

5. Francis Fukuyama, "The End of History?" *The National Interest* 16 (1989), 3–18; Fukuyama, *The End of History and the Last Man* (New York: Free Press, 1992). One now-dominant narrative holds, in contrast, that the bright, history-less future that Fukuyama envisioned was eclipsed by the terrible specter of terrorism on September 11, 2001. Others have argued, however, that that ominous date provided the architects of a "new American century" a distinct opportunity to launch new and highly profitable wars and extend the disciplines of a surveillance state, largely in continuity with policies preceding 2001; the onset of a "War on Terror" simply provided a mobilizing pretext to continue and extend policies of imperialism and American exceptionalism consistent with Fukuyama's fantasy. The latter argument finds ready substantiation in a comparison of *Rebuilding America's Defenses: Strategies, Forces, and Resources for a New Century*, a white paper from the Washington, DC-based Project for a New American Century (2000), and *The National Security Strategy of the United States of America,* published by the (George W. Bush) White House in 2002. In the words of economist Paul Romer, "a crisis is a terrible thing to waste."

can and should achieve through their own virtue and effort. Only individuals with a grossly malformed sense of entitlement would lay claim to the sort of public subsidy that is routinely offered to corporations, though of course at a far greater scale, and of course without the burden of the pejorative but manifestly accurate label "welfare" (let alone "socialism") being affixed. Least of all is the federal government obligated to change the fundamental structures that create and accelerate economic inequality, or hold the most notorious architects of impoverishment publicly accountable, lest cataclysmic harm be done to "the economy"—the latter understood not in terms of public health and sustainability, but of the volume of financial transactions and the accumulation and concentration of wealth, the only measures that count under capitalism. Of course, it is wholly unremarkable (in the world spun by corporate-owned broadcast media) that the "less government" screed never extends to diminishing the United States' unprecedented and unparalleled global military supremacy, at whatever cost. That supremacy is required, in order at any time to "send a message" about "our resolve"—though this should not be understood to constitute any obligation to ensure the safety of actual people in other lands, beyond strictly delimited "national interests."[6]

Reality in the United States is bleaker than these messages allow. Although the headline is unlikely to hold through a whole news cycle, in reality, racial disparities in the United States continue to worsen.[7] Deregulated and publicly subsidized corporations extract,

6. It might be objected that my presentation is tendentious, lifting up only the perspective of the most recalcitrant blowhards at, for example, Fox News. But Fox News is "the most trusted news source in America," according to polls (Pamela Engel, *Business Insider*, June 10, 2014), and the far-away frontrunner among Republicans and self-identified conservatives; at the other end of the spectrum of corporate-owned broadcasting, MSNBC comes in last, despite its popularity among Democrats and self-described liberals.

7. To document a point painfully obvious to millions in the United States seems precious. Columnist Gary Younge makes the point ably enough in "The Truth about Race in America: It's Getting Worse, Not Better," *The Nation*, June 9–16, 2014.

and export to overseas accounts, profits from the labor of millions, while escaping the burden of federal taxes. Oil companies direct a legislative onslaught against the established science warning of irreversible and catastrophic climate change. In the United States, an ideologically activist Supreme Court has determined that even democracy is a commercial commodity available to the highest bidder (*Citizens United v. Federal Electoral Commission*). And as the Occupy movement has forcefully emphasized, not least through its effective use of the slogan "we are the 99%," unprecedented inequalities of wealth and power put the lie to many a claim of social progress since the 1960s. (Arguably, the fact has gained sporadic attention in the Western press not primarily because of the Occupiers' unflagging efforts, but because now the grinding impoverishment long familiar to two-thirds of the world's population is afflicting the sacrosanct "middle class" of developed nations as well, obliging candidates for public office to give it at least cursory lip service.)

That the explosion of economic inequality is neither accidental nor natural has been illuminatingly demonstrated by journalist Naomi Klein. Her brilliant analysis of the ongoing "sacking" of the global economy (what Brazilians call *el saqeo*) and the maintenance, under the guise of neoliberal economic policy, of a permanent state of crisis throughout the world is, in my view, a concise and lucid articulation of the premise of this volume. Since the 1970s, Klein shows, "using moments of collective trauma to engage in radical social and economic engineering" has become "the preferred method of advancing corporate goals" in country after country, and now quite decidedly in the United States, in a pervasive regime that she calls "disaster capitalism."[8] From Klein's perspective, the precipitous

8. Naomi Klein, *Shock Doctrine: The Rise of Disaster Capitalism* (New York: Metropolitan Books, 2007), 9; Klein, "Daylight Robbery, Meet Nighttime Robbery," *The Nation*, August 16, 2011.

collapse of the US economy in 2007—a climax to years of carefully organized plunder, normalized in subsequent years with impunity for the responsible parties on Wall Street and massive bonuses for financial executives who used the crisis to turn a profit—is unusual only for scale, and for the transparency of corporate management of US economic policy.

I would be testing my reader's patience to attempt any fuller description of our political situation in the early twenty-first century. My point is simply to observe the gap between the most salient challenges of our time and the overarching storylines that dominate "our" media. If we knew of the world only what we were told on cable news programs, it would appear that the maladapted activists of the 1960s and 1970s, with their call for revolutionary change, clearly offered nothing that anyone today genuinely needs.

Nor, the gravest pundits insist, should the morally serious imagine that any other world is possible. There are, at last, no realistic alternatives but to adjust one's attitude to the current relationships of power. The predominant mode of much broadcast punditry—ridicule and ad hominem invective aimed at dissenting views—makes the point: only fools would fail to see the inevitability of the present order.

Limitations of space compel me to describe in monolithic terms a picture that is of course more complex, but the picture should be recognizable to my readers. Decades ago, Noam Chomsky and Edward S. Herman published their study of "the political economy of the mass media," detailing the mechanisms and orientation of corporate-owned sources of information as a "propaganda model."[9]

Bruce Worthington expresses doubts (introduction above) that Klein has adequately identified capitalism itself as the root cause of present crises. I take Klein to mean by "disaster capitalism" not just one objectionable variety of capitalism, but the primary form capitalism takes in our day. Her indictment of capitalism as such is clear as well in her more recent *This Changes Everything: Capitalism vs. the Climate* (New York: Simon and Schuster, 2014).

The years since have only intensified the patterns they described, as deregulation has allowed a handful of gigantic international media corporations to consolidate holdings of most of the broadcast, print, and electronic media in the world.[10] The trumpeted democratizing potential of the Internet is imperiled, as I write, by a sweeping rules change proposed by the F.C.C. that would grant "fast-lane" access to the largest Internet service providers, allowing unprecedented corporate control of the widest source of information on the planet. While it is tempting to attribute the tendentiousness of corporate news and entertainment media simply to the constant pursuit of profit, the cumulative effect is greater and more pernicious, as David Graeber suggests:

> It could well be said that the last thirty years have seen the construction of a vast bureaucratic apparatus for the creation and maintenance of hopelessness, a giant machine designed, first and foremost, to destroy any sense of possible alternative futures. At its root is a veritable obsession on the part of the rulers of the world—in response to the upheavals of the 1960s and 1970s—with ensuring that social movements cannot be seen to grow, flourish, or propose alternatives; that those who challenge existing power arrangements can never, under any circumstances, be perceived to win.

9. Edward S. Herman and Noam Chomsky, *Manufacturing Consent: The Political Economy of the Mass Media* 2nd ed. (New York: Pantheon, 2002). I applied their "propaganda model" to the role of churches in US culture in "A Famine of the Word: A Stringfellowian Reflection on the American Church Today," in *The Bible in the Public Square*, ed. Cynthia Briggs Kittredge, Ellen B. Aitken, and Jonathan Draper (Minneapolis: Fortress Press, 2008), 184–96.
10. Robert W. McChesney, *Rich Media, Poor Democracy: Communication Politics in Dubious Times* (Champaign: University of Illinois Press, 1999; with a new preface, New York: New Press, 2000). In 2012, the six corporations controlling an estimated 90 percent of US media were GE (owning Comcast, NBC, Universal Pictures, and Focus Features, among other holdings); NewsCorp (owning Fox, the *Wall Street Journal,* and the *New York Post,* in addition to Harper publishing); Disney (ABC, ESPN, Pixar, Miramax, etc.), Viacom (MTV, BET, Paramount Pictures, etc.), Times Warner (CNN, HBO, *Time,* Warner Brothers, etc.), and CBS (Showtime, *60 Minutes,* etc.). Subsequent transactions have changed the lineup but not the concentration of media power in a few corporate "hands."

The end result is "a pervasive climate of fear, jingoistic conformity, and simple despair that renders any thought of changing the world seem an idle fantasy."[11] It is all the more telling in this light that the Occupy Wall Street protesters were compelled to depend on a system of hand signals and the "human microphone" to communicate, after the New York Police Department prohibited their use of megaphones and electronic sound equipment. So far as official organs are concerned, it appears, the revolution may not even be amplified. (As Bruce Worthington observes, it may instead be *acoustic.*)

Living after History Failed to End

If there is a bright side to the present crisis, Nancy Fraser suggests, it is that analysis of capitalism's dangerous instability is now so obvious that it is frankly discussed even outside the circle of self-styled Marxists.[12] The unusual attention given to French economist Thomas Piketty's meticulous analysis of the dynamics of inequality is a case in point, though his proposed remedy—a progressive, global tax on capital—is so eminently rational and moral as to be doomed to fail, if left to the whim of current legislatures.[13]

Indeed, the triumph of capitalism is obvious enough even to die-hard Leftists, though they understand the consequences with more gravity than one will encounter in the celebratory corporate media. "There exists only one lord and master, and only one system," wrote liberation theologian Franz Hinkelammert in 1995; the empire of global capitalism "is everywhere. . . . The consciousness that an

11. David Graeber, *Debt: The First Five Thousand Years* (Brooklyn: Melville House, 2011), 382.
12. Nancy Fraser, "Behind Marx's Hidden Abode," *New Left Review* 86 (2014): 55–72.
13. Thomas Piketty, *Capital in the Twenty-First Century*, trans. Arthur Goldhammer (Cambridge, MA: Harvard University Press, 2014). Journalist Eric Alterman writes, "The chances that significant national action will be undertaken to improve the lives of the vast majority of our citizens have fallen to nearly zero, should such action be perceived to conflict with the interests of any subset of the super-rich, regardless of how small their number or how trivial its cost" ("The Power of Piketty's *Capital*," *The Nation*, May 12, 2014).

alternative exists is lost. It seems that there are no longer alternatives."[14] Marxist theorist Göran Therborn emphasizes that rising economic inequality is neither accidental nor insignificant, describing it as constituting the "killing fields" of our time; but he is under no illusion that revolutionary change is a foreseeable possibility, now that Marxist political theory and historiography are largely academic exercises sundered from any meaningful political movement.[15] The end of nominally Communist nations has not brought the end of history, only the final evidence of their bankruptcy, as was already clear enough to the multitudes in 1968, in Immanuel Wallerstein's analysis. We stand now in a "time of systemic transition," he writes, of "deep uncertainty, in which it is impossible to know what the outcome will be. History is on no one's side"—so much for the purported "determinism" of Marxist thought!—"but we do not and cannot know how others will act to affect it, too." But those in control of the capitalist machinery have also abandoned confidence in its durability, Wallerstein observes. They are no longer trying "to preserve the existing system (doomed as it is to self-destruction); rather, they will try to ensure that the transition leads to the construction of a new system that will replicate the worst features of the existing one—its hierarchy, privilege, and inequalities." The looting of the US economy, which reached a conspicuous climax in 2007–2008, illustrates the point.[16]

14. Franz Hinkelammert, "The Crisis of Socialism in the Third World," in *Cultura de la Esperanza y Sociedad sin Exclusión* (San José, Costa Rica: DEI, 1995), 5–38.
15. Göran Therborn, *The Killing Fields of Inequality* (Cambridge: Polity, 2013); Therborn, "After Dialectics: Radical Social Theory in a Post-Communist World," *New Left Review* 43 (2007): 114.
16. Immanuel Wallerstein, "New Revolts against the System," *New Left Review* 18 (2007): 38. The point is well illustrated by comments made by "the super rich" at the World Economic Forum in Davos, 2015: see Alec Hogg, "As Inequality Soars, the Nervous Super Rich Are Already Planning Their Escapes," *The Guardian*, January 23, 2015.

Remarkably, multitudes persist in the conviction, concisely expressed in the slogan of the World Social Forum meeting in Porto Alegre in 2001, that "another world is possible." The long-term policy prescriptions on offer from the Left are often sweeping, morally compelling, and seemingly completely impractical in the present moment.[17] The practices Leftists enjoin for the present are more modestly phrased, however. Therborn encourages "a certain *defiant humility*" as "the most adequate intellectual stance. Defiance before the forces of capital and empire, however powerful. Humility before the coming new world and the learning and unlearning that it will call for."[18] Immanuel Wallerstein urges "actions that we can take, in the short run, to minimize the pain that arises from the breakdown of the existing system, and from the confusions of the transition," including incremental and electoral moves "in order to obtain more material benefits for those who have least; greater protection of judicial and political rights; [and] measures to combat further erosion of our planetary wealth and conditions for collective survival."[19] Both, like other Leftists, enjoin robust inquiry and conversation adequate to understanding the dynamics of our present moment.

We must regard it as significant that throughout the last two decades, as we have witnessed tectonic shifts in global capitalization, progressive social movements have mobilized millions of people to

17. Wallerstein contrasts the "spirit of Davos" with the "spirit of Porto Alegre" ("Structural Crises," *New Left Review* 62 (2010): 133–42; compare Jon Sobrino's contrast of "the civilization of capital" and "the civilization of the poor," *No Salvation Outside the Poor* (Maryknoll, NY: Orbis Books, 2008). Alain Badiou offers as a succinct formulation of "the Communist hypothesis" that "the logic of class . . . is not inevitable; it can be overcome" ("The Communist Hypothesis," *New Left Review* 49 [2008], 29–42). At the end of his argument that debt is the oldest form of economy, usually structured through unequal power relationships to benefit the powerful, David Graeber declares at last that "we are long overdue for some kind of Biblical-style Jubilee: one that would affect both international debt and consumer debt" (*Debt*, 390). I cite these authors to convey something of the "inconceivably" utopian tone of actually imagined alternatives.

18. Göran Therborn, "After Dialectics," *New Left Forum* 43 (2007).

19. Wallerstein, "Structural Crises."

protest neoliberal policies and to draw as much attention to the inner workings of "disaster capitalism" as possible—from the 1999 World Trade Organization conference in Seattle to the XL Pipeline protests, continuing as I write. To draw the line at 1999 is of course arbitrary. The Seattle protests were preceded by the largest anti-war protests in recorded history, mounted, as Noam Chomsky has cheerfully noted, even *before* the launch of the Gulf War in 1991 (to name another date routinely dropped from official history).[20] These depended on lessons learned in the Vietnam anti-war movement, the civil rights movement, Gandhi's campaign for Indian nationalism, and US labor movements stretching back to the nineteenth century—and so on.[21] The Occupy movement in the United States has itself been hailed as having "demonstrated the power of people in motion"; though "it vanished after a few months . . . it transformed our political debate," "transformed the national discourse concerning inequality and corporate power," and opened "the prospect of a democratic revolution."[22] It is "the first major public response to thirty years of class war," Chomsky has declared, revealing that "the public narrative can be changed by the public itself."[23]

I invoke these realities of crisis and popular protest to name the context in which the various practices of contemporary biblical

20. As Iraq "imploded" in the summer of 2014 (News Services), news media "background" usually cast their eyes as far back as the US (bombardment and) invasion in 2003; sometimes skipping further back to the Balfour Declaration, and occasionally, skipping again over a wealth of interesting and relevant developments, back to the traditionally ascribed split between Shi'a and Sunni in 632. The year 1991 was notoriously invisible in US media.

21. The requisite references include the classics by Gene Sharp, *The Politics of Nonviolent Action*, 3 vols. (Boston: Porter Sharp, 1973), and Howard Zinn, *A People's History of the United States*, rev. ed. (San Francisco: HarperSanFrancisco, 2005 [1980]).

22. Institute for America's Future president Robert Borosage, SEIU official David Rolf, and activists Leah Hunt-Hendrix and Max Berger, writing in a forum on "Progressive Strategies in a Populist Moment," *The Nation* 299, no. 1–2 (2014).

23. Greg Ruggiero in the editor's foreword to Noam Chomsky, *Occupy: Reflections on Class War, Rebellion, and Solidarity*, 2nd ed. (Westfield, NJ: Zuccotti Park Press, 2013).

scholarship take place, and to focus attention on at least one aspect of social and civic responsibility shared by biblical scholars today.

Our situation is helpfully illumined by brief reflection on the state of *theological* scholarship. I hasten to acknowledge the historical relationship between the two disciplines, which was established precisely to mark off a field of historical inquiry and, at the same time, to define it in relationship to Christian dogmatics. That is a constraint against which a significant proportion of biblical scholars continue to chafe today. My point in making an analogy between the two disciplines is not to (re)subordinate biblical scholarship to dogmatics, but simply to make an analogous point about the ideological constraints at work when scholarly fields are construed according to preordained definitions of what counts as "religion" or "the religious." To the extent that other biblical scholars identify themselves (ourselves) with the work of *theology,* this is also a way to name our *theological* responsibility.

As Ivan Petrella points out in an impassioned manifesto, the poverty of the majority of the world's people is the material context in which theological scholarship takes place today; and the paramount theological challenge of our time is the general *failure* of theology, even (and in Petrella's view, particularly) theologies of liberation, to address that material reality effectively. (How much more, one rightly wonders, is this the case with theologies that make *no* claim to social relevancy?) Despite their profusion, Petrella writes, contextualized theologies remain "powerless to face the spread of zones of social abandonment. They're powerless because the upsurge of race, ethnicity, gender, and sexuality as organizing axes for liberation theology has blurred the fact that *material deprivation,* that is, the deprivation that comes from one's class standing in society, *remains the most important form of oppression.*"[24]

Petrella's indictment of current academic theological writing, in particular liberation theology (which he takes as its most radical extreme), might be extended, with appropriate modifications, to biblical scholarship as well. He writes that in general, global *economic* marginalization "recedes from view while the *theological* exclusion" of one or another group "comes to the forefront. . . . Helping people become theologians [we might substitute: *biblical scholars*] is given priority over helping people lift themselves from social misery. Obviously, a class choice has been made." The result, Petrella concludes, "is not a theology of liberation, it is a theology of inclusion for the middle class."[25] To the anticipated protest that biblical scholarship is properly concerned with the *past,* not with contemporary issues, I would respond that the protest is an indefensible evasion of the civic responsibility owed our global neighbors, and a refusal to practice professionally the "engaged" biblical scholarship to which Elisabeth Schüssler Fiorenza called members of the Society of Biblical Literature in her 1987 presidential address.[26] It is also a failure to recognize our own contingent place in a single history that includes the ancient world. That failure is not accidental; it is the result of the ideological constraints of our own age.[27]

24. Ivan Petrella, *Beyond Liberation Theology: A Polemic* (London: SCM, 2008), 80–81, emphasis added. The phrase "zones of social abandonment" comes from Giorgio Agamben, *Homo Sacer: Sovereign Power and Bare Life*, trans. D. Heller-Ronzen (Stanford: Stanford University Press, 1995). Alain Badiou observes that the proliferation of identities and subjectivities (which Petrella observes are the focus of much contemporary theology) are generated within a capitalist cultural regime to which they are eminently suitable: "Capital demands a permanent creation of subjective and territorial identities in order for its principle of movement to homogenize its space of action; identities, moreover, that never demand anything but the right to be exposed in the same way as others to the uniform prerogatives of the market" (*Saint Paul: The Foundation of Universalism*, trans. Ray Brassier [Stanford: Stanford University Press, 2003], 14). I thank Bruce Worthington for drawing my attention to the quotation.

25. Petrella, *Beyond Liberation Theology*, 56.

26. Elisabeth Schüssler Fiorenza, "The Ethics of Interpretation: Decentering Biblical Scholarship," *JBL* 107, no. 1 (1988): 3–17.

In what follows I seek to name the constraints operating in several overlapping spheres that biblical scholars inhabit and to suggest practices that may help us to resist those constraints.

The Constraints on Higher Education

Many, if not most, biblical scholars are employed primarily in institutions of higher education. I expect they will need no primer in the deteriorating situation faced by more and more of their institutions, but it is nevertheless important to name specific aspects of what Henry A. Giroux has labeled the neoliberal "war on higher education."[28] As an acquiring editor, I converse daily with teachers facing wage stagnation or freezes, required and under- or uncompensated overload and administrative assignments, deferred or cancelled sabbaticals, involuntary furloughs and leaves of absences, and a generally tense, sometimes even antagonistic atmosphere created by administrators who are eager to prove their institutions financially "competitive." New scholars in particular, but not only they, face a daunting job market. According to a variety of studies published on the website of the American Academy of Religion, in *The Chronicle of Higher Education,* and the Auburn Center for Theological Education, a majority of full-time instructors in religious studies (like their colleagues in other fields) are "vulnerable" faculty, working in adjunct, part-time, temporary, or non-tenured assignments. Openings and opportunities for advancement are often dependent on academic publications, causing a hopelessly glutted publication market at a time when academic book publishing is decreasing in size.

27. On the notion of ideological constraint, see, in particular, Fredric Jameson, *The Political Unconscious: Narrative as a Socially Symbolic Act* (Ithaca, NY: Cornell University Press, 1981).
28. Henry A. Giroux, *Neoliberalism's War on Higher Education* (Boston: Haymarket Books, 2014).

Students face increasingly insurmountable levels of student loan debt, caused by spiraling education expenses (an increasing proportion of them administrative) that were at first supported by federal loan programs. These debts are now exacerbated by the abrupt reduction or cessation of that federal support so that the bulk of available student loans are "private," that is, corporate-owned, with unsustainably high interest rates. Caught between rising costs and student attrition, higher-education institutions are forced into unattractive decisions: to reduce or compromise programs, to lay off faculty, to close departments. The editors of *The Economist* observe that more generous federal budgets led universities and colleges to proliferate and overdevelop to a point of redundancy, and suggest that the current forced reductions in faculty and course offerings and the closing of campuses are but marks of the painful transition to a more appropriate (if not a more equitable) distribution of resources. The editors cannot, however, disguise their enthusiasm for the "implosion," and the concomitant rise in automated online education, since in their view these mark the accelerated transition to a more efficient system that will deliver properly prepared candidates for an increasingly automated world economy.[29]

Humanities departments (including religious studies, or departments of philosophy, history, languages, culture and ethnic studies, etc., where religious programs are given temporary shelter) are particularly vulnerable, since their contribution to an increasingly automated and financialized global economy is far from obvious. This will surprise few readers. The explanation of convenience, which humanities departments labor mightily to dispel, is that humanities majors are less "employable" than their counterparts. But in his

29. "Creative Destruction: A Cost Crisis, Changing Labour Markets, and New Technology Will Turn an Old Institution on Its Head," *The Economist,* June 28, 2014. The phrase "creative destruction" is much bandied about in the corporate world without any hint of irony, a point not lost on Klein, *Shock Doctrine*, op. cit.

discussion of literary studies departments in particular, Terry Eagleton offers a different explanation:

> The impotence of liberal humanism is a symptom of its essentially contradictory relationship to modern capitalism. For although it forms part of the "official" ideology of such society, and the "humanities" exist to reproduce it, the social order within which it exists has in one sense very little time for it at all.[30]

Humanities departments, Eagleton writes, "are part of the ideological apparatus of the modern capitalist state. They are not wholly reliable apparatuses," however, "since for one thing the humanities contain many values, meanings, and traditions which are antithetical to that state's social priorities." At last, the value of humanities departments

> is a question of the power-relations between the literary-academic institution, where all of this occurs, and the ruling power-interests of society at large, whose ideological needs will be served and whose personnel will be reproduced by the preservation and controlled extension of the discourse in question.[31]

Instructors in religious studies at public universities may have the hardest go of it. Religious studies scholars in the field themselves are increasingly aware that their subject matter is a rather wobbly construct,[32] which tends to overlap with other fields of study to an extent that approaches the vanishing point.[33] The majority of religious studies courses offered in the United States are biblical studies courses, however, and the majority of biblical studies courses are offered not at public universities, but at private colleges and

30. Terry Eagleton, *Literary Theory: An Introduction*, 2nd ed. (London: Blackwell, 1996), 176.
31. Ibid., 177.
32. T. Fitzgerald, *The Ideology of Religious Studies* (New York: Oxford University Press, 2003).
33. I offer a personal anecdote that I suspect is not unusual. Several years ago I proposed a course in American civil religion in a religious studies program at a state university. The course was, at length, approved, but only after polite, but pressing questions from curriculum committee members from the history and sociology departments who offered courses with significant overlap.

universities, many of them affiliated with Christian churches or denominations, as well as at seminaries. If this trend continues, it suggests that the general public understanding of the biblical materials will depend increasingly on a form of knowledge production (scholarship and education) that is more oriented than not toward congeniality with Christian self-identity, indeed, toward Christian *formation*, and that this formation may take predominantly Evangelical or Fundamentalist directions (as is explicitly the case already at many institutions).[34]

The Ends of Biblical Studies

Phrasing this issue in terms of "public" versus "private," or "secular" versus "church-affiliated" institutions, neatly misses the point. It would be as inappropriate to insist that critical biblical studies can be taught only by "secularists" as it would to suggest that only "true believers" can properly appreciate the Bible.[35] My concern is with the *ideological context* that shapes both the content of biblical studies and the purposes toward which instruction in Bible is implicitly, and often quite explicitly, directed. Two particular observations may serve both points and hint toward more general realities.

34. Textbook adoption data for 2009–11 indicated that courses introducing the Bible, Hebrew Bible, and New Testament accounted for fully 45 percent of all religious studies adoptions in the United States (PubTrack). A 2003 survey conducted by the American Academy of Religion found that 60 percent of public universities offered *no courses in biblical studies at all*; an update in 2008 found similar results. Yet 72 percent of biblical studies courses were *required* by their institutions, suggesting an ideological investment on the part of the relevant private universities in the formation of their students. In 2013, the largest single institutional adoption of a biblical studies textbook reported to PubTrack was at an ultra-conservative Christian university; the textbook was authored by a faculty member (and was not adopted elsewhere).
35. Market research commissioned some years ago by Fortress Press initially described distinct "profiles" of faculty members in biblical studies, including "confessional" and "secularist" profiles, the latter correlated with work in public universities or in religious studies (rather than theology) departments. Further analysis of the data gathered revealed, however, that 40 percent of so-called "secularist" scholars were ordained ministers in their denominations, suggesting that the statistical profiles were something less than descriptive.

Eagleton's comments above regarding the normal ideological serviceability of the humanities might be applied to biblical scholarship as well. I take as one example Steven Friesen's eye-opening study of the ways poverty in the Greco-Roman world has been presented in a dozen standard academic New Testament textbooks, published between 1904 and 1975. But I should use the singular: there is *one* way in which these textbooks, when they make any mention at all of economic aspects of the first-century Greco-Roman environment of Paul's congregations, generally depict a robust economy and an upwardly ambitious middle class. Friesen concludes that "the twentieth-century mainstream consensus on economic issues in the Pauline assemblies was tedious. There was little progress on the topic [of poverty] and little curiosity about it." Even in scholarship attentive to "social status" published beginning in the 1970s, "economic inequality . . . never gained a foothold as a significant topic of conversation"; to the contrary, "our preoccupation with 'social status' is the very mechanism by which we have ignored poverty and economic issues."[36] Elsewhere, Friesen has suggested that the explanation is to be sought in "an unacknowledged bias": "Instead of remembering the poor, *we prefer* to discuss upwardly mobile individuals and how they coped with the personal challenges of negotiating their ambivalent social status." He proposes that we should label this systematic bias "capitalist criticism": "after all, why should the burden of self-disclosure fall only on the shoulders of Marxist critics?"[37]

The phenomenon to which Friesen points, a general avoidance of certain topics and perspectives in biblical studies, is primarily the result of participation in twentieth-century capitalist culture and

36. Steven Friesen, "The Blessings of Hegemony: Poverty, Paul's Assemblies, and the Class Interests of the Professoriate," in *The Bible in the Public Square*, 121 n. 8; 124–25.

37. Steven Friesen, "Poverty in Pauline Studies: Beyond the So-called New Consensus," *JSNT* 26, no. 3 (2004): 332–36.

ideology, not of either "secularism" or "religious" identity—unless, that is, we recognize its consonance with the practices and discourse of the American *civil* religion. As Robert N. Bellah has described that religion, it includes not only a generally unquestioned assumption of the nation's sacred purpose, but also a fundamental endorsement of capitalism, if not, indeed, the sacralization of capitalist ideology. A triumphant (and triumphalist) "ideology of individualism" is central to American mythic self-identity, Bellah wrote. He observed, however, that in the twentieth century, "individualism" was far more often opposed to the power of government than to the power of international corporations, even though the latter are far less subject to external restraint.[38] Corresponding to the ideology of industrial capitalism, "Americans tend to treat social problems"—like poverty—"as problems of personal morality"; efforts at collective social responsibility are routinely characterized as smacking of "socialism." Within American civil religion, socialism is the arch heresy.[39]

The larger cultural context in which biblical scholarship takes place, then, may be characterized by the privatization of religious symbols and the representation of true religion as compatible with the American civil religion. "Religion" is thus implicitly defined as incompatible with challenges to the regnant ideology of capitalism, except where it can be trivialized as the whimsical idiosyncrasies (or in properly economical terms, the consumerist choices) of "radicals."

38. Robert N. Bellah, *The Broken Covenant: American Civil Religion in Time of Trial* (Chicago: University of Chicago Press, 1975; 2nd ed., 1992), 115. Chapter 5, on "The American Taboo on Socialism," is one of the least discussed aspects of Bellah's work. The theory of American civil religion, which posits aspects of religion—sacred myths, rituals, sacred times and spaces, and so on—to American public life, has become a subfield of academic religious studies since Bellah's inaugural essay "American Civil Religion," *Daedalus* 96, no. 1 (1967): 1–21.

39. Bellah, *The Broken Covenant*, 116. I learned to recognize and study the history and dynamics of American civil religion under Richard A. Hughes at Pepperdine University; his introduction to the topic is *Myths America Lives By*, with a foreword by Robert N. Bellah (Urbana: University of Illinois Press, 2003).

Even when that context has a pervasive influence on the "findings" of biblical scholarship, interpreters themselves may be unaware of that influence, or even deny its relevance outright. The thoroughgoing privatization of religious symbols is often presented as the observation of a "Constitutional" distinction between "church and state," "politics and religion." But of course, familiarity with United States *civil* religion, with its unique combination of nationalist and capitalist ideologies, immediately exposes the artificiality of that distinction. In practice, more often it is those discussions of religious symbols that call into question the inevitability or "naturalness" of capitalist power relationships, especially as these are now shaped by neoliberal policy, that are regarded as inappropriately and dangerously "politicized."[40] The pattern has characterized the invidious campaign of the Institute for Religion and Democracy to pressure denominations and seminaries to discipline, marginalize, or remove moderate and left-leaning members of theological faculties,[41] as well as Glenn Beck's notorious attack, on the Fox Network, on even mildly social-democratic impulses as omens of "socialistic" liberation theology.[42]

The construal of "the religious" as congenial with civil religion has particular consequences for biblical studies because the latter is often

40. Another anecdote may make the point. In 2002, the ISAIAH coalition of hundreds of Christian, Jewish, and Muslim congregations convened to present to invited Minnesota legislators a brief legislative agenda reached by consensus. The agenda was fairly innocuous, including increased funding for early childhood programs and shelters for victims of domestic abuse. Representatives of the Democratic-Farmer-Labor (DFL) party announced that their caucus had already endorsed all the presented items as their legislative agenda for the session. Republican legislators, in contrast, objected that they "resented" feeling "pressured" by the "illegitimate" intrusion of religion into politics. Most adamant in his insistence on the separation of church and state was the Speaker of the Minnesota House, who had appeared in the pulpit of a local church the previous Sunday to ask for support in an upcoming election.

41. The IRD was founded in 1981 by neoconservative theologians and provided initial funding by conservative foundations and, in 1985, by the US Intelligence Agency. The Institute's website is www.theird.org; a brief introduction to its antagonistically conservative agenda is provided by Political Research Associates at www.publiceye.org/magazine/v20n1/clarkson_battle.html.

42. See T. Jefferson, "Glenn Beck: Liberation Theology and Social Justice," *GlennBeck.com*, July 13, 2010, http://www.glennbeck.com/content/articles/article/198/42891.

assumed to have particularly *religious* ends. As an academic editor as well as an occasional seminary instructor, I have in mind the premise, often quite explicitly stated as a norm in seminary and Christian university classrooms as well as in the editorial offices of academic publishers who seek to prepare textbooks for those classrooms, that the test of the value of one or another line of biblical interpretation should be serviceability in the pulpit. That is, "will it preach?" or "*how* will it preach?" The norm has value, of course. Members of religious congregations are overwhelmingly the primary "end consumers" of religious and theological discourse. Their expectation that their clergy will be well educated in critical issues of interpretation is important (though it appears less common, in practice, than other criteria of evaluation). Furthermore, pulpits can often be used to mobilize tremendous popular energy in the cause of social justice, as is evident in coalitions formed and forming today throughout the United States and, of course, beyond.

But preachers, as well as seminary professors of liturgics and homiletics, know all too well the stringent constraints on the average Sunday morning sermon. Professional clergy in particular—those who depend on maintaining congenial relationships with the congregations who pay their salaries—feel and often express, if only to other clergy, the pressure to avoid the risk of disappointing expectations. (As an ordained priest in the Episcopal Church, I have been grateful for the occasions when my colleagues in staff positions have discussed just this pressure quite candidly.) Historians of American Christianity attribute a large proportion of the decline of "mainline" Protestant denominations after the 1960s to those churches' involvement in civil rights, women's movement, and anti-war causes, as well as movements for Black Power, reparations for slavery, Central American solidarity, Sanctuary, and the acceptance, ordination, and consecration of marriages for gay, lesbian, and transgender persons.[43] Time after time, congregants who felt compelled to agitate for these causes found themselves unwelcome in their own congregations and left to pursue what they understood to be their responsibilities in other venues.[44] To the extent their congregations were left populated by, and often substantially controlled by, more conservative members, professional clergy—especially those responsible for the maintenance of old, impressive, yet increasingly dilapidated church buildings—have been especially vulnerable to pressure to conform. Upton Sinclair's quotation, "It is difficult to get a man to understand something, when his salary depends upon his not understanding it" may not be applicable to the vast majority of clergy; but if we substitute "men and women," and "proclaim" for "understand," I think a number of my own clerical colleagues would admit that the point has weight.[45] Even when clergy members dedicate their efforts to social justice advocacy,

43. In the Episcopal Church, the critical point is often identified with the 1967 General Convention budget, which authorized committing million annually to "programs related to the urban crisis" (Episcopal Church Archives). In 1969, Presiding Bishop John Hines, who championed this commitment, also brought forward the *Manifesto* of the National Black Economic Development Conference, which called for churches and synagogues to commit 0 million to reparations for slavery. The church's executive council rejected the reparations clause--but its consideration was sufficient to outrage and alienate numerous Episcopal congregations (William L. Sachs, Thomas P. Holland, *Restoring the Ties That Bind: The Grassroots Transformation of the Episcopal Church* [New York: Church Publishing, 2003], 151 n. 2).To some more conservative observers, the decline of mainline churches is no reason for alarm. The "problem of liberal Protestantism" is simply a surrender to a hostile "post-Christian" culture, and if "the future looks grim" for liberal seminaries, this is the appropriate and inevitable consequence of their own abandonment of a stoutly Evangelical Christian mission (Ben Witherington, "Ancient Future: The Future of Seminary Education," *Patheos*, October 21, 2011, http://www.patheos.com/blogs/bibleandculture/2011/10/21/ancient-future-the-future-of-seminary-education).
44. It is *outside* the churches that I have met dozens of such lifelong activists, and I have been impressed how often they have described their *congregational* formation as decisive for their sense of vocation. I continue to find it peculiar that the exodus of such individuals should be regarded within churches as "losses," as if their retention, albeit in uncomfortable silence, would be preferable. Especially those churches that aspire to be "missional" might look upon such former members, now at work in "the world," as striking successes.
45. Upton Sinclair, *I, Candidate for Governor: And How I Got Licked* (Los Angeles: University of California Press, 1935), 109.

they may be keenly aware of the constraints of capitalist ideology that define the acceptable limits of how "social justice" may be defined.

I hasten to add that this point should not be understood primarily in personal terms. This is an *institutional* dynamic, ably described decades ago by lay theologian William Stringfellow:

> . . . [T]he church becomes confined, for the most part, to the sanctuary and is assigned to either political silence or to banal acquiescence. Political authority in America has sanctioned this accommodation principally by the economic rewards it bestows upon the church. The tax privilege, for example, to which the church has acceded, has been a practically conclusive inhibition to the church's political intervention save where it consists of applause for the nation's cause. Furthermore, the tax preference, or political subsidy, the church has so long received has enabled, perhaps more than anything else, the accrual of enormous, if unseemly, wealth. In the American comity, the church has gained so huge a propertied interest that its existence has been overwhelmingly committed to the management of property and the maintenance of the ecclesiastical fabric which that property affords.[46]

My broader point, to use the jargon of political theory, is that churches (meaning the larger denominational structures, with seminaries, presses, and various levels of judicatories, as well as local congregations) are among the premiere *sites of ideological contestation* in US society.[47] When that fact is not recognized, or when clergy, and the seminary professors who prepare them, fail to address the fact deliberately and directly, the result may be an institutional acquiescence in the dominant ideological currents of the civil religion. To the degree biblical scholarship is evaluated by its

46. William Stringfellow, *Conscience and Obedience* (Dallas: Word Books, 1977), 102.

47. Louis Althusser's discussion of ideology is important here: his 1970 essay "Ideology and Ideological State Apparatuses" is included among other essays in *On Ideology* (London: Verso, 2008). On this and other theories of ideology, see Terry Eagleton, *Ideology: An Introduction*, 2nd ed. (London: Verso, 1991); Jan Rehmann, *Theories of Ideology: The Powers of Alienation and Subjection* (Boston: Haymarket Books, 2014).

serviceability to "church life," that institutional acquiescence becomes a chronic pressure on the practice of scholars.[48]

Terry Eagleton's remarks on the serviceability of criticism in the humanities, literary criticism in particular, seem particularly appropriate in this regard:

> The power of critical discourse . . . is the power of "policing" language—of determining that certain statements must be excluded because they do not conform to what is acceptably sayable. It is the power of policing writings itself, classifying it into the "literary" and "non-literary," the enduringly great and the ephemerally popular. . . . It is the power of certificating or non-certificating those who have been judged to speak the discourse better or worse. Finally, it is a question of the power-relations between the literary-academic institution, where all of this occurs, and the ruling power-interests of society at large, whose ideological needs will be served and whose personnel will be reproduced by the preservation and controlled extension of the discourse in question.[49]

A similar "policing" of language may be observed with regard to biblical scholarship, and the larger realm of discourse it is imagined to support and inform (including the homiletical and catechetical, etc.). What is "acceptably sayable" by preachers or professors may be more or less "historically critical," more or less "pastorally sensitive," more or less "orthodox," depending on the polity and ethos of one or another congregation, one or another denomination. But in order to be considered *responsible* as biblical scholarship within the dominant ideology (in Eagleton's phrase, able to be "certificated"), discourse regarding the biblical writings must be confined to the distant and isolatable past; or, if the interpreter ventures to address the present, his or her discourse must respect the fundamentally *religious* character of the biblical writings and of the meaning they carry, "religious" here

48. See my earlier essay "A Famine of the Word" (cited in n. 9).
49. Eagleton, *Literary Theory*, 177.

necessarily remaining vague enough to be blurred with the premises of the civil religion.[50] Wherever the distance between ancient "Christian origins" and contemporary Christianity is *collapsed*, whether in congregational life or the university or seminary classroom, such "policing" will seem superfluous. The premises of civil religion, which normally are not the subject of sustained reflection, let alone resistance, in either churches or academic settings, readily shape the ambiguity of the language about what counts as "religious." On the other hand, to the extent that discourse about the Bible deviates from the carefully circumscribed parameters of "the religious," we should expect an effective ideological system to rule such discourse *not* "acceptably sayable." As we have seen, that is just what has happened on occasions when the Institute for Religion and Democracy has effectively "policed" discourse by securing the disciplining, marginalization, or removal of theological faculty members. Where the ideological system is particularly effective, we should expect to see successfully "certificated" persons police themselves.[51]

50. The alternatives may be illustrated by two leading textbooks in New Testament studies. Bart Ehrman's *The New Testament: A Historical Introduction to Early Christian Writings*, 5th ed. (New York: Oxford University Press, 2011), is criticized by some educators for its general restriction to *history*. In contrast, D. Moody Smith, Robert Spivey, and Clifton Black continue in the current edition of their textbook "to affirm the necessity of viewing and seeking to understand those writings as products of *an ancient religious community* and its leaders"; it is the religious nature of the texts that they consider most relevant to contemporary readers (*Anatomy of the New Testament*, 7th ed. [Minneapolis: Fortress Press, 2013], xxv; emphasis added).

51. I have encountered remarkably efficient self-discipline on the part of clergy—as when, on the eve of the Sunday preceding George W. Bush's launch of the Iraq War in 2003, two Episcopal priests told me, in separate conversations, that they would avoid saying anything related to the war from the pulpit lest they be perceived by congregants as "Bush-bashing." I also encountered it from faculty colleagues in a Roman Catholic college theology department, in the months before an earlier President Bush's bombardment of Iraq in 1991, who cautioned me against discussing "just war" theory in the introduction to theology course because "the case for this war is so clear." The same colleagues illustrated exemplary self-discipline by removing the adjective "feminist" from departmental course descriptions in advance of the arrival of a new and purportedly more conservative archbishop.

Putting Biblical Scholarship in Its Place

So where does that leave us—"us" meaning specifically those involved in biblical scholarship who recognize, and seek to resist, the dominant ideological constraints of our age?

As a biblical studies editor at a premier academic press, I remain convinced that there is an important place for strong, clear, precise, and innovative scholarly writing regarding the Bible, the history that shaped it, and the history that shapes us as we engage it today. Given the sort of ideological "slant" to scholarship on the Bible that Steven Friesen has described (see above), a countervailing alternative discourse that deliberately attends to the historical dynamic of exploitation and class struggle—in the ancient world and in our own context—is both necessary and, to my eyes, salutary.

But publishing exercises in interpretive virtuosity, whether practiced in terms of traditional exegesis or critical theory, will not be enough. That is so partly because of the changing environment of academic publishing. The late André Schiffrin has ably documented the dismaying consolidation of print publishing (including academic publishing) in the hands of giant media conglomerates. Their goal, in stark contrast to the norm that informed previous decades of publishing, is simply to amass the largest profit possible in the shortest time, by the buying and selling of imprints.[52] The consequent pressure even on university presses to show a substantial annual profit is as deleterious to their work as it is a departure from their traditional mission.[53] In contrast, the smaller market of "religious publishing"—which includes self-styled and self-published "end-time prophecies" as well as their glossier, upscale mass-market equivalents,

52. André Schiffrin, *The Business of Books: How the International Conglomerates Took Over Publishing and Changed the Way We Read* (London: Verso, 2001); Schiffrin, *Words and Money* (London: Verso, 2010).

53. Scott Sherman, "University Presses under Fire," *The Nation*, May 6, 2014 .

forbidden Amish love "bonnet-rippers," and an explosion of "spiritual self-help" books—continues to expand. Entrusting an important message to an academic press remains an important way to communicate clearly and directly with an academic readership, but it is no longer the dominant media signal regarding religious knowledge in US culture (and probably has not been for a long time).[54]

It is at least as important for scholars in their classrooms, clergy in their church buildings, and publishers at their desks as they contemplate imaginary (as distinct from "implied") readers, to focus their efforts quite strategically on these social sites as learning sites and as sites of ideological contestation. In this light, several practices seem especially important for learning sites.

First, we should avoid and resist the limitation of discourse about the Bible to "religious" discourse, more appropriately the domain of "religious" persons and "religious" institutions. Given the pervasive and perduring relevance of the biblical legacy in US culture,[55] its interpretation remains a matter of public concern, and should be engaged as such. (This will mean complicating and questioning the claim that the Bible is primarily a *personal* possession and that merely "academic" interpretation must yield to the views of pastors, pious relatives, etc.) We should ensure that the use of pronouns is consonant with this practice, in classrooms and church sanctuaries alike: does "we" mean, however covertly, "we Christians"? Or "we global citizens who regard the biblical legacy with critical eyes"?

We should name the ideological environment in which the Bible is engaged. (One useful technique might be to ask students to report adjectives and noun phrases linked to the Bible in their own lived

54. For a larger historical perspective, see Nathan Hatch, *The Democratization of American Christianity* (New Haven: Yale University Press, 1991).

55. See Gene M. Tucker and Douglas A. Knight, eds., *Humanizing America's Iconic Book* (Missoula, MT: Scholars Press, 1982).

contexts; another, to describe different "ways of reading" the Bible in various settings today.) Stated religious identities ("I'm Catholic") should not enter classroom discussion without a simultaneous discussion of *American civil religion* and the question of identification with or loyalty to that religion. The nature and claims of the civil religion deserve careful and open discussion and, often, resistance, in all these sites.

We should *discuss* and *analyze* aspects of this ideological environment, not least as a way of *modeling critical thinking* (and critical theological method as a "religious" virtue). If it is worthwhile teaching students about the program of "demythologizing" the ancient world ("three-story universe!" "angels and demons!"), it is even more worthwhile to engage in the demythologization of our own world ("the invisible hand of the market," "what the market requires," the auto-generativity of capital, the mystification of "job creation" and "where wealth comes from," etc.).[56] Distinguishing a global "devastating pillage" from "the market" is a common enough practice elsewhere; it can be in US classroom and congregational settings as well.[57]

56. There is a clear homology between scholarly debates over the Roman economy and the contemporary global economy, suggesting that ideological currents are equally influential in both discussions. *The Cambridge Companion to the Roman Economy* (ed. Walter Scheidel [Cambridge: Cambridge University Press, 2012]) frankly discusses the relevance of slavery, "markets and violence," "relations of domination," and conquest and "predation." Such candor has yet to penetrate mainstream New Testament scholarship, where (for example) Bruce J. Malina can flatly state that in the first-century world, terms like *poor* and *rich* had no relationship to "'class' or economic rank at all" (*The New Testament World: Insights from Cultural Anthropology*, 3rd ed. [Louisville: Westminster John Knox, 2001], 97). See my essay "Diagnosing an Allergic Reaction: The Avoidance of Marx in Pauline Scholarship," *Bible and Critical Theory* 8, no. 2 (2012): 1–13. It is as unusual to hear contemporary economists or politicians recognize that US prosperity is the result of centuries of slavery, colonization, and labor and resources expropriated through conquest, though the historical point is incontestable.

57. With regard to the mystification "the market," a Jesuit conference held in San Salvador in 1994 readily distinguished globalization under the agency of "the IMF, World Bank, Interamerican Development Bank, U.S. Agency for International Development, European Community, UN Development Program and their ilk," which Central Americans experienced as "a more devastating pillage than what its people underwent 500 years ago with the conquest

We should resist the inevitable protest (from students, administrators, juridical authorities, or colleagues) that such contextualizing work is illegitimate "politicization" of a subject matter that must be kept unrelentingly "religious."

Finally, however, it will be important not to overvalue the significance of biblical scholarship as such. It is but a single, particular discourse, relevant and important but not all-sufficient in the struggle for fundamental social change that is here in view. Involvement in direct action campaigns, solidarity with adjacent mobilizations of people, and being explicit about the connections between one's scholarly work and those commitments, if any, are vital. As Ivan Petrella points out, the most important work carried out in "zones of social abandonment" will be organized and led by persons with a variety of preparations and training, foremost among them lawyers and social workers, perhaps. The biblical scholar (like the theologian) may perform the most useful service by supporting others, even in work for which he or she is not particularly qualified.[58]

I am under no illusion that these arguments will be compelling to all my readers. The ideological context in which we all work remains real and powerful, regardless of the depth of our recognition of it. Indeed, the ideological construction of "religion" virtually ensures

and colonization," from "the market." Noam Chomsky cites the report in *World Orders Old and New* (New York: Columbia University Press, 1994), 179. As an editor and writer, I am chagrined that those seeking more precise citation will be frustrated; Chomsky's citation is "Jaramillo, *Third World Resurgence* 42/43 (1994)." Neither previous citations nor the index, provided by Columbia University Press, take us any further, nor does an extensive Google search. I am alarmed at the difficulty I had in tracking what should be a significant citation, but also grateful for Professor Chomsky's ardent pursuit of "Third-World" references (not otherwise familiar to "The World Wide Web"). I am also impressed that a world of scholarship exists just beyond the reach of "global" electronic media. For those devoted to footnotes, I offer a more readily verifiable reference: twice-deposed (both times at US taxpayer expense) Haitian President Jean-Bertrand Aristide readily distinguished the centuries-long village markets of Haiti, "free markets" in every sense of the word, from the austerity programs dictated from distant imperial capitals: *Eyes of the Heart: Seeking a Path for the Poor in the Age of Globalization*, ed. Laura Flynn (Monroe, ME: Common Courage, 2000), 9–10.

58. See the final chapter of Petrella, *Beyond Liberation Theology*.

that many practitioners can afford safely to ignore the question altogether. Further, the "commodification of dissent" determines that a volume like this may prove attractive primarily to a market segment that already identifies with labels like "progressive" or "radical," and thus (in ecclesiastical terms) preach only to the choir, rather than evoke a general moment of self-criticism throughout the discipline.[59] Nevertheless, if a volume like this one can encourage such efforts in solidarity by showing sympathetic biblical scholars that they are not alone in their commitment to the cause of social change, it will provide an important and valuable service.

59. The phrase "commodification of dissent" I owe to (fellow chorister) Davina C. Lopez, as well as immense gratitude for her critical and helpful reading of this essay and helpful comments throughout though, of course, I remain responsible for any infelicities, inaccuracies, or misapprehensions that stand here.

4

Solidarity! Conditions Apply

Christina Petterson

Introduction

Recently, at an academic conference on history of emotions, a keynote speaker was moved to wonder why "the affective turn" was happening now.[1] The suggestions were many, and ranged from the inadequacies of post-structuralism to people's realization of the crucial role that emotions and the body play in our lives. What no one entertained out loud was the idea that "the affective turn" is yet another example of the extreme individualism that so-called

1. The whole notion of 'the turn' is connected with trends in critical theory, as for example 'the linguistic turn,' 'the corporeal turn' and now the 'affective turn' which designates the turn to affect, which is usually connected with the work of Spinoza, and taken up as a philosophical concept in Deleuze and Guattari's work.

cutting-edge scholarship has been producing since "the linguistic turn," which took place in the early 1990s.

While biblical studies, with a few exceptions, have yet to turn towards affect,[2] there are plenty more options available for measuring the claim that the individual has become the ultimate horizon of contemporary biblical scholarship and that such a horizon is consistent with the logic and workings of capital. By focusing on the individual, systemic change is curtailed, leaving behind a cultural resignation that urges us to focus only on ourselves.[3] By this I mean an unprecedented proliferation of reading strategies that focus on the reader, strategies that are conditioned by identity politics and thus produce sedative readings, which do nothing to challenge the system itself.[4]

In this article, I will focus on two areas of biblical studies since the 1990s that operate with such a limited horizon: literary readings and postcolonial criticism. Needless to say these are very broad categories, and I will not be able to address them all in depth nor cover all of the literature. What I hope to do is address the way in which these areas have produced various ideologies of reading, which have managed to focus the debates on individual readers, identity formation, and difference. After arguing that this concept of self is constituent of capitalism, and thus cannot provide any sense of collective opposition, I will shift to the biblical text in the third and final section. The focus on the text is an attempt to move beyond the individual subject, while retaining the emphasis on the socioeconomic context.

2. But see the 2014 call for papers for the Bible and Emotions program unit at the Society of Biblical Literature, and Reading, Theory and the Bible.

3. Thanks to Bruce Worthington for pressing this point.

4. In this article, I place autobiographical and postcolonial analyses under such a heading, but gender and queer readings would also fit snuggly under this umbrella. For an exploration of this, see Teresa Hornsby, "Capitalism, Masochism, and Biblical Interpretation," in *Bible Trouble: Queer Reading at the Boundaries of Biblical Scholarship*, ed. Terese J. Hornsby and Ken Stone (Atlanta: Society of Biblical Literature, 2011).

Reading the Readers: Fernando Segovia and Stephen Moore

Beginning with Fernando Segovia's early attempts at theorising contextual criticism and reader constructs in *What is John*, this section will then move on to literary criticism, of which Stephen Moore is sine qua non. In his conclusion to *What is John?*[5] Fernando Segovia undertakes a reading of the various analyses in the volume according to a grid that maps out different reading constructs and strategies.[6] Segovia focuses on "how the real readers [in this book] address and deal with their own status and role as real readers in the reading, interpretation, and evaluation of the Gospel."[7]

Segovia constructs two readers that constitute the end poles of a spectrum: the universal reader construct, which is a reader, who does not identify his or her location, and thus proceeds without historical or cultural context; and the real reader construct, which is historically situated and culturally conditioned, that is, thoroughly contextualized. The universal reader construct is descriptive (in relation to the "reality" it describes), objective and value free, while the real reader construct is a constructor of "reality," subjective and value-oriented. This is Segovia's primary axis. Secondary axes are related to these two constructs, so that the real reader may be analyzed according to a social/individual reader axis and a compliant/resistant reader axis. The universal reader may be analyzed according to the first-time/multiple reader axis, the historical/textual reader (which reads the text either as if one were in a different time or culture or attempting to match the implied reader of the text), and the naïve/

5. Fernando F. Segovia, "Reading Readers of the Fourth Gospel and Their Readings: An Exercise in Intercultural Criticism," in *What Is John? Readers and Readings of the Fourth Gospel*, ed. Fernando F. Segovia (Atlanta: Society of Biblical Literature, 1996).

6. Jennifer Bird uses Segovia's grid to perform an ideological critique of selected interpretations of 1 Peter. See Jennifer Bird, "Reading the Readers Ideologically: Prolegomena to a Study of 1 Peter," *The Bible and Critical Theory* 2, no. 3 (2006).

7. Segovia, "Reading Readers of the Fourth Gospel," 240

informed reader axis, which emphasizes former knowledge of subject matter. In her article on reading the readers, Jennifer Bird produced this helpful diagram (stylistically modified):

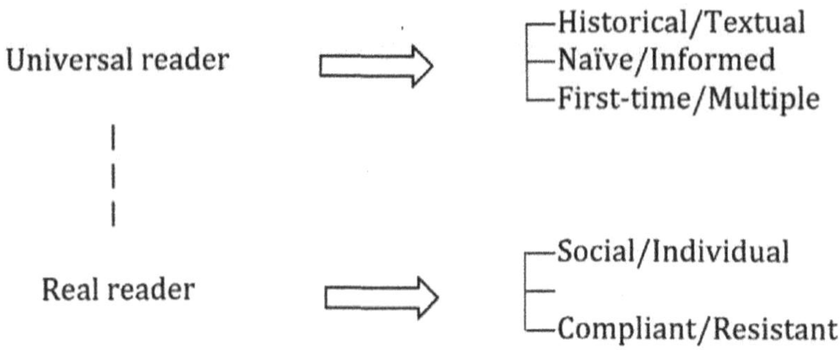

While the universal reader constructs him- or herself as outside the text, the real reader construct is unfolded in an autobiographical fragment, embedded within the reading in a more or less obvious connection with the reading in general. It is worth noting that this main axis—the universal/real reader—also constitutes a moral standpoint. We are left in no doubt of which is the acceptable position—the hint is in the second axis of the universal reader, where the historical reader *pretends* to match the time and culture of the text.[8] I will return to this below, but now would like to examine how this cultural criticism relates to other criticisms that directly invoke the "I" and its experiences, such as autobiographical criticism (Jeffrey Staley) and personal criticism (Ingrid Rosa Kitzberger). Are these various I's conceptualized differently? Do they speak from the same central or marginalized positions and do they address the same issues? Do they draw on the same claims to truth and self?

8. Ibid., 242.

A good place to begin is in Stephen Moore's survey of the field of autobiographical criticism (also known as personal criticism, autobiographical criticism, confessional criticism, autocritography, the New Belletrism, and the New Subjectivism as interchangeable).[9] Pondering a number of articles from the anthology *Reading from this Place*, Moore expresses disappointment in the real reader, introduced in Segovia's article on hermeneutics of the diaspora.[10] Moore is disappointed because Segovia insists on configuring the real reader socially.[11] Even if the reader proclaims that he or she is a believer or German or claiming to "read myself," Segovia understands this as part of a larger socio-religious, sociocultural, or socio-educational context. The reader is always socially embedded and the readings thus have an importance within the social environment they come from. Even so, Moore wants to read Segovia as an individual, and if Segovia does not provide the fodder for entertainment, then Moore must speculate as to the reason. First, he notes Segovia's representation of himself in the depersonalizing particulars of a passport or a census form, and then goes on to ask whether or not this "hermeneutic of the diaspora" cries out for "personal testimony, autobiographical instance, first-person disclosure?" Second, he wonders whether the discrimination that Segovia hints at is too painful to detail in personal terms, at which point he decides not to push any further.[12] Another interpretation is possible, which is not rooted in the individual:

9. Stephen D. Moore, "True Confessions and Weird Obsessions: Autobiographical Interventions in Literary and Biblical Studies," *Semeia* 72 (1995): 19 n. 2. See also p. 21, where he, following Nancy K. Miller, identifies personal (confessional, autobiographical) criticism as entailing "an explicitly autobiographical performance within the act of criticism."

10. Fernando F. Segovia, "Toward a Hermeneutics of the Diaspora: A Hermeneutics of Otherness and Engagement," in *Reading from This Place 1: Social Location and Biblical Interpretation in the United States*, ed. Fernando F. Segovia and Mary Ann Tolbert (Minneapolis: Fortress Press, 1995).

11. In "Reading Readers of the Fourth Gospel." Segovia's axis of the real reader also has the possibility to be individualist, namely in psychological approaches.

12. Moore, "True Confessions," 27.

Segovia simply cannot conceive of the individual in the way that Moore wants, because Segovia insists on the social as the ultimate horizon of interpretation.

In contrast to Segovia's communal focus, we have the autobiographical, or the personal reading as seen for example in the anthology *The Personal Voice in Biblical Interpretation* edited by Ingrid Rosa Kitzberger. As both words suggest, these readings focus on the individual reader, with more than just a suggestion of the autonomous individual's unique status and the reading in question as *my* personal experience. Or as Kitzberger puts it: "The truth is, there is no 'true' reading, but the truth is always personal."[13] This authority sheltered in experience is characteristic of readers who claim a defined perspective to read from, and at the level of criticism, it becomes difficult to challenge. As Richard Rohrbaugh points out in his response to the *Semeia* volume on autobiographical criticism, it is difficult to respond to something one does not understand.[14] And that is exactly what the experiential narratives do. They lock, or at least attempt to lock the interpretation into a highly specialized private experience, which one as a critic is hesitant to challenge for the fear of *ad hominems*.[15] A significant reason for this hesitation is that the methodology is opaque, as Peter-Ben Smit points out in his review of Kitzberger's second contribution to the field: "One would like to know what *method* apart from random self-reflection one could use to do this. In spite of [Jeffrey] Staley's admirable knowledge of extra-

13. Ingrid Rosa Kitzberger, "Border Crossing and Meeting Jesus at the Well: An Autobiographical Re-Reading of the Samaritan Woman's Story in John 4:1-44," in *The Personal Voice in Biblical Interpretation*, ed. Ingrid Rosa Kitzberger (London: Routledge, 1999), 122.
14. Richard L. Rohrbaugh, "A Social Scientific Response," *Semeia* 75 (1995).
15. I have wrestled with analyzing the autobiographical performances of Ela Nutu and James A. Smith's contributions to Fiona Black's edited volume on autobiography and culture in Christina Petterson, "Review of Fiona Black (ed.), *The Recycled Bible: Autobiography, Culture and the Space Between*," *The Bible and Critical Theory* 4, no. 2 (2008).

theological disciplines, one does not learn this (nor does one from his monograph or any of the other contributions in this volume)."[16]

In another anthology on autobiography, Roland Boer's contribution provides a Marxist critique of this literary trend, which culminates in a potted history of the private individual and 'human rights' where Boer shows how the rising individual is connected to the increasing importance of private property within capitalism:

> And so we find, within capitalism, that the private individual is an inviolable unit, the mark of which may be found in the legal system that has developed within the current socioeconomic dispensation. Its task is primarily twofold, the protection of private property and of the private individual.[17]

Boer insists that this is the context within which the phenomenon of autobiographical criticism and its assumption of truth, its claims to authenticity, and its emphasis on ownership of personal stories must be understood. That this is important is evident from the following comment by Stephen Moore in his article: "Autobiography by any other name? Assuredly. Self-Indulgent? Perhaps. But whom should I indulge instead? The stern fathers of our discipline (as it is so aptly named)?"[18] This comment assumes the narrative of the straitjacket, with which Moore ends his article, and is a quote from Jane Tompkins: "This one time I've taken off the straitjacket, and it feels so good",[19] where the discipline against which one is rebelling is cast

16. Peter-Ben Smit, "Review of Ingrid Rosa Kitzberger (ed.), *Autobiographical Biblical Criticism: Learning to Read between Text and Self* (2003)," *RBL* 10 (2004). Emphasis in original. Cf. Ingrid Rosa Kitzberger, ed. *Autobiographical Biblical Criticism: Learning to Read between Text and Self* (Leiden: Deo, 2003).
17. Roland Boer, "He/brew(')s Beer, or, H(om)ebrew," in *The Recycled Bible: Autobiography, Culture and the Space Between*, Semeia Studies, ed. Fiona C. Black (Atlanta: Society of Biblical Literature, 2006), 63. This volume is, strictly speaking, not an anthology on autobiography per se, but, as the title indicates, encompasses this feature as one out of several. There are contributions that do not deploy this way of reading. The three former compilations (*Semeia* 72 and Kitzberger's two volumes) are more focussed on this particular theory.
18. Moore, "True Confessions," 32.

as an apparatus into which one is, well, disciplined. The struggle is thus only between Moore and biblical studies (he can indulge either himself or the stern fathers), where Moore always casts himself as standing on the outside of this implied ideal of totality.[20]

In their astute diagnosis of the politics of difference,[21] Rosalind O'Hanlon and David Washbrook see this principle of self-representation as indicative of the "desire to be seen on the side of the dispossessed against power, working with their strange voices and different stories, subverting dominant cultures and intellectual traditions 'from within the academy,'" which shows up in these self-representations.[22] O'Hanlon and Washbrook's study is a critique of Gyan Prakash's post-foundational history and self-representation within the disciplines of history and anthropology, and I shall return to this in the following section. Here, I would like to gesture towards the perennial outside position, which holds up historical exegesis as the power broker of biblical studies, against which one must resist and demarcate with words such as *traditional*, *conservative*, *essentialist*, and *foundationalist*. However, much is lost in this process, which I will discuss in the final section.

The Postcolonial Subject

The personal experience as the ultimate horizon of interpretation has also found its way to postcolonial biblical studies. The currents in postcolonialism, however, are, according to Segovia, an extension of cultural studies.[23] As Segovia charts the move via his own

19. Ibid., 23 and 43, citing Jane Tompkins, "Me and My Shadow" from *New Literary History*, Moore, "True Confessions," 24.
20. The notion of an implied ideal of totality is borrowed from Fredric Jameson's critique of post-structural philosophies in Fredric Jameson, *The Political Unconscious: Narrative as a Socially Symbolic Act* (Ithaca, NY: Cornell University Press, 1981), esp. 37–38.
21. Rosalind O'Hanlon and David Washbrook, "After Orientalism: Culture, Criticism, and Politics in the Third World," *Comparative Studies in Society and History* 34, no. 1 (1992).
22. Ibid., 166.

transformation, he shows the step from the contextual voice of biblical studies to the potentially subversive voice of postcolonial studies. The first step, that of the contextual voice, implicates us all, whether we acknowledge it or not. The methods we choose, the passages we include in our interpretation, the chapters we omit, the contexts we reconstruct are all bound up with who we are in all our identity formations and social locations. What Segovia calls "the postcolonial voice," however, seems to be one of attitude, in recognizing that this contextuality is empowering for those not usually associated with power. This is, of course interesting, given that one of the main criticisms of postcolonial critics, most forcefully expressed by Arif Dirlik, Aijaz Ahmad, and the above-mentioned article by O'Hanlon and Washbrook,[24] is the negligence on behalf of postcolonial critics to contextualize their postcolonial condition. However, the particular context, which the critics call for, and which *is* patently ignored, is that of the economic possibilities that generated them. This failure to articulate the socioeconomic conditions of their own subjectivity is like something that is likewise avoided in biblical postcolonial studies, which has been recognized in engagements by David Jobling and Roland Boer.[25] But the contextualization that *is* given by postcolonial readers—and that legitimates, or authenticates

23. Fernando F. Segovia, "My Personal Voice: The Makings of a Postcolonial Critic," in *The Personal Voice in Biblical Interpretation*, ed. Ingrid Rosa Kitzberger (London: Routledge, 1999), which indicates a number of stages of consciousness in the process of the Segovian self. Intrigued as I am with the recollection of the "I" of young Segovia intruding into an article, to which the reviewer took much offense, I will focus on the last two stages, "The irruption of the personal voice," connected with cultural studies, and "The entrenchment of the personal voice," connected with postcolonial studies, since these positions seem to address some of the issues raised.

24. Aijaz Ahmad, *In Theory: Classes, Nations, Literatures* (London: Verso, 1992); Arif Dirlik, "The Postcolonial Aura: Third World Criticism in the Age of Global Capitalism," *Critical Inquiry* 20, no. 2 (1994); O'Hanlon and Washbrook, "After Orientalism."

25. Roland Boer, "Marx, Postcolonialism, and the Bible," in *Postcolonial Biblical Criticism: Interdisciplinary Intersections*, Bible and Postcolonialism, ed. Stephen D. Moore and Fernando F. Segovia (London: T&T Clark, 2007); David Jobling, "'Very Limited Ideological Options': Marxism and Biblical Studies in Postcolonial Scenes," in *Postcolonial Biblical Criticism*. See

the biblical analysis—amounts to an account of ethnic origins and feelings of displacement, ambivalence or hybridity—a self-othering of sorts. Some of Musa Dube's postcolonial work is a case in point here.[26] To this list we may also add works by Fernando Segovia,[27] Tat-siong Benny Liew,[28] Stephen D. Moore,[29] and Archie Lee.[30] Or, in the case of biblical scholars from the colonizing side, we often find a description of the moral obligation that has made a given scholar realize his or her complicity in colonialism and the accountability that arises from such a realization. Here, the work of Jeffrey Staley comes to mind,[31] as does the work by Judith McKinlay,[32] and myself.[33]

Aijaz Ahmad defines post-structuralism as a radicalized version of metropolitan literary theory designed to fill the redoubled vacuum left after the renouncing of socialism and nationalism.[34] To carve out postcolonial theory from this larger umbrella term, we may appropriate Roland Boer's contribution to the first collection of essays in the Bible and Postcolonialism series edited by R. S. Sugirtharajah.[35]

also Boer's introduction to *A Vanishing Mediator?: The Presence/Absence of the Bible in Postcolonianism*, Semeia 88 (Atlanta: Scholars Press, 2001), 1–12.

26. Musa Dube, "Savior of the World but Not of This World: A Postcolonial Reading of Spatial Construction in John". in *The Postcolonial Bible*, Bible and Postcolonialism, ed. R. S. Sugirtharajah (Sheffield: Sheffield Academic, 1998); Musa W. Dube, "Consuming a Colonial Cultural Bomb: Translating Badimo into 'Demons' in the Setswana Bible (Matthew 8.28–34; 15.22; 10.8)," *JSNT* 21, no. 73 (1999).
27. Segovia, "Biblical Criticism and Postcolonial Studies."
28. Tat-siong Benny Liew, *Politics of Parousia: Reading Mark Inter(Con)Textually* (Leiden: Brill, 1999).
29. Stephen D. Moore, *Empire and Apocalyse: Postcolonialism and the New Testament* (Sheffield: Sheffield Phoenix, 2006).
30. Archie C. C. Lee, "Returning to China: Biblical Interpretation in Postcolonial Hong Kong," *BI* 7, no. 2 (1999).
31. Jeffrey Lloyd Staley, *Reading with a Passion: Rhetoric, Autobiography, and the American West in the Gospel of John* (New York: Continuum, 1995); Staley, "Changing Woman: Postcolonial Reflections on Acts 16.6–40," *JSNT* 21, no. 73 (1999).
32. Judith E. McKinlay, *Reframing Her: Biblical Women in Postcolonial Focus*, Bible in the Modern World (Sheffield: Sheffield Phoenix, 2004).
33. "Moses and Abraham go Arctic," *Biblical Interpretation* 16 (2008) and "Mission of Christ and Local Communities in Acts" in *Identity Formation in the New Testament*, WUNT 227, ed. BengtHolmberg & Michael Winnige (Tübingen: Mohr Siebeck, 2008).
34. Ahmad, *In Theory*, 34.

In his essay, "Remembering Babylon: Postcolonialism and Australian Biblical Studies," Boer determines postcolonialism as constitutive of the postmodern moment, namely "in terms of a dialectical conjunction between globalization and disintegration."[36] Globalization, meaning the worldwide dominance of capitalist modes and relations of production that took place after 1989, generates the accelerated and dialectically converse process of disintegration, which includes reification (of human relations), fragmentation (of social life and the production process), and commodification (of everything).[37] As Boer notes, while the pace and intensity of globalization and disintegration under late capitalism is unprecedented, the seeds for this phase were sown in the sixteenth century—to which we shall return shortly. In postcolonialism, then, this dialectical opposition is at its most intense, from which he concludes that "this opposition is a determinative feature of postcolonialism as such." While his first example concerns the intensification of globalization in the wake of decolonization, his second example concerns that of Aboriginal art, which became significantly popular in the 1980s and 90s.[38] This interest, Boer states, was due to the interest of the international art market, which meant that the importance of a "distinct and local cultural form" was raised, and that this provided a profile for Aboriginal art. However, as Boer also notes, the object itself, Aboriginal art, changes in the very instance of contact with the market.[39]

35. Roland Boer, "Remembering Babylon: Postcolonialism and Australian Biblical Studies," in *The Postcolonial Bible*, Bible and Postcolonialism, ed. R. S. Sugirtharajah (Sheffield: Sheffield Academic 1998).
36. Ibid., 25.
37. Ibid., 26.
38. Ibid., 27.
39. This means that artwork that displays a commonly recognized feature of traditional Aboriginal art (the characteristic dots, strokes, and native animals) and a spiritual theme (connection to land or dreaming) is recognized as such. Some of the very radical political art that slams the discrimination of the Australian government, its commodification of Aboriginal spirituality,

Boer's example may be extended to the general commodification of indigenous and other "exotic" or "ethnic" identities, which is currently taking place and celebrated at a global scale.[40] To understand this process, as well as the reading strategies we have been exploring, we can turn to the larger socioeconomic framework, namely that of the imperial machine, as theorized and articulated by Michael Hardt and Antonio Negri in *Empire*,[41] which expands the points from Boer indicated above. Hardt and Negri point to the *production of locality* as a central feature of the global flows of capital and empire. The notion that there is something authentic and natural about the local, which is celebrated as difference, heterogeneity, and authenticity over against the homogenization of globality, misunderstands the fact that the local is a product that feeds in to the imperial machine.[42] The imperial machine celebrates the local as naturally ethnic and very authentic precisely because it raises capital: there is a large demand for this kind of market, to which the example of Aboriginal art testifies. So not only is the truth claim inherent in the personal contextualization a natural market outcome of the liberal notion of the individual as discussed above, but the cultural critics, the contextual critics, and the postcolonial critics are also all constructions of and contributors to the machine, despite all efforts and desires to the contrary.

and its neglect of the material reality of the Aboriginal people is not regarded as indigenous or Aboriginal art. I have explored some of these issues in relation to the production of an Inuit identity in Christina Petterson, *The Missionary, the Catechist and the Hunter: Foucault, Protestantism and Colonialism*, Studies in Critical Research on Religion 4 (Leiden: Brill, 2014), 173–76, also page 9.

40. See Graham Huggan's concept of "the postcolonial exotic" expounded in *The Postcolonial Exotic: Marketing the Margins*, repr. (London: Routledge, 2006). And of course, John L. Comaroff and Jean Comaroff, *Ethnicity, Inc* (Chicago: University of Chicago Press, 2009), is a must in this regard.
41. Michael Hardt and Antonio Negri, *Empire* (Cambridge, MA: Harvard University Press, 2000).
42. Ibid., 45.

Postcolonial readings of the Bible generally address unequal power relations, the liberating potential of the text, and the use/abuse of the biblical text in the history of colonialism.[43] These do not necessarily have to be directly connected with personal experiences, as Sugirtharajah's work shows. However, the highly influential postcolonial toolbox developed by Homi Bhabha, especially the concepts of hybridity, mimicry, and ambivalence, is also, albeit obliquely so, based on the experience of an individual.[44] Thus, readings using Bhabha will (perhaps inadvertently) reproduce this individualizing focus in the biblical material.[45]

The postcolonial critic is thus doubly constructed by a capitalist framework: both as an individual—a feature that is common to postmodernist literary conventions—and as an Other, a feature particular to the postcolonial trend.[46] Both of these strains of interpretation are individualist, and in their eclipse of socioeconomic issues, also ahistorical. In her response to the first *Semeia* volume dedicated to postcolonialism, Susan VanZanten Gallagher warned that "without concrete historical grounding, a postcolonial

43. See, for example, R. S. Sugirtharajah, *Postcolonial Reconfigurations: An Alternative Way of Reading the Bible and Doing Theology* (London: SCM, 2003); Sugirtharajah, *The Bible and Empire: Postcolonial Considerations* (Cambridge: Cambridge University Press, 2005).

44. In a review of R. Muñoz-Larrondo, *A Postcolonial Reading of the Acts of the Apostles* (New York: Peter Lang, 2012), I expressed frustration at the author's use of hybridity, which was modified beyond recognition because of Muñoz-Larrondo's unease with its implications for early Christianity as well as his own background. I had not, at the time, thought through to what extent Homi Bhabha's universalized categories are grounded in his own experience, but following Ahmad and Dirlik, I regarded them more as an expression of his class position. If we submit to the experiential and more individualist view, then Muñoz-Larrondo's experience is just as valid as Bhabha's, although the question remains, why use them in the first place, then, if they are not adequate to express the issues at hand? As an attempt to move beyond the individualism, see Joseph Marchal's effort to use Bhabha to decenter Paul by investigating the possibilities for the audience's agency.

45. See, for example, John W. Marshall, "Hybridity and Reading Romans 13," *JSNT* 31(2008); Robert Paul Seesengood, "Hybridity and the Rhetoric of Endurance: Reading Paul's Athletic Metaphors in a Context of Postcolonial Self-Construction," *Bible and Critical Theory* 1, no. 3 (2005).

46. This may be noted in the seemingly endless proliferation of sub-disciplines corresponding to ethnic and/or national identities at SBL and AAR, for example.

metanarrative dismantling the colonial myth is an elusive abstraction, airless and impotent."[47] She noted that in spite of the wealth of context-specific detail, the contributions to the volume nevertheless gestured toward "some kind of central experience of 'colonisation' and 'resistance' that has manifested itself in human history over countless centuries and in all-too-many cultures. . . ." David Jobling has echoed this criticism in his response to the first volume in The Postcolonial Bible series from Sheffield: "Simple links between biblical and current situations, whether they leave the Bible looking bad or good, convey no lasting benefit."[48] Finally, the studies that belong under what Stephen Moore calls the "X and Empire brand of postcolonial biblical criticism"[49] also tend towards this ahistoricism, in their desire to compare the Roman Empire with the American or Chinese Empire. Thus, paradoxically, the tendency to collapse the distance between empires then and now renders historically attentive studies *ahistorical.*

To bring all of these points together before we move on to the next section, it must be emphasized that postcolonialism does not, indeed cannot, undermine or be seen apart from the individualism of postmodern, capitalist subjectivity. That fractured self, toward which Fredric Jameson gestures in *The Political Unconscious* in his historicization of psychoanalysis, is part and parcel of the fragmentation and reorganization of the subject since the beginnings of capitalism.[50] Thus the postcolonial subject and postcolonial

47. Susan VanZanten Gallagher, "Mapping the Hybrid World: Three Postcolonial Motifs," *Semeia* 75 (1996): 232.

48. Jobling's contribution in "The Postcolonial Bible: Four Reviews," *JSNT* 74 (1999): 118. See also his "Very Limited Ideological Options," esp. 194.

49. See the survey of these works in Moore, *Empire and Apocalypse*, 17–19.

50. Jameson, *Political Unconscious*, 47. Jameson notes that the emergence and success of psychoanalysis was dependent on a social development, of which the autonomization of sexuality is a highly significant feature, indeed *the* preliminary feature, that conditions the articulation of desire and the possibility to speak of drives, phallus, repression, and so on. Sexuality as a mere bodily function is sexuality as a "banal innerworldly event" a part of social

criticism is consistent with the logic of capital, and produces a form of resistance that can easily be accommodated within capitalism, given the seemingly endless ability of capitalism to absorb resistance (as long as it is individual).

The Role of History

It seems, then, to have become important to contextualize ourselves, but not the text. The way this is carried out, as outlined above, shows how this focus eclipses not only the historical context but also the socioeconomic concerns of said self and text. Both Stephen Moore and Fernando Segovia use historical research as synonymous with traditional, conservative, and institutional exegesis.[51] In "Biblical Studies 'after' Theory," which Stephen Moore co-authored with Yvonne Sherwood,[52] the advent of theory in biblical studies was cast in a "dichotomy of the literary and the historical,'"[53] or synchronic/

life, which also means that its ability to function as symbolic field is limited: "Its symbolic possibilities are dependent on its preliminary exclusion from the symbolic field" (49). *The Political Unconscious* was written in 1984, before the explosion of body and sexuality analyses, and yet it diagnoses the limited political possibilities of such analyses. As an example see what seems to be a shift in Judith Butler's theorization of body from *Bodies that Matter: On the Discursive Limits of "Sex"* (New York: Routledge, 1993) to *Bodies in Alliance and the Politics of the Street* (http://www.eipcp.net/transversal/1011/butler/en). Does Butler return to a more phenomenological approach, an approach with which she began? See her "Sex and Gender in Simone De Beauvoir's *Second Sex*," *Yale French Studies* 72 (1986). If so, then the very need to return to the phenomenology she left behind in the turn to the materiality of bodies could signal the limited political efficacy (outside of identity politics) of the body as theorized in *Bodies that Matter*.

51. For Segovia, see the place of the historical critic in his personal narrative: Segovia, "My Personal Voice," 27–29. Also, the moral condemnation of the universalism of the historical critic, who pretends to match the time of the text, "Reading Readers of the Fourth Gospel," 242. For Moore, it appears to be constitutive of his work. Stephen D. Moore, *Literary Criticism and the Gospels: The Theoretical Challenge* (New Haven, CT: Yale University Press, 1989), xiii–xxii.
52. Stephen Moore and Yvonne Sherwood, "Biblical Studies 'after' Theory: Onwards Towards the Past Part One: After 'after Theory', and Other Apocalyptic Conceits," *BI* 18, no. 1 (2010). This article, and the following two instalments in *Biblical Interpretation* has since been gathered in Stephen D. Moore and Yvonne Sherwood, *The Invention of the Biblical Scholar: A Critical Manifesto* (Minneapolis: Fortress Press, 2011).
53. Moore and Sherwood, "Biblical Studies 'after' Theory," 24.

diachronic, a dichotomy that, according to Moore and Sherwood, served to minimize the impact of high/critical theory on the field: "To invite the accusation that one's work was 'ahistorical' was to put oneself beyond the pale of 'serious' biblical scholarship and beyond the kinds of questions that the guild was predisposed to recognize as the ones that really mattered."[54] Leaving aside the fact that this statement comes from the two biblical scholars that have taken most delight in positioning themselves on the outside of the "traditional" realm of biblical scholarship—the one as an oscillating agnostic, the other from English literature—the dichotomy, false or not, is an entrenched one, which is clear from a glance in the program of the annual meeting of the Society of Biblical Literature. Moore and Sherwood speculate whether the situation might have been different if the historiographical turn in literary theory (resulting in, e.g., postcolonial theory) had been at the forefront of biblical literary criticism. Given the equal entrenchment in historical studies over the intrusion of post-structuralism into the discipline of history, the probable answer is no.[55]

However, the question is of course whether one, in the dismissal of history, has thrown out the baby with the bathwater? The answer to this question depends on what one sees as a historian's task and whether one regards the accusation of being "ahistorical" as praise or curse.[56]

54. Ibid., 25.

55. For a good introduction to this issue in history in general, see Ann Curthoys and John Docker, *Is History Fiction?* 2nd ed. (Sydney: University of New South Wales Press, 2010). For an introduction to the development that considers biblical studies, a must read is Elizabeth A. Clark, *History, Theory, Text: Historians and the Linguistic Turn* (Cambridge, MA: Harvard University Press, 2004).

56. David Jobling is the scholar who has done much work in attempting to straddle Marxist historical interpretation and post-structuralism. See in particular his considerations in David Jobling, "'Forced Labor': Solomon's Golden Age and Question of Literary Representation," *Semeia* 54 (1991).

The difference lies between what Jameson calls positive and negative hermeneutics, where positive hermeneutics "tends to filter out historical difference and the radical discontinuity of modes of production and their cultural productions" and negative hermeneutics uses "the narrative raw material shaped by myth and 'historical' literatures to sharpen our sense of historical difference."[57]

The point of view in this article is to follow the path of negative hermeneutics, and to emphasize our sense of historical difference. Not only does this mean exercising suspicion toward individualist categories and fragmentation, but also toward such a basic thing as translation. Not enough attention has been given to the extent that Bible translations tend to "update" the biblical texts and make them accessible to a modern reader.[58] The most extreme form of this heavy-handed positive hermeneutics is to be found in the principle of dynamic equivalence—a trend that incidentally arose at the same time as post-structuralism.[59]

Such a negative hermeneutics would follow Ellen Meiksins-Wood and E. P. Thompson, who regard historical analysis an important way of thinking in non-capitalist terms.[60] Of course this is a tricky venture, given that we are immersed in capitalist conceptual categories, but we can at the very least attempt to, as Meiksins-Wood

57. Jameson, *Political Unconscious*, 117.

58. See for example the Good News Bible and NIV's translations of translation of the verb *asaf* in 1 Kings 10:26. In older (pre- or early capitalist) translations, *asaf* is translated as "gathering together," but in the Good News Bible and NIV it is translated as "build up" and "accumulated," respectively. In particular, "accumulate" is a word that we should carefully note, in that this is one of the basic principles of the circulation of capital in Marx's analysis in *Kapital*.

59. For an introduction to dynamic equivalence and bible-translation see Roland Boer, *Last Stop before Antarctica: The Bible and Postcolonialism in Australia*, 2nd ed., Semeia Studies (Atlanta: Society of Biblical Literature, 2008), 135–40. See also Christina Petterson, "Translation Techniques: Modern Versions," in *The Oxford Encyclopedia of Biblical Interpretation*, ed. S. L. McKenzie (Oxford: Oxford University Press, 2013).

60. E. P. Thompson, *The Making of the English Working Class* (New York: Vintage Books, 1966); Ellen Meiksins-Wood, *Democracy against Capitalism: Renewing Historical Materialism* (Cambridge: Cambridge University Press, 1995).

puts it, "challenge the universality of its constituent categories."[61] Rewriting all texts in terms of either Self, Other, or contemporary imperialist politics does not help us use the biblical texts as a reservoir for thinking in non-capitalist terms. In New Testament, important source texts to such a venture could be the collective as it appears in the body of Christ in 1 Corinthians 12, Romans 12:3-8, and Ephesians 1:23; 4:7-16; 5:21-33 as examples of pre-individualist thinking. Another important groups of texts are the various models of household in the Hebrew Bible and the New Testament. The New Testament households are more often than not analysed as distinct entities abstracted from their socio-economic contexts and imbued with notions of public and private space. However, a more thorough historicization could yield results which challenge such a disembedded understanding of household and provide source material for communal living.

One example of negative hermeneutics is provided by David Jobling, who constantly challenges postcolonial criticism to historicize. In his article "Very Limited Ideological Options," to which we have already referred, Jobling urges us to present responsible "translations," that is, to consider "how words of power spoken within one pervasive mindset are capable of being heard within another."[62] The example he uses is that of the Jubilee, debt-remission, which occurs in two different biblical texts: Leviticus 25 and Deuteronomy 15. As Jobling notes, the ideological basis for this remission is that God owns everything, but he argues that this means two different things in the texts, one of which is shaped by a tributary mode of productions, and the other through the household mode of production, which then produces two different theologies (one state-centred and the other household-centred).[63] Finally, he asks, "What

61. Meiksins-Wood, *Democracy against Capitalism*, 13.
62. Jobling, "Very Limited Ideological Options," 194.

might God's ultimate ownership of everything mean within late capitalism, what it is *capable of meaning*?" to which he responds that "until we know how to answer such a question, perhaps we should be sparing of analogies [between ancient and modern empires]."[64]

A second example, triggered by the process of translation, is the increasing use of capitalist nomenclature in the translation of ancient texts. In his commentary on 1 and 2 Kings from 2000, Walter Brueggemann claims that the account of Solomon in 1 Kings 10 parallels "what we of late have come to call 'the global economy'" and that Solomon is "at the center of a huge commercial enterprise in which wealth from every transaction comes to Jerusalem from every direction."[65] I agree with Brueggemann that the narrative is constructed so as to place Solomon at the center; the disagreement concerns at the center of what?

However, is it possible to speak of Solomon's appropriations of resources in terms such as "global economy" or "commercial enterprise"? Roland Boer notes that biblical scholars, who deal with social and economic questions, have a tendency to deploy a capitalist (or neoclassical economic) nomenclature when dealing with ancient texts, and that what ends up taking place is the perpetuation of the myth that capitalism is everywhere "in various stages of its long path to maturity."[66] This means that while Brueggemann uses this terminology to critique what he calls the "uncaring massive force" of global economy,[67] he actually ends up reaffirming it as a ubiquitous

63. By using mode of production Jobling refuses to grant capitalism a privileged ubiquitous presence, since the very category of 'mode of production' builds in the difference between modes of production. Jobling, "Forced Labor."

64. Jobling, "Forced Labor," 195

65. Walter Brueggemann, *1 & 2 Kings*, Smyth & Helwys Bible Commentary Series (Macon: Smyth and Helwys, 2000), 135.

66. Roland Boer, "The Sacred Economy of Ancient 'Israel,'" *Scandinavian Journal of the Old Testament* 21, no. 1 (2007): 35. See also Roland Boer, *The Sacred Economy of Ancient Israel*. Library of Ancient Israel (Louisville: Westminster John Knox), 2014.

67. Brueggemann, *1 & 2 Kings*, 138.

force, naturalizing capitalism as a deeper human drive. That is, it is "natural" for human beings to pursue profit, but these ancients didn't quite know how to do it as well as we do—incidentally an argument advanced by Adam Smith in *The Wealth of Nations.*[68]

These two examples serve to indicate the problems of thinking historically about the biblical texts, and how important it is to historicize the texts, and emphasize the distance between the world of the text from our contemporary situations, lest we produce unintended complacent readings in place of radical politics. This also means that it is necessary to historicize our own place, not (only) in terms of categories of identity, but in terms of our immersion in capitalist categories. Reproducing the economic categories of capitalism, as Brueggemann does, urges the reader to find solutions within that self-same system, and not outside it.

There are several ways of approaching this problem. One way is to enhance the strangeness of the biblical texts by focusing on other categories apart from the individual, but rather the collective, and to try and understand the differences in conceptualizing collectivity in the ancient world.[69] Connected to this is Jameson's approach to history, which is based on that of Louis Althusser, and the access to history exclusively through its effects. This means that history is in effect "inaccessible to us except in textual form," with the consequence that the object under examination "brings into being

68. In his chapter on agricultural systems, he concludes an exposition of trade in ancient societies with the following: "All systems either of preference or of restraint, therefore, being thus completely taken away, the obvious and simple system of natural liberty establishes itself of its own accord." Adam Smith, *An Inquiry into the Nature and Causes of the Wealth of Nations*, Modern Library (New York: Random House, 1937 [1776]), 651.

69. I have tried to do this in an article called "Imagining the Body of Christ" in *Sexuality, Ideology and the Bible: Antipodean Engagements*, ed. C. Blyth and R. Myles (Sheffield: Sheffield Phoenix Press, forthcoming). I am still thinking through some of these issues relating to history and historical approaches, but in that article, I try to read the body of Christ and the community in 1 Corinthians in terms of Philo's *diairesis*, in order to bring out the radical alterity in the conceptualisation.

that very situation to which it is also, at one and the same time, a reaction."[70] Not only does this mean that history necessarily takes shape as a reconstruction of events unavailable to us, but also that a context independent of the material in question is an illusion, since the context necessarily derives from precisely textual material.[71]

Another way would be to examine the process of domestication of the biblical texts and how history has worked to shut down and exclude various interpretative possibilities, which could have had radical consequences for the theological and thus epistemological developments of the West. Imagine, for example, how the superstructures of the West would have looked, if John's gospel had not been part of our Bible? Can this be reconciled with Slavoj Žižek's point in "The Fragile Absolute":

> The past is not simply past, but bears with it its proper utopian promise of a future Redemption; in order to understand a past epoch properly, it is not sufficient to take into account the historical conditions out of which it grew—one also has to take into account the utopian hopes of a Future that were betrayed and crushed by it—that which was "negated," that which did not happen—so that the past historical reality was the way it was. What the proper historical stance "relativizes" is not the past, but paradoxically, *the present itself*—our present can be conceived only as the outcome (not of what actually happened in the past, but also) of the crushed potentials for the future that were contained in the past.[72]

Conclusion

I am currently working with eighteenth-century handwritten German manuscripts and was astounded by how foreign and

70. Jameson, *Political Unconscious*, 67.
71. A similar approach to history emerges from Henri Lefebvre's spatial analyses in *The Production of Space*, trans. Donald Nicholson-Smith (Malden: Blackwell, 2005).
72. Slavoj Žižek, *The Fragile Absolute: Or, Why is the Christian Legacy Worth Fighting For?* (London: Verso, 2000), 89–90. See Neil Elliott's deployment of this in *The Arrogance of the Nations: Reading Romans in the Shadow of Empire*, Paul in Critical Contexts (Minneapolis, MN: Fortress Press, 2008), 159–61. Thanks to Bruce Worthington for suggesting this quote.

different they appear to me in comparison with the biblical material. This is no doubt due to a host of different reasons (such as the actual dusty manuscripts, with brown fingerprints and ink-splatters), but also because the biblical texts have been tamed, and their radical alterity subdued over centuries. Whilst literary readings perhaps seem radical when regarded over against a stifling clerical tradition, their radical nature remains academic and promotes, indeed celebrates, individualism. Postcolonialism follows this trend, and leaves behind the programmatic sociopolitical focus of liberation theology, which is regarded as one of its influences, yet remains exceedingly difficult to discern. What I have argued for in this article is historization of text and of self, in order to bring out the true radical nature of the material we work with and the cannibalistic socioeconomic conditions with which we approach them.[73]

73. This article is roughly based on a couple of papers given at international and annual meetings of the Society of Biblical Literature: "Autobiography and the Real Reader"' from Vienna 2007; "King Solomon and the Global Economy" and "Class, Hybridity, and the Bible: Does It Work?" both from San Francisco 2011. A version of the latter was given as "Biblical Inequality and Our Sphere of Concern: On the Failure of Postcolonial Biblical Criticism" at a research seminar at the Theology Programme at Otago University, Dunedin. I would like to thank the people present for comments and suggestions. Also, this article has benefited from discussions with Jorunn Økland, Robert Myles, and Roland Boer.

PART II

Global Crisis and the First Testament

5

On the Feasibility of Subsistence Economics

Roland Boer

> Come, my beloved,
> let us go forth into the fields,
> and lodge in the villages.
> –Song of Solomon 7:11

I would like here to explore the possibility that subsistence economics may be viable today. Rather than offer a somewhat idealistic image, full of bucolic bliss, backyard vegetable gardens and chicken yards, I am interested in the specific economic structure of what may be called subsistence survival. For that economic analysis, my focus is ancient southwest Asia, the larger context in which ancient Israel (southern Levant) was found, and thereby the context of the production of the Hebrew Bible. In fact, given that the southern Levant was always politically, culturally, and economically marginal, subsistence survival was the normal and dominant economic form for much of its history. In order to develop my argument, I draw on material across ancient southwest Asia for two reasons: first, it indicates the context in which ancient Israel functioned; second, it draws together relevant evidence for an area—the southern Levant—that is notably short on concrete data concerning economic forms.[1] I also refer from time to time to biblical texts where they are relevant, but we should be perpetually wary of reading them as simple references to reality. Biblical material is notoriously slippery when it comes to such matters. For this reason, I also rely on recent archaeological material from the territory where ancient Israel rose briefly, before it became an imperial province. The following analysis outlines, first, the nature of subsistence economics in the ancient world, with its crops, herds, kinship, and household structures. Then, after indicating the persistence and temporal range of subsistence survival, I ask whether it is viable today, and, if so, what may need to be adapted to make it work.

Before proceeding, I should say a few words on why the focus on subsistence economics is less common in biblical scholarship than it should be. The reason lies as much with specific methods of analysis as it does on the socioeconomic—and thereby ideological—context in which we do our work. It is no accident that the dominant way of analyzing the ancient world is a neoclassical one. By neoclassical I mean the approach to economics that derived from the classical economists such as Adam Smith, David Ricardo, and Thomas Malthus.[2] Neoclassical economics removed the political and social concerns of the earlier classical economists and focused on reducing economics to a "science." That is, it sought to de-historicize, de-

1. Crucially, the use of parchment rather than clay tablets in the southern Levant means that records apart from the slippery material in the Hebrew Bible are few and far between.
2. Roland Boer and Christina Petterson, *Idols of Nations: Biblical Myth at the Origins of Capitalism* (Minneapolis: Fortress Press, 2014).

socialize, and individualize economics, so that it merely explained the world through the eyes of dominant powers. It is no accident that such an approach arose first in Europe and then North America. The result is a method now refined to three assumptions concerning economic activity and indeed human nature: economic systems naturally achieve equilibrium ("crisis" then needs to be explained); individuals are rational actors that seek their own advantage (*homo economicus*); the market is a mechanism to itself, outside social and political forces. It is obvious that such assumptions arise from an ideal as to what capitalism should be rather than what it really is. But what happens with this reductionism is that it enables what is called economics imperialism.[3] Having excised matters of class, institutions, history, and even religion from economic analysis, this redefined neoclassical economics then engaged in colonizing these and every other area of the social sciences and humanities—and continues to do so vigorously today. Particularly from the 1980s onwards (with the "fall" of communism) the extraordinarily narrow principles of rationality and equilibrium became a "universal grammar" for analyzing human behavior, institutions, history, geography, neural networks (neuroeconomics), and even religion.[4] This economics imperialism has also been applied to reconstructing the economies of ancient Israel within the context of ancient southwest Asia.[5] My essay

3. Ben Fine and Dimitris Milonakis, *From Economics Imperialism to Freakonomics: The Shifting Boundaries between Economics and Other Social Sciences* (London: Routledge, 2009); Dimitris Milonakis and Ben Fine, *From Political Economy to Economics: Method, the Social and the Historical in the Evolution of Economic Theory* (London: Routledge, 2009).

4. See, for instance, Lionel Robbins, *An Essay on the Nature and Significance of Economic Science* (London: Macmillan, 1935 [1932]); Gary S. Becker, *The Economic Approach to Human Behavior* (Chicago: University of Chicago Press, 1976); Rachel McCleary, ed., *The Oxford Handbook of the Economics of Religion* (Oxford: Oxford University Press, 2010); Larry Witham, *Marketplace of the Gods: How Economics Explains Religion* (Oxford: Oxford University Press, 2010). Polanyi's curt reply is to the point: "No human motive is per se economic" (Karl Polanyi, *Primitive, Archaic and Modern Economies* [Boston: Beacon, 1971 (1968)], 63).

5. I have counted at least four such projects: the International Scholars Conference on Ancient Near Eastern economies (coordinated by Michael Hudson); the Vienna START project; the

is then written as a resistance to this kind of economic analysis, which stretches its imperialism to argue that even in ancient Israel, human beings were "partly capitalist."[6]

Subsistence Economics

> *Le premier point est que la communauté de village existe encore comme élément essentiel d'une structure économique (et politique).*[7]

Crops and herds—these are two economic components of subsistence survival. As for the crops, their variations depended on rainfall patterns and soil types,[8] but in the southern Levant they included glume wheats (emmer and einkorn), barley, and lentils, while minor crops included various types of peas, chickpeas, grapes, figs, dates, olives, and nuts. There is nothing particularly stunning here, for these are high-yield crops with a range of benefits. But what is most interesting is the way labor was organized to grow such crops. Did farmers own their own fields, passing them on as an inalienable inheritance from generation to generation? No, for the situation was quite different, especially in what Soviet-era Russian scholars called the pattern of field shares in the village-commune,[9] a technique that

Dutch "Economy of Ancient Mesopotamia" group; and odd coterie from Stanford University inspired by Ian Morris.

6. Guillermo Algaze, *Ancient Mesopotamia at the Dawn of Civilization: The Evolution of an Urban Landscape* (Chicago: University of Chicago Press, 2008), 42.

7. Mario Liverani, "Communautés de village et palais royal dans la Syrie du IIème millénaire," *Journal of the Economic and Social History of the Orient* 18 (1975): 163–64.

8. The minimum rainfall for dry farming is 200–350 mm per annum, although this varied according to region, from wetland niches and well-watered floodplains to areas with an annual rainfall as low as 150 mm. David Hopkins offers a full survey of rainfall and climate matters for the Levant, along with a judicious assessment of water conservation techniques (Hopkins, *The Highlands of Canaan: Agricultural Life in the Early Highlands* [Sheffield: Almond, 1985], 79–108, 171–87).

9. Igor M. Diakonoff, "The Commune in the Ancient East as Treated in the Works of Soviet Researchers," in *Introduction to Soviet Ethnography*, ed. Stephen P. Dunn and Ethel Dunn (Berkeley: Highgate Road Social Science Research Station, 1974), 2:519–48; Diakonoff, "The Rural Community in the Ancient Near East," *Journal of the Economic and Social History of the Orient* 18, no. 2 (1975): 121–33; Diakonoff, "The Structure of Near Eastern Society before

has also been called *musha‘* farming.[10] Instead of fields as private property, the land around the village was divided into field-shares, usually non-contiguous with one another. These were often long, rather narrow strips, able to be plowed in long furrows. But the

the Middle of the Second Millennium B.C.," *Oikumene* 3 (1982): 35; Diakonoff, "General Outline of the First Period of the History of the Ancient World and the Problem of the Ways of Development," in *Early Antiquity*, ed. Igor M. Diakonoff and Philip L. Kohl (Chicago: University of Chicago Press, 1991), 34–35; Diakonoff, "Early Despotisms in Mesopotamia," in *Early Antiquity*, 88; Ninel B. Jankowska, "Communal Self-Government and the King of the State of Arrapha," *Journal of the Economic and Social History of the Orient* 12 (1969): 233–82; Jankowska, "Asshur, Mitanni, and Arrapkhe," in *Early Antiquity*, 253; L. S. Vasil'ev and I. A. Stuchevskii, "Three Models for the Origin and Evolution of Precapitalist Societies," *The Soviet Review* 8.3 (1967): 28–32; Roger P. Bartlett, *Land Commune and Peasant Community in Russia: Communal Forms in Imperial and Early Soviet Society* (London: Palgrave Macmillan, 1990). I understand "village-commune" and "village community" here as covering a complex range, from farmstead through hamlet to village. Roberts provides an insightful discussion of the variability of terminology (Brian Roberts, *Landscapes of Settlement: Prehistory to the Present* [London: Routledge, 1996], 15–19). The population of the village-commune was typically between 75–150 people, although often smaller settlements had less than 75 (Douglas A. Knight, *Law, Power, and Justice in Ancient Israel*, Library of Ancient Israel [Louisville: Westminster John Knox, 2011], 122–23).

10. The term *musha‘* was first used by Samuel Bergheim in the late nineteenth century (Bergheim, "Land Tenure in Palestine," *Palestine Exploration Fund Quarterly* 26, no. 3 (1894): 191–99). Significant studies followed in the twentieth century: Robert McCormick Adams, "Property Rights and Functional Tenure in Mesopotamian and Rural Communities," in *Societies and Languages of the Ancient Near East: Studies in Honour of I. M. Diakonoff*, ed. J. N. Postgate et al. (Warminster: Aris and Phillips, 1982), 1–14; Helga Seeden, and Muhamed Kaddour, "Space, Structures and Land in Shams ed Dīn Tannīra on the Euphrates: An Ethnoarchaeological Perspective," in *Land Tenure and Social Transformation in the Middle East*, ed. Tarif Khalidi (Beirut: American University of Beirut Press, 1984), 495–526; Abraham Granott, *The Land System of Palestine in History and Structure* (London: Eyre and Spottiswood, 1952); Jacques Weulersse, *Paysans de Syrie et du Proche Orient* (Paris: Gallimard, 1946); Amos Nadan, "Colonial Misunderstanding of an Efficient Peasant Institution," *Journal of the Economic and Social History of the Orient* 46 (2003): 320–54; Amos Nadan, *The Palestinian Peasant Economy under the Mandate: A Story of Colonial Bungling* (Cambridge, MA: Harvard University Press, 2006; Ya'akov Firestone, "The Land-equalizing Mushâ‘ Village," in *Ottoman Palestine*, ed. Gad G. Gilbar (Leiden: Brill, 1990), 91–130; Birgit Schäbler, "Practicing Musha‘: Common Lands and the Common Good in Southern Syria under the Ottomans and the French (1812–1942)," in *Rights to Access, Rights to Surplus: New Approaches to Land in the Middle East*, ed. Roger Owen (Cambridge, MA: Harvard University Press, 2000), 241–309. To the advantage of those who have studied these practices closely, for the Ottoman period maps of *musha‘* field systems, or at least post-*musha‘* landscapes that retain the patterns of earlier practices, have been published: Tony Wilkinson, "The Tell: Social Archaeology and Territorial Space," in *Development of Pre-State Communities in the Ancient Near East*, ed. Dianne Bolger and Louise C. Maguire (Oxford: Oxbow, 2010), 58; Weulersse, *Paysans de Syrie et du Proche Orient*, fig. 37.

key was that they were periodically reallocated, every one or two years. Members of the village would therefore find themselves with different land shares on each occasion.[11] In the same way that the land shares were regularly reallocated, so also was the produce, for it went into the common pool of the village, there to be threshed and ground, sorted and cleaned, dried and preserved. From there it was reallocated to members of the village-commune.

How were these processes decided? It may have been by lot, but more often it was determined by a village mayor, or council of elders, or all the able-bodied men.[12] Here we encounter what is ultimately

11. The relevant term from the Hebrew Bible is *ḥelĕqat haśadeh*, more often functioning as a metaphor (Gen. 33:19-20; Ruth 4:3, 2 Sam. 14:30-31; 2 Kgs. 9:21, 25; Jer. 12:10; Amos 4:7; note also the verb *ḥlq*, "apportion" in Jer. 37:12). This is not, as it is so often rendered, a field or plot of land, but a movable and reallocated land share. In this light, it is possible to understand the various references to "boundary" or "landmark" (Deut. 19:14; 27:17; Prov. 22:28 and 23:10; Job 24:2; Hos. 5:10), to "the lot (*gôral*) of their *naḥălâ*" (Josh. 14:2; see also 18:2-10), as well as to the "measuring rope" (*ḥebel*), the semantic field of which actually includes an "allotted portion" of land (Deut. 3:4, 13-14; 32:9; Amos 7:17; Mic. 2:5; Zeph. 2:6-7; Zech. 1:16; 2:5; Ps. 16:6; 78:55; 105:11). A consistent thread of some awareness of this approach to agriculture may be found among biblical commentators, albeit with more or less specificity: Albrecht Alt, *Kleine Schriften zur Geschichte des Volkes Israel* (Munich: Beck, 1959), 3:348–72; K. H. Henrey, "Land Tenure in the Old Testament," *Palestine Exploration Quarterly* 86 (1954): 5–15; Josef Kohler, "Gemeinderschaft und Familiengut im israelitischen Recht," *Zeitschrift für Vergleichende Rechtswissenschaft* 17 (1959): 217–22; Edward Neufeld, "The Emergence of a Royal-Urban Society in Ancient Israel," *Hebrew Union College Annual* 31 (1960): 32; Karl Elliger, "Allotment," in *The Interpreter's Dictionary of the Bible*, ed. George Arthur Buttrick (Nashville: Abingdon, 1962); Marvin L. Chaney, "Ancient Palestinian Peasant Movements and the Formation of Premonarchic Israel," in *Palestine In Transition: The Emergence of Ancient Israel*, ed. David Noel Freedman and David Frank Graf (Sheffield: Almond, 1983), 64–65; Stephen A. Kaufman, "A Reconstruction of the Social Welfare System of Ancient Israel," in *In the Shelter of Elyon: Essays on Ancient Palestinian Life and Literature in Honour of G.W. Ahlstrom*, ed. W. Boyd Barrick and John R. Spencer (Sheffield: JSOT, 1984), 280; Niels Peter Lemche, *Early Israel: Anthropological and Historical Studies on the Israelite Society Before the Monarchy*, trans. Frederick H. Cryor (Leiden: Brill, 1985), 196–98; Christopher J. H. Wright, *God's People in God's Land: Family, Land, and Property in the Old Testament* (Grand Rapids, MI: Eerdmans, 1990), 70; Shunya Bendor, *The Social Structure of Ancient Israel: The Institution of the Family (Beit'Ab) from the Settlement to the End of the Monarchy* (Jerusalem: Simor, 1996), 141–60; Anne M. Kitz, "Undivided Inheritance and Lot Casting in the Book of Joshua," *Journal of Biblical Literature* 119 (2000): 601–18.

12. This process was part of the wider pattern of customary law, for which see the comprehensive study by Knight, *Law, Power, and Justice in Ancient Israel*, 115–56.

a problem with the agricultural system of the village-commune, a problem that concerns its social relations (see further below). These involved the kinship-household, in which the kinship structures were deeply patriarchal. No matter how flexible genealogies may be, no matter how much a household (a social unit that included animals) may be characterized by the rhythms and flows of life, it was a social structure determined by the older men. The most telltale sign of this situation is where the partner in a reproductive pairing would go. If the woman went to the man's household, then she was under his and ultimately the oldest male's direction; if a man went to a woman's household, then both were under the control of the headman of that household.[13] So also with the patterns of allocation in a village-commune, each of which was usually coterminous with the kinship group.[14] Even in its most representative form, the process of decision making involved the able-bodied men. More often, and especially in the southern Levant where Israel appeared late on the scene, the reality was more often a council of elders (or "fathers"), along with a village headman.[15]

13. Mieke Bal calls this "virilocal" and "patrilocal" marriage, in contrast to the misleading designation of patrilocal and matrilocal (Bal, *Death and Dissymetry: The Politics of Coherence in the Book of Judges* [Chicago: University of Chicago Press, 1988]; David Jobling, "Feminism and 'Mode of Production' in Ancient Israel: Search for a Method," in *The Bible and the Politics of Exegesis: Essays in Honor of Norman K. Gottwald on His Sixty-Fifth Birthday*, ed. David Jobling, Peggy L. Day, and Gerald T. Sheppard [Cleveland, OH: Pilgrim Press, 1991], 239–51).

14. Jankowska, "Communal Self-Government," 239–53; J. David Schloen, *The House of the Father as Fact and Symbol: Patrimonialism in Ugarit and the Ancient Near East* (Winona Lake, IN: Eisenbrauns, 2001), 155–65; Mario Liverani, *Israel's History and the History of Israel*, trans. Chiara Peri and Philip Davies (London: Equinox, 2005), 21–22.

15. Jankowska, "Communal Self-Government," 274–76; Igor M. Diakonoff, "Commune in the Ancient East," 532, 540. See Diakonoff for the detailed terminology (Diakonoff, "The Structure of Near Eastern Society," 7–100). Traces may be found in the biblical *zĕkēnîm* and *ziqnê hā'îr*, "elders" and "elders of a town" (Deut. 19:12; 21:3; Josh. 20:4; 1 Sam. 16:4; Ruth 4:2). A number of studies deal with the councils of elders, mayors, and even assemblies, in Bronze Age Emar, Ugarit, Alalakh, and Israel (Michael Heltzer, *The Rural Community in Ancient Ugarit* [Wiesbaden: Reichert, 1976], 75–83; Paula M. McNutt, *Reconstructing the Society of Ancient Israel* [London: SPCK, 1999], 100–101, 176; Liverani, *Israel's History and the History of Israel*, 22; Daniel E. Fleming, "The Integration of Household and Community Religion in Ancient

The other dimension of subsistence survival concerns our four-footed friends, above all the domesticated goat and sheep, along with bovines for traction. Over a long process that began in the tenth millennium BCE, human beings, animals, and crops experienced a fundamental shift in their relationships.[16] The reasons are unclear, although the most persuasive analyses focus on a mix of social, economic, cultural, and environmental factors in which mutual agency brought about a decisive change in the mode of production and the sense of how life itself should be lived. Over some four millennia, the good-tempered and social ruminants—goats, sheep, and then later pigs—mutated. Through restriction of movement, controlled breeding, and regulation of feeding, lactation became sustained, wool became longer and more amenable to human use, and the animals became smaller than their wild relatives. Plants too changed, becoming dependent on human beings for reproductive success, just as human beings became thoroughly dependent on these

Syria," in *Household and Family Religion in Antiquity: Contextual and Comparative Perspectives*, ed. John Bodel and Saul M. Olyan (Malden, MA: Blackwell, 2008), 39; Knight, *Law, Power, and Justice in Ancient Israel*, 72–73).

16. Earlier reconstructions suggested the eighth century for this process (Ofer Bar-Yosef and Richard H. Meadow, "The Origins of Agriculture in the Near East," in *Last Hunters, First Farmers: New Perspectives on the Prehistoric Transition to Agriculture*, ed. T. Douglas Price and Anne-Birgitte Gebauer [Santa Fe: School of American Research Press, 1995], 39–94), but in a significant update by Melinda Zeder, these developments have been pushed back to the tenth millennium (Zeder, "The Origins of Agriculture in the Ancient Near East," *Current Anthropology* 52 [2011]: 295–96), an idea first proposed in Soviet-era Russian scholarship (L. V. Danilova, "Controversial Problems of the Theory of Precapitalist Societies," *Soviet Anthropology and Archeology* 9, no. 4 [1971]: 269–328). One should consult the following references with this in mind (Peter M. M. G. Akkermans and Glenn M. Schwartz, *The Archaeology of Syria: From Complex Hunter-Gatherers to Early Urban Societies [ca. 16,000-300 BC]* [Cambridge: Cambridge University Press, 2003], 68–79; Brian Hesse and Paula Wapnish, "An Archaeozoological Perspective on the Cultural Use of Mammals in the Levant," in *A History of the Animal World in the Ancient Near East*, ed. Billie Jean Collins [Leiden: Brill, 2002], 465–67; Benjamin S. Arbuckle, "Caprine Exploitation at Erbaba Höyük: A Pottery Neolithic Village in Central Anatolia," in *Archaeozoology of the Near East VIII: Proceedings of the Eighth International Symposium on the Archaeozoology of Southwestern Asia and Adjacent Areas*, ed. Emmanuelle Vila, Lionel Gourichon, Alice M. Choyke, and Hijlke Buitenhuis [Lyon: Maison de l'Orient et de la Mediterranee, 2008], 345–66).

plants for their own survival. The brittle stalks of wild grains became thicker and stronger, thereby able to germinate better, ripen longer, and produce larger yields. "Naked" seeds developed, the easier to thresh, and two-row barleys became six rows.

By the time of the fourth millennium, through a long process of trial and error, the nature of herds became stabilized. Across varied times and places, the herds were invariably comprised of one-third goats and two-thirds sheep, with pigs used in more well-watered areas.[17] Why? Both types of animals are versatile, providing milk, fibers, meat, hide, and bones. Goats especially are able to eat almost anything and manage extreme heat and cold, as well as shortage of food and water, extremely well. Sheep are not quite as flexible, but they too can travel far from water resources and eat pastures that goats do not need. A further reason is risk aversion. If disease afflicts one of the species, the other part of the herd will survive. And due to the high breeding rate of both animals, herd size can be restored in a few seasons.[18] Analysis of bone remains indicates that sheep and goats

17. Pigs are limited to the 250 mm isohyet, much higher than that required by sheep and especially goats. Caroline Grigson, "Shiqmim: Pastoralism and Other Aspects Animal Management in the Chalcolithic of the Northern Negev," in *Shiqmim I*, ed. Thomas E. Levy (Oxford: British Archaeological Reports, 1987), 219–41. Remains of pig bones indicate fluctuation in the use of pigs over time, with abundant distribution during the Chalcolithic, declining to a low in the Late Bronze Age, rebounding for a while in the early Iron Age in a few places, until full resurgence in the Hellenistic era (Brian Hesse, "Pig Lovers and Pig Haters: Patterns of Palestinian Pork Production," *Journal of Ethnobiology* 10 [1990]: 195–225; Hesse and Wapnish, "Archeological Perspective," 468–70; Brian Hesse and Paula Wapnish, "Can Pig Remains Be Used for Ethnic Diagnosis in the Ancient Near East?" in *The Archaeology of Israel: Constructing the Past, Interpreting the Present*, ed. Niel Asher Silberman and David Small [Sheffield: Sheffield Academic, 1997]). Rather than blaming this patchy pattern on an emerging ideological aversion to porcine products (and investing wasted energy on using such data to determined ethnic awareness), it is better to focus on the limited possibilities of pigs within subsistence survival. They may provide good quality meat, but they do not cope well with temperature extremes, require relatively high levels of water, and do not provide fiber or milk for human consumption

18. Aharon Sasson provides a detailed and sophisticated zooarchaeological study of the remains of animal bones in "The Role of Cattle and Economic Strategies in the Bronze and Iron Age at Tell Beer-Sheba, Israel," in *Archaeozoology of the Near East VI: Proceedings of the Sixth International Symposium on the Archaeozoology of Southwestern Asia and Adjacent Areas*, ed. Hijlke Buitenhuis et al. (Groningen: Centre for Archeological Research and Consultancy,

were culled regularly to maintain a healthy herd, with females living longer due to breeding. All parts of the animals were used, rather than select portions characteristic of luxury consumption and breeding for commercial reasons. As for the bovines, remains indicate that they were few in each village and that they lived to a relatively ripe old age, when they were finally slaughtered for a repast of tough old meat at a festival or two.[19] Once again, careful use of resources is the key, for cows consume an extraordinary amount of water and fodder.[20] These animals were therefore used for traction, being shared around in the village for plowing and hauling heavy loads.[21]

I close this brief account of the structures of subsistence economics with a question: why did human beings gather in settlements, in village-communes in the first place? The usual answer focuses on security: human beings preferred the support of others, the reality of more regular food supply, and collective defense against marauding bands. However, this misses a crucial incentive, especially in light of the many problems connected with collective life—intensive labor, new diseases from the refuse of settled communities and the vermin they encouraged, and a lower life expectancy (about thirty years). That incentive was alcohol, an item often neglected in accounts of the origins of human collective living. The products may loosely

Rijksuniversiteit, 2005), 208–21; Sasson, "Reassessing the Bronze and Iron Age Economy: Sheep and Goat Husbandry in the Southern Levant as a Model Case Study," in *Bene Israel: Studies in the Archaeology of Israel in the Bronze and Iron Ages in Honour of Israel Finkelstein*, ed. Alexander Fantalkin and Assaf Yasur-Landau (Leiden: Brill, 2008), 113–34; Sasson, *Animal Husbandry in Ancient Israel: A Zooarchaeological Perspective on Livestock Exploitation, Herd Management and Economic Strategies* (London: Equinox, 2010).

19. The story of the Golden Calf (Gen. 32) contains a trace of the value of such bovines.

20. The species of cow in ancient southwest Asia had five times the body mass of a sheep or a goat, yet it sucked up to twenty-five times the amount of water. A cow needs approximately fifty liters of water per day, more in hot weather, while a sheep or a goat needs two to three liters. For this reason, a cow can range no more than sixteen kilometers from a water source, while sheep and goats can be up to thirty kilometers away.

21. Sasson estimates that a village of one hundred people would need three hundred sheep and goats, and only twelve bovines (Sasson, *Animal Husbandry*, 56).

be termed "beer" and "wine," for the intoxicating liquids produced were far from what we would associate with such terms.[22] Some have argued persuasively that the first human communities gathered not purely for the production of grain for bread, but also for alcoholic beverages. Early archaeological material from ancient Mesopotamia and Egypt points to the possibility that it was the production of beer from barley and wheat that enticed human beings together in more settled social forms.[23] In Mesopotamia, approximately 60 percent of the total cereal crop was barley, and up to 40 percent of the whole cereal crop was used for brewing.[24] Extensive data from the third millennium to the Persian era indicates how important alcohol really was, with sacred drinking clubs (*marziḫu*), payment of rations for ancient estate workers including beer, with extra portions for pregnant women or the celebration of the completion of a building stage.[25] So crucial was the supply that the brewers themselves are

22. For instance, *šēkār* in Hebrew was a fermented drink somewhere between beer and wine, a kind of brandy, as found in Lev. 10:9; Deut. 29:5; Prov. 20:1 (Michael M. Homan, "Beer, Barley, and *šēkār* in the Hebrew Bible," in *Le-David Maskil: A Birthday Tribute for David Noel Freedman*, ed. R. E. Friedman and W. H. C. Propp [Winona Lake, IN: Eisenbrauns, 2004], 25–38; Michael M. Homan, "Did the Ancient Israelites Drink Beer?" *Biblical Archaeology Review* 36, no. 5 [2010]: 78; Lawrence E. Stager, "Ashkelon on the Eve of Destruction in 604 B.C.," in *Ashkelon 3: The Seventh Century B.C.*, ed. Lawrence E. Stager, Daniel M. Master, and J. David Schloen [Winona Lake, IN: Eisenbrauns, 2011], 8). Stories of wine and even beer abound in the Hebrew Bible, revealing its crucial role. Noah's vineyard and drunkenness is perhaps the most well-known (Gen. 9).
23. Jeremy Geller, "Bread and Beer in Fourth-Millennium Egypt," *Food and Foodways* 5, no. 3 (1993): 255–67; Robert J. Braidwood, "Did Man Once Live by Beer Alone?" *American Anthropologist* 55 (1953): 515–26.
24. H. S. Corran, *A History of Brewing* (London: David and Charles, 1975), 15.
25. Pierre Briant, *From Cyrus to Alexander: A History of the Persian Empire*, trans. Peter T. Daniels (Winona Lake, IN: Eisenbrauns, 2002), 432, 435; Anne Goddeeris, *Economy and Society in Northern Babylonia in the Early Old Babylonian Period (ca. 2000 - 1800 BC)* (Leuven: Peeters, 2002), 362; James M. Lindenberger, *Ancient Aramaic and Hebrew Letters*, ed. Kent Harold Richards (Atlanta: Society of Biblical Literature, 2003), 91; Kristin Kleber, "Von Bierproduzenten und Gefängnisaufsehern: dezentrale Güterverteilung und Buchhaltung in Eanna," in *Approaching the Babylonian Economy: Proceedings of the START Project Symposium Held in Vienna, 1–3 July 2004*, ed. Heather D. Baker and Michael Jursa (Münster: Ugarit, 2005), 289–322; Jane M. Renfrew, "Vegetables in the Ancient Near Eastern Diet," in *Civilizations of the Ancient Near East*, ed. Jack M. Sasson (Peabody, MA: Hendrickson, 2006), 197; Theodore J.

named, the beers and wines distinguished between ordinary and good quality, and the high volumes of these blessed liquids recorded. In early Mesopotamia and Egypt, bakeries and breweries or wineries were not separate affairs, but parts of the same building that was itself the central installation in a town.[26] The reason was that yeast (crucial for beer, wine, and bread) appears naturally in some areas in higher concentrations. People soon found that some containers attracted this strange substance that made beer or wine ferment and bread rise, so they kept using those same containers. And since yeast is a living organism, it stays and multiplies. In short, the production of alcoholic beverages is inseparable from the production of bread. This makes profound sense, for why else would humans exchange the relatively light and efficient work of hunting and gathering for the much more labor-intensive cultivation of crops? It is not for nothing that the way of referring to food and drink, even from the early days of Sumer and Akkad, was "beer and bread."[27]

Is This Viable?

Even with such a good incentive, the question remains as to whether subsistence economics is viable in our day and age. Time and again I have been asked this question in various ways, especially with a view to the Bible's normative role concerning economics. For example, one person from a secular commune, which seeks to live in ways different from capitalism, asked me what models are available for

Lewis, "Family, Household, and Local Religion at Late Bronze Age Ugarit," in *Household and Family Religion in Antiquity: Contextual and Comparative Perspectives*, ed. John Bodel and Saul M. Olyan (Malden, MA: Blackwell, 2008), 74–76; Wolfgang Heimpel, *Workers and Construction Work at Garšana* (Bethesda, MD: CDL, 2009), 105–14.

26. Corran, *A History of Brewing*, 19–22; Roger Protz, *The Ultimate Encyclopaedia of Beer* (London: Carlton, 1995), 201–203; Geller, "Bread and Beer," 258–59; Lawrence E. Stager, Daniel M. Master, and J. David Schloen, ed., *Ashkelon 3: The Seventh Century B.C.* (Winona Lake, IN: Eisenbrauns, 2011), 13–29.

27. Piotr Michalowski, *Letters from Early Mesopotamia*, ed. Erica Reiner (Atlanta: Scholars Press, 1993), 27.

them and others. Another mentioned that she has been considering deeply a way of living that is economically, socially, and environmentally responsible. Another, from nothing less than a Christian communist community, offered the wisdom of long experience in living in such a fashion and asked for more information concerning biblical economics. A younger person from an urban environment gave me an insight into the way young people are eschewing the pursuit of a "successful" career, with its empty appurtenances of expensive cars, a big house, and 1.8 children. Instead, they seek new ideas for modes of engaging communally in a way that is informed by an agenda of widespread and fundamental social transformation.

It would be easy to dismiss such a question as a theological one, a dismissal based on the crude assumption that theology is either "ideological" (the European variation) or a pseudo-discipline (the North American variation). That such an objection is more the sign of older or newer petty turf wars than any serious consideration of theology should be obvious. The question may also be dismissed as appropriate to the practice of primitive peoples in an ancient time, inapplicable to the "advanced" economic structures of today. Instead, with the global population well past the seven billion mark, we need all that technology can provide in order to feed the world's population—fertilizers, genetic modification, intensive mono-cropping, and so on. Apart from the dubious nature of the claim that these features of agro-business are really all that efficient and necessary,[28] it is also worth noting how persistent and widespread the practice of subsistence economics is in very different modes of production. It has been identified in medieval Europe, seventeenth-century North America, pre-1873 Japan, Russia, the Maghreb, pre-

28. For instance, within capitalism the widespread production of beef is deeply wasteful and hardly necessary.

Ottoman and Ottoman periods, Iraq until the revolution of 1958, and twentieth-century Greater Syria and Greece.[29]

The reasons for the attractiveness of subsistence economics are not difficult to find: it functions at an optimal level, is all-inclusive, diverse, secure, and stable. First, it operates according to optimal rather than maximal (profit-based) engagement with nature, preferring modes of animal husbandry, crop management, and human population at well below the environment's carrying capacity. As one example, this approach prefers animals that have minimal impact on their environment, rather than the bovines that suck up water and fodder as though they were nothing. Compare the daily provision of "ten fat oxen" to Solomon's mythical court (1 Kgs. 4:23), oxen that may well be illustrated by the Egyptian practice of fattening cows so much that they could no longer walk and had to be transported in carts. Yet Solomon provides but one of a number of images of patriarchs, kings, and landlords with vast herds, including sheep, goats, oxen, donkeys, and occasionally camels, images that become simultaneously metaphorical signals of power and wealth

29. Granott, *Land System of Palestine*; Liverani, "Communautés de village"; Jerome Blum, *The End of the Old Order in Rural Europe* (Princeton, NJ: Princeton University Press, 1978); Adams, "Property Rights," 1–14; Mario Liverani, "Communautés rurales dans la Syrie du IIe millénaire A.C.," in *Les communautés rurales 2e Partie: Antiquité Recueils de la Société (Congrès de Varsovie, 1976)*, Paris: Dessain et Tolra, 1983), 147–85; Hopkins, *Highlands of Canaan*, 257–58; Roberts, *Landscapes of Settlement*, 15–37; McNutt, *Reconstructing the Society of Ancient Israel*, 67–72, 174; Tony Wilkinson, *Archaeological Landscapes of the Near East* (Tucson: University of Arizona Press, 2003); Warren O. Ault, *Open-Field Farming in Medieval England: A Study of Village By-Laws* (London: Routledge, 2006 [1973]); Wilkinson, "The Tell"; Philippe Guillaume, *Land, Credit and Crisis: Agrarian Finance in the Hebrew Bible* (Sheffield: Equinox, 2012), 28–42. I would add here a recent personal experience in a village in Transylvania. In a part of the world—Eastern Europe—that has experienced the ravages of capitalism more than most since the "shock therapy" of the 1990s, old and trusted methods have returned. As we were walking through the village, my host and I came across a herd of goats and sheep. I inquired about their numbers and was told they were 1/3 goats and 2/3 sheep, with regular culls and an optimal size of about sixty. The ubiquity of this practice raises the question about its function within very different modes of production. Here Marx's observation is valid: specific components that are found in more than one mode of production have quite different functions in relation to the specific whole one is analyzing.

as well as images of unbelievable excess that may contain an undercurrent of disapproval (for instance, Gen. 12:16; 13:2–6; 20:14; 24:34; 30:25–43; Job 1:2; 42:12). By contrast, an optimal approach is not geared for the sake of prestige, power, profit, or greed, but to ensure survival in the lean time that is always just around the corner.

All of this has a direct bearing on the question of surpluses. If one follows the myth of Adam Smith, then the production of surplus for the purpose of trucking, bartering, and exchanging is supposed to be a basic, inescapable feature of human existence.[30] But is this true for subsistence economics? Not at all, for the production of small surpluses was a necessary feature of survival, a reserve to carry the group over a bad harvest, drought, burnt crops, animal disease, or any other untoward but all too common event that threatened survival (see, for example, Gen. 42:1). Planning for surplus is thereby a response to ever-present uncertainty rather than a strategy for profit.[31] Something is always left over for an emergency if one systematically under-utilizes pasturage, water, and resources.[32]

30. Adam Smith, *The Wealth of Nations* (London: Modern Library, 1776 [2000]), I.2.1; I.4.2.

31. Marshall Sahlins, "Tribal Economics," in *Economic Development and Social Change: The Modernization of Village Communities* (New York: Natural History Press, 1971), 30; C. G. Widstrand, "The Rationale of Nomad Economy," *Ambio* 4 (1975): 146–53; Tim Ingold, *Hunters, Pastoralists and Ranchers: Reindeer Economies and their Transformations* (Cambridge: Cambridge University Press, 1980), 134–40; Michael Jochim, *Strategies for Survival: Cultural Behavior in an Ecological Context* (New York: Academic Press, 1981), 210; Mario Liverani, "Ville et campagne dans le royaume d'Ugarit: Essai d'analyse economique," in *Societies and Languages of the Ancient Near East: Studies in Honour of I. M. Diakonoff*, ed. Muhammad Dandamaev et al. (Warminster: Aris and Phillips, 1982), 253; Peter Rowley-Conwy and Marek Zvelebil, "Saving it for Later: Storage by Prehistoric Hunter–Gatherers in Europe," in *Bad Year Economics: Cultural Responses to Risk and Uncertainty*, ed. Paul Halstead and John O'Shea (Cambridge: Cambridge University Press, 1989), 40–56; Sasson, *Animal Husbandry*, 7–10. And if one should not have a particular item needed for subsistence survival, such as flint or bitumen, then one sought those items locally, at the nearest place possible. The friction of distance and assumptions of subsistence economics prevented anything more extensive (Ianir Milevski, *Early Bronze Age Goods Exchange in the Southern Levant: A Marxist Perspective* [London: Equinox, 2011]).

32. Brian Hayden, "On Territoriality and Sedentism," *Current Anthropology* 41 (2000): 109–11; Richard W. Redding, "A General Explanation of Subsistence Change: From Hunting and Gathering to Food Production," *Journal of Anthropological Archaeology* 7 (1988): 56–97; Richard

Second, subsistence economics seeks not choice portions characteristic of ruling class practices, not the luxury foods that seek to mark that class and those who aspire to it from the common herd. Rather, it is all-inclusive, making use of everything, whether all parts of animals, every possible part of a plant, or whatever else one makes or finds. Nothing is wasted, for if it can be used it will be, and then again. Third, diversity is crucial, for this provides security in the long term—diversity in terms of food, shelter, and minimizing the risks of disease. In my earlier discussion, diversity appeared in terms of animal species, but it was also a feature of the range of crops grown. Fourth, diversity ensures security by reducing risk: one does not suffer catastrophically when disaster hits, for another part of the herd will be there.[33] Nonetheless, this way of phrasing the point is to focus on the security of human life in an environment that could at any time threaten that security. But that is to separate human beings from their natural environment in all its unpredictability. Rather, security is for the natural environment as a whole.

These features lead to the final point: subsistence economics is stable, through well-tried strategies. Indeed, this economic approach was the stable basis of ancient southwest Asia. That observation requires a revaluation of usual accounts of ancient economies (going back to Herodotus), according to which crisis and collapse are what happens when an empire falls, when a palatine economic system or

W. Redding, "Subsistence Security as a Selective Pressure Favoring Increasing Cultural Complexity," *Bulletin on Sumerian Agriculture* 7 (1993): 77–98.

33. L. W. Binford, *Constructing Frames of Reference: An Analytical Method for Archaeological Theory Building Using Hunter-Gatherer and Environmental Data Sets* (Berkeley: University of California Press, 2001), 193; C. R. Wharton, "Risk, Uncertainty, and the Subsistence Farmer: Technological Innovation and the Resistance to Change in the Context of Survival," in *Studies in Economic Anthropology*, ed. George Dalton (Washington: American Anthropological Association, 1971), 152–80; Jennifer Piro, "Pastoral Economies in Early Transcaucasian Communities from the Mid-4th to 3rd Millennium BC.," in *Archaeozoology of the Near East VIII*, 451–64; Jennifer Piro, *Pastoralism in the Early Transcaucasian Culture: The Faunal Remains from Sos Höyük* (PhD thesis, New York University, 2009).

one of tribute-exchange breaks apart, and when a supposed "dark age" ensues. These periods of supposed "chaos" were frequent and lengthy, the longest taking place in the third millennium, in the "dark age" of the sixteenth and early fifteenth centuries, and then the twelfth to tenth centuries BCE. But we need to ask, collapse and chaos for whom? From the perspective of the ruling class it is indeed collapse and the ensuing period is a prolonged time of crisis.[34] The sources of wealth have been removed, the palaces and temples destroyed, the estate system or patterns of tribute and exchange have been dismantled, and power has been lost.

Yet, from the perspective of the subsistence economics of the village-communes, a "collapse" actually means a blessed relief from various means of extraction.[35] We can hardly expect the peasants, laborers, and common people to sit back and wait for such much-desired collapses to happen (see Neh. 9:36--37). From the Habiru through to archaeological signals of urban destruction by the town's own exploited class, these various groups were more than keen to hasten the demise.[36] Indeed, in the Amarna Letters, the Habiru

34. Marc van de Mieroop offers an outline of the "collapse" after 1200, albeit from the perspective of the ruling classes and their states (van de Mieroop, *A History of the Ancient Near East ca. 3000-323 BC*. 2 [Oxford: Blackwell, 2007], 191–206). Even Norman Yoffee, who sets out in neo-evolutionary terms to describe the emergence and collapse of states from the perspective ordinary people, cannot avoid this statist assumption of "collapse" (Yoffee, *Myths of the Archaic State: Evolution of the Earliest Cities, States, and Civilizations* [Cambridge: Cambridge University Press, 2005], 131–60).

35. Gale A. Yee, "Recovering Marginalized Groups in Ancient Israel: Methodological Considerations," in *To Break Every Yoke: Essays in Honor of Marvin L. Chaney*, ed. Robert B. Coote and Norman K. Gottwald (Sheffield: Sheffield Phoenix, 2007), 13–15. On peasant movements more generally, see Eric R. Wolf, *Peasants* (Englwood Cliffs: Prentice-Hall, 1965), 106–109; James C. Scott, *Weapons of the Weak: Everyday Forms of Peasant Resistance* (New Haven, CT: Yale University Press, 1985).

36. As an example, Late Bronze Age Hazor shows signs of the burning of monumental structures in the lower city and on the "acropolis," aimed at the symbols and reality of ruling class power (Nimrod Marom, and Sharon Zuckerman, "Applying On-Site Analysis of Faunal Assemblages from Domestic Contexts: A Case Study from the Lower City of Hazor," in *Household Archaeology in Ancient Israel and Beyond*, ed. Assaf Yasur-Landau, Jennie R. Ebeling, and Laura B. Mazow (Leiden: Brill, 2011), 51–53).

become ever stronger and threaten town after town, making for heart-warming reading.[37] Their slogans had wide appeal, as we find in the words of 'Abdi-Aširta, one of their leaders:

> Let us drive out the mayors from the country that the entire country be joined to the 'Apiru, . . . to the entire country. Then will (our) sons and daughters be at peace forever. Should even so the king come out, the entire country will be against him and what will he do to us?[38]

In that light, I suggest that the statement that there was no king in Israel and that "all the people did what was right in their own eyes" (Judg. 17:6; 18:1; 19:1; 21:25; see also 1 Kgs. 22:17; 2 Chron. 18:16) may be seen as a positive image. In response to such threats, a petty despot like Rib-Hadda did well to fear revolt: "I am afraid the peasantry will strike me down."[39] Semi-nomadic pastoralists too were ready to join in, for throughout Mesopotamian history, their annual and usually "peaceful" migration "could be transformed into aggressive campaigns if the power of the centralized state was weak."[40] The outcome was highly desirable: no longer do the young men and women have to work periodically or permanently on the palatine estates; no longer does the despised usurer-merchant-tax-collector call with his thugs to collect a debt slave or take a portion of the herd or some of the girls for his sexual usage; no longer do the temple and palace suck away the foodstuffs needed for subsistence survival. I would suggest that the mythical accounts of the Tower of Babel (Genesis 11) and Sodom and Gomorrah (Genesis 18–19) embody such a perspective in their own way, as do the warnings

37. William L. Moran, *The Amarna Letters* (Baltimore: Johns Hopkins University Press, 1992), 137–223, 230–31, 235, 262, 265–68, 269–70, 273, 274–75, 280, 283–84, 297–98, 300, 307–308, 317–19, 326–34, 340–41, 343, 345, 346–47, 349, 364).

38. Ibid., 143; see also Igor M. Diakonoff, "Syria, Phoenicia, and Palestine in the Third and Second Millennia B.C," in *Early Antiquity*, 295; Liverani, *Israel's History and the History of Israel*, 27–28.

39. Moran, *Amarna Letters*, 148.

40. Nelly V. Kozyreva, "The Old Babylonian Period of Mesopotamian History," in *Early Antiquity*, 99.

of 1 Samuel 8, the parable of the bramble in Judges 9:8-15, the long account of the failings of the kings of Israel and Judah and the eventual punishment in 1–2 Kings, and the account of the resistance by the "people of the land," and myriad other groups in Ezra-Nehemiah to the imposition of an imperial regime of plunder with the return of the exiles.[41] It is telling that during such times the records of loans, debts, and the obligatory labor tied in with loans, disappear.[42] This is not due to some "dark age," lacking civilization, but rather another signal of the dominance and desirability of subsistence economics. The reality, therefore, is that during the long periods when despots and potentates were laid low, subsistence economics dominated. Always in the background during imperial times, subsistence economics would once again come into its own, much preferred by the majority.

Optimal, all-inclusive, diverse, secure, and stable—to these I would add an observation from Marshall Sahlins: "There are after all two roads to satisfaction, to reducing the gap between means and ends: producing much or desiring little."[43] Subsistence designed for survival opts to desire little. No wonder this approach has been so resilient through human history. In our own day, terms such as environmentally sustainable and economically equal might be used for such an approach. I find it intriguing that in the marginal area of the southern Levant, or ancient Israel, this was the dominant economic form, being eclipsed from time to time (the brief period of the little kingdom and then under imperial control as a province) yet reasserting itself once again.

41. On the class dimensions of the resistance in Ezra-Nehemiah, see Roland Boer, "No Road: On the Absence of Feminist Criticism of Ezra-Nehemiah," in *Her Master's Tools: Feminist and Postcolonial Engagements of Historical-Critical Discourse*, ed. Vander Stichele Caroline and Todd Penner (Atlanta: Society of Biblical Literature, 2005), 233–52.

42. Marc van de Mieroop, "A History of Near Eastern Debt?" in *Debt and Economic Renewal in the Ancient Near East*, ed. Michael Hudson and Marc van de Mieroop (Bethesda: CDL, 2002), 81.

43. Sahlins, "Tribal Economics," 49.

Yet, there is a problem. The social relations of subsistence economics were determined by the kinship-household (see earlier), relations that were not particularly favorable in terms of gender and age, and in relation to outsiders. I have yet to hear an argument in favor of kinship as a model of human organization. Kinship may provide some level of security and social cohesion in particular circumstances, but it is inevitably geared toward abuse of the young, of women, and of the elderly. Patriarchal and hierarchical, it is hardly a model for human flourishing. In our own day, "family values" ultimately means the all too present patterns of physical, emotional, and at times sexual abuse. Growing up means that one has to come to terms with the way one's parents, siblings, and other relatives have damaged you.

In that light, I suggest that subsistence economics may be viable only if it dispenses with social forms that are hierarchical and abusive, that seek security at the cost of women, outsiders, and the vulnerable. It requires, not a return to some idealized and mythical earlier practice, when the world was a simpler and happier place, as the conservatives would have us believe.[44] Rather, if it is to be workable, subsistence economics requires very different types of social organization and determination. It would be primarily collective, in a dialectical form of collective life that enables individual flourishing that in turn strengthens the collective. It would also have robust sanctions in light of the fact that human beings often seek to do the worst rather than the best to one another. In that way, subsistence economics may well provide a model for those seeking a different

44. "It may be worth noting in passing that when Marx and Engels spoke of 'primitive communism', they *never* entertained such a simplistic thesis, for they always used to protest against what they called the idea of a primitive 'El Dorado' and tirelessly insisted upon the fact that even in the most primitive societies, there would seem to exist at least three forms of inequality: between men and women; between senior and junior generations; and between autochthons and foreigners" (Maurice Godelier, *The Mental and the Material: Thought, Economy and Society*, trans. Martin Thom [London: Verso, 1986 (1984)], 78).

path. It would be one that is environmentally and economically sustainable, communal, optimal, all-inclusive, diverse, secure, and stable, but also one that has gender, ethnic, and sexual equality. A pipe dream in our day and age? Not at all, for many communities—both local and national—around the world have provided and continue to provide ample examples, seeking ways to make such an approach work.

6

Occupying the Temple in Ancient Judah

Resisting Debt Abuses, from Jerusalem to Wall Street

Matthew J. M. Coomber

Introduction

The burden of overwhelming debt is an injustice that afflicts people across gender, race, and—to some extent—economic class. Whether indebted through the use of credit cards, unexpected medical bills, or the purchase of a home, debt not only affects US citizens' daily purchasing powers, but also their abilities to access education and medical care, and even the choice to have children.

Whereas in the biblical world debt was a condition to be avoided at all costs, Western capitalism has given debt a far more positive spin and central role in our lives: in fact, our system runs on credit and debt. For many people, falling into unsustainable levels of debt is not the result of irresponsible behavior; it is an inevitable outcome of chasing the *American Dream*, the central part of the United States' cultural and historical folklore that states that if you work hard, you can climb the fiscal ladder. Compared to many nations, the United States does offer opportunities for economic advancement—albeit with uneven playing fields for reasons including but not limited to, an individual's race, gender, economic class, and sexual orientation—but to climb the ladder almost always demands taking out loans that will take decades to repay, making debt a systemic issue in our economy. And at the same time that many people's life choices are dictated by the debts that they are coerced into accumulating in their pursuits of the American Dream, those who have positioned themselves as creditors within this system enjoy a secure stream of income off the hard work of their neighbors.

Since the United States government does not ensure education above the high-school level, federal and private lending agencies are relied upon to assist citizens in attaining levels of education that are now needed for financial security. Due to woeful transportation systems in much of the United States, and because almost all of our cities and towns are designed with car ownership in mind, people commonly take on debt in order to purchase automobiles. Because homes cost too much for most anyone to purchase outright—especially considering how many other debts they are servicing for higher education, cars, medical expenses, and so on—and because our culture promotes homeownership as an ideal, people commonly agree to fifteen or thirty years of debt to purchase houses. Without taking on considerable debt, our society's political and financial structures will not allow the vast majority of our citizens to contribute to society beyond what a high-school degree level can offer, drive to the jobs that they work, or purchase homes to return to after a hard day's work. For most all US citizens, debt is not an option; it is a prerequisite to attain basic levels of comfort in our society.[1]

Debt is now required to give individuals hope in a better tomorrow while allowing the United States to benefit from the talents and skills of those who could not otherwise afford to fulfill their potential, or get to work.

The Gamble of Debt in Domestic and International Capitalism

Ultimately, debt is a gamble that—in our current capitalist system—most everyone is forced to play. And as in a gambling hall, the field of play is slanted to the benefit those who run the tables. Casino magnates play the odds in their favor, and so have political and financial elites—for millennia. This has been made all too clear in the wake of the 2008 financial crisis, when the perpetrators profited from their poor choices, and the customers were left holding the bill.

Different Rules for Different Players

In addition to the years of stress caused by the repayment of the debts into which United States citizens are coerced to engage, student loans and mortgages also come with dire risk, as witnessed in the wake of the 2008 economic crisis. Many of those who bought homes before the collapse of the housing market now find that their mortgage debt is greater than the value of their houses; more than four million other households have found their home investments ending in foreclosure.[2] Thousands who invested in their futures through engaging in high levels of student-loan debts—the average debt incurred for a bachelor's degree is above $35,000—from tradespeople to PhD graduates, now struggle to navigate a job market that offers

1. Sarah Amandolare, "The Student Loan Crisis: How Middle-class Kids Get Hammered," *Los Angeles Times*, February 10, 2014, http://articles.latimes.com/2014/feb/10/opinion/la-oe-amandolare-student-loan-defaults-20140210.
2. "Student Debt Levels – Now Averaging More Than ,000 – Surprise To Half Of 2013 College Grads," *Fidelity.com*, May 16, 2013, www.fidelity.com/inside-fidelity/individual-investing/college-grads-surprised-by-student-debt-level-exceeds-35000.

few opportunities for employment.[3] With just over 41 percent of doctoral graduates finding tenure-track positions in their field, support groups like Versatile Ph.D. and the Beyond Academia Conference have worked to find other opportunities for doctoral graduates who have spent years to achieve their credentials only to be weighed down with six-digit debts.[4] It is in situations like these, when circumstances outside the borrower's control turn debt from a promise of opportunity into a crippling burden, that the debtor is left to suffer while those who hold the controls of our fiscal and political institutions enjoy the benefits.

The exploitative nature US capitalism's system of credit and debt, and its many dangers, became fully exposed in the 2008 financial crisis. Despite being ignited by the shady dealings of fiscal elites, whose voracious appetites had trumped their responsibly toward those whose money they managed, consumers paid the price. Right before Merrill Lynch's collapse, for example, their former CEO John Thain spent $1.22 million on redecorating his office.[5] While the outcome was catastrophic for millions, Thain now enjoys the seat of chairman and CEO of CIT Group.

Through the misleading of investors in order to use their money to invest in loans that were doomed to failure (harming both investors and the borrowers whom they led into ill-advised mortgages and investments), the United States was nearly dragged into a second great depression. While outrage was palpable, little was done to root out the rot at the system's core. Many of those responsible for the catastrophe were baled out as their victimized borrowers—and

3. Ibid.
4. Rebecca Tuhus-Dubrow, "The Repurposed Ph.D.: Finding Life After Academia—and NotFeeling Bad About It," *New York Times*, November 1, 2013, http://www.nytimes.com/2013/11/03/education/edlife/finding-life-after-academia-and-not-feeling-bad-about-it.html?_r=0.
5. Jessica Pressler, "Wall Street's Golden Throne: This Commode Costs a Load," *New York Magazine* 45, no. 11 (2012): 65.

taxpayers—were left to pay the price of their recklessness. In fact, JPMorgan Chase CEO Jamie Dimon received $29 billion US dollars of taxpayer money to clean up former competitor Bear Sterns' collapse, with no obligation to repay from JPMorgan Chase's own funds. How did Dimon strike such an amazing deal? He was also serving as a director of the New York Fed at the time. As a result of this massive conflict of interest, funded entirely by taxpayer money, his personal stock portfolio enjoyed a $90 million jump. Dimon, a billionaire, swelled his own coffers during—and as a result of—the same crisis that left millions unemployed and without homes.[6]

While those who control our economic system's debt profit handsomely, even when the economy fails, the accumulation of capital is not the only goal in Western capitalism. Elites also position themselves to continue controlling the rules to their advantage. Whereas casinos value the *gamble of game* for attaining wealth, ruling and financial elites have also used the *gamble of debt* as an instrument of societal control on both domestic and international levels. This is not a new development in economic systems, but one of the central goals of trade and extraction economics, for millennia.

From the Local to Foreign, and Back Again

While the necessitation of debt and the harmful loss of self-autonomy that accompany it are highly visible in US society, our citizenry are certainly not the only victims to international capitalism's harmful effects. World economic systems exert pressure on multiple levels, both domestic and foreign; a world economic systems' center (traditionally a dominant nation) places pressure on the systems' regions (weaker states) to produce greater and greater amounts of capital, whether that capital takes the form of stockpiles of grains

6. Ibid., 50–59, 63.

and produce, as found in an agrarian societies, or cultivating the future values of stocks and government bonds. Such pressures from the systems' center, in turn, place pressure on peripheral regions' local officials to extract greater and greater capital from their workers and producers. At some point, when the pressure becomes too great, unbalanced, or both, the seals of the mechanism begin to give way, which can lead to the system's collapse or some adaptation to the economic system, usually as a result of revolt among the disenfranchised. Such a moment was witnessed in the outrage that was expressed through the Occupy movement.

A call for action from the Canadian anti-consumerist organization Adbusters drew protestors to create a shantytown at the heart of the United States', and arguably Western capitalism's, financial system. While the on-site numbers were modest, the virtual protest—taking place through social media outlets and continual news coverage—started an ongoing conversation on the nature of Western capitalism, giving the world a chance to take a hard look at how an elite few take the lion's share while the majority suffer under the weight of their ambition. The media attention and conversations that the occupation of Wall Street sparked has an unexpected and overlooked affinity with a conversation that took place in ancient Judah and is found in the prophetic writings of the Old Testament.

Where the Bible Joins the Conversation

A Connecting Thread Across Time

Like the bankers of Wall Street, it appears that Judean creditors also enjoyed a secure yet ruthless profit stream from those who, in order to survive in an evolving Judean society, were given little choice but to enter into devastating levels of debt. While the economic systems that affected the debtors of ancient Judah were vastly different from those systems that control debtors today, the Hebrew prophets appear to have railed against creditors who enriched themselves by lending at the expense of the vulnerable. It is through the ongoing problem of debt entrapment that we find a thread that connects the ancient prophetic voice with the struggles that face so many in our own time and, therefore, give these ancient writers a voice in our modern world.

As modern debt systems that coerce people into debilitating loans are not simply the products of regional economics, but rooted in international systems and interests, so too were the debt struggles of the ancient Judeans. While international economic engagement can be a positive force for international cooperation and help to create economic balance—which it does, to some extent—trade is far more often used as a means through which powerful states or financial entities can exert both economic and strategic control, chipping away at weaker nations' autonomy.

Dangers of Reinventing the Past in Our Image

The Bible can function like a sort of magical window through which one sees only their own beliefs, ideology, or preconceived notions. It is for this reason—the temptation to force the Bible into our own image—that readers and interpreters need to exercise caution when relating biblical texts to their own time. It is all too easy to create loosely constructed links between our world and that of the ancient kingdoms of Israel and Judah, falsely treating the writings of the Old Testament as contemporary texts that address contemporary issues. To ignore the vast differences between the biblical world and our own not only disrespects the complexities of these texts and the time-locations of those who wrote them, but it also ignores the intricacies of the issues that we face in the modern world.

However, while the agrarian economy of ancient Judean and international capitalism today are incredibly different in a number of ways, the effects of debt exploitation on these systems' most vulnerable members are similar. Ruling elites use credit and debt to seize control of both farmlands and the labor potential of those who work them, resulting in displacement, impoverishment, and a lack of independence for both individuals and their communities. It is through this connecting thread of exploitation that we find new meaning within biblical complaints against economic injustice that are attributed to eighth-century BCE Judah, when the kingdom was absorbed into Assyria's trade-and-tribute system. At the same time, this thread that spans both time and culture can uncover new meaning in prophetic voices that can address the modern-day injustices of domestic and international debt exploitation.

A Biblical Foothold for Addressing Modern-Day Debt

A good foothold for exploring these connections between biblical texts and modern debt abuses is found in two prophetic complaints against land seizures: Isaiah 5:8-10 and Micah 2:1-2. Both of these texts condemn land seizures and are attributed to Judah's late eighth-century entrance into Assyria's trade/tribute economy. Micah. 2:1-2 proclaims, "Woe to those who plan wickedness and make evil on their beds; at the morning light they act upon it because the power is in their hand. They desire fields and they steal them, and houses, and they take them away. They oppress man and his house, man and his inheritance" (author's own translation). The authors of Isaiah 5:8 level a similar complaint: "Woe to those who join house to house, who touch field to field until there is no place to sit in the midst of the land" (author's own translation).[7] While you can see that both

7. The ways in which the words for house (בית) and (מבית) are used in Isa. 5.8 and Mic. 2.1-2 suggest the authors were addressing agricultural real estate and a small landholding,

passages attack people who take land from their neighbors—land being the central means of livelihood in an agrarian economy—they don't tell us who was taking the land, who was losing it, or what was suddenly allowing these land grabs to happen. Such contextual gaps have to be filled with something and the most common filler has been either "wealthy merchants" or "corrupt judges" conspiring against "poor farmers." However, new light can be shed on these texts through a greater understanding of how agrarian societies tend to behave during shifts from subsistence farming (cultivation for the good of the community) toward specialized farming (cultivation for tribute or trade)—as took place in late eighth-century Judah.

Considering the swift and widespread economic developments of late eighth-century Judah, several biblical scholars have recently argued that Isaiah 5:8-10 and Micah 2:1-4 did not simply scold a few wicked individuals who undermined an otherwise just Judean legal system, but respond to an evolution in Judah's economic strategy, which benefited Judah's elites at the cost of the kingdom's largely autonomous subsistence communities.[8] This hypothesis is supported by the social-scientific model of cultural-evolutionary theory, which reveals a recurring pattern that arises, regardless of culture or time, when agrarian communities are absorbed into world systems of trade. Evidence of this pattern is widespread in both eighth-century Judah and as a result of our international capitalist economy.

respectively; see William L. Moran, "The Conclusion of the Decalogue: Ex 20:17–Dt 5:21," *Catholic Biblical Quarterly* 29, no. 4 (1967): 543–54.

8. Marvin L. Chaney, "Whose Sour Grapes? The Addressees of Isaiah 5:1–7 in the Light of Political Economy," in *The Social World of the Hebrew Bible: Twenty-Five Years of the Social Sciences in the Academy*, eds. Ronald A. Simkins and Stephen L. Cook (Atlanta: Society of Biblical Literature, 1989); D. N. Premnath, *Century Prophets: A Social Analysis* (Atlanta: Chalice, 2003); Matthew Coomber, *Re-Reading the Prophets Through Corporate Globalization: A Cultural-Evolutionary Approach to Understanding Economic Injustice in the Hebrew Bible* (Piscataway, NJ: Gorgias, 2010).

The Theory of Cultural Evolution in Late Eighth-Century Judah

The Theory

Cultural-evolutionary theorists like Morton Fried, Gerhard Lenski, Allen Johnson, and Timothy Earle find that when agrarian societies are absorbed into world systems of trade, administrative elites employ systems of debt exploitation in order to refocus rural communities' productive efforts from the needs of the producers to the desires of ruling elites, both domestic and foreign. Such changes in regional economics are doubly true in the case of subsistence-centered agrarian societies which, by their nature, benefit the producer more than state goals.[9]

Traditional subsistence-farming strategies are designed to spread risk and minimize effort in order to produce enough food and goods for the community while creating a small surplus for minimal exchange and to weather unsuccessful growing seasons. When practiced well, these systems give their participants a good degree of self-sufficiency and security, while also minimalizing labor. But as such outside influences as emboldened domestic leaders and/or foreign powers encroach and pressure farmers into producing larger and larger surpluses for trade or tribute, subsistence farming's traditional risk and labor-reducing strategies become a hindrance to the interests of the elites.

As a region's economic goals evolve, so does agrarian culture. Rendered obsolete by new trade and/or tribute demands, rural producers are coerced into abandoning the risk-reducing strategy of growing a variety of crops for the very risky specialized cultivation of crops that will benefit political administrators, whether used for trade or for the payment of an empire's occupying forces.[10] As crop failures

9. A. W. Johnson and T. Earle, *The Evolution of Human Societies: From Foraging Group to Agrarian State* (Stanford: Stanford University Press, 2001), 26–28.

inevitably come due to disease or insufficient rainfall—dangers that subsistence strategies are designed to prevent—farm communities have few options but to turn to high-interest survival loans, which administrators are all-too-happy to offer. As subsequent crop failures lead to spiraling debt, administrators foreclose on their debtors' lands and consolidate them into large estates. Former semi-autonomous subsistence farmers are then transformed into wage-laborers on the lands that they once controlled for their own benefit.

When empowered administrative classes' desires eclipse the needs of the producers, those in control take steps to hoard the benefits of the new economic system while rural producers suffer the effects of displacement.[11] This process, called *latifundialization*, gives administers full control over the lands' productive capabilities and mirrors the complaints lodged against those who desired fields and stole them and who touched field to field until there was no place to sit in the midst of the land (Isa. 5:8; Mic. 2:1-4).

Evidence of this recurring pattern is found across continents and throughout the ages,[12] but why is this recurring pattern of debt exploitation found in such varied societies as Bronze Age Palestine, Hellenistic Greece, medieval England and Japan, and late twentieth-century Vietnam? Like the path water takes down a mountain, latifundialization offers the fastest route to revenue production. And if one wishes to attain the surpluses that are needed for trade and tribute, the patterns found in cultural-evolutionary theory offer an expedient way to ensure control over both the land and the people who work to release its productive capabilities. Outside of the Bible,

10. R. Boer, *The Sacred Economy of Ancient Israel* (Louisville: Westminster John Knox, 2015).

11. Johnson and Earle, *The Evolution of Human Societies*, 2001), 24–27; M. H. Fried, *The Evolution of Political Society* (New York: Random House, 2001), 186; S. K. Sanderson, *The Evolution of Human Sociality: A Darwinian Conflict Perspective* (Lanham, MD: Rowman and Littlefield, 2001).

12. Coomber, *Re-Reading the Prophets*, 67–71, 88–97.

such patterns are found in the developments that took place during Judah's late eighth-century archaeological record.

Cultural-Evolution in Judah

Whether late eighth-century Judah had an established kingdom or was an emerging state—an ongoing topic of debate—discoveries in the region reveal that Judah experienced an economic and demographic transformation that involved a heightened production of goods to serve trade and/or tribute to appease the Assyrian Empire.[13] In addition to a sudden boom in population, within a single generation Judah experienced a sevenfold extension of Jerusalem's fortified areas, the construction of massive defensive walls and fortresses in the Negev, an introduction of standardized weights and scales, and an expansion of the region's irrigation systems.[14] This time also witnessed the emergence of farm communities in previously uncultivated areas, a centralization of olive oil and wine production, and a sudden expansion of Judean fruit-processing facilities.[15]

In addition to evidence of increased specialized cultivation, the signs of heightened trade activity can also be seen in the sudden appearance of Nile River shellfish, fine woods, and other luxury imports in Jerusalem.[16] All of these developments would have

13. Israel Finklestein and Neil Silberman, "Temple and Dynasty: Hezekiah, the Remaking of Judah and the Rise of the Pan-Israelite Ideology," *Journal for the Study of the Old Testament* 30, no. 3 (2006): 263–65.
14. Mario Liverani, *Israel's History and the History of Israel*, trans. Chiara Peri and PhilipDavies (London: Equinox, 2005), 155.
15. Israel Finkelstein and Nadav Na'aman, "The Judahite Shephelah in the Late 8th and Early 7th Centuries BCE." *Tel Aviv* 31, no. 1 (2004): 73–75.
16. A. Faust and E. Weiss, "Judah, Philistia, and the Mediterranean World: Reconstructing the Economic System of the Seventh Century B.C.E." *Bulletin of the American Schools of Oriental Research* 338 (2005): 71–92; Henk K. Meinis, "Molluscs," in *Excavations at the City of David 1978–1985*, eds. A. de Groot and D. T. Ariel (Jerusalem: Institute of Archaeology, Hebrew University of Jerusalem, 1992), 129.

required heightened administrative control, resource coordination, and increased trade activity.

The fact that these advances unfolded in a region that had been composed of small, scattered farm communities prior to the late eighth century reveals a developing political economy that eclipsed the relatively low-maintenance subsistence strategies of previous generations. This gives credence to the idea that prophetic complaints against Judean land seizures did not condemn isolated instances of corruption, but a total restructuring of Judah's economy.

While the hardships of the Judean farmers cannot be known for certain, Assyria's demands for tribute and increased access to the empire's trade routes offered Judean rulers both new problems and also new opportunities for economic development. As explained above, it is logical that such opportunities led ruling elites to coerce rural producers into abandoning traditional low-risk subsistence farming for the high-risk specialized cultivation of cereals, olives, and grapes for export or as tribute to their Assyrian masters. A channeling of local produce from local consumption to foreign markets, combined with higher-risk cultivation, led to crop failures, survival loans, and subsequent foreclosures, allowing Judah's rulers to consolidate family-held lands under their control. As is often the case in such periods of societal transformation, those reluctant to abandon their traditional subsistence strategies would likely have been coerced through a combination of force and levying of heavy taxes upon "inefficiently" produced grains.[17] As Judah's economy took a sharp turn toward the advantage of ruling elites, rural producers suffered the kinds of displacement and oppression that enraged the authors of Isaiah 5 and Micah 2.

Before the Judean debt-exploitation scenario above is tied to debt exploitation in the modern world, a few things need to be made

17. Chaney, "Whose Sour Grapes?" 107.

clear. Social-scientific models do not offer proof of what happened in the ancient past, but show us expected patterns that need to be critically examined against existing data and continually improved upon.[18] That stated, considering extensive data that shows a late eighth-century centralization of Judah's economic efforts and a major shift toward the production of goods to be consumed outside of the producers' family units, to assume the presence of recurring cultural-evolutionary patterns of exploitation isn't only justified, it is to be expected. But a key question remains: How can evidence of cultural-evolutionary theory in ancient Judah relate to trade exploitation in the modern world? Considering that cultural-evolutionary patterns are reveal an ongoing cycle of abuse that transcends both culture and time, trade-based debt exploitation in the modern world does not simply represent the negative consequences of global capitalism, but the latest manifestation of a cycle that has repeated itself for millennia, and which the Hebrew prophets appear to have addressed in their own time. It is through such connections that Micah and Isaiah find relevance to the modern world.

"Globalization," from Then to Now

Despite the vast differences between ancient Assyria's methods of extraction and trade and those of international capitalism, these two systems are connected by common economic motivations: the drive to dominate weaker states, increase wealth, and expand. And while capitalism enjoys technological, organizational, and strategic advances that would have been unimaginable to the Assyrians, their ancient system should not be seen as unrelated to ours: it is an ancestor. Joachim Rennstich explains that while technologies, improvements in agrarian techniques, and systems of management

18. Lester Grabbe, *Ancient Israel: What Do We Know and How Do We Know It?* (London: T&T Clark, 2007).

and control between successive world systems advance, "the driving logic—human agency—of this process remains the same [as] its context changes, constituting a 'social learning algorithm' of evolutionary change that is at work at all levels of the world system process—from the individual to the change of the world system itself."[19] Although our current global financial system has developed into a far more efficient and expansive system from its Assyrian, Babylonian, and Persian ancestors, the driving factors of profit and control—and their subsequent impacts on agrarian communities—are common. It is this connecting thread that gives prophetic complaints against late-eighth century land seizures a legitimate voice in addressing debt exploitation in the twenty-first century. Perhaps the best approach for exploring what we can learn from such connections between ancient and modern uses of debt as a weapon of control is to examine a way in which debt has been used to exert compliance on impoverished populations within the structures of international capitalism. To understand international capitalism's cultural-evolutionary effects, it is helpful to understand how it developed into its present state.

The Rise of International Capitalism

Bretton Woods and the Dawn of a New Debt

In 1944, with the Axis powers facing what was being seen as an inevitable defeat, forty-four Allied countries sent delegates to the United States to take part in the United Nations Monetary and Financial Conference at Bretton Woods in New Hampshire, where they developed a fiscal strategy for handling the needs of a post-

19. Joachim Karl Rennstich, "Three Steps in Globalization: Global Networks from 1000 BCE to 2050 CE," in *Globalization and Global History*, eds. Barry K. Gills and William R. Thompson (London: Routledge, 2006), 2:205.

war global economy. Considering the massive losses to life and infrastructure during the war, the conference delegates had taken on a daunting task.

During the Bretton Woods Conference, the delegates agreed that the only way to ensure a lasting post-war peace and political stability was to increase revenue in the developing world, reconstruct war-torn regions, and secure employment for returning troops. To their credit, the delegates sought—or at least entertained—an egalitarian approach of shared prosperity that would eradicate such destabilizing factors as poverty and hunger through the rebuilding of infrastructure, correcting nation-members' balance of payments, and assisting in the economic development of poorer countries.[20] In an effort to attain these goals, the conference created two powerful international financial instructions, or IFIs: the International Bank for Reconstruction and Development (now known as The World Bank), and the International Monetary Fund, or IMF.

The original mandate of the World Bank and IMF was to help poorer states settle their debts and provide low-interest loans for post-war reconstruction and development. But in a move that *The Economist* called "ludicrous" and a "process of political chaffering more than an objective attempt to achieve equity,"[21] Britain's delegates demanded greater voting powers for the IMF's and the World Bank's largest donors; the rationale was that these nations would finance most of the two institutions' development activities. As a result, tools for egalitarian growth quickly became weapons for societal control. Greater voting powers among the wealthiest nations allowed the world's most powerful states to craft a world economic

20. A. K. Kuhn, "United Nations Monetary Conference and the Immunity of International Agencies," *American Journal of International Law* 38, no. 4 (1944): 663; William Fellner, "Widow, Orphan, and the Poor in Ancient Near Eastern Legal and Wisdom Literature," *Journal of Near Eastern Studies* 21 (1962): 129–39.
21. "Bretton Woods," *The Economist CXLVII*, no. 5266 (1944): 138.

system that promoted their own interests and cultural values while many impoverished countries watched helplessly as their economic well-being became increasingly dependent on the financial goals of the so-called *First World*.[22] One of the most powerful weapons used by the IMF and World Bank for the achieving these goals has been the debt system of *conditionality loans*.

Societal Control and Abuse through Conditionality Loans

The stated purpose of conditionality loans was to provide highly indebted poor countries (HIPCs) with access to development funds while protecting them from abusive private-market lenders. But unlike conventional loan debt, in addition to requiring interest payments these conditionality loans give lenders the power to attach pro-growth conditions that borrowers are obligated to fulfill. The rationale is to help HIPCs achieve long-term stability by rooting out harmful domestic policies: that is, rooting out corruption and/or practices that obstruct foreign investment, thus lowering the risk for creditors who might be wary of lending to unstable states. Cheryl Payer notes that conditionality loans can be highly useful in their ability to "change host government policies [that are] adverse to foreign investment, including unwillingness to release promising acreage to exploration."[23] However, while these loan conditions can serve as an asset to HIPCs, their debt obligations can cause more harm than good.

Despite the benefits that conditionality loans offer (e.g., bringing in financial expertise and rooting out deeply entrenched corruption), conditionality loans have been widely criticized for penetrating too deeply into the political and economic workings of borrowing

22. Coomber, *Re-Reading the Prophets*, 144–49.
23. Cheryl Payer, *The World Bank: A Critical Analysis* (New York: Monthly Review Press, 1982), 204.

countries and causing harm to rural communities. Several domestic policies that are seen as impediments to a country's participation in the international markets, such as protectionist measures and traditional land-management strategies, often serve as lifelines for small-scale farming communities that cannot otherwise compete in the international markets with farmers from more technically advanced and wealthier nations.[24] Even lands set aside for wildlife conservation or for cultural or spiritual reasons can be opened to oil and mineral exploration if lending IFIs deem it necessary. And beyond allowing lending nations to dictate borrowers' economic policies, these debt schemes also allow creditors to penetrate deeply into borrowers' political, educational, and even military decisions, threatening the national autonomy of HIPCs.[25]

The abuses that result from conditionality-loan debts have not only raised the ire of human rights groups, non-governmental organizations, and those who suffer under this form of debt exploitation, but leading economists have also voiced their concerns. In 1998, the US Congress formed a commission of economic experts, headed by Allen Meltzer, to make recommendations on the United States' interactions with the world's most powerful IFIs. In their report, the Meltzer Commission expressed dire concerns over the coercive and intrusive consequences of the IMF's conditionality loans. The commission claimed that these loans' far-reaching powers stretched beyond the limits of economic nation building to wield "too much power over developing countries' economic policies," and that "the use of IMF resources and conditionality to control the economies of developing nations often undermines the sovereignty

24. R. G. Carter, "Leadership at Risk: The Perils of Unilateralism," *Political Science and Politics* 36, no. 1 (2003): 18.
25. Michael Bujazan et al., "International Agency Assistance to Education in Latin America and the Caribbean, 1970–1984: Technical and Political Decision-Making," *Comparative Education* 23, no. 2 (1987): 164.

and democratic processes of member governments receiving assistance."[26] As in previous world systems, debt obligations were used on both domestic and international levels to ensure financial and social control.

International Capitalism's Shift in Strategy

The methods used to wield debt as a form of control in global capitalism reveal an important break from the strategies of previous world systems, such as that of the Assyrians, Persians, Romans, and other empires of the biblical world. Whereas previous world systems, from the ancient world up to the British Empire, revolved around an imperial state that functioned as the system's core—exerting its control over its peripheral states—our modern system's core is found in the boardrooms of IFIs that exert control over peripheral states and peoples via fiscal dominance and debt allocation. Lester Thurow writes that even at the system's core, "instead of a world where national policies guide economic forces, [our current] global economy gives rise to a world in which extra-national geo-economic forces [our international financial institutions] dictate national economic policies."[27] In line with the phrase "tail wagging the dog," our global economy is based on the health of financial entities that are controlled by the financial elites of the wealthiest nations rather than the well-being or desires of any of its participants or, indeed, their governments.

While the inner workings of our current world system function in vastly different ways from earlier systems, its rise has had similar overall effects on agrarian communities. As agrarian practices are

26. The Meltzer Commission, *The Meltzer Report* (Washington DC: United States Congress, 1999).

27. Lester Thurow, *The Future of Capitalism: How Today's Economic Forces Shape Tomorrow's World* (New York: William Morrow, 1996), 127.

refocused from the well-being of producers to the well-being of those administrators who engage in trade and/or pay imperial tributes or loan interest to an IFI, producers suffer increased poverty and displacement while elites enjoy greater wealth and power. Twentieth-century Tunisia's experience with conditionality loans and trade liberalization offers both useful examples of how these abuses unfold while also revealing a number of justice concerns that the Judean prophets—who could never have imagined the size or scale of our world system—might be able to address.

The Example of Debt Abuses in Twentieth-Century Tunisia

Tunisia's independence from France in 1957 not only brought about a new era of self-rule, but it also marked the beginning of a cultural revolution that placed its leaders' desire for participation in global capitalism above the nation's entwined agrarian and socio-religious traditions. Tunisia's ruling elite understood that they needed to force cultural change at home in order to benefit from this new world system. Debts, both issued and received, served as their primary means to that end.

While the IMF used conditionality loans to ensure the interests of international capitalism's primary sponsors and benefactors (the system's core), Tunisia's ruling elites (peripheral actors) used these loans to control their citizenry. IFI loan conditions that moved Tunisia's economy toward liberalization enabled Tunisia's rulers to overturn centuries-old subsistence traditions, replacing them with an agrarian sector that redirected its focus from providing for the producers to strengthening the markets through specialized cultivation and trade, thus increasing wealth *and* power among elites. This modernization of Tunisia's agrarian sector was in line with an IMF mandate to address a common mid twentieth-century concern: stunted economic development was the result of dysfunctional attachments to traditional production strategies.[28] This strategy of using international and domestic debt obligations proved highly lucrative for Tunisia's political elites and their supporters, opening new avenues of trade and ensuring the approval of supporting IFIs. But the consequences were dire for many rural communities who suffered from the effects of their administrators' ambitions.

President Bourguiba and the First Wave of Tunisia's Cultural Evolution

In a single masterstroke, Tunisia's first president, Habib Bourguiba, restructured his country's farm sector, uprooted centuries-old religious traditions and ways of life, and cut off the main revenue stream of his chief political rival, Tunisia's religious elite. During President Bourguiba's first two weeks in office he consolidated the majority of the nation's subsistence landholdings by closing the public *habous*: vast Muslim land endowments that were established by the Ottomans in the sixteenth century.[29]

The public *habous*, which were to be used in ways that would be "pleasing to God," could never be privatized through sale, gifting, or inheritance.[30] While familial *habous* concentrated wealth amongst Tunisia's elites, public *habous* served a far more egalitarian purpose: offering peasants access to communal farmlands that provided food for the community while also generating revenue for the religious establishment that managed them. In addition to offering arable land for subsistence cultivation, public *habous* also funded schools and

28. Matthew Coomber, "Prophets to Profits: Ancient Judah and Corporate Globalization," in *Bible and Justice: Ancient Texts, Modern Challenges*, ed. Matthew Coomber (London: Equinox, 2011), 224–25.

29. Lisa Anderson, "Prophets to Profits: Ancient Judah and Corporate Globalization," in *Bible and Justice: Ancient Texts, Modern Challenges*, 235.

30. David S. Powers, "Orientalism, Colonialism, and Legal History," *Comparative Studies in Society and History* 31, no. 3 (1989): 536.

charitable hospitals for the peasants who worked these lands. However, once seized in the name of national development during President Bourguiba's first wave of reforms, efforts that had once been focused on the well-being of the producers who had worked these lands for hundreds of years were now refocused on the cultivation of grapes, olives, citrus fruits, and dates for foreign appetites.[31]

After consolidating the public *habous* lands, the Tunisian government worked to secure control over those lands that were owned and operated by family-held subsistence farms; their strategies for seizing these lands are in step with those of earlier economic systems. The government punished those small-scale farm communities that were reluctant to abandon their traditional risk-reducing subsistence strategies for the high-risk specialized cultivation of export crops, and its accompanying high costs of refrigeration, storage, and transportation. The result is not surprising: a mixture of crop failures and high-interest survival loans caused many scale farms to fall into foreclosure, before being consolidated into large estates that supported Tunisia's participation in the global economy.

Through using Tunisia's IMF debt obligations and their liberalizing conditionality clauses, the country's ruling elite consolidated its power over an increasingly government-dependent labor force.[32] Dovetailing with debt exploitation in previous world systems, the Tunisian government's exploitative lending practices highlight that debt not only generates wealth but also serves as a powerful weapon of domestic societal control. A world system that

31. Samir Radwan et al., *Tunisia: Rural Labour and Structural Transformation* (London: Routledge, 1991), 29, 89–91; Stephen J. King, *Liberalization Against Democracy: The Local Politics of Economic Reform in Tunisia* (Bloomington: Indiana University Press, 2003), 75.
32. Douglas E. Ashford, "Succession and Social Change in Tunisia," *International Journal of Middle East Studies* 4, no. 1 (1973): 36.

was fashioned by the financial elites of international capitalism (the system's core) created an environment that demanded an international capitalist worldview, thus enabling Bourguiba to alter Tunisian culture (a periphery state) in ways that benefited both foreign and domestic elites at the cost of the nation's most vulnerable. Another example of such twentieth-century transformations is found in Libya, where Colonel Muammar al-Gaddafi restructured Muslim doctrine to facilitate economic liberalization in his own land.[33]

Internationally, Tunisia's debts to the world system's core were used to restructure the domestic economy for the world system's benefit. Domestically, Tunisia's rulers harnessed the terms of the debt conditions to force highly unpopular reforms, which uprooted deeply embedded socioeconomic institutions. This move did not only increase the Tunisian government's power by seizing control over the country's agrarian efforts, it also neutralized the influence of a religious establishment that opposed the consequences of international capitalism on Tunisia's poor.[34] In the end, subsistence communities' self-sufficiency was replaced with government dependency; as debt systems handed control of Tunisia's arable lands over to the country's rulers, displaced farm workers became increasingly vulnerable to government demands.

Echoing neo-Assyrian methods for consolidating economic power, Tunisia's ruling elite further strengthened their control over their economy by gifting state-backed corporations to loyal supporters.[35] As a result of these reforms, by the end of the 1980s, the country's wealthiest three percent controlled a third of Tunisia's

33. Lisa Anderson, "Obligation and Accountability: Islamic Politics in North Africa," *Daedalus* 120, no. 3 (1991): 107.

34. Coomber, *Re-Reading the Prophets*, 193–97.

35. J. N. Postgate, ed., *Neo-Assyrian Royal Grants and Degrees* (Rome: Pontifical Biblical Institute, 1969), 9–16; Rhys Payne, "Economic Crisis and Policy Reform in the 1980s," in *Polity and Society in Contemporary North Africa*, eds. I. William Zartman and William Mark Habeeb (Boulder, CO: Westview, 1993), 144.

farmlands, while the poorest forty-six percent held a meager eight percent, and to devastating effect.[36]

Debt and Displacement as Means of Societal Control

While economic shock can lead to civil unrest, it can also be a powerful tool for coercing populations into accepting changes that run counter to their own interests.[37] In the initial trauma of losing their traditional way of life, displaced subsistence producers sought low-wage jobs on government-controlled estates. However, with a desire to keep overhead costs to a minimum, employment opportunities for displaced farmers were scarce, forcing large numbers of rural workers into urban centers where they fulfilled the Tunisian government's need for low-wage labor for building Tunisia's developing infrastructure.[38] Although the desperation that accompanied this exodus to Tunis and other urban centers led to occasional rioting and unrest, the government successfully quelled revolts through the use of brutal tactics; by the end of the 1970s, torture and imprisonment were a mainstay in the government's strategy for coping with resistance to President Bourguiba's economic, social, and religious policies.[39]

The Tunisian government's use of debt to increase wealth of its rulers and to enact societal control over their people is not unique, but reflects common patterns in world systems expansion. Rulers of fourth-century Milan exerted control over peasants by driving them into debt through a manipulation of food prices. Regional leaders in

36. Lokman Zaibet and Elizabeth Dunn, "Land Tenure, Farm Size, and Rural Market Participation in Developing Countries: The Case of the Tunisian Olive Sector," *Economic Development and Cultural Change* 46, no. 4 (1998): 835–36.
37. See Naomi Klein, *Shock Doctrine: The Rise of Disaster Capitalism* (New York: Metropolitan Books, 2007).
38. N. A. Ziadeh, *Origins of Nationalism in Tunisia* (Beirut: Librarie du Liban, 1969), 41.
39. Nigel Disney, "The Working Class Revolt in Tunisia," *Middle East Research and Information Project Reports* 67 (1978): 12–14.

fifteenth-century China used debt to remove religious dietary taboos, creating greater revenue through newly opened access to foreign appetites.[40] And in the early 1990s, both Peruvian and Vietnamese ruling elites employed debt schemes to increase revenue and force displaced peasants into urban centers where they could be exploited as low-wage laborers.[41] While the means used to expand world systems may change, a sudden rise in trade activity most often leads to the sort of exploitation that is referenced in prophetic complaints against Judean land seizures.

The Hebrew Prophets And Modern Debt Exploitation

The world system into which Judah was absorbed was vastly different from our current system of global capitalism; global capitalism profits from the investment *potential* of trade goods, rather than actually *possessing* those goods. So how can the consequences of Tunisia's entrance into our modern economic system, which is focused on appeasing the desires of stockholders rather than a single government, relate to an Assyrian world system that was focused on hoarding luxury goods and building supplies for its rulers? Despite the differences between how present and previous world systems function, we can learn a lot from debt weaponization in different world systems; while the methods and goals of wealth accumulation may change, the wounds that they inflict on rural producers are relatively the same.

Whether in Roman Milan, medieval Japan, or twenty-first century Chiapas, rising world systems lead to a centralization of production that displaces farm communities, while those at the helm of the

40. C. A. Bayly, "'Archaic' and 'Modern' Globalization in the Eurasian and African Arena: c. 1750–1850," in *Globalization in World History*, ed. A. G. Hopkins (London: Pimlico), 52–53.
41. Michel Chossudovsky, *The Globalization of Poverty*, 2nd ed. (Quebec: Global Research, 2003), 180–83, 221–22.

system enjoy increased wealth and power. As argued above, this link can help us to uncover new connections between ancient and current debt abuses, while also revealing a previously unrecognized relevance that prophetic texts have for addressing economic exploitation in our own time. Three particular areas of connection are the use of foreign obligations to enforce unpopular domestic change, the economic and physical displacements that result from land seizures, and the ways in which rulers harness resulting desperation to redirect labor efforts and sustain socioeconomic change.

While conditionality was not used in ancient Judah, tribute obligations to the Assyrian Empire could have been used to press through the kinds of societal change that are found in the archaeological record. The rapid rise of late eighth-century Judah's administrative accomplishments, including the centralization of agrarian production, would not have been easy to achieve; changes like these uproot traditional economic and religious ways of life, as found in Tunisia and other periphery nations in a variety of world systems.[42] The threat of Assyrian punishment for not fulfilling tribute obligations could have given Judah's rulers the needed leverage to coerce autonomous communities into enduring what would have otherwise been unacceptable reforms. As in the case of Peru and Vietnam in the 1990s, Judean leaders could have exploited the vulnerability of displaced farmers—having lost their traditional livelihoods through land-consolidation schemes—to transform semi-autonomous agriculturalists into low-wage laborers on the newly irrigated desert lands that were developed during this time. Perhaps some of their efforts, when not working the fields, were also redirected toward the numerous and massive construction projects that emerged in the late eighth century.

42. Coomber, *Re-Reading the Prophets*, 128–32.

Another question raised through cultural-evolutionary understandings of late eighth-century Judah is whether the kingdom's ruling elite was solely responsible for debt schemes and the displacement of rural producers. While ruling elites are the most likely perpetrators of the land seizures found in Isaiah and Micah, exploitative debt practices in our current and earlier cultural-evolutionary cycles show that another group could have exploited Judean farm workers: neighboring Judean farm workers.

Whereas interpretations of Isaiah 5:8-10 and Micah 2:1-4 usually focus on urban-based merchants who may not have known their victims, new or increased pressures to meet trade and tribute obligations, as well as the fear of falling into crippling debt and foreclosure, may have altered intra-community relationships and caused shifts in allegiance among producers. Such relational changes are common during cultural evolutionary shifts,[43] and are certainly found in Tunisia's twentieth-century transformation, souring friendly relations between wealthy and poorer farmers.

A Tunisian farmer named Majoub remembers that before President Bourguiba's reforms, ". . . the rich were kind. If they knew someone did not have clothes and food, then they would go find them to help them out. At harvest time, everyone helped out. Sometimes the rich would give you a piece of land and allow you to use their tractors."[44] But Majoub saw all of that change as powerful landowning elites seized the nations farming cooperatives, joining field to field:

> Times have changed. Morality has changed. The rich don't feel anything for the needy. They even fear the poor. They don't want the poor living near them or having land near them because they will ask for things. They don't even want the poor to raise a chicken near

43. Johnson and Earle, *Evolution of Human Societies*, 250; Patrick Nolan and Gerhard Lenski, *Human Societies: An Introduction to Macrosociology*, 9th ed. (Boulder, CO: Paradigm, 2004).

44. King, *Liberalization Against Democracy*, 86–87.

them because it would sneak on their land. Hajj Naouar [a powerful landowner], who lives next door, wants us all to move. His workers only work the land [and do not farm for themselves]. He said, "Don't raise your animals and let them eat my grass." Some of his workers had to sell their cows and look for other work.[45]

In addition to simply cutting off support, many of those who escaped debt—either through greater access to resources or the luck of having better access to water—worked to seize the lands of their neighbors, by lending to them at extortionate rates or by using their influence to drive them out of business.

Corruption in the Courts

Another example of the friendly relations in Tunisia being replaced by a culture of betrayal is found in the manipulation of legal and political channels, as referenced in Micah 2:1. When a wealthy farmer named Abdelkader was awarded a loan worth $280,000 to buy the latest refrigeration technology, a group of small-scale farmers tried to form a refrigeration cooperative in order to stay competitive and maintain markets viability. As local administrators were considering the co-op's loan application, Abdelkader and his colleagues used their influence in the local governing body to ensure that the loan request was dropped.[46] Majoub's observations on Abdelkader's actions follow a common breakdown of community ties that occurs as new trade opportunities emerge. Such a scenario draws attention to the possibility that while Judah's rulers were likely the perpetrators who attached "field to field" (Isa. 5:8), economic exploitation may not have been a strictly top-down affair: it could also have moved horizontally across social lines, pitting small-scale farmers against one another (cf. Mic. 7:5-6). Perhaps subsistence farmers who weathered a few bad

45. Ibid., 87.
46. Ibid., 93.

harvests took advantage of their neighbors' misfortune, lending at high interest rates.

The sufferings inflicted upon farm workers who lose their lands to debt and foreclosure is often exacerbated by corruption in the courts of law, offering another possible point of connection between the effects of debt abuse in Judah and in the modern world. As large privatized estates overtook smaller collective farmlands in Tunisia, the displacement of agrarian workers became widespread. A peasant named Hadi, who found employment on a privatized cooperative, noted how his country's new economic system did not care about the well-being of agrarian workers but reshaped itself toward the benefit of Tunisia's wealthiest citizens. Hadi lamented,

> Small farmers are being run out of farming. The government doesn't want to divide the land into small parts. They are distributing it hundreds of hectares at a time, so the poor can't afford it. Wealthy people . . . will go to the *'umda* [local federal-government representatives] and plan on getting the land in one person's hands. Later they will divide the money with the *'umda*. I know that they aren't using technical criteria for [land distribution], because people like me who studied agriculture can't get any.[47]

Nur Eddine, another Tunisian laborer who is respected in his community as a capable and educated farmer, also expressed his frustration with these corruptive practices. Having been passed over for a land grant by a wealthier neighbor, despite his farming experience, he complained, "How could they give all that land to those people? . . . My brother has a diploma but he can't get a job. We don't know the right people for those kinds of jobs."[48] The involvement of *'umda* in these land transactions offers an interesting parallel to land seizures and distributions in ancient Judah. Hadi's

47. Ibid., 87.
48. Ibid., 83.

and Nur Eddine's accounts of government-backed administrators allocating farmlands to wealthy elites during a period of rapid trade development provides new insights for the work of Ludwig Köhler and John Dearman, who consider the phrases from Micah 2:1, ". . . in the light of day they do it" and ". . . for it is in the power of their hand," to refer to the involvement of Judean judges.[49] Such a connection could resonate and be used by those communities who work to oppose such systems of cronyism in both rural and urban areas, such as Jamie Dimon's assignment to take over Bear Stearns and make a handsome personal profit in so doing.

Conclusion

The weaponization of debt in our current world system of international capitalism functions in new and wider-reaching ways in its bid to create wealth for those at its financial core, as well as control of its peripheral regions and members. The systems of debt that it employs, such as conditionality loans, place IFI in exceedingly powerful positions from which to control the nations who come to them for aid. Furthermore, the ruling elites of HIPCs who enter their nations into conditionality loans have commonly used them to enact highly unpopular domestic reforms, giving them increased societal control and access to wealth.

While the Assyrian systems of extraction and control were far more crude and inefficient than those of today, they too enabled the Assyrian Empire to control peripheral states in the late eighth century. And reading the archeological record through a cultural-evolutionary perspective, it appears that Judean elites used these pressures to enact their own systems of control. Upon reading texts

49. Ludwig Köhler, *Hebrew Man*, trans. Peter R. Ackroyd (London: SCM, 1956), 151; John Dearman, *Property Rights in the Eighth-Century Prophets: The Conflict and its Background* (Atlanta: Scholars Press, 1988), 46.

like Isaiah 5:8-10 and Micah 2:1-4 in light of cultural-evolutionary theory and archaeological evidence, we find that the prophetic voices that cried out against economic exploitation and displacement—and are attributed to a time of massive economic change—have a special relevance in addressing the complaints that are lodged against systemic exploitation in our modern world.

Yes, our system has vastly different ways than that of the Assyrians, but the two are not divergent in every way. Underlying motivations, the use of debt for control, and the suffering of those who are left at the margins of the system—as well as the transgressions of those who cause their suffering—relate to the biblical cries against the exploitation of the vulnerable, be it the foreclosure of a farming cooperative in rural Tunisia or of a family's home in Detroit. The problem, as a whole, is not new, and neither is the courage of some to take a stand and cry "injustice" in the face of what seem to be untouchable economics systems and insurmountable centers of power. But that did not stop the prophets from speaking out, nor should it stop activists in our present time.

The prophetic voice, time and again, speaks out against the kinds of systems and injustices with which we contend. But quoting the Bible in the face of injustice is not enough. Simply standing before the house-and-field-joiners of our time and quoting Isaiah, Micah, or the story of Naboth's vineyard won't change our world, alone. What these biblical passages *can* do is show Jews and Christians the disconnect between their scriptural traditions and how our capitalist system exploits millions of people around the world, including those in our communities. What these biblical passages *can* do is to help us see our cause for justice in new ways, reminding us that we are not alone in the noble struggle for economic equality. Passages like those found in the Hebrew prophets can inspire us to write and educate one another on the failings of our system. And hearing the impassioned pleas of the ancient prophets can encourage us to endure, engage, and protest our way to a brighter and more just future.

7

The Global Crisis of Debt in Context

Biblical and Postcolonial Reflections on the Ideology of Empire

Robert Wafawanaka

Introduction

Recent national and international crises have challenged many concerned individuals to take a serious look at the global state of affairs and their apparent causative factors. In particular, the nascent Occupy movement has brought our attention to many rotating crises such as poverty, debt, homelessness, injustice, ecological disasters, and gross income inequalities between the rich and the poor.[1] This movement has highlighted an explosion of social and political issues in various parts of the world. Despite its waning power, the

1. The major distinction is drawn between the wealth, power, and influence of the global minority 1 percent as opposed to that of the majority 99 percent.

movement has forced us to confront the reality of our world and ponder the implications of a world defined by injustice, poverty, and inequality on the one hand, and excessive wealth, influence, and power on the other. Socially concerned individuals have been at work documenting the serious nature of this divide. Indeed, some have offered creative and radical solutions to address these global crises. Others have even formulated theological and spiritual alternatives to the status quo that has historically benefited the few.[2] The task of this essay is to contribute to this discussion by focusing on the crisis of debt, especially as it relates to the Two-Thirds World in general, and Africa in particular. Through postcolonial reflections, the text of Naboth's vineyard is used as a symbolic case study of the ideology of power and the victimization of those who are powerless and lack political capital. Consequently, this narrative provides an interpretive lens on our own modern crises including the global crisis of debt.

A Brief History of the Occupy Movement

According to its proponents, the Occupy movement began in 2011 when protesting members of the 99 percent streamed into and occupied Zuccotti Park in New York City to express their indignation toward big banks and corporations as well as government bailouts of multinational companies. The movement eventually spread around the globe particularly to Africa and the Middle East. It highlighted the idea that "the status quo is unjust and unsustainable and that a new social contract is urgently necessary."[3] Occupy theologians[4] like Joerg Rieger and Kwok Pui-lan have

2. See Joerg Rieger and Kwok Pui-lan, *Occupy Religion: Theology of the Multitude* (New York: Rowman and Littlefield, 2012); and Adam Bucko and Matthew Fox, *Occupy Spirituality: A Radical Vision for a New Generation* (Berkely, CA: North Atlantic Books, 2013).

3. Rieger and Pui-lan, *Occupy Religion*, 2. This well-documented book captures the movement at its height including personal reflections, electronic resources, why it began, its claims, and what

indeed attempted to describe the basic tenets of a theology of the multitude. While Occupy had a global reach,[5] the movement arrived in Richmond, Virginia, where this author resides, in October 2011. Protesters occupied parts of the capital city of Richmond including Brown's Island for several weeks. Extensive coverage of the movement was done by the late publisher of the *Richmond Free Press,* Raymond H. Boone, a fearless advocate of justice for the disenfranchised and a champion of civil rights. When the city threatened to arrest protesters, Boone decided to allow protesters to camp on his front yard, in view of the residency of the Mayor of Richmond, who had expelled the protesters from the city. To the mayor's consternation, the protesters camped at the publisher's home for several weeks.[6]

Like the mass movements of the 1960s and 1970s, the Occupy movement, led mostly by young people,[7] protested global economic and social inequality, injustice, and greed, and sought to change the status quo.[8] It also highlighted how consumerism benefits the powerful elite who promote it. Rieger and Pui-lan describe the world as facing "an unprecedented crisis" because

> While living standards have increased for some, inequality is more pronounced today than ever before and affects more people than ever. Large and growing parts of humanity are forced to struggle for survival

God, church, and theology of the multitude might look like. Social media also played a crucial role in the spread of this movement.

4. The term "occupy movement" is a recent phenomenon that took root in 2011. The phrase "Occupy theologians" is used to refer to those who espouse the views of this movement. The practitioners of this movement seek "to challenge traditional ways of thinking about religion and the space that religion is supposed to inhabit" Rieger and Pui-lan, *Occupy Religion*, 4.
5. Rieger and Pui-lan state that the movement went global on October 15, 2011, when protesters in 952 cities in 82 countries took to the streets (*Occupy Religion*, 19).
6. These events were extensively covered in the editions of the *Richmond Free Press* of October 27, November 23, December 1–3, December 8, 2011, and January 5, 2012. I thank the *Free Press* for giving me these crucial dates.
7. Bucko and Fox, *Occupy Spirituality*, xix–xx; Rieger and Pui-lan, *Occupy Religion*, 2, 31.
8. Rieger and Pui-lan, *Occupy Religion*, 5; Bucko and Fox, *Occupy Spirituality*, 4–15.

> every day, even in the wealthiest countries. Inequality in the United States, a country that often takes pride in being the leader for others to emulate, is especially troublesome.[9]

While reflecting on the state of poverty in the United States fifty years after President Lyndon B. Johnson's 1964 declaration of the "War on Poverty" (and also nearing the fiftieth anniversary of Martin Luther King Jr.'s "Poor People's Campaign"), I noted that "the reality of poverty is reflected on the streets of many of America's inner cities and rural areas on a daily basis" and concluded that "the very idea of poverty in the United States, one of the richest nations on earth, may seem ironic or troubling to some," hence the war on poverty needs to continue.[10]

The social transformation that needs to take place must be a global effort because "we need each other more now than at any other time in history."[11] While we constitutionally tend to separate religion and politics, Rieger and Pui-lan argue that "politics and religion are not fundamentally opposed in many of our traditions—the idea that they can be separated is a modern misconception."[12] They are right because this view is supported by some biblical scholars, including Jerome C. Ross who argues that while "political structures were sacralized" on the one hand, "on the other hand, cultic structures were politicized."[13] This insight is clarified by the biblical picture of religion and politics as not separate entities in ancient Israel. In

9. Rieger and Pui-lan, *Occupy Religion*, 25, 57.
10. See Robert Wafawanaka, "Is the Biblical Perspective on Poverty that 'There Shall Be No Poor amongYou' or 'You Will Always Have the Poor with You?'" *Review & Expositor* 111, no. 2 (2014): 107–20, esp. 108, 120.
11. Rieger and Pui-lan, *Occupy Religion*, 59. This is the basis of their proposal for a theology of the multitude. Even the idealized American Dream is a vanishing or unattainable dream for many (63, 98). The "protestant ethic" of hard work does not equal to success any more. Cf., Max Weber, *The Protestant Ethic and the Spirit of Capitalism,* trans. Talcott Parsons (New York: Scribner, 1958).
12. Rieger and Pui-lan, *Occupy Religion*, 76.
13. Jerome Clayton Ross, *The History of Ancient Israel and Judah: A Compilation* (Pittsburgh: Dorrance, 2003), 2.

fact the balance between the vertical and horizontal dimensions of the social order was crucial to the smooth functioning of society. Such a balance sought to ensure justice and equity in the land.[14] For the most part, the biblical narrative shows this connection. For example, the prophets largely functioned as political advisors to the kings and they provided the necessary checks and balances on the monarchy.[15] In Ross's words, "Yahwistic prophetism was Yahwistic tribalism's check on the monarchy."[16] Nathan's clever indictment of King David's misdeeds proved that the king, however great, was not above the law of the land (2 Sam. 11–12).[17] Similarly, Isaiah functioned as a political advisor to King Ahaz during the Syro-Ephraimitic War of 734–733 BCE (Isaiah 7–8). Three decades later, he was also an advisor to King Hezekiah when Sennacherib, king of Assyrian, besieged Jerusalem in 701 BCE (2 Kings 18–20). Likewise, the prophet Jeremiah presided over the political affairs of Judah when Jerusalem fell to Babylonian King Nebuchadnezzar in 598–597 and 587–596 BCE (Jeremiah 37–39; 52:1-34; cf. 2 Kings 24–25). In that role, he preached an unpopular message as he advised the Judean king and citizens to capitulate to Babylon and prepare for exile. As a true prophet, Jeremiah also dispelled Israel's false sense of security in the protection of the temple with these angry and haunting words,

14. See the classic essay of F. Charles Fensham, "Widow, Orphan, and the Poor in Ancient Near EasternLegal and Wisdom Literature," *JNES* 21 (1962): 129–39. Simply stated, "It is not possible to appreciate and respect God without appreciating and respecting other people" (Rieger and Pui-lan, *Occupy Religion*, 104, 128).

15. However, prophets like Obadiah sought to defend the punishment that had been visited on Jerusalem bycriticizing the Edomites for assisting the Babylonians in their invasion of the city due to its perceived sin. On the other hand, kings like Ahab, a son of the great King Omri, were viewed as the architects of the evil that destroyed the nation, especially because Ahab's kingship was dominated by the evil acts of his Phoenician Queen Jezebel. But ideologically, the Bible has nothing good to say about Northern (Israelite) kings as they all, without exception, interestingly "walked in the way of Jeroboam, the man who caused Israel to sin" (1 Kings 12). It should be noted that Jeroboam I, the first king of the Northern Kingdom, is vilified for breaking up the United Kingdom of David and Solomon, the so-called "Golden Age."

16. Ross, *History of Ancient Israel and Judah*, 34.

17. See Deut. 17:14-20 on the law of the king.

> Thus says the Lord of hosts, the God of Israel: Amend your ways and your doings, and let me dwell with you in this place. Do not trust in these deceptive words: "This is the temple of the Lord, the temple of the Lord, the temple of the Lord." For if you truly amend your ways and your doings, if you truly act justly one with another, if you do not oppress the alien, the orphan, and the widow, or shed innocent blood in this place, and if you do not go after other gods to your own hurt, then I will dwell with you in this place, in the land that I gave of old to your ancestors forever and ever. (Jer. 7:3-7, NRSV)[18]

This kind of indictment reveals the imbalance of religious and political structures in ancient Israel. Other prophets, including Minor Prophets like Amos and Micah, also spoke vehemently against the lack of social justice in their day.[19]

Occupy theologians (simply, theologians who have participated in the event, or represent the ethos of the movement) have asked where God can be found in this unjust and unequal world. They generally agree that God does not identify with the establishment, but rather with "the least of these" (Matt. 25:45), the oppressed (Luke 1:46–55), those on the streets and lanes of cities (Matt. 22:9; Luke 14:21), and with the lowly (1 Cor. 1:26–29).[20] Adam Bucko, an advocate for homeless kids in New York City, wrote an essay titled "My God Lives on the Street," which chronicles the work he is doing with street children. To the question "Where is God?" he answers, "He is here on this street, lying naked in the gutter. He is here on this street, homeless . . . waiting for our love."[21] Biblical tradition portrays a God who identifies with the oppressed, such that "the liberation of the

18. Biblical citations are taken from the New Revised Standard Version.
19. For a more extended discussion of the prophets, see Robert Wafawanaka, *Am I Still My Brother's Keeper? Biblical Perspectives on Poverty* (Lanham, MD: University Press of America, 2012), esp. ch. 3. Bucko and Fox argue that prophets got mad, as did Mahatma Gandhi, Martin Luther King Jr., and Jesus, because "moral outrage is and always has been a light that sets fire to social change" (xxv).
20. Rieger and Pui-lan, *Occupy Religion*, 87, 98, 107. See also Willy Schottroff and Wolfgang Stegemann,eds., *God of the Lowly: Socio-Historical Interpretations of the Bible*, trans. Matthew J. O'Connell (Maryknoll, NY: Orbis Books, 1984).

poor and the oppressed is . . . at the heart of what it is to know God and to worship God."[22] This idea is equally fitting for biblical scholars whose task should be to translate the message of the Scriptures for the transformation of society. Robert McAfee Brown expresses this well when he writes, "To make a 'preferential option' for such people is to leave the safe world of head trips, engage in foot trips to such places, and help the oppressed organize to challenge the oppressors."[23]

In their collaborative work, Adam Bucko and Matthew Fox discuss the elements of a radical spirituality brought about by the Occupy movement. Their observations are in the form of a free-flowing and at times philosophical conversation between them. They believe this new spirituality, grounded in monasticism, nature, and humanity, and divorced from the normal order of our world, "has the potential to change both individual lives and the world as a whole."[24] As Bucko explains it,

> Occupy at its best is not about fixing the existing system or imposing a new fixed rule. It's about something much more powerful than that. It's about pioneering a new way of living that is based on a daily practice of putting aside our egos and figuring out what it means to create a community and a world that works for all.[25]

21. See Bucko and Fox, *Occupy Spirituality*, 56–58, 131, 224; see also the reflections of "J.M.," 115. The father of Latin American liberation theology, Gustavo Gutiérrez, responding to the question of where the poor are for whom the church makes a "preferential option," makes a similar statement by stating that the poor are not in church but "dwell in the *barrios*, the slums; they are tenant farmers trying to scratch a living out of the wretched pieces of land the wealthy *patrón* rents to them at exorbitant rates." See Robert McAfee Brown, *Unexpected News: Reading the Bible with Third World Eyes* (Philadelphia: Westminster, 1984), 114.
22. Rieger and Pui-lan, *Occupy Religion*, 98. See the work of pioneering liberation theologian James H. Cone, *God of the Oppressed* (Maryknoll, NY: Orbis Books, 2003).
23. See Brown, *Unexpected News*, 115. Adam Bucko challenges academicians by stating: "When Occupy Wall Street began and spaces around the world were being occupied by young people standing up to greed and power, seminaries remained open with their students tucked safely inside. Shouldn't they have instead been closing down and sending their students to the streets to live with the Occupiers? Isn't that where Jesus would have been?" See Bucko and Fox, *Occupy Spirituality*, 154–55.
24. Bucko and Fox, *Occupy Spirituality,* 21.
25. Ibid., 179–180.

Theologian Matthew Fox agrees and says that life should not be about endless greed or endless consumption, because nothing is infinite, including the earth and its resources.[26] He adds, "The truth is we have an *entire economic system based on rendering us addicts from the time we are young children*—that is the deep shadow behind consumer capitalism and its trillion-dollar advertising industry. It feeds on human weakness: greed and avarice. That is why we need a new economics."[27] In attempting to create a better alternative world, Bucko and Fox conclude their vision of a spiritual democracy by arguing that "we can't have a democracy that is of the people, by the people, and for the people if we have an economic system that is of the few, by the few, and for the few—or of the corporations, by the corporations, and for the corporations."[28]

The global crises that the Occupy movement has underscored need to be addressed by all human beings, both rich and poor, because "we're all in the same boat; we rise and fall, sink *and* swim together."[29] As W. R. Brookman states, "We have a commonality one with another . . . the rich and the poor do have relationship."[30] The social and economic disparities highlighted by the Occupy movement compel us as human beings to think critically about the fate of our world. As previously stated, "the challenge is radical transformation of the human tendency toward self-care without regard for the other. We ought to seriously wrestle with the implications of a world of extremes—extreme wealth on the one hand, and extreme poverty on

26. Ibid., 184, 187. Fox adds, "Life is not here to serve the economy, the economy is here to serve life," that is, all forms of life and ecosystems on Earth (184–85, 203). Bucko retorts, "What we need is a democratization of this enterprise, so everyone can benefit and live" (186).
27. Ibid., 200, emphasis in original. In addition to greed (avarice), the early church had identified seven deadly sins including pride, wrath (anger), sloth (laziness), gluttony, envy, and lust.
28. Ibid., 216.
29. Ibid., 226, emphasis in original.
30. W. R. Brookman, *Global Scenes of Biblical Injustice: Glimpsing the Poor and Oppressed in Today's World* (Lanham, MD: University Press of America, 2012), 2.

the other. The two are not mutually exclusive either."[31] The crisis of debt is but one problem that both rich and poor need to confront because it is often the poor who are helplessly caught in the vicious cycle of debt. As a result, it is the poor who finance the rich while the rich continue to impoverish them through high interest rates and revolving debt. The unequal creditor-debtor relationship leads to the creation of what Lazzarato defines as "the indebted man." He writes,

> Through consumption, we maintain an unwitting relationship with the debt economy. We carry within us the creditor-debtor relation—in our pockets and wallets, encoded in the magnetic strip on our credit cards. Indeed, this little strip of plastic hides two seemingly harmless operations: the *automatic* institution of the credit relation, which thereby establishes *permanent* debt. The credit card is the simplest way to transform its owner into a permanent debtor, an 'indebted man' for life.[32]

The crisis of debt is a global phenomenon felt most acutely in the developing world such as Africa, to which we now turn.

The Crisis of Debt in Africa

Although Africa is the world's richest continent in terms of natural resources,[33] it is now grappling with grinding poverty and misery as well as political, social, and economic instability. It is ironic that

31. Wafawanaka, *Am I Still My Brother's Keeper?* 6.
32. See Maurizio Lazzarato, *The Making of the Indebted Man: An Essay on the Neoliberal Condition*, trans. Joshua David Jordan, Semiotext(e)/Intervention Series 13 (Los Angeles: Semiotext(e), 2011), 20. Emphasis original. Lazzaroto adds, "The debtor-creditor relationship . . . intensifies mechanisms of exploitation and domination at every level of society, for within it no distinction exists between workers and the unemployed, consumers and producers, working and non-working populations, retirees and welfare recipients. Everyone is a 'debtor,' accountable to and guilty before capital. Capital has become the Great Creditor, the Universal Creditor" (7).
33. *The Economist*, September 14, 1996. The paper states that Africa has 40 percent of the world's hydro-electric power; most of the world's diamonds and chromium; 50 percent of the world's gold; 70 percent of cocoa; 60 percent of coffee; 50 percent of palm oil, etc. (68). Cited in *Biblical Interpretation in African Perspective,* ed. David Tuesday Adamo (Lanham: University Press of America, 2006), 223.

in the postcolonial era, Africa can hardly afford to feed itself and is burdened with a debt crisis that it cannot repay.[34] The crisis of leadership in Africa has also contributed to some of its problems.[35] To understand the debt crisis and Africa's current designation as the "poverty trap," we must take into account its history of colonialism and Western imperialism. While Africa may have many natural resources, the historical "scramble for Africa" and its resources, as well as those of other continents, has resulted in the current reality where most people in Africa and other developing countries are poor and survive on only one to two dollars a day.[36] Despite globalization and progress in technology and other areas, the poor die of poverty, preventable diseases, and many other causes.[37] On a global scale, the gap between the rich and the poor continues to widen.

African scholars have addressed Africa's debt crisis. According to Musa Dube, the Lord's Prayer in the Gospel of Matthew addresses many global issues including the reality of debt in Africa. With much insight, she interprets the meaning of this familiar text in a global context.[38] Dube argues that in the Palestinian agrarian economy under Roman imperial rule, most people had personal debts ranging from loans to imperial and temple tax. Notably, as in the Old Testament context, those who failed to pay their debts were most

34. See Robert Wafawanaka, "Poverty in the Old Testament in African Perspectives," in *Biblical Interpretation in African Perspective*, ed. David Tuesday Adamo (Lanham, MD: University Press of America, 2006), 223–58.

35. See George B. N. Ayitteh, *Africa Betrayed* (New York: St. Martin's, 1992); Ayitteh, *Africa in Chaos*(New York: St. Martin's, 1998). In addition to neocolonialism in Africa today, these crises have also led some to call for a "second liberation" of Africa to rid the continent of oppressive regimes, or the ludicrous calls for "re-colonization" due to the mistaken belief that Africans cannot rule themselves. See Adamo, ed., *Biblical Interpretation in African Perspective*, 226.

36. See Wayne Grudem and Barry Asmus, *The Poverty of Nations: A Sustainable Solution* (Wheaton, IL: Crossway, 2013), 19.

37. See Jeffrey D. Sachs, *The End of Poverty: Economic Possibilities for Our Time* (New York: PenguinBooks, 2005), 20–25, and also Brookman, *Global Scenes of Biblical Injustice*, 52–65.

38. See Musa Dube, "To Pray the Lord's Prayer in the Global Economic Era (Matt. 6:9-13," in *The Bible in Africa: Transactions, Trajectories, and Trends*, eds. Gerald O. West and Musa W. Dube (Leiden: Brill, 2000), 611–30.

likely imprisoned or enslaved. Moreover, this was part of "systemic structures that lock many responsible, hard-working individuals and nations into a vicious cycle of poverty and debts."[39] In her view, "The Lord's Prayer vision indicates that to place impossible debts on people through oppressive and exploitative international or national policies are inconsistent with the rule and will of God in heaven or on earth."[40] Thus, the Lord's Prayer is a clarion call to action leading to "national and international economic restructuring—a restructuring that frees the oppressed from exploitative systems; a restructuring that calls those in positions of power to abandon their unjust economic strategies . . . [by] seeking and formulating healthy and fair national and international economic policies."[41] In addition, Two-Thirds World nations are all too familiar with debt as "some countries owe more than they produce as a whole nation, yet the loans they have received have hardly improved their lives. Indeed, most of these Two-Thirds World countries are ensnared in worse forms [of] colonization than in the pre-independence era."[42]

Elsewhere, I have investigated some of the causes of poverty in Africa and they include colonialism, political and economic instability, non-democratic processes, incompetent leadership, and corruption. Thus I concluded that "ironically, the suffering that Africa has endured in the post-colonial period is quite unlike that of the colonial period."[43] My investigation also revealed that in the case of Zimbabwe, our British colonial masters did not believe Africans

39. Ibid., 622.
40. Ibid., 622–23.
41. Ibid., 623–24.
42. Ibid., 624.
43. Wafawanaka, "Poverty in the Old Testament in African Perspectives," 224–26, esp. 226. For more causes of poverty, see Sachs, *The End of Poverty*, ch. 3. Temba Mafico expresses the same sentiment in "Land Concept and Land Tenure in Israel and African Tradition," in *Postcolonial Perspectives in African Biblical Interpretations*, Global Perspectives on Biblical Scholarship 13, eds. Musa W. Dube, Andrew M. Mbuvi, and Dora R. Mbuwayesango (Atlanta: Society of Biblical Literature, 2012), 243.

were capable of ruling themselves, as the former Rhodesian rebel Prime Minister Ian Douglas Smith once infamously claimed that majority rule would come "not in a thousand years." When majority rule came to Zimbabwe in 1980, Paul L. Moorcraft published his appropriately titled book *A Short Thousand Years.*[44]

What can we learn about debt from the Lord's Prayer? Dube concludes that "the Lord's Prayer presents us with an alternative model: forgiveness. The alternative is that Christian communities, nations, and institutions must clear the tangles of yesterday and today's exploitative structures, and work to build a realm of equality, justice, peace and self-sufficiency."[45]

A Brief History of Colonialism in Africa and the Struggle for Land

Postcolonial studies have shed much light on the process of colonial expansion and the effect of European imperialism around the world. Scholars have shown how the colonizers often acted with theological justification. They viewed themselves as the conquering Israelites whose goal was to spread the Christian gospel and convert the "heathens" or "savages," regardless of the fact that "Africans are notoriously religious."[46] For example, the Scottish missionary, Thomas Pringle states, "Let us subdue Savage Africa by justice, by kindness, by the talisman of Christian truth."[47] In these conquest stories, imperial masters and missionaries saw themselves as reenacting the biblical paradigm in which they were the victorious conquerors. Biblical interpreters such as Musa Dube have correctly

44. Paul L. Moorcraft, *A Short Thousand Years: The End of Rhodesian Rebellion*, rev. ed. (South Africa: Galaxie, 1980).
45. Dube, "To Pray the Lord's Prayer," 625.
46. John S. Mbiti, *African Religions and Philosophy*, 2nd ed. (Oxford: Heinemann, 1990), 1.
47. D. Hammond and A. Jablow, *The Myth of Africa* (New York: Library of Social Science, 1977), 44, cited in Musa Dube, *Postcolonial Feminist Interpretation of the Bible* (St. Louis: Chalice, 2000), 9.

argued that the colonizers traveled to other people's lands to teach, but never to learn from their subjects at the "contact zone."[48] Under the guise of commerce and the spread of Christianity, they went to dispossess others and possess for themselves. The colonized victims were often seen and treated as the biblical Canaanites, fit to be degraded, devalued, and subjected to the *ban* or *herem.*[49] The *ban* meant the destruction and dedication of all life to Yahweh. According to Joshua 6:17, "the city and all that is in it shall be devoted to the Lord for destruction." John Collins, Professor of Old Testament Criticism and Interpretation at Yale Divinity School explains, "We should not be surprised that the Israelites, like other peoples, gloried in the destruction of their adversaries. What is troubling in the biblical text is the claim that such action is justified by divine command."[50] According to the book of Deuteronomy, there would be blessings of land occupation by following such draconian measures. Consequently, curses were pronounced for failing to obey such laws (Deut. 8:1-20; 27:11 – 29:29). It is with this divine mandate that Israel sets out for the land of Canaan. Robert Allen Warrior, a Native American scholar, argues that our reading of the Exodus narrative often ignores "those parts of the story that describe Yahweh's command to mercilessly annihilate the indigenous population."[51]

48. Dube, *Postcolonial Feminist Interpretation of the Bible*, 67–69.

49. See Robert Wafawanaka, "'The Land is Mine!' Biblical and Postcolonial Reflections on Land with Particular Reference to the Land Issue in Zimbabwe," in *Postcolonial Perspectives in African Biblical Interpretations*, 221–34.

50. John J. Collins, *Introduction to the Hebrew Bible.* Second Edition (Minneapolis: Fortress Press, 2014), 201. He adds: "The entire history of Western colonialism involved claims of divine authorization for transparently selfish interests. The most glaring example is perhaps the conquest of North America by white settlers of European origin and the near eradication of Native Americans" 202. He cautions that we should not be oblivious to the fact that "the unprovoked conquest of one people by another is an act of injustice and that injustice is often cloaked with legitimacy by claims of divine authorization" ibid.

A twentieth-century literary "masterpiece," Joseph Conrad's *Heart of Darkness*,[52] eloquently describes the Imperial Britain's negative image of Africa. With reference to British colonial expansion in southern Africa, Dora Mbuwayesango writes in the *Global Biblical Commentary* that "to get ownership of the arable lands, the settlers killed and displaced the indigenous peoples from their ancestral lands. They justified their barbaric acts on the pretext of civilizing the indigenous peoples, and the missionaries who came with them saw this settlement as an occasion to convert the 'natives' to Christianity."[53]

The whole history of the "scramble for Africa," or the rush of European countries to possess the lands and wealth of Africa in the nineteenth century, began at the Berlin Conference of 1884. At this gathering, European powers met and planned to seize African lands with impunity, and divide them among themselves.[54] Eventually it became evident that European explorers and missionaries wanted to simply possess the best African lands for themselves, without the consent of the native inhabitants. Many Africans were driven to less fertile areas or to other countries, or they became tenants on their own traditional lands.[55] This practice was also noted in many other parts of the world during the period of colonial expansion.

51. Robert Allen Warrior, "A Native American Perspective: Canaanites, Cowboys, and Indians," in *Voices from the Margin: Interpreting the Bible in the Third World*, New Edition, ed. R. S. Sugirtharajah (Maryknoll, NY: Orbis Books, 2000), 279.
52. See Robert Hampson, ed., *Joseph Conrad: Heart of Darkness: With the Congo Diary* (London: Penguin Books, 1995).
53. See Dora R. Mbuwayesango, "Joshua," in *Global Bible Commentary*, ed. Daniel Patte (Nashville: Abingdon, 2004), 64–73, esp. 64.
54. Dube clarifies, "To start with, at the Berlin conference of 1884, where the European imperial powers met to divide the map of Africa amongst themselves and to draw a constitution on how to do it, the role of missionaries among other agents of imperialism, was recognized and given its rightful place" (*Postcolonial Feminist Interpretation of the Bible*, 4).
55. Musa Dube and Gerald West, eds., *The Bible in Africa: Transitions, Trajectories, and Trends* (Boston: Brill, 2000), 152–53; Dube et al. eds., *Postcolonial Perspectives*, 15–16.

Christianity's complicity with imperial governments and administrations has been amply demonstrated by many scholars and researchers.[56] This global history of the colonization of Africa leading to the scramble for African lands begins with European explorations around the world dating back to the late fifteenth century. More recently, some critics have identified "a new scramble for Africa," which is also expressed elsewhere around the world. Michael Hardt and Antonio Negri write, "Whereas European states led the scramble a century ago, today it is primarily corporations dividing up the spoils under the cover of complex forms of global governance."[57] Writing in *Reading from This Place*, Mary Ann Tolbert paints a grim picture of the connection between Christianity and imperialism in human history. She states,

> As a First World biblical scholar . . . I found it impossible to avoid the realization of the devastation and misery brought to most of the inhabited world by the imperialist expansion of European nations into the lands and cultures of Africa, Asia, and the Americas during the fifteenth to nineteenth centuries. Much of this expansion was justified by and indeed fueled by calls to 'spread the gospel to the nations.' What this 'godly pilgrimage' left in its wake was the devastation of rich and influential cultures, complete restructurings of traditional land allocations, and the deaths of millions of generally peaceful, cooperative people.[58]

56. Rieger and Pui-lan, *Occupy Religion*, 128. They argue, "the history of Christianity has been so enmeshed with colonial enterprises like the Crusades, the conquest of the Americas, the colonization of Africa and Asia, and the suppression of other cultures and religions," ibid. Others simply call it "to kill in the name of Christ" (Bucko and Fox, *Occupy Spirituality*, 190).
57. See Michael Hardt and Antonio Negri, *Commonwealth* (Cambridge, MA: Harvard University Press, 2009), 231. They add, "From the diamond mines of Sierra Leone to the oil fields of Uganda, forms of mineral-extraction capitalism, often in the hands of foreign corporations and under the protection of informal militias, has come to dominate local economies."
58. Mary Ann Tolbert, "Christianity, Imperialism, and the Decentering of Privilege," in *Reading from this Place: Social Location and Biblical Interpretation in Global Perspective*, vol. 2, eds. Fernando F. Segovia and Mary Ann Tolbert (Minneapolis: Fortress Press, 1995), 2:348.

Struggles to reclaim lost land have occurred in many places. Given biblical Israel's history of extensive conquest and imperial domination, the question of the land is an especially sensitive one. Biblical history depicts the ancient Israelites as being mostly under the domination of some empire—Egyptian, Assyrian, Babylonian, Persian, Greek, and Roman Empires—except for brief periods of freedom during the Davidic monarchy (the so-called Golden Age) and the Hasmonean era following the Maccabean Revolt.[59] There have been struggles for land in South Africa due to the apartheid system that long discriminated against the majority blacks. Two decades after independence in 1994, it appears that a small percentage of whites in South Africa still own most of the arable land. The question of land ownership and redistribution is still problematic along racial lines. Some researchers contend that "land reform has fallen far short of expectations."[60] Others argue that about 25 percent of the land is "in the hands of the state" while 75 percent is "privately owned."[61] Researchers argue that in Kenya, the Mau Mau Uprisings were primarily caused by Kenyans who sought a fair share of their land from their former British colonial masters.[62]

59. See Hershel Shanks, ed., *Ancient Israel: From Abraham to the Roman Destruction of the Temple*, 3rd ed., (Boston: Prentice Hall, 2011); Ross, *History of Ancient Israel & Judah*; and Michael D. Coogan, ed., *The Oxford History of the Biblical World* (Oxford: Oxford University Press, 2001). For a discussion of imperialism in New Testament times, see Richard A. Horsely, ed., *Paul and Empire: Religion and Power in Roman Imperial Society* (Harrisburg, PA: Trinity Press International, 1997). Horsely begins the discussion by unequivocally stating that "Christianity was a product of empire" (1). For more recent discussion, see David M. Carr, *An Introduction to the Old Testament: Sacred Texts and Imperial Contexts of the Hebrew Bible* (Chichester: Wiley-Blackwell, 2010); and David M. Carr and Colleen M. Conway, *An Introduction to the Bible: Sacred Texts and Imperial Contexts* (The Chichester: Wiley-Blackwell, 2010).

60. See Edward Lahiff, "Q&A: Land Reform in South Africa." Cited at www.pbs.org/pov/promisedland/land_reform.php. Accessed 6 May, 2015.

61. See Frans Cronje, "How much of SA's land is really in black hands?" 27 February, 2012. Cited at www.politicsweb.co.za/opinion/how-much-of-sas-land-is-really-in-black-hands. Accessed 6 May, 2015.

62. See for example, Ngũgĩ wa Thiong'o, *Decolonising the Mind: The Politics of Language in African Literature* (Nairobi: EAEP, 1981).

Ancient (pre-colonial) Africa was characterized by the Egyptian Empire and the great kingdoms of Ghana/Gold Coast, Benin/Nigeria, Mali, Songhai, Aksum, Kush/Meroe/Ethiopia, and Great Zimbabwe. Much trade and commerce flourished in these kingdoms. African indigenous institutions run by elders, headmen, chiefs, and kings brought success to these renowned kingdoms. However, the glories of these ancient kingdoms, just like any other civilization, did not last forever. Eventually these kingdoms declined and collapsed due to colonization by the Portuguese, British, French, Dutch, Spanish, Belgians, Germans, Turks, and Italians. The greatness of ancient Africa has been documented by historians like Basil Davidson in books such as *The African Past, Lost Cities of Africa, African Kingdoms,* and *Africa in History.* In his book, *African Saga*, Stanlake Samkange wrote, "Long before Europeans dominated Africa, Africans had organized large empires with a high civilization, great cities, and a flourishing economy based on agriculture, mining and trade."[63] Writing in *Decolonising the Mind*, famed Kenyan writer Ngũgĩ wa Thiong'o further explains,

> The land question is basic to an understanding of Kenya's history and contemporary politics, as indeed it is of twentieth century history wherever people have had their land taken away by conquest, unequal treaties or by the genocide of part of the population. The Mau Mau military organization which spearheaded the armed struggle for Kenya's independence was officially called the Kenya Land and Freedom Army.[64]

63. See Stanlake J. T. Samkange, *African Saga: A Brief Introduction to African History* (Nashville: Abingdon, 1971), 141. Other kingdoms of West Africa were Kanemu-Bornu, Hausa States—Oyo, Benin, Ashanti, and Fante (148–162). Those of southern and central Africa were Luba Kingdoms, Lunda Empire, Manikongo Empire, Bunyoro and Buganda, Azania and Zanj and the Rozwi Empire of (Great) Zimbabwe (163–78); Basil Davidson, *Africa in History: Themes and Outline*, rev. ed. (New York: Collier Books, 1991). It should be noted that while these African kingdoms are sometimes referred to as "empires," they did not exercise global rule beyond their immediate borders as did European empires. It is thus more appropriate to refer to them as "kingdoms."

64. Ngũgĩ wa Thiong'o, *Decolonising the Mind*, 44.

The issues of land, freedom, political, and economic independence have defined much of the history of Africa in the postcolonial era. The struggle for land in countries like Zimbabwe is no exception to this history and background of colonialism and imperial expansion.

The question of the land in Zimbabwe dates back to the close of the nineteenth century when British imperialist Cecil John Rhodes "discovered" Zimbabwe in 1890 and appropriately named it after himself as Rhodesia. It would be almost a century of British rule before Africans reclaimed their independence and renamed the country Zimbabwe in 1980.[65] Imperial power and the struggle for land in Africa is reminiscent of a classic biblical land struggle as reflected in the story of Naboth's vineyard in 1 Kings 21, to which we now turn.

Case Study of Naboth's Vineyard: The Ideology of Royal Power

The story of Naboth's vineyard as recorded in 1 Kings 21 illustrates the typical ideology of ancient Near Eastern royal power. It is a familiar tale of injustice and retribution, power and powerlessness, the perpetrator and the victim, possession and dispossession. The contrasting power dynamics in this text are also reflected in modern history. Using postcolonial hermeneutics, we will revisit the story of Naboth's vineyard in order to understand the larger historical world of colonial expansion and the subsequent seizure of traditional lands.

The story features Queen Jezebel as the ultimate villain. The writer, the Deuteronomistic Historian (DH), paints Jezebel as "the most wicked woman in the history of Israel, perhaps because she was a very powerful queen."[66] Kyung Sook Lee states that DH's portrayal of Jezebel as a wicked foreign woman is evident in two

65. See Henry V. Moyana, *The Political Economy of Land in Zimbabwe* (Gweru: Mambo, 1984); and "Land Issue – Fact Sheet" at http://www.raceandhistory.com/Zimbabwe/factsheet.html
66. See Kyung Sook Lee, "1 and 2 Kings," in *Global Bible Commentary*, 112.

narratives—her persecution of Yahweh's prophets, and her masterminding of Naboth's murder. These Jezebel texts interrupt an older narrative about a royal dispute with a local landowner, which the royal court illegally won. While the story blames the foreign queen who domineers over her inept husband, it is truly a story of royal tyranny and abuse of power. It illustrates how those with power may act with impunity, but the story also dispels this notion.

The story naturally falls into two parts. The first half (vv. 1-16) narrates the account of Naboth's murder and the second half (vv. 17-29) describes the Prophet Elijah's reaction to this crime. The narrative begins with King Ahab who plans to acquire the plot of land next to his winter palace in Jezreel to use as a vegetable garden. We should note that this property is neither free nor available, because it belongs to Naboth the Jezreelite. By the time the story concludes, Ahab has broken half of the commandments in the Decalogue—idolatry, covetousness, false witnessing (lying), stealing, and killing (see Isa. 5:8; Mic. 2:1-2).[67] He cannot enforce the Israelite concept of land tenure, which clearly states, "The land shall not be sold in perpetuity, for the land is mine; with me you are but aliens and tenants" (Lev. 25:23). In other words, land ultimately belongs to Yahweh and is not for Ahab to take. The effect of this legal stipulation is to prevent class divisions between those who could afford to accumulate land and those who could not. Similarly, the spoils of war are not for Ahab to spare as he spared the life of King Ben-hadad. Warren Wiersbe puts it this way: "Ben-hadad was the man Ahab should have killed but he set him free; and Naboth was the man Ahab should have protected, but Ahab killed him."[68]

67. See Warren W. Wiersbe, *Be Responsible: Being Good Stewards of God's Gifts* (Colorado Springs, CO: Victor, 2002), 160–64.
68. Ibid., 160.

In its present context, the story of Jezebel provides a perfect rationale for the eventual seizure of Naboth's land. Jezebel, Ahab's Phoenician wife, has a different land tenure view than her husband's. She views everything from a typical oriental despotic position: land is a commodity to be bought and sold—or forcibly taken, if one desires it. At least Ahab understands Israelite land tenure, which explains why he sulks after Naboth refuses to sell or exchange his property.

Since Naboth refuses to sell his property because it is his family's inheritance (*naḥalah*), Ahab returns home "resentful and sullen," pouting like a child. The king sulks and appears weak but he does not force matters because he knows that he, even as king, is not above the Deuteronomic law of the king (Deut. 17:14-20). As a foreigner, Jezebel, while apparently aware of this law by virtue of her marriage to Ahab, however, does not recognize or adhere to it. She is everything that her husband is not. Ahab is portrayed as an inept king, completely under the influence of his wife. Jerome Walsh and Christopher Begg describe Ahab as "petty and ineffectual, domesticated by the forceful and unscrupulous Jezebel."[69] The historian's view of Ahab is similar to his view of Solomon, whose marriage to a thousand foreign women caused him to sin and stray from the Lord (1 Kings 11:1-41, esp. vv. 1-13). It is apparent that the DH's misogynistic tendency to blame foreign women for the fall of Israelite men is also seen in his portrayal of Delilah as the cause of Samson's final undoing (1 Sam 13:1—16:31). Yet Samson himself is portrayed as the unbridled Incredible Hulk.

It is therefore not surprising that Jezebel, Ahab's Phoenician wife, takes a leading role in the matter of the vineyard of Naboth. Her rap sheet is notoriously long: she introduced the Baal cult in Israel. She

69. See Jerome T. Walsh and Christopher T. Begg, "1–2 Kings," in *The New Jerome Biblical Commentary*,ed., Raymond E. Brown, Joseph A. Fitzmyer, and Roland E. Murphy (Englewood Cliffs, NJ: Prentice Hall, 1990), 160–85, esp. 173.

tried to kill all the prophets of the Lord. King Ahab fled to report to her about Elijah's annihilation of Baal's prophets. Jezebel threatened Elijah's life so that he went on the run. In our text, Jezebel mocks Ahab as a weak and ineffective king who does not exercise his royal powers to get what he wants. The limitations Israelite law imposed on kingship (Deut 17:14–20) do not seem to apply to her. So she arrogantly promises that she herself will give him the vineyard of Naboth, as if it is within her right to do so.

As a powerful queen, Jezebel literally takes over Ahab's royal prerogatives. She writes letters in his name and seals them with his seal, sending them to the elders and nobles of Jezreel. She tells the local leaders to proclaim a fast as if there was a special need or a great calamity (see, e.g., Judg. 20:26; 1 Sam. 14:24; 2 Chron. 20:3), or a grave sin that threatens the peace of the whole community (1 Sam. 7:6). She instructs the elders and nobles to place Naboth in a prominent place that suggests honor, but actually makes him a target. Moreover, two "scoundrels" or worthless fellows with nothing to lose falsely testify against him. Jezebel seems to know that two or three witnesses are needed to corroborate charges in a trial for a capital offense (Deut. 17:6; 19:15). The charges of blasphemy and treason against God and the king, respectively, warrant a death penalty (see Exod. 22:28–29; Lev. 24:15–16; 2 Sam. 16:9). Once convicted, Naboth is taken outside and stoned to death.

All of Jezebel's wishes are carried out as she instructed, thus creating a way for Ahab to illegally take possession of Naboth's property. According to Old Testament scholar C. L. Seow, "The office of the king has been usurped by a foreigner and corrupted with the king's acquiescence, if not consent. Neighbor has turned against neighbor. Those who are entrusted with the responsibility of upholding justice have perverted it. . . . The law is manipulated to perpetrate gross injustice."[70] In contemporary culture, the injustices against the populace have been heightened in recent cases of police brutality involving Trayvon Martin in Florida, Michael Brown in Ferguson, Missouri, Eric Garner in New York, and recently, Freddie Gray in Baltimore.

The prophet Elijah suddenly appears on the scene. Despite Jezebel's schemes, it is Ahab the king who is charged with murder and illegal possession of property (see Exod. 20:13, 17; Deut. 5:17, 21). Ahab did nothing to stop his imperious wife from expediting his own wish. He is not innocent for his inaction but equally guilty. Providing the necessary checks and balances, the prophet proclaims an oracle of doom against the king. He will face a dishonorable death shortly (see 1 Kgs. 22:38). Jezebel too will die a disgraceful death. Unfortunately, as Lee has noted, it seems that for the DH, Ahab's and Solomon's marriages to foreign women caused all their troubles. But as the kings of Israel and Judah, they should bear the ultimate responsibility for the deeds and misdeeds of their associates, including their wives. In his work on the translation of the Naboth text in the Tshivenda Bible, Elelwani Farisani argues for a sociological reading of the text that brings out the "ideological power play" in the text. Such a translation empowers the marginalized and blames not only Jezebel, but King Ahab as well for the crimes against Naboth.[71]

This text sheds light on the problem of royal abuse and social injustice. It is equally relevant in modern history where a similar pattern of dispossession and forcible land seizure has been executed. Temba Mafico argues that "African and Israelite history . . . in ancient and modern times is full of examples of land being seized from a traditional group of people by a more powerful group."[72] He cites

70. See Choon-Leong Seow, "The First and Second Books of Kings: Introduction, Commentary, and Reflections," in *The New Interpreter's Bible*, ed. Leander E. Keck (Nashville: Abingdon, 1994), 3:157.

71. See Elelwani Farisani, "Ideology, History, and Translation Theories," in *Postcolonial Perspectives,* 199–217, esp. 215.

examples of seizures of African lands, as well as Israelite occupation of Canaanite land, the case of Naboth's vineyard, and Solomon's treatment of Israelite land as a commodity in the tenth century BCE. He correctly argues that Solomon had "a more radical departure from the traditional land holding practices" because he gave away Israelite land to the Phoenicians as payment for his building excesses (1 Kgs. 9:10–14).[73] Ultimately, this led to the political crisis that broke up the United Kingdom. Similarly, Europeans seized traditional lands for economic reasons, which impoverished or deprived Africans of the land of their progenitors.[74]

The Naboth text also demonstrates the illegitimacy of business transactions between unequal parties. The king's party has political and economic clout while Naboth relies on tradition and the rule of law. The king is even willing to use the power and the appeal of money to violate the law he knows too well. This struggle also takes place today between rulers and subjects, between large corporations and small businesses, between powerful nations and dependent nations. The prophetic word of judgment provides recourse and redress for acts of injustice. For the contemporary world, the same prophetic word and the Bible's message of justice have provided material and emotional comfort to those who are wronged. Despite its efficacy, at least it has the effect of stirring the conscience of nations.

The text has described in vivid detail how injustice can easily escalate. Covetousness leads to perjury and murder as one violation gives way to another. The story concludes with King Ahab repenting for his misdeeds but one wonders if it is a genuine expression of remorse or an attempt to reduce his sentence. Is the king sorry for his

72. Mafico, "Land Concept and Tenure in Israel and African Tradition," 234–44, esp. 241.
73. Ibid., 242.
74. Ibid., 243.

sin, or is he sorry that he has been caught? God, however, will delay his punishment but the king will reap the consequences of his actions or failure to take appropriate action.

The conclusion of this story describing Ahab's punishment and death in the Aramean war is in 1 Kings 22. Elijah's prophecy is fulfilled as the text somberly declares, "So the king died, and was brought to Samaria; they buried the king in Samaria. They washed the chariot by the pool of Samaria; the dogs licked up his blood, and the prostitutes washed themselves in it, according to the word of the Lord that he had spoken" (1 Kings 22:38). As for Jezebel, 2 Kings 9:30–37 portrays the queen as meeting a particularly violent death at Jehu's hands, and her corpse is eaten by dogs. In 2 Kings 10:11, Jehu is described as killing the rest of the members of Ahab's house including his seventy sons. Thus Jehu wipes out the Baal cult from Israel (2 Kings 10:28) as retribution for Jezebel's crimes.

While the DH might have intended to portray the wickedness of a foreign woman who brought her gods and religion into the Israelite kingdom, our focus on the ideology of royal power is undiminished. Jezebel represents the power of empire that brought its gods and influence throughout the world. Many of the crises the world is experiencing, including the debt crisis, are directly related to the social, political, and economic system empire has established.[75]

75. In this study, "empire" refers to the period of colonial and imperial domination of the world by Europeancountries from the fifteenth to the twentieth centuries. However, the turn of the twentieth century has produced a new type of empire as defined by Hardt and Negri. They write, "At the end of the last millennium a genuinely new global situation had emerged, which set in motion new processes of governance and began to establish new structures of global order. A new Empire was being formed that was qualitatively different from the previous existing imperialisms, which had been based primarily on the power of nation-states." See Hardt and Negri, *Commonwealth*, 203. They add, "On the emerging imperial system was imposed a central authority [the United States] through which all global decisions were to pass" (206). The other key players in this new global order are China, the European Union, India, Japan, and Russia.

Power versus Powerlessness

The Naboth text is one of the most revealing incidents about the oppression and injustice done to the powerless during the early Israelite monarchy (1 Kgs. 21:1-29).[76] Many scholars have reacted to this narrative on the oppressive nature of kingship in different ways. Bruce Malchow calls it "a good example of social injustice in the monarchic period," and for Richard Nelson, it is simply "royal tyranny."[77] Norman Habel has identified six land ideologies in the Hebrew Bible and views the story of Naboth as a case of conflicting ideologies of land, namely, royal and peasant (or ancestral household).[78] Closely related to Habel's view is Ferdinand Deist's analysis of the Naboth story and its parallels to the South African situation. Deist maintains that this narrative has "*two perceptions of land ownership*: Naboth sees land as an inalienable gift from God; to Ahab it is a commercial article that can change hands."[79]

This text has more to do with power imbalance than simply a land dispute. Commenting on the narrative, I. G. P. Gous brings out this point clearly:

76. See Wafawanaka, *Am I Still My Brother's Keeper?* 88.
77. Bruce Malchow, Social Justice in the Hebrew Bible: What is New and What is Old (Collegeville, MN: Liturgical Press, 1996), 60; Richard D. Nelson, First and Second Kings (Atlanta: John Knox, 1987), 138–45. See also Robert K. Gnuse, You Shall Not Steal: Community and Property in the Biblical Tradition (Maryknoll, NY: Orbis Books, 1985), 74–75; Leslie J. Hoppe, Being Poor: A Biblical Study (Wilmington, DE: Glazier, 1987), 50–52; and John Gray, I and II Kings: A Commentary, 2nd ed. Old Testament Library (London: SCM, 1970), 433–44. This story is the central focus of the essays in Hendrik L. Bosman, I. G. P. Gous, and Izak J. J. Spangenberg, eds., Plutocrats and Paupers: Wealth and Poverty in the Old Testament (Pretoria: J. L. van Schaik, 1991).
78. The six land ideologies are royal, agrarian, theocratic, prophetic, ancestral household, and immigrant. Norman Habel argues that the poor and the Canaanites have no right to land and therefore can be made slaves of the empire at the will of the monarchy. See Habel, The Land is Mine: Six Biblical Land Ideologies (Minneapolis: Fortress Press, 1995), 30–32.
79. Ferdinand Deist, "Biblical Studies, Wealth and Poverty in South Africa: Retrospect and Prospect," in Plutocrats and Paupers, 252, emphasis in original. Deist proceeds to illustrate two conflicting views of community, economy, law, religion, culture, and righteousness in the Naboth narrative (pp. 253–54).

> Since the king (actually the queen) was more powerful than he [Naboth], he could use his power to dispose of Naboth in an underhand way. Hence the point at issue in this passage is political rather than economic poverty. Naboth and his followers did not suffer want because they did not have possessions; they lacked the *power* to resist the actions of the king. In addition Naboth had no right of appeal.[80]

Naboth's inability to resist the advances of the king makes him a helpless victim of a scheming wife aided by a powerful king. In both the story of Naboth's vineyard and the David and Bathsheba incident (2 Sam. 11–12), Karen Lebacqz finds "abuse of kingly power" through "deceit and violence" because the king desires something he cannot have without violating a law.[81] Once again, this narrative closely resembles the reality of imperialism, the subsequent seizure of native lands in Africa and around the world, and the crises that ensue.

A View from the Other Side: Implications

After the murder of Naboth and the illegitimate seizure of his land, the prophet Elijah appears on the scene to pronounce judgment upon King Ahab. The prophetic word of judgment essentially condemns the king's evil deeds and announces the end of Ahab's dynasty. Though the Lord delays the punishment due to his repentance, his fate and that of his sons is already sealed. Justice demands the punishment and end of Ahab's house. According to Volkmar Fritz, the intention of this "fictional example of royal despotism" is to demonstrate that royal power has become "an instrument of murder to which the free citizen is cruelly exposed."[82]

80. I. G. Gous, "City and Countryside: A Sociopolitical Perspective on Wealth and Poverty in ancient Israel," in Plutocrats and Paupers, 169, emphasis added. Deist adds that 1 Kings 21 "shows the extent to which the peasant community was at the mercy of the crown and officialdom." See "The Historical Scene in which the Old Testament was Enacted," in Plutocrats and Paupers, 119.
81. Karen Lebacqz, Justice in an Unjust World: Foundations for a Christian Approach to Justice (Minneapolis: Fortress Press, 2007), 109.

While we tend to read biblical narratives from the perspective of the dominant party or identify with the conquerors and victors, reading such narratives from the perspectives of the victims can bring new insights. In reading the Exodus story from a Native American perspective, or "with Canaanite eyes," Robert Allen Warrior exposes those parts of the narrative that we tend to ignore—Yahweh's command to mercilessly annihilate the indigenous peoples.[83] While Yahweh gives no such command in the Naboth text, or offers a prohibition, the ideology of ruthless seizure of property and land in our history seems to be informed by biblical conquest narratives, or our failure to read the Naboth story from the perspective of the powerless victim. On a global scale, our challenge is to confront ideologies of power, conquest narratives, and indiscriminate land seizures, as well as the concomitant crises.

Though few comparable prophetic figures are found in modern situations of injustice, the world has witnessed liberation struggles aimed at the attainment of justice as well as reclaiming land that was lost during imperial expansion. Often led by charismatic political figures, Africa waged liberation struggles for land rights and independence. This era ranges from Ghana's independence in 1957 to South Africa's independence in 1994, a nearly four-decade period. While the independent period itself is barely six decades old, by contrast, the colonial period in Africa stretches for some five centuries (the fifteenth through the twentieth century). Within this long stretch of history, we have witnessed many conquest narratives, land struggles, quests for liberation, eventual attainment of independence, and the reacquisition of native lands.

82. See Volkmar Fritz, *1 & 2 Kings: A Continental Commentary*, trans. Anselm Hagedorn. (Minneapolis: Fortress Press, 2003), 211.

83. Warrior, "A Native American Perspective," 279.

First Kings 21 provides a useful window and entry point into the larger world of injustice, inequality, oppression, and land seizures on a global scale. Naboth becomes victim to a powerful king and as a result loses his life and land in this power struggle. Elijah holds the king accountable. Interpreted in a global context and with reference to Africa in particular, this story is an apt example of the excesses and abuse of power when directed toward innocent and powerless victims. The history of colonialism and imperial expansion has affected the entire world and resulted in the mistreatment and suffering of indigenous peoples. This description is true of biblical history as it is of American, Asian, South American, Australian, British, and African history. Naboth's account is a microcosm of similar patterns of abuse and oppression on a global scale. The crises that theologians are addressing, including the crisis of debt, make much more sense in the context of this larger global history, politics, and economy.

8

Food, Power, and Ecological Hermeneutics

Reading Joseph with Monsanto

Gregory P. Fewster

Introduction

The integration of an environmentally sensitive accent into contemporary biblical criticism is well practiced. On one hand, those scholars embarrassed by Christian anti-environmentalist sentiments often adopt an apologetic tone in their work, suggesting that it is not fair to read environmental domination out of key texts. Passages such as Genesis 1:26-27 or Matthew 21:18-20//Mark 11:13-21 are sanitized and others, like Romans 8:19-23, are promoted.[1] On the other hand, those less invested in a literalist hermeneutic urge the

1. Richard Bauckham's perspective is perhaps one of the most significant voices here, suggesting that we recover a holistic approach to the Bible. This means that we can reread "dominion passages" like that found in Genesis 1 once we see how the biblical writers situate humanity within the created order. See Bauckham, *The Bible and Ecology: Rediscovering the Community of Creation*, Sarum Theological Lectures (Waco, TX: Baylor University Press, 2010), 37.

rejection of dominative sentiments, encouraging readers to move beyond these and care for the earth that Western Christianity has so long destroyed.[2] Common to both of these approaches is a hermeneutical reorientation, a response to the realization that the human race has not been very kind to our planet and that Christianity has been, at the very least, complicit in such wrongdoing. We have recognized a crisis and sought to respond to it. However, in my experience, the ecologically friendly position tends toward fairly limited readings: human antagonists repeatedly injure Mother Nature and those creatures that depend on her for survival. And what is the solution? Kyoto accords, hybrid cars, and bird-friendly coffee beans.[3] We reform the system to provide a more environmentally sensitive way of doing business. Is this the best we can do? These surface-y solutions pair with surface-y readings of biblical texts based upon an "earth consciousness."[4] The tie between the manipulation of the environment and global capital remains an insidious fixture inherent to these types of solutions, perhaps to the extent that our focus on reducing our carbon footprint and having more ethically grown coffee beans distracts from the force that continues to drive the relentless purge of natural resources—the global capitalist economy.

2. Norman Habel's category of "suspicion," where the interpreter to is to begin by suspecting that the text bears out an anthropocentric bias, characterizes this approach. See Habel, "Introducing Ecological Hermeneutics," in *Exploring Ecological Hermeneutics*, ed. Norman C. Habel and Peter Trudinger (Atlanta: Society of Biblical Literature, 2008), 4; and recently Jeffrey S. Lamp, *The Greening of Hebrews? Ecological Readings in the Letter to the Hebrews* (Eugene, OR: Pickwick, 2012).
3. Bauckham's critique of "stewardship" as a popular solution is well made (*Bible and Ecology*, 1–36), though his own proposal is rather unremarkable (see n. 1).
4. See Norman C. Habel, "Introducing the Earth Bible," in *Readings from the Perspective of the Earth*, The Earth Bible Project I, ed. Norman C. Habel (Sheffield: Sheffield Academic, 2000), 26. These fairly strict "guides" of the Earth Bible project place strict limits on the types of interpretations we can make. These guides can be seen in Habel, "Introducing Ecological Hermeneutics," 2; Habel, "Guiding Ecojustice Principles," in *Readings from the Perspective of the Earth*, 38–53.

My goal in this article is to highlight the connection between economic power and the manipulation of the environment, specifically through the production of food, and how this affects human agency and well-being. On a general level, this observation problematizes contemporary (esp. liberal Christian) efforts at ecological hermeneutics as ineffective, so long as the underlying paradigms that enable ecological manipulation are seen as redeemable. Much of the potential thrust of an ecological hermeneutic is lost, so long as this attitude remains.

Illuminating for this argument is the conduct of the multinational corporation Monsanto, currently the world leader in genetically modified organisms (GMOs). Repeated crises follow in the wake of Monsanto's dealings, enabling new interpretive moments for the bible reader. In this case, I wish to turn attention to the story of Joseph, found in Genesis 37–50. The point of this exercise is not to engage in fanciful allegorizing of Joseph and Monsanto. Instead, I want to explore how an ecological crisis, helped along by Monsanto, interacts with current religious convictions and the sacred text(s). This single horizon of experience allows a reorientation to both a reading of the Joseph story and a relationship to corporate farming. The story of Joseph read alongside the Monsanto crisis alerts us of the centrality of food to any sort of political or economic power, regardless of the particular economic system in place (late capitalist or otherwise). In a world at the mercy of a failing corporate minority, food is the place where control may be recovered.

Reformulating an Ecological Hermeneutic

The word "crisis" is a buzzword found consistently in the vocabulary of ecological critics, likely part of the trend of apologetic response to Lynn White's "The Historical Roots of our Ecological Crisis."[5] It is strange, however, that in the relevant publications, rarely is this crisis clearly delineated or defined. At best, readers are reminded of the dangers of deforestation or carbon emissions. The notion that our world is in jeopardy and responsible global citizens ought to stem the tide, flows liberally from article to article. Yet, popular exhortations pander to "ecological awareness" and call for more coordinated attempts at "creation care."[6] Many Christian exegetes recommend that the biblical narrative promotes a harmony between humanity and the earth, which is our home.[7] Such a response, in fact, fits nicely with White's conclusion: that the ecological crisis is actually a religious crisis, to which the response also must be religious.[8] I suppose the result of rereading our religious texts with new ecologically sensitive eyes is a nice thing and certainly fits within the general scope of postmodern political exegesis, in which we appreciate the situatedness of our interpretive efforts. But, Lynn White's article is old and his explanation for a so-called ecological crisis requires some reworking. In almost forty years since White

5. See Lynn White, "The Historical Roots of our Ecological Crisis," *Science* 155 (1967): 1203–1207. Ernst Conradie's brief sketch of the history of the discipline readily acknowledges that the early attempts at ecological hermeneutics were defensive ones. Notably, he finds such attempts inadequate (Conradie, "What on Earth is Ecological Hermeneutics? Some Broad Parameters," in *Ecological Hermeneutics: Biblical, Historical and Theological Perspectives*, ed. David G. Horrell et al. (London: T&T Clark, 2010), 295.

6. See, for example, Kathleen Fischer, "Christian Spirituality in a Time of Ecological Awareness," *Theology Today* 76 (2010): 169–81; Fred van Dyke et al., *Redeeming Creation: The Biblical Basis for Environmental* Stewardship (Downers Grove, IL: InterVarsity, 1996); and the essays in Robert James Berry, ed., *The Care of Creation: Focusing Concern and Action* (Downer's Grove, IL: InterVarsity, 2000). Also, see Rosemary Radford Ruether's "Ecology and Theology: Ecojustice at the Centre of the Church's Mission," *Interpretation* 65, no. 4 (2011): 354–63, who promotes an ecojustice perspective—deriving from covenantal and sacramental traditions—that embraces recycling and other reformatory methods. My use of the term "creation care" is meant to be a direct allusion to the 2012 Annual Meeting of the Evangelical Theological Society. I did not attend the conference.

7. Jeanne Kay argues that the biblical view of God, nature, and humanity is "a belief in nature as a tool for divine justice: beneficent nature is a reward for religious observance, and a deteriorating environment is God's punishment for idolatry or immorality" (Kay, "Human Dominion over Nature in the Hebrew Bible," *Annals of the Association of American Geographers* 79, no. 2 [1989]: 215). See more recently, Theodore Hiebert, "Reclaiming the World: Biblical Resources for the Ecological Crisis," *Interpretation* 65, no. 4 (2011): 341–52.

8. See White, "Ecological Crisis," 1207.

published, attempts to hold off ecological destruction have been minor and ineffective, in spite of significant shifts in the views of Western Christianity (i.e., now they care more about the environment). Why has Green Christianity failed so miserably?

Slavoj Žižek observes that today's cultural capitalism incorporates within it the cost of "giving back." Fair Trade everything ensures that the individual and the environment that produced the commodity are treated fairly and with respect, which ultimately results in temporarily assuaging the guilt of consumption.[9] It is no surprise that hipster Christians flock to purchase at Starbucks and other like-minded corporations, in order to make what has been construed as the morally upright and ecologically sensitive choice. This is perplexing. Feelings of guilt prompted many middle-class North Americans (like me) to take a more holistic look at the environment and the humans who work the land. We can clearly see the once invisible hand of capital at work in the manipulation of both worker and environment at the same time. Žižek's observation is incisive, however. It suggests that the capitalist paradigm is a totalizing system, limiting our ability to think creatively outside of it. Thus, "solutions" to the problem of eco-economic crisis, like Fair Trade coffee, TOMS shoes, and grass-fed beef only result in the further multiplication of markets.[10]

9. See esp. Slavoj Žižek, *First as Tragedy, Then as Farce* (London: Verso, 2009), 51–55. Similarly, from within the discourse of agriculture and food studies, researchers contest the depiction of "local" and "organic" options as truly alternative. Instead, this represent smaller-scale attempts to wiggle into the global market. Alternatively, it might suggest that the market system inhibits our ability to think outside of its boundaries. See Hilary Tovey, "'Local Food' as a Contested Concept: Networks, Knowledges and Power in Food-based Strategies for Rural Development," *International Journal of Sociology of Agriculture and Food* 16, no. 2 (2009): 21–35. Albert Arce, "Sources and Expressions of Power in Global Food Coordination and Rural Sites: Domination, Counter-domination and Alternatives," *International Journal of Sociology of Agriculture and Food* 16, no. 2 (2009): 2–20, identifies the increasing complexity of food production models (and their interpretation) and how these alternatives compete within the local *qua* global market.

10. This sentiment, echoing that made by Žižek, is attacked by Celia Deane-Drummond, suggesting that opposition to the market system in relation to ecological concerns has not yet gone deep enough. See Deane-Drummond, *Eco-Theology* (Winona, MN: Saint Mary's, 2008), 17–19.

This neurosis is precisely what the capitalist economy requires and encourages in order to perpetuate itself.[11] This helps to understand what I have described above as lack of creativity in many efforts toward an ecological hermeneutic.

With that said, David Horrell has argued that a positive ecological hermeneutic incorporates a dialectic between ancient text and contemporary context, which includes attention to contemporary science.[12] Clive Hamilton's interpretation of current environmental science is striking: climate crisis has climaxed such that human agency cannot head it off. To think otherwise is a naïveté derivative of a post-Cold War American conservatism that has reified leftist environmentalists as the new enemy of the state.[13] That is to say that while conservative voices that deny climate change and its harmful effects may be wrong, they are correct to disparage the pathetic reformative efforts of the Left. Chris Hedges insightfully identifies a longstanding trend of liberal voices in America being seduced and silenced by the delights of capital. By buying into the myth of reformation, choice, and market solutions, Hedges's so-called "liberal class" has efficiently destroyed its ability to provide a viable voice of resistance against the powerful and minority corporate class.[14]

> The liberal class, which clings to the decaying ideologies used to justify globalism and imperialism, which has refused to defy the exploitation or

11. See especially Bruce Worthington, "Jesus the Pervert: A Žižekian Response to Mark 11.15-17," *BI* 22 (2014): 172–74.
12. See David G. Horrell, *The Bible and the Environment: Towards a Critical Ecological Biblical Theology*, Biblical Challenges in the Contemporary World (London: Equinox, 2010), 124–26.
13. See Clive Hamilton, *Requiem for a Species: Why We Resist the Truth about Climate Change* (Washington, DC: Earthscan, 2010), 1–32, 98. See also Chris Hedges, *Death of the Liberal Class* (Toronto: Vintage Canada, 2010), 19–58, on the notion of "permanent war" (102–108) on Cold War politics and the silencing of the Left; and, more briefly, Žižek, *First as Tragedy*, 33–34.
14. See Hedges, *Death*, esp. 195. This book was written before the Occupy movement got underway, which is therefore a major blindspot in Hedges conclusions. Since then, Hedges's participation in the movement signals his support of this militant anti-capitalist voice that cuts across more traditional Left–Right political dichotomies. See esp. Chris Hedges and Joe Sacco, *Days of Destruction, Days of Revolt* (New York: Nation Books, 2012), 225–72.

> galvanize behind militants to halt the destruction of the ecosystem, has become a useless appendage.[15]

This aptly describes the liberal Christian voice in ecological hermeneutics. Any attempt to (re)formulate a ecological hermeneutic needs to come to terms not only with a very pessimistic outlook for the fate of the planet, but with the ideologically complex discourses about eco-economic crisis. But, what about Monsanto?

Ecological Crisis and the Monsanto Corporation

For years, criticisms of Monsanto, GMOs, and corporate farming have been flying fast and thick. Much of the debate has to do with health and whether or not GMOs are safe for human consumption or healthy for our ecosystems. Alternatives to GMO crops include organic produce that supposedly does not benefit from the big-name chemical herbicides. One perspective on this issue appears in an article in the *Boston Review* by plant pathologist Pamela Ronald.[16] Her moderate stance rides a fine line, promoting genetic engineering while articulating some weaknesses in the present system. She suggests that humans have been breeding organisms to manifest productive traits for thousands of years, often with the result that second-generation crops will not manifest the same traits for which the parent seeds were bred. Genetic engineering allows farmers to spray fewer harmful chemicals on their crops, requires less tillage of fields, and so on. Not only are these developments healthier for the individual consumer, they have higher scale benefits like reduced

15. Hedges, *Death*, 194. In spite of Hedges's use of terms like "militant," his extensive coverage of global conflict for over a decade has revealed the inherent problems of violent resistance (see *Death*, 197–99).
16. See Pamela Ronald, "The Truth about GMOs," *Boston Review*, September 6, 2013, http://bostonreview.net/forum/pamela-ronald-gmo-food.

greenhouse gas emissions in the production process. So what is the problem with GMOs?[17] Ronald perceives the following trend:

> Much of the concern relates to a general distrust of large corporations, in particular, Monsanto, which produces a large proportion of the world's seeds. GE opponents fear that such corporations are taking advantage of farmers. Yet one need only observe the overwhelming farmer adoption of GE crops in the United States and elsewhere to conclude that the GE crop varieties on the market are useful to farmers. It is unlikely that experienced and skilled farmers would buy GE seeds if their farm operations did not benefit economically.[18]

Ronald's hesitancy is not with Monsanto *per se*. She wants to see the benefits of GE seeds equally available for farmers in the developing world and a system that regulates the seed trade.

Ronald's view parallels current trends in ecological hermeneutics, in which the present system is praised for its few benefits and some simple reforms are proposed. Similar reformative strategies have been proposed elsewhere, notably in the branding and mass-production of organic food.[19] However, her proposals highlight the insidious nature of the global capitalist paradigm in food production. In the above quote, farmers are depicted as free agents with the unrestricted ability to choose what seeds they plant. This is the capitalist myth of the free market, which is directly antithetical to Ronald's stated concern for the archetypal poor farmer. Monsanto, the world's top producer of

17. Deane-Drummond identifies this argument as fairly typical of moderate proponents of GE crops (*Eco-Theology*, 22). Notably, after a brief survey of GMO use globally, she argues that "GMOs have more often than not been used for the purpose of commercial gain for particular specialist markets, without adequate consideration of the overall impact on either local ecology or global trade, and in many cases leading to gross injustices towards those who are most vulnerable to exploitation" (24).
18. Ronald, "GMOs." Note her use of the acronym GE rather than GMO.
19. For example, A&W's "better beef" campaign, which boasts environmentally responsible ranches and (mostly) grass-fed beef (see http://awbetterbeef.ca). In my two years as an employee at Costco Wholesale, I noticed a significant increase in organic and gluten-free products. Regardless of the intent, multinational fast-food chains and megastores like Costco are seeking more environmentally responsible options, catering to the growing market for such products.

GMOs, has a long and bleak history, not only of producing harmful products, but in the suppression of information and the manipulation of government bodies that would otherwise wreak havoc on profit margins. As if the PCB and Agent Orange controversies of the 1960s and 1970s were not enough to blight their reputation, contemporary products such as rBGH milk, Bt Cotton, and the Roundup Ready soybean continue to attract media attention and manipulate farmers who lack the capital or political clout to affect any sort of successful resistance.

Again, Pamela Ronald seems to be under the impression that the current landscape of seed production allows farmers an unrestricted and educated choice regarding what they can plant in their fields. The appearance that heritage seeds are an equal and viable option for the farmer, and that "organic" and GMO food is an equal choice for the consumer, reflects what Marxist theorists call an illusion of choice. Ronald seems unable to appreciate the power dynamic that stems from Monsanto's vast capital resources. These result in the overwhelming control of the seed market such that not only is Monsanto able to slant the options heavily in their favour, but they are able to keep the consumer unaware of their lack of choice.[20]

I am not interested in engaging in-depth the abundant examples of Monsanto's duplicitous and oppressive business practices or the negative impact of their products on the environment, however. This is a common strategy in ecological hermeneutics, which "reminds" us of how many bad things we do to the earth.[21] Regardless of

20. This principle is the thesis of Andrew Bard Schmookler, *The Illusion of Choice: How the Market Economy Shapes Our Destiny* (New York: State University of New York Press, 1993). Arce briefly identifies this phenomenon specifically with respect to the grocery market ("Sources and Expressions," 7). See also Clive Hamilton's discussion on choice, preference, and market coercion (Hamilton, *The Freedom Paradox: Towards a Post-Secular Ethics* [Sydney: Allen and Unwin, 2008], 38–44, 61–67).

21. I think it also feigns expertise in ecological science. I am not a scientist, but I am trained in discourse analysis, hence my alternative approach.

the "truth" about Monsanto's products or conduct, there exists an interesting and somewhat polarized discourse surrounding Monsanto. Here, Monsanto exists as a discursive object in relation to which those dubbed conspiracy theorists combat the corporate-sponsored scientific PR machines. More interesting than wading through the mess to arrive at the actual state of affairs is to observe the discursive politics at play as a case in point of the connection between capital, power, and food production.[22] Consider the reception of Monsanto's rBST milk and their Bt cotton.

One of Monsanto's early efforts was what they called recombinant bovine somatoropin (rBST), also known as recombinant bovine growth hormone (rBGH), a modified hormone designed to promote lactation in cows.[23] Unfortunately, the milk coming from cows injected with rBGH significantly increases the risk of cancer while the antibiotics used to remedy mastitis in the cows (a very common occurrence thanks to rBGH) increases antibiotic resistant strains of bacteria. Despite these controversial findings, Monsanto's rBGH was reasonably well received in many countries and continues to be FDA approved in the United States. However, the reception of the hormone has been plagued with withheld and manipulated scientific testing and corporate bullying, as Mari-Monique Robin's interviews reveal.[24] The information publicized about the impact of rBGH milk

22. See Mike Reynolds, "How Does Monsanto Do It? An Ethnographic Case Study of an Advertising Campaign," *Text* 24, no. 3 (2004): 329–52, for a discourse analysis of Monsanto's advertising machine.

23. "Recombinant" indicates that they have genetically manipulated a commonly occurring hormone, in this case by combining it with the bacterium *E. coli*.

24. See Marie-Monique Robin, *The World according to Monsanto: Pollution, Corruption, and the Control of our Food Supply: An Investigation into the World's Most Controversial Company*, trans. George Hollock (New York: New Press, 2010), 89–130. Lisa Mills argues that there was a surprising amount of consensus among scientists regarding the effects of rBGH milk. The significance of the findings was at issue. For example, what levels of risk are acceptable for humans? (Mills, *Science and Social Context: The Regulation of Recombinant Bovine Growth Hormone in North America* [Montreal: McGill-Queen's University Press, 2002], 103–4). While Mills's research accesses much of the same information as Robin's interviews, the interviews

on humans had become so manipulated that Canada's rejection of the hormone was made on the basis of the negative effects on the cows, not human consumers.[25] In the United States, acceptance was partially afforded by a consistency in farming practices. For example, the use of antibiotics in dairy farming is already very common, thus the table was set for rBGH to succeed.[26] This example reveals a troubling division of policy across North America. Monsanto's ability to successfully market a harmful farming supplement was based on existing corporate farming procedures and political clout of capital.

Bt cotton is a breed of cotton implanted with an insect-repelling gene derivative of the bacteria *Bacillus thuringiensis* developed also by Monsanto. This genetic modification allows the cotton plant to have increased resistance to harmful insects, thus reducing the need for expensive chemical pesticides. Monsanto has gained control of the cotton seed market in India, such that it is nearly impossible for peasant farmers to purchase alternative seeds. This may not be an issue if it were not for the failure of the Bt cotton to live up to its expectations. Bt seeds are not as successful at repelling insects as claimed. As a result, many farmers must still resort to chemical pesticides to ensure a positive yield. Robin's study suggests that many Indian farmers have racked up massive debts to maintain their cotton farms, and farmer suicide rates have increased since the adoption of Bt cotton.[27] On the other hand, a recent study denies a resurgence

reveal more behind-the-scenes dealings with Monsanto and certain government regulation bodies.

25. An excellent study of Health Canada's rejection of rBGH can be found in R. Steven Turner, "Of Milk and Mandarins: rBGH, Mandated Science and the Canadian Regulatory Style," *Journal of Canadian Studies/Revue de'études canadiennes* 36, no. 2 (2001): 107–30. See also discussion in Mills, *Science and Social Context*, 104–20. Notably, one of Heath Canada's concerns was the reliability of the animal tests and "bad experimentation" by Monstanto itself (127).
26. See Mills, *Science and Social Context*, 124.
27. See Robin, *World according to Monsanto*, 290–306. It should be noted that suicides of this type are relatively common in India relative to crop failure and massive debt. According to this study, Bt cotton is responsible for aggravating that already tragic cultural script.

in farmer suicides, and promotes the overall success of Bt cotton in India.[28] The implications of this study are probably more damning than sensationalist reports of farmer suicides. Monsanto's presence in India dates back to the late 1940s, encouraging monoculture farming and the purchase of expensive pesticides that are able to combat the insect problem initiated by monoculture farming in the first place. The real trouble with Bt cotton is its use in non-ideal growing conditions combined with poor education for farmers on how to properly use the product.[29] In these contexts, crop failure and increased indebtedness encourage debt hounding directed especially to farmers of lower social status.[30] This speaks to a rather more complicated economic context in India, in which Monsanto can thrive by hiding in the layered mess of food production and money-lending, avoiding direct responsibility for the failure of their product and the devastation of small-time Indian farmers.

In light of these cases, it is difficult to validate Monsanto's pledge for Integrity, Dialogue, Transparency, Sharing, Benefits, Respect, to Act as Owners to Achieve Results, and to Create a Great Place to Work.[31] From an ecological perspective, the manipulation and control of food production, and thus consumers, is intimately tied to the global market, without which Monsanto would be unable to exercise such totalizing control. The uneven distribution of power is tied to capital worth, allowing Monsanto to run rampant over the defenseless poor and the land they work. But, given that consumers enjoy a very limited set of options as far as the purchasing of food from different sources, what are they supposed to do—boycott and

28. See Guillaume P. Gruère et al., "Bt Cotton and Farmer Suicides in India: Reviewing the Evidence," *International Food Policy Research Institute Discussion Paper 00808*, 2008, 40–43, at http://www.ifpri.org/sites/default/files/publications/ifpridp00808.pdf

29. Ibid., 43. Also, Robin, *World according to Monsanto*, 295.

30. Gruère, "Bt Cotton and Farmer Suicides in India," 36–37.

31. Explication of this pledge can be found online at http://www.monsanto.ca/whoweare/Pages/monsanto-pledge.aspx.

starve? Monsanto is a critical agent in affecting our relationship to food, food production, and environmental destruction. In the following section, I will explore the interaction of food, power, and consumers in the story of Joseph. Monsanto and the GMO enterprise figures prominently in framing the types of questions asked of the text. Attention is given to the occasions where dominative power is asserted when issues of food are at stake, especially in Joseph's rise to power in the Egyptian court and Joseph's manipulation of his family in Canaan and Egypt.

Joseph the Farmer

Reading the Bible with Monsanto is not a novel insight. In a recent article, William O'Brien briefly observes the failure of Monsanto in its promise to put biotechnology to the task of feeding a hungry world. He proposes that the story of Israel's exodus from Egypt provides some "ancient biblical wisdom [that] can empower us to take on the high-tech and politically sophisticated iniquities of the Monsantos of the world."[32] Upon their deliverance out of slavery, the wandering Israelites bemoan lack of food. God's provision of manna and the stipulations of its consumption and storage remind us of a God who provides enough to go around. Hoarding and the control of the food is antithetical to God's vision of a people liberated from slavery.[33] This is a fair insight and potentially instructive for small communities typified by the wandering Israelites.

On the other hand, this insight reads like much postcolonial criticism, posing a strong bifurcation between the oppressor and oppressed. The Exodus story aligns itself against the evil Egyptian Empire and those who would mimic such oppression in controlling God's gift of creation. However, the circumstances surrounding

32. William O'Brien, "Finding Manna in the Age of Monsanto," *Tikkun* 47, no. 2 (2012): 47.
33. Ibid., 68, 69.

Israel's Egyptian experience complicates this simple narrative. The need for food, so prevalent in the wilderness wanderings, was an experience familiar to the patriarchs.

Joseph's story may not be the most obvious place to go in a piece on ecological hermeneutics. However, agriculture plays a very prominent role in the tale. As Hans Jensen remarks, "it . . . remains a story about bread."[34] Joseph as a dreamer and dream-interpreter launches his political career in Egypt as Pharaoh's right hand and administrator of food. This contentious and unexpected rise to power invites some consideration on the basis of ecology.

Dreams, Food, and the Rise to Power

While Jacob's preference for his son Joseph instigated feelings of bitterness among Jacob's other sons, the young Joseph did not help these relationships. Early in Genesis 37, the narrator has Joseph describing a peculiar dream in which his brothers' wheat sheaves bow down to his own sheaf. The resentment of the brothers deepens with this obvious reversal of birthright, though such reversal was already well established among Abraham's descendents. This brief episode sets up Joseph as a dreamer, establishes a crude relationship between

34. Hans J. T. Jensen, "The Bible Is (Also) a Myth: Lévi-Strauss, Girard, and the Story of Joseph," *Contagion: Journal of Violence, Mimesis, and Culture* 14 (2007): 51. This is the important feature of interest for this article. The historicity of the Joseph story is, of course, highly contested by critical scholars (W. F. Albright, "Historical and Mythical Elements in the Story of Joseph," *JBL* 37 [1918]: 111–43, is a classical example). However, the question, "did these events actually happen?" amid a quest for origins is a stale effort and actually unhelpful in historical analysis (see B. H. McLean, "The Crisis of Historicism: and the Problem of Historical Meaning in New Testament Studies," *Heythrop Journal* 53 [2009]: esp. 220). Rowe's article highlights many of the issues present when attempting to account for the historical accuracy and significance of particular elements of the Joseph narrative (Ignacio Márquez Rowe, "How Can Someone Sell His Own Fellow to the Egyptians?" *VetTest* 54, no. 3 (2004): 335–38). More importantly, the Joseph narrative was important in the development of ancient Hebrew and Jewish identities as an explanation of their emergence as a nation and a way to make sense of their present enslavement. Further, this narrative has continued to impact the formation of Christian identity through its inclusion in Christian canons.

food and power, and has the immediate effect of a close shave with death and his sale to the Midianites.[35]

Joseph's relationship to power is characterized by peaks and valleys. He goes from favorite son to Potiphar's slave, head slave in Potiphar's household to prison inmate, and so on. As a prison inmate, Joseph turns from dreamer to dream-interpreter, a trait that will continue to advance his political positioning. It is striking that both of the officials who come to Joseph with their dreams had a relationship with the Pharaoh on the basis of food and drink. In keeping with this theme, the content of the dreams themselves involve the very items of food and drink with which they had previously served the king. Joseph's interpretations identify agricultural success with political prosperity—budding grapes will see the cupbearer restored while hungry birds will feast on the body of the baker. This marks a significant gain for the cupbearer, even if not the baker. The cupbearer's restoration puts him in a close position to the Pharaoh, a position that Joseph is able to marshal in his favor. When it happens that the Pharaoh has his own set of unsettling dreams, the cupbearer is able to recommend Joseph's services. The connection between food and power is potent. Political elites—especially kings—can elevate the consumption of food and drink to a level of prestige and excess that goes far beyond essential sustenance. Food and drink provide privileged position to those who participate in the excesses of the court and the cupbearer gains the Pharaoh's ear. Joseph is obviously

35. Ron Pirson, argues that the brothers incorrectly identify the bowing down of the sheaves with Joseph as a king over them. Joseph's eventual dominance would be to the Egyptians (see Pirson, *The Lord of the Dreams: A Semantic and Literary Analysis of Genesis 37–50*, JSOTSup 355 [Sheffield: Sheffield Academic, 2002], 47–50). James Ackerman makes the more striking observation that the coming of the brothers to Egypt plays out as an unexpectedly delayed fulfillment of the sheaf dream. The doubling of the "bowing down" (with the second instance being the true fulfillment) allows ample space for Joseph to wield his power. Interestingly, it is the fulfilling of the power play that allows Joseph to be reinstated as a brother. See Ackerman, "Joseph, Judah, and Jacob," in *Modern Critical Interpretations: Genesis*, ed. Harold Bloom (New York: Chelsea House, 1986), 89–95.

not oblivious to this dynamic, since he requests that the cupbearer, when re-established, remember Joseph.

Pharaoh's dreams mark a climax as the final and most significant set of dreams. The content of the dreams are given twice, as the second time is a recounting of the dreams to Joseph. When Joseph is called to the Pharaoh (thanks to the cupbearer's recommendation), Joseph indicates that the two dreams are recapitulations of the same basic message: after a seven-year period of agricultural plenty, seven years of famine will commence. The second retelling of the dreams adds a significant detail: the seven thin and ugly cows and the seven withered ears of corn gain nothing from consuming the seven fat cows and the seven full ears. These dreams are unsurprisingly cryptic and unnatural, as dreams tend to be—what kind of plant eats other plants?

For those familiar with the impact of Monsanto's corn varieties in Mexico, the proposition of freak corn that consumes robust and healthy corn is an all-too-familiar image. To many contemporary North American eyes, small, misshapen, and multi-colored corn may not look very appetizing. But these unfamiliar cobs represent the genetic base for biodiversity and thus the potential for a healthy and resistant crop. Monsanto's push for the sale of GMO corn in Mexico has been moderately successful, resulting in crossbreeding between native varieties and Monsanto's patented varieties (i.e., Bt corn, developed for pest resistance).[36] This type of random

36. See David Quist and Ignacio H. Chapela's important study "Transgenic DNA Introgressed into Traditional Maize Landraces in Oaxaco, Mexico," *Nature* 414 (2001): 541–43. Robin notes that NAFTA disables Mexican restriction of the corn trade, which is, in turn, heavily subsidized the United States (*World according to Monsanto*, 245). The response to Quist and Chapela's article has been contentious to say the least, due to some errors in their research and the underhanded blackballing by undercover representatives of Monsanto. See Robin, *World according to Monsanto*, 248–53; Kenneth A. Worthy et al. "Agricultural Biotechnology Science Compromised: The Case of Quist and Chapela," in *Controversies in Science & Technology: From Maize to Menopause*, ed. Daniel E. Kleinman et al. (Madison: University of Wisconsin Press, 2005), 135–49.

crossbreeding lacks the fine-tuned gene placement that Monsanto's engineered corn enjoys and produces wild and vagrant corn plants with giant stocks and puny, unhealthy ears. Prospects are dim for the future for Mexico's corn biodiversity and their main staple food. Native corn is not replaced by a superior variety, but by genetic freaks that are useless for human consumption. In Mexico, as in Pharaoh's dream, the good ears are swallowed up by the bad ears.

It is, as yet, unclear how the corn crisis in Mexico will unfold, or what can be done to allow the Mexican people access to edible corn. The story of Joseph, however, holds better prospects as his interpretation of Pharoah's dream is followed by a suggested solution to the problem of famine. This solution—to store enough grain during the years of plenty to last for the years of famine—almost seems like common sense, yet it is framed in a clever way. Joseph's suggestion to search for a man who is discerning and wise (אִישׁ נָבוֹן וְחָכָם, 41:33) to oversee the collection and distribution of the corn is well placed since the rest of the "wise men" (חֲכָמֶיהָ, 41:8) at court have been disgraced already by their inability to interpret the dream.[37] This episode marks another step in Joseph's climb—the Pharaoh sets him up as overseer of the royal palace and Joseph is able to oversee his solution to the food shortage.

My reading of Joseph thus far can identify two notable characteristics. First, he develops a keen eye for the relationship between food and power, as evidenced earlier by his relationship to the cupbearer. Second, faced with a food shortage crisis, Joseph is able to come up with a creative solution that seemingly defies

37. W. Lee Humphreys does not think that the Egyptian wise men are presented as fools so much as the story is meant to elevate Joseph (Humphreys, *Joseph and His Family: A Literary Study*, Studies on Personalities of the Old Testament [Columbia: University of South Carolina Press, 1988], 149–50). It is hard to see one without the other. See also Lindsay Wilson, *Joseph, Wise and Otherwise: The Intersection of Wisdom and Covenant in Genesis 37–50*, Paternoster Biblical Monographs (Carlisle: Paternoster, 2004), 125–26, for comments on the connection between wisdom, wise men, and the interpretation of dreams.

conventional wisdom.[38] Interestingly, this latter insight comes to fruition as a kind of public wisdom that takes place in Pharaoh's court, allowing him to achieve a powerful position in the court.[39]

Joseph the Administrator

With Joseph's impressive display, he is vaulted to a position of high authority in the realm of Egypt. In this case, Joseph's control over a food surplus in a time of need across the Egyptian Empire makes him the caretaker of life and death. It is this position of authority that allows Joseph to meet his family again, since those living in Canaan are faced with a food shortage as well. I do not wish to labor over the details of Joseph's interactions with his brothers as they come to Egypt for assistance. However, I do want to highlight some of the interesting occasions where power dynamics are established vis-à-vis food.

I briefly suggested above that when at court, Joseph was able to capitalize upon the Pharaoh's weak position created by the impending threat of starvation. Food shortage (especially that resulting from natural disaster) has a limiting effect upon human free agency. Thus, food itself is a valuable resource that disrupts conventional wisdom and enables new ways of acting. This can be seen further on in the Joseph story, when Joseph decides to imprison Simeon and send his other brothers back to Canaan to retrieve Benjamin, Joseph's only full brother. When the brothers

38. Joseph's rise is not predicated entirely upon God's provision. Pirson makes the incisive observation that while God is deemed to be the giver and interpreter of dreams, there is much that Joseph himself does that extends beyond the limits of the provided interpretation. Joseph acts as the interpreter of divine insight but also is able to tactfully secure a position of power for himself (*Lord of the Dreams*, 87–90). I suggest that in this case, the prospect of famine is frightening for the leader of Egypt and thus Joseph's ability to see a solution to the problem is timely. It is an odd thing to give such authority to a foreigner, but I think that, faced with starvation, people make rash decisions.
39. See Wilson, *Joseph, Wise and Otherwise*, 237.

return home and recount their story, Jacob is distressed that he has lost his son Simeon to the Egyptians in addition to his previous loss of Joseph. Jacob makes the uncomfortable decision to save Benjamin's life at the cost of Simeon's and does allow his sons to return to Egypt. At the beginning of Genesis 43, however, the famine becomes so severe that the food brought back from Egypt runs out and Jacob is forced to reconsider his previous decision. Jacob sends his sons back to Egypt, along with Benjamin this time, to purchase more grain from the Egyptians. The way in which Jacob discusses his predicament with his sons (Gen. 43:11-14) and the way Jacob's sons express their predicament to Joseph later on (Gen. 44:14-34) demonstrates that Jacob and his family experience some emotional confliction. But against his better judgment and perhaps a certain sentimentality towards the offspring of his favorite wife, Jacob acts in order to feed his family.[40]

Fortunately for Jacob's family, Joseph acts with benevolence to the brothers, even after he jerks them around a little more. Because of Joseph's high position in the court he is able to secure a home for his family in Egypt. Not only are the children of Israel secured a place to live with access to food, they seem to be differentiated from the native Egyptians regarding subsequent administrative decisions across the land. The famine becomes so lengthy that the people of Egypt and Canaan can no longer pay for grain to feed themselves. In order to survive, they sell themselves and their land into slavery to Joseph.[41]

While the point of this essay is not to read against the grain and criticize Joseph into oblivion, the way in which Joseph uses his

40. Ackerman ("Joseph, Judah, and Jacob," 95–96) highlights favoritism as an important theme in the patriarchal narratives, especially with respect to favoring the younger. Here, favoritism toward Benjamin is only heightened by Joseph's perceived death.

41. This is certainly an interesting reversal from when Joseph was sold into slavery. I do not think that the Israelite settlers in Goshen were included in this group since later after the death of Jacob, these sons, for fear of Joseph's retribution, attempt to make themselves Joseph's slaves. It is unlikely they would do this if they already were considered slaves.

control of Egypt's food to essentially enslave the entire population is striking. Here, we can see two sides to this issue. The one who controls the production and distribution of food has the power to control the very lives of the people who depend on that food to survive. On the other hand, those who do not have free access to food must and will go to great lengths to feed themselves, including selling their bodies and the potential to control their own food resources in the future. Joseph positions himself much like Monsanto has positioned itself in the global food market, where they have a commanding control of food itself as well as those who produce and consume it (i.e., everyone).[42] Slavery has been a recurring theme in Joseph's story and will continue as such in Exodus when the children of Israel become slaves in Egypt and strive for their freedom. Our contemporary experiences with Monsanto's totalizing control of food heightens an awareness of Joseph's action in this case. It is almost with a sense of outrage that we read of Joseph, one previously sold as a slave himself, who could accept the proposed bondage of the Egyptians and Canaanites.[43] The conduct of Monsanto today provides a foil against overly romanticized pictures of Joseph as an agent of divine wisdom and providence. In addition to his questionable role as slavemaster, Clarke Cochran reminds us that Joseph's actions in Egypt essentially prepare his people for slavery to the Egyptians.[44]

42. Eric Lowenthal argues that the handing over of the livestock in exchange for food was a way for Joseph to destabilize the power of the wealthy, perhaps for the benefit of the poor and that the people of Egypt were never actually adopted as slaves (Lowenthal, *The Joseph Narrative in Genesis* [New York: Ktav, 1973), 125–30.

43. Though Lowenthal (*Joseph Narrative*, 130) argues that the "modern moralist" should not hold Joseph responsible in this case. See also, for example, Stone's analysis of Joseph in which he is interpreted as an ideal ruler and one who succeeds in ethical living where Adam failed (Timothy J. Stone, "Joseph in the Likeness of Adam: Narrative Echoes of the Fall," in *Genesis and Christian Theology*, ed. Nathan MacDonald et al. [Grand Rapids, MI: Eerdmans, 2012], 62–73). Other sympathetic readings include Victor P. Hamilton, *The Book of Genesis: Chapters 18–50*, NICOT (Grand Rapids, MI: Eerdmans, 1995), 618. Readings such as this seem to glaze over some of the grittier details of the narrative.

Conclusion

In this chapter I have tried to think about the ancient story of Joseph together with the contemporary story of Monsanto as an exercise in ecological hermeneutics. I am interested in a number of insights evoked by the exercise. First, the relationship between food and power is ubiquitous if not exceedingly complex. Second, the control of food can often result in a very unequal power dynamics. In both the case of Monsanto and in the Joseph story, a minority in control of food production and distribution can wield an unprecedented magnitude of power in the face of a disenfranchised majority. Third, this majority will act in opposition to conventional wisdom or personal desire when faced with a food shortage, thus putting themselves in a vulnerable position for further domination. This was a striking feature of the Joseph story and it occurred again and again with different characters in slightly different circumstances. Here, the story rebounds toward our contemporary scenario. Monsanto thrives on a discourse of ecological catastrophe and food shortage. How will we feed the world? Their solution is monoculture mega-farms of GMO produce and, faced with certain starvation, the disenfranchised majority can do nothing but acquiesce. But there are opportunities for resistance.

Our universal experience of Monsanto's domination contrasts the story of Joseph, in which his relationship to power is characterized by a slow rise to power. This story allows us to see how much food production and distribution can be effective in shifting power dynamics. As I have already gleaned from Chris Hedges, food becomes a place where the 99 percent can begin to take back control of their own lives from the ruling corporate class. Solutions will

44. Clarke E. Cochran, "Joseph and the Politics of Memory," *The Review of Politics* 64, no. 3 (2002): 430.

not necessarily come in the form of a primitivizing of our food production system. Indeed, irreparable damage has already been done to the global environment such that this is not possible. The freak corn in Mexico is a chilling fixture in the erosion of the earth's biodiversity. The localization of our food system has its appeal. At best, this results in slow, steady changes that tend to be geared toward the established middle class, without much consideration about those for whom healthy food is an ill-afforded luxury. How many city-dwellers really know how to be effective farmers, anyways? It is more likely, however, that such antithetical efforts may be co-opted by the capitalist markets just like organic farming and Fair Trade coffee.

A more apocalyptic outlook witnesses the destabilizing of the capitalist system, at least as we know it. Perhaps food shortages due to lack of transport resources will doom urban food deserts to destruction. Drastic changes resulting from unavoidable ecological disaster may force revolution and not reform. This is the reality we ought to live in light of, without a naïve hope that crisis can be averted. The clarion call of the Hebrew Bible is hinted at in Genesis 44, in which Judah's desire to return to Egypt for grain is for the benefit of future generations, even at the possible expense of his own life.[45] Desire for the future generation developed in the Hebrew Bible is the expectation of the righteous remnant, characterized by the preservation of the nation but at the expense of catastrophic human loss. Perhaps amidst the expectation of environmental disaster and the destruction of food resources, the anticipation of a surviving remnant is an opportunity for hope. To be clear, this is not a call for some otherworldly and immaterial expectation. Jensen notes that "the Hebrew Bible never loses sight of the material basis of existence. . . . It does not look forward to an ethereal existence in Heaven or elsewhere where there is no question of food."[46] A strong connection

45. See Ackerman, "Joseph, Judah, and Jacob," 97.

to the land and the material realities of existence is central to an effective ecological hermeneutic and an opportunity for the survival of the community.

46. Jensen, "The Bible Is (Also) a Myth," 50.

PART III

Global Crisis and the Second Testament

9

Homelessness, Neoliberalism, and Jesus' "Decision" to Go Rogue

An Analysis of Matthew 4:12-25

Robert J. Myles

As our dominant ideological climate, the age of neoliberal policy, pragmatism, and consensus has, often unknowingly and uncritically, filtered into our everyday lives, our thought processes, and even our interpretations of the Bible. It has, in the words of David Harvey, "become hegemonic as a mode of discourse. It has pervasive effects on ways of thought to the point where it has become incorporated into the common-sense way many of us interpret, live in, and understand the world."[1] James Crossley's recent book, *Jesus in an Age of Neoliberalism*, has begun to uncover a number of these ideological peculiarities within historical Jesus research. He successfully exposes,

1. David Harvey, *A Brief History of Neoliberalism* (Oxford: Oxford University Press, 2005), 3.

among other things, how Western individualism has influenced the construction of Jesus within both historical and popular quests.[2] In this chapter, I want to bring a similar lens to bear on the connection between Jesus and homelessness as it is constructed within Gospel exegesis and scholarship, in particular the beginnings of Jesus' itinerant ministry within the Gospel of Matthew. In doing so, I will undertake a re-reading of Matthew 4:12-25 using Marxist exegesis that attempts to embed both Jesus and the first disciples in a structured social world as it is encoded within the Matthean text. This should assist in disrupting narratives of neoliberalism in the world before the text as they shape and distort our dominant hermeneutical filters.

Built upon classical liberal and economic ideals, neoliberalism refers to the contemporary political movements emphasizing open markets, small government, privatization, and personal moral and economic responsibility. Its advent is usually associated with the Reagan and Thatcher era of the 1980s, and then was continued through the so-called "Third Way" policies beginning in the 1990s. It has now become a political orthodoxy across many Western democracies in which governments, whether left-wing or right-wing, focus more on managing the economy as best they can within neoliberal conditions than on "traditional" ideological stances. Within this matrix, homelessness is usually interpreted as a "choice" made for lifestyle reasons or individual moral and/or economic failings.

It is not uncommon to find interpretive connections between Jesus and homelessness in contemporary biblical scholarship. For all practical purposes, Jesus' itinerant ministry was a homeless one.[3] A

2. James G. Crossley, *Jesus in an Age of Neoliberalism: Quests, Scholarship and Ideology* (Sheffield: Equinox, 2012).

3. Some interpreters argue that Jesus cannot possibly be homeless in Matthew because he has a house (*oikos*) in Capernaum (Matt. 9:10, 28; 12:46; 13:1, 36; 17:25). However, we ought to avoid conflating the related but distinct terms "house" and "home" in English, even though

popular reconstruction of Christian origins developed by Gerd Theissen, for instance, describes the wandering charismatic followers of Jesus as essentially homeless, lacking family (having abandoned or renounced family), lacking possessions, and lacking protection. He writes:

> Giving up a fixed abode was an essential part of discipleship. Those who were called left hearth and home (Mark 1:16; 10:28ff.), followed Jesus, and like him became homeless. 'Foxes have holes, and birds of the air have nests; but the Son of man has nowhere to lay his head' (Matt. 8.20) is a saying which applied to them.[4]

As I have argued elsewhere, the connection interpreters often make between Jesus and homelessness, however, is overwhelmingly constrained by neoliberal thinking.[5] But it is at this nexus of Jesus and homelessness that a peculiar contradiction emerges: because Jesus is supposed to be the moral hero of the story, his homelessness becomes romanticized and the desperation and destitution that might typically accompany the experience gets extracted. If Jesus is, for Christians and/or biblical scholars, the ultimate object (or commodity) of theological and/or scholarly desire, in which Jesus functions in his salvific role as a mediator of our "surplus enjoyment" (*plus de jouissance*), then his homelessness acts as a fantasmatic screen, shielding us from the traumatic experience of homelessness proper and the apparent failure of our wider sociopolitical system in which homelessness remains a tangible political problem. In other words, homelessness is idealized in Jesus in a way that encourages us to

no distinction exists in Koine Greek: a house refers to a physical structure whereas a home refers to a much more complex notion of connection and orientation to a significant place of meaning. The conflation of these terms in English began during the rise of the bourgeoisie in the seventeenth century and assumes the emergence of capitalist modes of production and concepts of private property.

4. Gerd Theissen, *Sociology of Early Palestinian Christianity* (Philadelphia: Fortress Press, 1978), 10.
5. Robert J. Myles, *The Homeless Jesus in the Gospel of Matthew*, Social World of Biblical Antiquity 2.10 (Sheffield: Sheffield Phoenix, 2014).

effectively divert our critical attention from some of these inherent contradictions contained within our own contexts of reading.

Within many contemporary interpretations, Jesus' itinerancy is predominantly conceived of as the result of his own free choosing (or at least a pious response to the driving force of the Spirit). A heightening of Jesus' agency enables the re-inscription of the prominent neoliberal myth that most people "choose" to become homeless for lifestyle reasons. For example, writing at the highpoint of Thatcherism in the 1980s, the British Matthean scholar R. T. France suggests that Jesus' "chosen way of life is one of homelessness and insecurity . . . and his disciples were called to share his style of life. This was a matter of choice, not of necessity, as Jesus' family was probably a comfortable, if not affluent, 'middle-class' one."[6] The reverberations here of individual choice, homelessness as a lifestyle, and a universalizing estimation of the middle-class, is intriguing when viewed in tandem with neoliberal mantras espousing the centrality of individual responsibility. Similar reverberations emerge within some of the scholarly attempts to draw parallels between Jesus' itinerant ministry and the Greco-Roman philosophical school of the Cynics. It must be immediately cautioned, of course, that the Cynics' poverty was a chosen lifestyle, not one they were necessarily born into, as were peasants. In fact, most Cynics appear to have come from the educated elite and become "cynical" about Greco-Roman society. Stephen C. Barton sums up the contrast between the cynics and the itinerancy of Jesus and his disciples as follows:

> [W]here the Cynics adopt a deliberate asceticism as an integral part of the wise man's revolt against culture and return to nature, the gospels speak more of involuntary deprivation and hardship in consequence of faithful missionary discipleship; and where the Cynics seek to reform the

6. R. T. France, *The Gospel According to Matthew: An Introduction and Commentary* (Leicester: InterVarsity, 1985), 160.

> individual by a highly provocative onslaught on civilized conventions and popular opinion, there is in the gospels a positive summons to Israel and the nations to personal and social reform in preparation for the advent of God.[7]

In contrast to its conventional treatment in biblical studies, however, a range of scholarly perspectives on contemporary homelessness construct the issue as far more complex, often stemming from various economic and social crises, such as housing shortages, high unemployment, inadequate resourcing for the mentally ill, social distancing, and estrangement. This culminates in the creation of a vulnerable underclass, predisposing already at-risk members of society into episodes of homelessness.[8] For the critical theorist Slavoj Žižek, homelessness emerges (along with the underclass, the ghettoized, and the permanently unemployed) as a *symptom* of the late capitalist universal system; a reminder of the structural deficiencies that remain beneath the surface and negate the "totalitarian logic of the proper capitalist utopia."[9] Might we not also conceive of Jesus' apparent homelessness as a symptom of wider structural crises? Not necessarily as a result of capitalism, of course, but rather the systemic and structural violence of the agrarian society in first-century Palestine and Judea?

While Jesus' itinerancy, by which I mean his traveling from one place to the next, is an integral part of his ministry, Matthew's Gospel includes a number of other episodes that pre-empt a shift to the margins. The flight to Egypt (Matt. 2:13-23), for example, involves an infant forcefully displaced both geographically and politically from

7. Stephen C. Barton, *Discipleship and Family Ties in Mark and Matthew* (Cambridge: Cambridge University Press, 1994), 52.
8. See, for example: Laura Stivers, *Disrupting Homelessness: Alternative Christian Approaches* (Minneapolis: Fortress Press, 2011); Emily Meanwell, "Experiencing Homelessness: A Review of Recent Literature," *Sociology Compass* 6, no. 1 (2012): 72–85.
9. Slavoj Žižek, *The Plague of Fantasies* (London: Verso, 1997), 7.

his hometown (cf. 8:20; 13:54–58). Homelessness and displacement are not usually conditions that people freely choose to enact. Rather, external factors, often far beyond their control, influence their ability to act and react within a particular structured environment. The same is true within the narrative of Matthew's Gospel in which Jesus' actions must always be understood in relation to other events, characters, and external pressures. In what follows, I re-read the connection between Jesus and homelessness as symptomatic of wider social and political conditions as they are encoded within the text.

Structuring the Beginning of Jesus' Ministry (Matt. 4:12-25)

Matthew 4:12–25 contains four distinguishable scenes: first, the arrest of John the Baptist (vv. 12–16); second, the proclamation of the kingdom (v. 17); third, the call of the first disciples (vv. 18–22); and finally, the inauguration of itinerant ministry, healings, and the spread of Jesus' fame (vv. 23–25). We ought to exercise caution in our structuring of the text, however. In recent years a structuring of Matthew that views the opening words of 4:17 ("From that time Jesus began . . .") as constituting an introductory formula to a new major section of the Gospel has gained some traction.[10] A consequence of this structuring is that Jesus' displacement to Capernaum in 4:12–13 becomes isolated from subsequent events.

Key to this structuring is the much-disputed formula ἀπὸ τότε (from that time) in 4:17. Ulrich Luz points out that the inclusion of this clause is intended precisely to establish a connection with the preceding verses.[11] The Matthean text often uses the adverb τότε as a

10. Kingsbury adopts this threefold structure of Matt: the presentation of Jesus (1:1—4:16); the ministry of Jesus to Israel and Israel's repudiation of Jesus (4:17—16:20); and the journey of Jesus to Jerusalem and his suffering death and resurrection (16:21—28:20). He suggests that the formulaic phrase "From that time on Jesus began . . ." (4:17; 16:21) initiates each new narrative block. See Jack Dean Kingsbury, *Matthew: Structure, Christology, Kingdom* (Minneapolis: Fortress Press, 1975).

connective particle to link two events through an unspecified passage of time. F. Neirynck argues that enough narrative connections exist between 4:17 and 4:12–16 to warrant its inclusion in the same paragraph.[12] Indeed, as will be argued below, it is the eventual occurrence of the arrest of the Baptist which prompts Jesus to withdraw to Capernaum, go about calling the first disciples, and begin his itinerant ministry.

If taken together, the beginnings of the Matthean Jesus' ministry are best understood as an embedded *response* to the arrest of the Baptist, in addition to other social and political threads that are encoded within the text. While religious motivations for Jesus' ministry are certainly evident (and noted particularly by the eschatological context of proclamation of the kingdom), these must be balanced against the various political, economic, and social forces that drive his actions. A politicizing of these textures reveals that the arrest of the Baptist functions as a significant trigger for Jesus' "withdrawal" from Nazareth and the beginning of his ministry in Capernaum. As a result, the Matthean Jesus' itinerant ministry is from its very inception symptomatic of various crises within his wider sociopolitical environment.

Jesus Withdraws (Matt. 4:12-16)

After hearing of John's arrest, Jesus, sensing danger, withdraws (ἀνεχώρησεν) from Nazareth and settles in Capernaum. Commenting on Matthew 4:12–13, Luz supposes that

> Matthew does not provide information about the subjective motives of Jesus for his return. Jesus goes to Galilee for the sole and uncomplicated

11. Ulrich Luz, *Matthew 1–7*, trans. J. E. Crouch, Hermeneia (Minneapolis: Fortress Press, 2007), 192.
12. F. Neirynck, "ΑΠΟ ΤΟΤΕ ΗΡΞΑΤΟ and the Structure of Matthew," *ETL* 64, no. 1 (1988): 120–23.

> reason that it corresponds to the divine plan that he minister to 'Galilee of the Gentiles.' . . . This applies precisely to the move to Capernaum also. Matthew underscores through the allusions to the following quotation that the move corresponds to the divine plan. Why Jesus (biographically) left Nazareth and chose Capernaum as residence is of no interest to him.[13]

To recall a key discourse of neoliberalism, it is curious that Luz frames Jesus' movement in terms of a "choice" to enact God's divine plan. Even though Jesus' actions have economic, social, and political consequences, they are isolated from this context and treated as significant only insofar as they advance Jesus' soteriological role. A more careful reading of the text, however, reveals that the beginning of Jesus' ministry is not the result of an arbitrary choice. Rather, it begins with Jesus "hearing" (ἀκούσας) of John's arrest. This echoes Joseph's "hearing" (ἀκούσας) of Archelaus ruling over Judea in 2:22. Similarly, the verb used to denote Jesus' movement is the same used multiple times to describe Jesus' flight to Egypt: he is again prompted to withdraw (ἀναχωρέω) for safety and refuge. The verb ἀναχωρέω appears a number of times in Matthew in connection to episodes of sociopolitical danger, and typically describes the forced displacement of its subject (2:12, 13, 14, 22; 12:15; 14:13; 27:5).[14]

In his anti-imperial reading of this text, Warren Carter maintains that while John's arrest causes Jesus to withdraw into Galilee, "Jesus' withdrawal from the wilderness (around the Jordan) to Galilee is not for safety reasons (as in 2:12, 13, 14, 22)."[15] He points out that Jesus withdraws into a dangerous territory, occupied by the Roman client Herod Antipas, and is made more dangerous by the Baptist's arrest. Echoes to the previous displacement during 2:21–23, however, in

13. Luz, *Matthew 1–7*, 194.
14. Robert J. Myles, "Echoes of Displacement in Matthew's Genealogy of Jesus," *Colloquium* 45, no. 1 (2013): 33–34.
15. Warren Carter, *Matthew and the Margins: A Sociopolitical and Religious Reading* (Maryknoll, NY: Orbis Books, 2000), 113.

which Joseph avoids the centers of power in Judea by withdrawing to (the still-dangerous) Galilee suggests that a similar move might be occurring here. Sean Freyne reasons that "the frequent withdrawals of Jesus might be interpreted as indicative of his need for constant vigilance before the threat of Herod, especially since there seems to be a conscious avoidance of the Herodian towns of Sepphoris and Tiberias."[16] The threat of Herod lingers and continues to drive the actions of Jesus. Carter himself notes how, with Jesus' relocation, the "periphery" of Galilee symbolizes "a new and non-localized center" of divine presence.[17]

Other narrative elements provide further evidence that Jesus' response to John's arrest is symptomatic of external sociopolitical realities. The passive verb παραδόθη, for example, which alludes to the Baptist's arrest or "handing over" in 4:12, occurs a number of times toward the end of the Gospel with respect to Jesus' own arrest (26:2, 16, 21, 23, 24, 25, 45, 46, 48; 27:2, 3, 4, 18, 26) and thus makes a clear parallel between their shared fate: the final solution for outsiders who disrupt normalized society is extermination.

While Jesus' move to Capernaum is motivated by self-preservation, another ideological dimension to consider is that of "withdrawal" as a subversive political act. It is here that the verb ἀναχωρέω in the context of Matthew 4 is most evocative. In his treatise of violence, Žižek distinguishes between two broad categories of violence in the world: *subjective violence*, a more visible form performed by a clearly identifiable agent; and *objective violence*, which includes both a "symbolic" violence embodied in language and its forms, and "systemic" violence, or the consequences of the smooth functioning of our economic and political systems.[18] The Baptist's arrest, for

16. Sean Freyne, *Galilee: From Alexander the Great to Hadrian* (Wilmington, DE: Glazier, 1980), 222.
17. Carter, *Margins*, 113.

example, is not directly attributable to any one subject (e.g., Herod); rather, he and his disruptive/prophetic ministry of baptism is disposed of through objectively violent regulating mechanisms, in order that society may return to its smooth, uninterrupted functioning.

It is in addressing these less-than-obvious forms of systemic violence in the contemporary dominance of late capitalist-democracy that Žižek frames his argument not via a revolutionary "call to arms," but rather through the *inaction* of sitting back and waiting, by means of a patient, critical analysis. There is no need for a fake sense of urgency for "[t]he threat . . . is not passivity, but pseudo-activity, the urge to 'be active', to 'participate', to mask the nothingness of what goes on. People intervene all the time . . . [t]he truly difficult thing is to step back, to withdraw."[19] Similarly, he contends that "the task today is to resist state power by withdrawing from its scope, subtracting oneself from it, creating new spaces outside its control."[20] So too, Jesus' "withdrawal" from society functions as a time of escape. His forty days in the wilderness (4:1–11) is a period of abstinence and testing. In verse 12, upon hearing of the Baptist's arrest, Jesus further disengages from everyday life in Galilee. As we will see below, Jesus' announcement of a heavenly kingdom extends this space outside the scope of societal control, and is followed by the subtraction of fishermen from full participation in the reigning ideological-political order.

Geographical Intertexture

After his "withdrawal" in verse 12, Jesus moves to "Capernaum, by the lake, in the territory of Zebulun and Naphtali" (v. 13). In the first century, Capernaum functioned primarily as a seaside fishing village,

18. Slavoj Žižek, *Violence* (London: Profile Books, 2008), 1–2.
19. Ibid., 183.
20. Slavoj Žižek, *In Defense of Lost Causes* (London: Verso, 2008), 339.

on the northwest shore of the Sea of Galilee. Jesus' settlement here is denoted by the verb κατοικέω, which can mean to live, dwell, or settle (down) in an intransitive sense, but can also describe the action of inhabiting a body or space for a limited period of time.[21] Jesus' settlement in Capernaum, however, is not permanent; the town does not function as a site of enduring residence, nor does it feature subsequently as a point of orientation (and moreover, he later attacks it in 11:22-23).

The withdrawal to Capernaum might, in fact, render a certain psychological change for Jesus. In considering the itinerancy of Jesus' ministry from the context of Jamaican migration, Paul Zilonka suggests that villages like Nazareth usually foster strong kinship ties and the personal psychological impact of this transfer of residence involves considerable trauma. He writes that

> [w]hen Jesus permanently moved away from his family, his 'roots,' he was thrust into a new drama on the public stage. He would learn the deeper meaning of the proverbial statement, 'You cannot go home again.' Geographical changes, a change of neighborhood, leave permanent effects in the way a person thinks and acts."[22]

Within 4:15-16, the trauma associated with Jesus' withdrawal is immediately underscored by a prophecy citation. The citation, drawn from Isaiah 9:1-2, consists of the beginning of a poem declaring a new age and a new ruler, a promise of hope in the aftermath of displacement and defeat. Jesus' arrival in Capernaum is, accordingly, interpreted as the fulfillment of Isaiah's promise of deliverance, originally addressed to the devastated regions of northern Palestine

21. "κατοικεω," *BDAG* 425. The nrsv translation of κατῴκησεν in 4:13 as "made his home in," is problematic in that it fuels the illusion that Capernaum is a place of safety and stability for Jesus, and yet upon arrival he immediately begins an itinerant ministry. Other English translations are more restrained than the NRSV: the KJV, for example, says that Jesus "came and dwelt" there, and the NIV renders it as "he went and lived" there. Such translations grant the impermanence of Capernaum in its function as a home place for Jesus.
22. Paul Zilonka, "The Pain of Migration," *The Bible Today* 26, no. 6 (1991): 354.

of his day. The prophecy most likely concerns the historical situation described in 2 Kings 15:26 and 1 Chronicles 5:26, in which the Israelites from Naphtali are taken captive by the Assyrians during 733–32 BCE. The intertexture evokes the suffering that goes along with their deportation, but reconfigures it so as to associate Jesus with their hopes and desires of liberation. In the Isaiah text, a son from the house of David who brings salvation is promised (Isa. 9:6–7). In the Matthean text, this promise is applied to the ministry of Jesus, who, as a son from the house of David (Matt. 1:1), is retroactively heralded as a "liberated liberator."[23] As we will see below, Jesus' proclamation of the approaching kingdom extends this prospective for political dissent.

Heralding the Kingdom (Matt. 4:17)

Jesus' ministry begins with a "light [which] has dawned" (v. 16). Awakening to the reality of his sociopolitical predicament, Jesus proclaims, "Repent, for the kingdom of heaven has come near." His words not only echo the Baptist's proclamation in 3:2, but mark the dawning of a messianic age. Jesus' proclamation contains a sense of immediacy; beginning with an imperative to repent (μετανοεῖτε), and the inclusion of ἐγγίζω leading the second clause. This highlights the immanent closeness of the kingdom's realization. As mentioned above, the adjoining text in verse 17, "From this time [ἀπὸ τότε]," connects the proceeding clause of the Baptist's arrest to Jesus' subsequent withdrawal. This disrupts the romanticization of Jesus' break from home place as a lifestyle choice. Instead, the beginning of Jesus' ministry is constructed narratively in the context of forced withdrawal; his proclamation is situated as a *response* to the intrusion of external political realities.

23. Elaine M. Wainwright, *Shall We Look for Another? A Feminist Rereading of the Matthean Jesus* (Maryknoll, NY: Orbis Books, 1998), 101–18.

From a revolutionary perspective, the dawning of new light in the shadow of death (v. 16b) might evoke for the contemporary reader the Marxist concept of class consciousness. Georg Lukács argues that becoming conscious of one's concrete social position and its revolutionary potential changes being itself—that is, it transforms a passive working class into the proletariat as a revolutionary subject.[24] While in exile, Jesus becomes aware of his outsider status, which has occurred not because of individual moral or economic failure, but as a remnant of wider social and political forces and his God-given mission. The text retroactively transforms his abject social reality into a theological locus for organizing revolutionary power.

A Kingdom of the Heavens?

The phrase "Kingdom of the Heavens" (βασιλεία τῶν οὐρανῶν) occurs twenty-three times in Matthew and functions as an evocative and countercultural discourse of the prophetic imagination. The kingdom or *basileia* presents an alternative vision of reality, disrupting the Real (that is, the external dimension of experience as opposed to reality based on sense perception and the material order) that frames and sustains dominant arrangements of power in society and the totality of its alienating features. Within such a vision, the expendable homeless population, those at the very bottom of first-century society, are heralded a central place.

In his book *Heaven and Earth in the Gospel of Matthew*, Jonathan Pennington discusses the meaning of the *basileia* within his wider thesis concerning Matthew's thematic use of heaven and earth. He argues that the *basileia*, which has a variety of meanings including but not limited to the rule or reign over a kingdom in a spatial sense,

24. Georg Lukács, *History and Class Consciousness: Studies in Marxist Dialectics*, trans. Rodney Livingston (London: Merlin, 1971).

is both from heaven and heavenly. This naturally contrasts with the counterpoint of earthly kingdoms and earthly ways of governance.[25] As such, the expression is used as part of the thematic contrast between God's kingdom and the kingdoms of this world.[26] Elaborating on the theology of the kingdom, Pennington remarks that Matthew

> repeatedly shows that the social order of the kingdom of heaven is very unlike the present earthly order, and that the latter will eventually be replaced by the former (6:9–10). In addition to radical teachings . . . Matthew depicts the heavenly kingdom as one in which the mourning and poor in spirit are blessed (5:3, 4, 10–12), while those who are meek stand to inherit the earth (5:5). Equally topsy-turvy, the nature of the kingdom of heaven is such that the one who is lowly like a child will be the greatest therein (18:1–4; cf. 19:13–15), while the leaders in God's community should be the slaves of all (20:25–28; cf. 23:11). Those who give up everything for the heavenly kingdom will gain all back and more (19:26–29)—the first shall be last, and the last first (19:30).[27]

Moreover, by proclaiming the *basileia* as a form of countercultural rhetoric, the subjects of the present ideological-political constellation are compelled to confront the fact that it exists, and exerts power, only insofar as it is accepted as such by its subjects.

An important contribution to the discussion of the meaning of the *basileia* as it pertains to the issues of home and homelessness is developed by Halvor Moxnes in his book *Putting Jesus in His Place*. Drawing on the field of critical spatial theory, in particular the works of Henri Lefebvre and Edward Soja, Moxnes situates the kingdom within the category of "imaginary places," which function as a vision of how a real place might be imagined differently. In

25. Jonathan T. Pennington, *Heaven and Earth in the Gospel of Matthew* (Leiden: Brill, 2007), 328.
26. Pennington posits that "the 'of heaven' part . . . is not accidental or reverentially circumlocutionary, but serves a very powerful literary and rhetorical purpose: to contrast the world's kingdoms with God's." Ibid., 337–38.
27. Ibid., 340.

his words, the kingdom opens up a "third-space" of representation or imagination that presents plans for alternative ways of structuring places and material practices from that of the ideologies dominated by the elite; it thus works as a poignant criticism of present conditions.[28] Moxnes further suggests that for those "who had been uprooted from their place of identity, the sayings about the kingdom . . . served to reinstate them in a location that could give them a new identity."[29] One of the "imagined places" for the kingdom was located in the house and household. As we will see below, Jesus' first disciples are dislocated from their households and become (up)rooted in a new social location among fictive kin.

What might this mean with respect to Jesus' connection to homelessness? Aside from the homeless population functioning as a symptom of the reigning sociopolitical order, the conceptual spaces opened by the imaginary of the *basileia* facilitates the raising of questions about the objective violence that underscores social reality. In neoliberal societies, for example, the homeless are predominantly depicted as moral and economic failures, or worse, as victims incapable of effecting political change by themselves (without the help of the "more fortunate"). Similarly, in first-century Palestine, expendables, at the very bottom of the social hierarchy, were seen to lack intelligent or moral character and fell outside the purview of social responsibility.[30] According to Anthony J. Saldarini, the expendable class was for those whom society had no place or need. In a description that rings true of not only the modern homeless population but also the Matthean Jesus, he writes that expendables had been displaced for a variety of reasons including "population

28. Halvor Moxnes, *Putting Jesus in His Place: A Radical Vision of Household and Kingdom* (Louisville: Westminster John Knox, 2003), 108–109.

29. Ibid., 124.

30. Gerhard E. Lenski, *Power and Privilege: A Theory of Social Stratification* (New York: McGraw-Hill, 1966), 180–84.

pressures or [because] they did not fit into society. They tended to be landless and itinerant with no normal family life and a high death rate."[31] Although Jesus is associated with a family of artisans, he eventually descends the social ladder to occupy the socio-symbolic space of an expendable, and consequently is disposed of on the cross at Golgotha. Jesus' public proclamation of the *basileia* challenges the fantasy that homelessness exists as a private, individualized responsibility. Rather, it exposes homelessness as a product of systemic violence inherent within existing arrangements of social and political power.

Who Should Repent?

Because Jesus' proclamation involves the potential re-ordering of the wider ideological-political constellation, we ought to investigate the intended audience of Jesus' injunction to repent. Within Matthew, I contend, "repentance" signifies not merely a private religious encounter, but rather a corporate activity of social and political transformation.

The verb μετανοέω (and its related noun form ἡ μετάνοια) in its basic sense describes the changing of one's mind. It also conveys the idea of a total reorientation of behavior, "to feel remorse" and/ or "to be converted" in a variety of relationships and in connection to varied responsibilities of the moral, political, social, and religious spheres.[32] Contemporary theological understandings of repentance typically assume a *subjective* logic, with a focus on the individual. Because no specific character groups are designated by Jesus' call to repent, the imperative tends to be read in generic ways that place the burden of responding to moral failure on individuals (inadvertently

31. Anthony J. Saldarini, *Pharisees, Scribes and Sadducees in Palestinian Society*, 2nd ed. (Grand Rapids, MI: Eerdmans, 2001), 44.
32. "μετανοέω," *BDAG* 640.

re-inscribing a neoliberal emphasis on personal responsibility). With the exception of the generic proclamations in Matthew 3:2 and 4:17, however, the Matthean text only ever uses the verb in an *objective* sense (i.e., independent of a single conscious entity or subject).[33]

Repentance as a theme is not as strong within Matthew as it is in Luke: μετάνοια occurs only twice (Matt. 3:8, 11) both times in relation to the Baptist (compared to five in Luke); μετανοέω occurs five times (compared to nine in Luke), once from the Baptist (3:2), and four times from Jesus (4:18; 11:20; 11:21; 12:41). The Baptist declares that the Pharisees and Sadducees coming for baptism—scathingly referred to as a "brood of vipers!"—must "bear fruit worthy of repentance" (3:7–8). Jesus then continues in the tradition of the Baptist's prophetic speech with his own proclamation in 4:17. W. D. Davies and Dale Allison write that "Israel is called to turn to God and away from sin, to arise in moral earnestness from a sinful slumber and to gain a wakeful heart and sober thought."[34] Note here the corporate dimension: the call invokes all of Israel to change, including its social and political structures.

Similarly, the mention of repentance in 11:20–24 is also connected to corporate entities. On this occasion Jesus reproaches the cities (πόλεις) in which most of his deeds of power in Matthew 8–9 have taken place "because they did not repent." The term πόλις denotes a population center of varying size. Within the Greco-Roman world the term generally held strong political associations, particularly in terms of the city-state. While in the ancient world most people did not live in cities, they were (like their modern equivalents) "the

33. Within Matthew, repentance is not a prerequisite for following Jesus. When Jesus goes about instructing pairs of individuals to follow him (chs. 18–22) he does not ask them to repent. As we will see, this strengthens the claim for understanding Matthean repentance as a corporate, political act, over and above an individual, moralistic act of piety.
34. W. D. Davies and Dale C. Allison, *The Gospel According to Saint Matthew 1–7*, ICC (Edinburgh: T&T Clark, 1988), 306.

centres where justice was administered, trade carried on, records kept, scribes trained, armies recruited, labour organized, power exercised."[35] This implies that Jesus expected these centers of power to repent, in all their systemic and symbolic capacity, and by not doing so they open themselves to God's wrath (11:23-24).[36] This corporate dimension to repentance is also found in the final Matthean occurrence of μετανοέω in 12:41. Jesus confronts Israel as a collective body and his condemnation of "this generation" can be likened to the Hebrew prophets' theodicizing about the generation sent into Babylonian exile.[37]

As with the major Old Testament prophets, then, the Baptist and Jesus' calls to repentance are based on the conviction that radical change must occur on a societal level. The prophets warned against systemic violence present within the religious, social, and political structures of ancient Israel (e.g., Jer. 23:3, 13-17; 21:11-12; Mic. 3:9-10, and so on). Repentance, for the Matthean text, appears to have more to do with the reorientation of these structures than with individual piety. This brings us back to the meaning produced by Jesus' proclamation of the *basileia* if understood as a response to sociopolitical displacement: repentance in the Matthean text involves the turning away from sin and toward God of not merely *individuals* but rather *entire political systems*, including especially those city-states perpetuating asymmetrical social and economic relations.

35. J. W. Rogerson and John Vincent, *The City in Biblical Perspective* (London: Equinox, 2009), 4.

36. See especially G. E. M. Ste. Croix, *The Class Struggle in the Ancient Greek World* (Ithaca, NY: Cornell University Press, 1981), 425–41. Ste. Croix argues that the historical Jesus was essentially a prophet of the *chora* and avoided the *polis* until his fatal trip to Jerusalem.

37. The biblical background to Jesus' threats against these unrepentant cities is found in Isaiah and other prophetic writings. Jesus' comparison of Chorazin and Bethsaida to the fates of Tyre and Sidon (11:21) echoes the oracle against these cities in Isa. 23:2-4 (cf. 23:12; Ezek. 28:1-26). Moreover, the link between Sodom and Capernaum in Matt. 11:23 evokes Isa. 1:9-10a, which calls on Sodom as an example of both a destroyed and sinful city with exploitative rulers. In both these examples the cities are judged collectively, in tandem with the holders of political office.

Forming an Alternative Community (Matt. 4:18-25)

The first action Jesus takes after heralding the *basileia* is to form a community of disciples. Walking by the Sea of Galilee, Jesus calls two pairs of fishermen to leave their boats and follow him. Barton notes how the emphasis on brothers (ἀδελφούς) in 4:18–22, repeated twice, links to the notion that following Jesus involves joining a community "best understood as a brotherhood."[38] A comparison might be made to the contemporary homeless population that will often form small communities or networks that function as surrogates for family and home.

Analyzing the pericope through the social scientific model of collectivism and kinship, Louise Lawrence observes that

> [t]he disciples illustrate an individualistic and personal decision that opts for a 'universal' collectivist goal rather than a concern for the nuclear 'in-group' alone as defined by the amoral familism model. In some ways, these brothers show individualistic traits, their attachments are not fixed. . . . This example shows that there is a certain synthesis between individualistic and collectivist traits in Matthew's world.[39]

In this respect, the call of the first disciples can potentially facilitate a neoliberal emphasis on homelessness as a "lifestyle choice" in the world before the text, requiring a careful reading against the grain. Conventional interpretations frequently construct 4:18–22 as a *model* of faithful conversion to Christian discipleship. Jesus goes about calling two pairs of brothers to leave their former lives and reorient themselves around him and the kingdom. Craig Keener, for instance, suggests that the purpose of 4:18–22 is to "demonstrate people's proper response to God's rule . . ." but more than this, the text "provides Matthew's community [and by extension all Christians?]

38. Barton, *Discipleship*, 129.

39. Louise Lawrence, *An Ethnography of the Gospel of Matthew* (Tübingen: Mohr Siebeck, 2003), 241.

several examples of servant leadership and radical discipleship."[40] Likewise, Davies and Allison claim the text "serves an aetiological function, for it recounts the acts whereby Jesus began to make men into missionaries. This means that we have before us the birth of the Christian mission. Also before us is the birth of the church, the decisive moment when people first threw in their lot with the cause of Jesus."[41]

This paradigmatic framing of 4:18-22, no doubt influenced by dominant theological interests, however, can also function to unnecessarily obscure other possibilities of meaning. In fact, the application of a feminist hermeneutics of suspicion reveals a glaring ideological inconsistency: the emphasis on only male disciples filters out women who do not feature here. As we will see below, the predominant focus on these characters as examples of faithful discipleship has meant that the text's social and cultural texture have remained relatively underexplored.

Existing studies that attempt to accentuate the sociopolitical context of the text can also serve the interests of dominant ideologies. In his discussion of the ways in which 4:18-22 raises the issue of the disciples' relationship to wider society, for example, Carter describes their characterization as "voluntary marginal." He elaborates that this consists in their "choosing" to live a liminal existence in alternative households because of existing ideology, commitments, and visions of reality.[42] In his commentary, Carter draws on the social scientific criticism of Dennis Duling to construct a binary of "voluntary marginality" versus "involuntary marginality."[43] This construction,

40. Craig S. Keener, *The Gospel of Matthew: A Socio-Rhetorical Commentary* (Grand Rapids, MI: Eerdmans, 2009), 149.

41. Davies and Allison, *Matthew 1–7*, 404.

42. Warren Carter, "Matthew 4:18–22 and Matthean Discipleship: An Audience-oriented Perspective," *CBQ* 59, no. 1 (1997): 58–59.

43. Carter, *Margins*, 43–49; Dennis Duling, *A Marginal Scribe: Studies in the Gospel of Matthew in a Social-Scientific Perspective* (Eugene OR: Cascade Books, 2011), 125–28.

however, does not correspond to the reality that marginalization is always a dynamic process involving a combination of internal and external pressures and influences. While such models are intended to simplify, the lack of nuance and stark contrast between so called "voluntary" and "involuntary" categories functions to affirm the logic of neoliberalism: if marginality is voluntary, then the responsibility for its consequences lies with the individuals affected. Marginality in all its complexity always involves subjective, inter-subjective, and objective processes interacting with one another. Even purposeful or strategic ideologies and commitments that are marginal are always produced within a specific context. While it is reasonable to infer that by joining Jesus the disciples move further to the periphery, the implicit assumption among many interpreters is that these characters do not already occupy a marginal space. It is with this observation in mind that we explore the socioeconomic location of these characters in more detail. Accordingly, the label "in/voluntary" is employed below as a means of fragmenting these categories when discussing the disciples' "decision" to join Jesus.

Fishing for Fishermen

Repetition indicates that the shared occupation of Jesus' new followers is a major topic in the discourse of 4:18-22: the casting nets (τὰ δίκτυα) used to catch fish are mentioned three times; the occupation and activity of fishing appears twice (ἁλιεῖς); boat (πλοίῳ/πλοῖον) is used twice; and the sea/lake (θάλασσαν) is mentioned twice. Furthermore, the word-play in verse 19 is generated by their occupation: Jesus declares that he "will make you fish for people."[44]

44. For a detailed study of this phrase, see Wilhem H. Wuellner, *The Meaning of "Fishers of Men"* (Philadelphia: Westminster, 1967).

Does the disciples' shared occupation as fishermen mean they enjoy relative economic security or perhaps even prosperity? Daniel Harrington, for example, suggests that "[i]n light of the importance of the fishing business at the Sea of Galilee it is clear that the first followers of Jesus were leaving behind a secure and stable lifestyle."[45] Similarly, in documenting the extensive and economically significant fishing industry of the Sea of Galilee, Keener deduces that by leaving their livelihood these first disciples are making a major economic sacrifice. He claims that successful fishermen, even if not high on the social scale, were far better off than the peasantry.[46] Such interpretations intend to heighten the dramatic sacrifice these characters make in following Jesus, thereby heightening their function as role models of individual discipleship.

Recent social scientific scholarship, however, has challenged the belief that fishermen were financially secure. In examining the fishing industry as a sub-system within the political and domestic economy of first-century Galilee, K. C. Hanson identifies the "relationships between the various players within the sub-system: the Roman Emperor; Herod Antipas; the tax administrators; the brokers, tax collectors, and toll collectors; the fishing families; the hired laborers; the suppliers of raw goods and other produces; fish processors; and shippers and carters."[47] Hanson cautions that although fishing was an important component of the Galilean economy, "it was not the 'free enterprise' which modern readers of the New Testament may imagine. Even fishers who may have owned their own boats were

45. Daniel J. Harrington, *The Gospel of Matthew*, Sacra Pagina (Collegeville, MN: Liturgical Press, 2007), 72. Davies and Allison suggest that Peter, Andrew, James, John, and Zebedee appear to have belonged to the same fishing partnership which included a number of hired servants (cf. Mark 1:16-20; John 21:1-3). As such, they believe they were probably "from the (lower) middle class." Davies and Allison, *Matthew 1–7*, 397.

46. Keener, *Matthew*, 151–53.

47. K. C. Hanson, "The Galilean Fishing Economy and the Jesus Tradition," *BTB* 27, no. 3 (1997): 99.

part of a state regulated, elite-profiting enterprise, and a complex web of economic relationships" including heavy taxation that extracted wealth produced by the local industry and funneled it directly to support the lifestyle of projects of elite society.[48]

Hanson points out that the economic structures of the ancient Mediterranean "were not independent systems with 'free markets,' free trade, stock exchanges, monetization, and the like, as one finds in modern capitalist systems."[49] Rather, the mechanisms of the economy were structured in terms of the flow of benefits upward to the urban elites, and especially the ruling families (one might point out, of course, that the same is true within capitalism). We ought, therefore, to refrain from imagining individuals who "go to work;" rather their activity was embedded in various and complex domestic-economic and political-economic relationships including peasant families and households. Hanson forcefully argues that families of fishermen would fit broadly into the "peasant" strata of society and not in some kind of idealized and anachronistic "middle class."

Given all this, we might ask to what extent the conditions of these disciples' employment influence their "decision" to leave their livelihoods and to follow Jesus. At best, these fishermen have a precarious existence, marginal in economic security to landed peasants and the small minority of urban elites. It is not much of a stretch, then, to imagine a scenario in which their hardship would provoke them to abandon work and live as drifters, especially if they were heavily indebted. Indeed, the withdrawal of Jesus in 4:12 sets the scene for the in/voluntary withdrawal of the fishermen from their boats and from full participation in the reigning ideological-political order.

48. Ibid.
49. Ibid., 100.

Another important observation is that by leaving their households and following Jesus, these first disciples move further to the margins of first-century Palestinian society. Given the context of an honor and shame saturated culture, the male disciples' dislocation from the household means that their identities as householders and/or sons of the household are strained. As Moxnes puts it, for Jesus and the disciples to be "without a house, in no-place, was therefore to be deprived of a role either as a householder, which given his age would have been his normal position, or as a son in a household."[50] Accordingly, their already precarious social standing within the wider socio-symbolic order is threatened. Moxnes points out that the call to discipleship narratives are about leaving a place of social identity that defines, secures, and structures one's identity. He continues, "The young male followers of Jesus had left their established, if inferior, position in the male world and were in a liminal situation."[51] The withdrawal of the fishermen from their boats complements the withdrawal of Jesus following the arrest of the Baptist in verse 12. Just as Jesus is thrust to the outside, so too, the already marginal social statuses of the first disciples is exacerbated. An emphasis on this deviant aspect of their shared itinerancy potentially disrupts attempts at its romanticization. This inner group of followers represents the formation of an alternative community of displaced brothers, banded together as a surrogate home place or fictive kinship. Jesus features as the locus around which their revolutionary activity is mobilized; his vision of the *basileia* compels them into conscious in/voluntary action. The Matthean text is ardent to expand upon this early success of Jesus' challenge to the dominant ideological-political order, and so follows the call of the first disciples

50. Moxnes, *Jesus*, 96.
51. Ibid.

by narrating the positive reception of Jesus' call to action among the crowds.

An Itinerant Ministry Spreads

The final three verses of this text (4:23–25) provide an overview of Jesus' ministry activity within Galilee. His deeds include preaching the good news of the *basileia* and curing sickness among the people (cf. 9:35; 10:1). Jesus' withdrawal earns him fame among those located on, and sympathizers with, the margins of first-century Palestinian society. The reader is told that "[r]eports about him spread out into the whole of Syria." Moreover, "great crowds followed him," thus setting the scene for the Sermon on the Mount beginning in Matthew 5.

Matthew 4:23 includes the first use of εὐαγγέλιον (gospel/good news) in Matthew to summarize Jesus' message of the approaching *basileia*. But for whom is the "good news" intended? The above reading would suggest that Jesus' itinerant ministry offers hope of emancipation for those who are already dispossessed in some way; the revolutionary *basileia* he proclaims alludes to a vision of a more equitable social reality. In line with the prophetic stream of the Israelite tradition, those in positions of power, and institutions of power such as the πόλις (city), are ordered to "repent," to change their direction or face the consequences of cosmic destruction on the Day of Judgment.

The text describes the growth of Jesus' movement by identifying "great crowds" following him from Galilee but also from centers of power including Jerusalem and the Decapolis (ten cities). The emphasis on centers of power indicates a fervent and widespread movement of withdrawal from normalized society and suggests growth of a countercultural resentment that can be traced back to the instability of these ruling political institutions. This narration of mass withdrawal amplifies Jesus' own displacement as symptomatic of the smooth functioning of the wider sociopolitical order.

Conclusion

This chapter has considered how Jesus' apparent decision to begin an itinerant ministry is, in fact, precipitated by external crises, most prominently, the arrest of John the Baptist. In Matthew 3, the Baptist appears on the outside in the wilderness, dispensing prophetic speech and acts and drawing great crowds out to him from the urban centers. By the end of Matthew 4, Jesus is having a similar influence, but on a much greater scale. While the disciples, introduced in verses 18-22, serve as an inner-circle to Jesus, the crowds in verses 23-25 add an outer periphery to his itinerant network.

The external sociopolitical realities of Jesus' predicament are internalized in the character of Jesus as he engages his wider ideological-political environment. After withdrawing to Galilee Jesus publically announces the *basileia*—an imaginary space in which the symbolic order of society is reversed. Within this restructuring, displaced subjects, like Jesus, are afforded honor and uplifting, whereas the elite and retainers of the status quo are dishonored and dethroned. The vision is accompanied by an injunction to repent, not directed at individual men and women, but rather to the entire ideological-political constellation. Such prophetic dissent unsettles the sensibilities of the normalized population, and Jesus will ultimately be suppressed through lethal violence.

Jesus' first disciples are fishermen who abandon their fishing boats and their livelihoods to follow him. Their withdrawal is not arbitrary, but rather is integrated with their occupation and class struggle as it is encoded within the text. An emphasis on the socioeconomic realities specific to the fishing industry in first-century Palestine adds much needed complexity to the disciples' in/voluntary decision to leave the house and/or household structure.

As we have seen, some of the prevailing contemporary concerns of neoliberal ideology can both influence and limit biblical interpretation. Rather than presenting Jesus and his first disciples as individual, free-roaming, moral agents, able to make isolated economic choices, the Matthean text embeds these characters within a wider social and political context within which they are in constant negotiation. Far from "choosing" to become homeless and begin an itinerant ministry, Jesus is already a displaced and uprooted subject. The text, accordingly, gestures towards external sociopolitical realities that become internalized in Jesus as an experience of perpetual uprooting and displacement.

10

Romans 13:1-7

With an Eye to Global Capital

Bruce Worthington

> I think we should just trust our President in every decision that he makes and we should just support that.
>
> –Britney Spears[1]

Introduction

Within the history of modern, liberal, protestant biblical scholarship, interpretation of the Christian's role within the state apparatus has consistently been defined in relation to, and often in contradistinction to, Romans 13:1-7. This passage is a nasty hangnail to the free-thinking protestant theologian, a theologian armed with modernist notions of political freedom, one who cannot but read

1. "Britney Spears: Trust our President in every Decision." CNN. September 3, 2003. http://www.cnn.com/2003/SHOWBIZ/Music/09/03/cnna.spears.

the apostle Paul through the lens of Rousseau, Locke, and Hobbes. When modern western political theory, and modern western biblical interpretation converge on the issue of political ontology, the result has been a tradition that has been unable to reconcile Romans 13:1-7 with (strangely enough, quasi-Pauline) notions of freedom, political emancipation, and justice.[2] Might we know Paul better than Paul knows himself? Or is the rust on this ancient idea of political ontology too thick to make shine? Perhaps this passage would be easier to ignore, if not for its popular usage among some biblical scholars, ones who welcome the notion of political subjection, and the inference that political subjection is also theological subjection, and vice versa. If anything, the growing irrelevance of modern western statecraft within the context of global capital and its emerging power puts an interesting twist on the whole notion of political subjection in Romans 13:1-7, a point to which the history of interpretation has failed to catch up.[3]

2. Here, I am referring to the "canon" of modern Western political thought: J. J. Rousseau, *The Social Contract and Other Later Political Writings*, ed. Victor Gourevitch (Cambridge: Cambridge University Press, 1997), John Locke, *Two Treatises of Government*, ed. Peter Laslett (Cambridge: Cambridge University Press, 1988), and Thomas Hobbes, *Leviathan*, ed. Richard Tuck (Cambridge: Cambridge University Press, 1996). In *Two Treatises of Government*, Locke suggests "we must consider what state all men are naturally in, and that is, a state of perfect freedom to order their actions, and dispose of their possessions, and persons as they think fit, within the bounds of the law of nature, without asking leave, or depending on the will of any other man . . . a state also of equality, wherein all the power and jurisdiction is reciprocal, no one having more than another" (269). And Rousseau in *The Social Contract* suggests (in contradiction to theological justifications of authority) "I say, then, that sovereignty, since it is nothing but the exercise of the general will, can never be alienated, and that the sovereign, which is nothing but a collective being, can only be represented by itself" (57).
3. Given the complexities of power within the system of global capital, biblical interpretation has failed to take up the task of interpreting Romans 13:1-7 in light of a nuanced understanding of power. As power has been divested from the state and handed over to global capital, what difference does this now make in our reading of Romans 13:1-7? How does the ubiquity of global capital change the lens from which we read and theologize about Romans 13:1-7?

Methodology

The purpose of this paper is not to reveal a new historicist meaning hidden underneath the cryptic paeranetic of Romans 13:1-7. No, I have not found another useful ancient bas relief, and there is no new information on the written correspondence between Roman official X and their political subordinates Y (there are not enough bas reliefs of Nero or letters from Cicero in the whole world to solve this debate). Instead, my simple aim is to compare and apply the hermeneutical insights of Hans-Georg Gadamer and Jurgen Habermas to the interpretation of Romans 13:1-7, and suggest how the application of their hermeneutical methods lead to vastly alternative interpretations of the aforementioned biblical text. In an age when political ontology is being questioned by the political Left (Occupy Wall Street), the political Right (Tea Party libertarian movement), and made increasingly irrelevant by the ubiquity of global capital, the ongoing interpretation of Romans 13:1-7 is an important task for the theologian committed to economic and political justice. I conclude the paper by suggesting that a reading of Romans 13:1-7 that ignores the impact of global capital on contemporary power structures is naïve to the true force of global capital in the world, and fails to recognize the illocutionary (sometimes quite locutionary!) impact of global capital on biblical interpretation. For us, the Christian interpretive question is no longer "how does Romans 13 fashion my disposition toward the State?" (an outdated horizon), but now instead "how does Romans 13 fashion my disposition toward the true seat of authority in the world, that of global capital?"

Romans 13:1-7: A Brief History of Interpretation

History of interpretation is particularly important for Gadamer in *Truth and Method*, as "the hermeneutical experience is concerned with tradition."[4] There are three main streams of interpretation regarding the notion of political authority in Romans 13:1-7: (1) it is as it is (Paul's words mean what they ostensibly say); (2) it is not as it is (Paul's meaning is something other than the surface sense of his words); (3) it never was (Paul never said these words). The first method of interpretation, "it is as it is," is congenial to more conservative interpretations of Romans 13:1-7—authority is real, it is endowed by God, and it is sustained in the created order that should not be broken. In this interpretation of Romans 13:1-7, C. K. Barrett, Douglas Moo, John Stott, and others take up the enduring position:

> Accordingly it was the Christ believers' duty to maintain the machinery of the State, and to recognize in it God's own appointed means of preserving the stability and moral order of the world, and of putting his wrath into operation before the day of wrath.[5]

The "it is as it is" interpretive stream implies a certain realism to the imposition of power: authority is not a clever illocutionary act; rather it is made obvious in the created world, and understood through objective features of established political discourse. Here, there is a direct correspondence between celestial authority and its analogous manifestation in an ordered, rational cosmic hierarchy:

> The civil power has Divine sanction. Its functions are to promote well being, to punish not the good, but the wicked. Hence it must be obeyed. Obedience to it is a Christian duty and deprives it of all its terrors.[6]

4. Hans-Georg Gadamer, *Truth and Method*, 2nd ed. (New York: Continuum, 2004), 352.
5. C. K. Barrett, *A Commentary on the Epistle to the Romans* (New York: Harper and Row, 1957), 228.
6. William Sanday and Arthur Headlam, *A Critical and Exegetical Commentary on the Epistle to the Romans* (London: T&T Clark, 1901), 365. The notion of authority as a "double reference"

The "it is as it is" interpretive stream relies heavily on comparing Romans 13:1-7 to other contemporaneous appraisals of power—that of Josephus (*Bell. Jud.* II.vii.7), the Book of Wisdom (6.1-3), the Book of Enoch (xlvi.5), and the like, suggesting that Paul establishes a similar correspondence between celestial and civic authority.[7]

The notion of a one-to-one correspondence between celestial and civic authority has been challenged by the second, "it is not as it is" (or, Paul's meaning is not what it seems) interpretive stream. This interpretation highlights the fact that Paul himself suffered under unjust punishment from civic rulers (see Acts 16:22, 37; 2 Cor. 11:25), and elsewhere speaks against "the rulers of this age" with great hostility (1 Cor. 2:8), viewing principalities and powers in the celestial realm as "opponents" to the gospel (Rom. 8:38). Proponents of the "it is not as it is" interpretation of Romans 13 include our colleague in this volume Neil Elliott, who suggests that Paul was pragmatically concerned to ward off civil disturbances (like the tax riot in Puteoli, Suetonius's report of tumults, disturbances in Alexandria) that would put the Jewish members of the Roman congregation in deep danger, especially after their expulsion under Claudius in 49 ce.[8] In a similar vein, Robert Jewett argues that Paul's language of "willing submission" of all (Roman citizen or not) to

to both celestial authority and its analogous civic authority is also taken up by K. L. Schmidt, G. Dehn, O. Cullmann, and Karl Barth. See C. E. B. Cranfield, *The Epistle to the Romans* (Edinburgh: T&T Clark, 1979), 2:657.

7. Such a position seems to have also been taken up by the early church, shown in the writings of Justin Martyr, *Apology* 1.17; Tertullian, *Apology of Tertullian* 30, 39; See Clement of Rome in *Letter to the Corinthians*: "Give concord and peace to us and to all that dwell on earth . . . while we render obedience to Thine Almighty and most excellent name, and to our rulers and governors on the earth. Thou, Lord and Master, has given them power of sovereignty through thine excellent and unspeakable might, that we, knowing the glory and honour which Thou hast given them, may submit ourselves unto them, in nothing resisting Thy will."

8. Neil Elliott, *The Arrogance of Nations: Reading Romans in the Shadow of Empire*, Paul in Critical Contexts (Minneapolis: Fortress Press, 2008), 154. It should be noted that Elliott's reading of Romans 13:1-7 in *The Arrogance of Nations* does not avoid addressing the situation of the contemporary reader, and, in a sense, my reading is only an extension of his work in that book.

civic authority is a recognizable critique of Roman rule, one that makes Paul's hearers active agents, far removed from an authoritarian ethic of obedience.[9] Finally, T. L. Carter notes that the "slavishly deferential" tone in which Roman rule is characterized, and the recognizably implausible manner in which authority is articulated by Paul, would have tipped Paul's Roman audience towards a noticeably "ironic" reading of Romans 13:1-7.[10] Underlying the "it is not as it is" interpretive stream is the recognition that Romans 13:1-7 is incompatible with Paul's general hostility toward civic authority, and also, perhaps, incompatible with our modern, liberal, democratic notions of political consent.

The third interpretive stream, "it never was," is only an extension of the logic of "it is not as it is." The "it never was" interpretive stream relies on the ancient practice of interpolation, namely, that Paul never actually wrote Romans 13:1-7, thus explaining the apparent contradiction between the paraenetic of Romans 13:1-7 with the rest of his body of work. Such a position, taken up by James Kallas, R. M. Hawkins, Winsome Munro, and others, suggests that "Paul could not have ascribed such an exalted status to Rome without being not only hypocritical and servile, but untrue to his whole theological position."[11] This interpretive stream has been unpersuasive to the majority of biblical historians, as many cite the absence of corroborating textual variants to this hypothesis, and the existence of manuscript evidence (like P46) that can be cited as external support for the early, basic structure of Romans (including 13:1-7).[12] This interpretive tradition should not be casually overlooked, however,

9. Robert Jewett, *Romans: A Commentary*, Hermeneia (Minneapolis: Fortress Press, 2006), 787–90.
10. T. L. Carter, "The Irony of Romans 13," *NovT* 46, no. 3 (2004): 209.
11. James Kallas, "Romans XIII:1–7: An Interpolation," *NTS* 11 (1964–65): 365. See also R. M. Hawkins, "Romans: A Reinterpretation," *JBL* 60, no. 2 (1941): 129–40; Winsome Munro, *Authority in Paul and Peter* (Cambridge: Cambridge University Press, 1983), 79.
12. Elliott, *Arrogance of Nations*, 153.See also Richard Longenecker, *Introducing Romans: Critical Issues in Paul's Most Famous Letter* (Grand Rapids, MI: Eerdmans, 2011), 18.

as it indicates our deep modern, democratic urge to make sense of hostile, authoritarian, or violent biblical texts—even at the expense of our own historical rigor.

I have sketched out a brief history of interpretation in order that we might see this text within its various contestations—ranging from "it is as it is" (authority is normative) to the anarchic "it never was" interpretation. The sheer range of conclusions regarding Romans 13:1-7 is hardly Paul's own fault, rather it indicates an interaction with a wholly alternative horizon of political meaning—the clash of values between Paul's world and ours. Being situated in such a vast interpretive tradition is not a limit to the freedom of knowledge, but rather that which makes knowledge of Romans 13:1-7 possible.[13]

When in Rome? Gadamer Visits Romans 13:1-7

The reason we ask penetrating questions and come up with (sometimes silly) theories of interpolation is nothing other than our being influenced by the prejudices of modern western statecraft: the dialectic between Romans 13:1-7 and our historically effected consciousness presents an Otherness of the text that cannot be subsumed by critical (albeit sentimental) scholarship. The prejudices contained within our search for meaning in Romans 13 are not at all negative; they are indispensible elements, a necessary precondition for asking the proper historical question in the first place.[14]

No, let's be even more brutally honest with ourselves: the reason we are interested in interpreting Romans 13:1-7 is because it continues to appear false. This side of the Holocaust, we are correct to ask our absolutely historically conditioned question—*Is political authority really a reflection of celestial authority?* Looking honestly

13. Gadamer, *Truth and Method*, 354.
14. B. H. McLean, *Biblical Interpretation and Philosophical Hermeneutics* (Cambridge: Cambridge University Press, 2012), 184.

at the "use and abuse" of authority in the twentieth century (see here Holocaust, Gulag, Pol-Pot, Suharto, Sukarno, Pinochet, Saddam Hussein, George Bush x 2), the historically effected consciousness has an increased ethical responsibility to ask questions of any text that might support the violent endeavors of powerful civic authorities.

Gadamer's notion of the historically effected consciousness is a useful idea in this regard, as it banishes the notion of self-forgetfulness in biblical interpretation: we ask the question because it is immanent to our moral/ethical concerns.[15] When we approach interpretation of Romans 13:1-7, the historically effected consciousness does so because it seems a worthwhile endeavor, yet if we falsely imagine ourselves as "innocent from prejudices," the otherness of text can no longer address us in terms of meaning and effect.[16] Paradoxically, the historically conditioned question of justice (and our experience of its opposite) is not a limit to the freedom of knowledge, or a barrier to understanding Romans 13:1-7; rather, the condition of continually suffering under unjust civic authority is a precondition to understanding, in more acute terms, the strange world encountered in Romans 13:1-7.

When interpreters (scholars or not) endeavor to understand the seemingly perverse logic of Romans 13:1-7, we bring our own horizon of meaning to the level of consciousness, a self-reflective awareness in which our own historical orientation (and experience of political devastation) is made obvious in order to find biblical history meaningful.[17] I would like to push this further: the historically effected question is not an option among many different types of hermeneutical approaches, it is not a nifty trick of left-leaning biblical interpreters, nor should it be a novelty for those tired of standard

15. Gadamer, *Truth and Method*, 337.
16. Ibid., 335.
17. McLean, *Biblical Interpretation and Philosophical Hermeneutics*, 181.

historical-critical exegesis. Historically effected consciousness can do nothing but bring the tears and cries of those who suffer under oppressive civic authority to bear in their interpretation of Romans 13:1-7; and to do anything less is to bathe in the irrelevance of subject-centered rationality. So, I disagree with the common impression that a Gadamerian reading cannot address the ethical: the historically conditioned interpreter (one aware of his or her prejudices) is always bound to reflect on the ethical conditions that give rise to their profound historical question. The historically effected consciousness is confronted with a history that is mutually irreducible in content and complicated by its own nasty ethical potentiality, one like: there is no authority except which God has established (Rom. 13:1).

Given the western emphasis on parliamentary democracy and consent of the governed (a notion imbedded in modern western political theory) that influences our modern horizon of meaning, Romans 13:1-7 confronts us with a foreign, rudimentary, awkwardly religious approach to ancient statecraft.[18] The pre-theoretical, precognitive world of the ancient text (the world of the governed) is a cosmos of ordered rationality, one governed by reciprocity, patronage, and piety.[19] In the examples provided above (Josephus, Tertullian, Justin Martyr, etc.) we experience a strange depiction of the cosmos as ordered hierarchy, a world in which God selects and maintains political authority to reflect God's own interests in the world. What might be an affront to our modern democratic horizon of meaning—that God ordains government—is often perceived in antiquity as blessing to the poor and dispossessed. The notion that civic authorities are servants of God (Rom. 13:4) is not perceived as

18. I realize that "ancient statecraft" is an anachronism, but I think it helps in the definition of how we understand the phenomenon of ancient political organization(s).

19. Elliott, *Arrogance of the Nations*, 157.

hegemonic threat to an ideal notion of liberty, rather *it is good news* to those who suffer under them:

> Hear therefore, O ye kings, and understand; learn, ye that be judges of the ends of the earth. Give ear, ye that rule the people, and glory in the multitude of nations. For power is given you of the Lord, and sovereignty from the Highest, who shall try your works, and search out your counsels. Because, being ministers of his kingdom, ye have not judged aright, nor kept the law, nor walked after the counsel of God; Horribly and speedily shall he come upon you: for a sharp judgment shall be to them that be in high places. (Ws 6:1-5)

The strange ancient notion that God selects, appoints, and disposes of civic authorities brings us into contact with an ancient cosmos of ordered rationality, and while this strangeness is certainly not a property of the text (it would have seemed quite normal to ancient interlocutors), it becomes meaningful only when located within our own horizon of political meaning (modern, western democracy, etc.).[20] In our confrontation with this alternative horizon of meaning, a gap is created whereby the interpreter can see beyond the former limits of his or her own historically effected consciousness.[21] In this intermediate place of fusion, Romans 13:1-7 is no longer a separate object, rather it can be located within a tradition of interpretation, and the contingent nature of the ancient world (and ours as well) is revealed.[22] By a fusion of horizon, Gadamer does not plainly endorse the notion that horizons seamlessly blend together in a trialectical synthesis, nor do horizons always amalgamate together to form a new horizon of meaning. Instead, in our reflections on an ancient alternative horizon (like Rom. 13:1–7), we are brought into contact with an Otherness that reveals our own horizon even more acutely.

20. McLean, *Biblical Interpretation and Philosophical Hermeneutics*, 191.
21. Gadamer, *Truth and Method*, 388.
22. McLean, *Biblical Interpretation and Philosophical Hermeneutics*, 192.

Here, Gadamer is in agreement with Emmanuel Levinas—the irreducible qualities of the Other (the pre-theoretical, ordered cosmos of Rom. 13:1-7) can never be fully known and analyzed as an object separate from a historically conditioned consciousness.[23] Like Levinas, a Gadamerian fusion of horizons engenders an open determinacy within a dialogical framework: the reiterability of historical documents is best accomplished through a self-reflective awareness of their interpreter. As mentioned above, this fusion of horizons can be an ethical act itself—one where *the questions we ask of the text remain immanent to our own moral/ethical concerns*. In light of the continued oppression of political subjects dominated by leaders who consistently seek transcendent justification for their acts, the historically effected consciousness has an ethical mandate to question this theological justification of power and thereby seek new, inexhaustible conditions of knowledge—so that we might not remain the same.

Habermas and the Pauline Ideological Insight

The application of Habermasian and Gadamerian hermeneutics is quite helpful in identifying both the locutionary and illocutionary elements of Romans 13:1-7.[24] In articulating a fairly standard depiction of reified civic authority (they are God's servants), Paul makes a rather common, self-evident statement of affairs, one that reflects the popularly held belief of power as divinely ordained (Josephus, *Wisdom*, *Enoch*, Justin Martyr, Tertullian etc.). In explicating a fairly conservative notion of ancient statecraft, Romans 13:1-7 makes a clear *locutionary* statement about civic authority,

23. Ibid., 263.
24. For a fuller explanation of Habermas's use of performative speech utterances, see Jürgen Habermas, *The Theory of Communicative Action: Reason and the Rationalization of Society*, trans. Thomas McCarthy (Boston: Beacon, 1984), 1:288–338, and J. L. Austin, *How to Do Things with Words* (Cambridge, MA: Harvard University Press, 1975).

expressing the state of affairs in a propositional manner.[25] Such an approach identifies with common imperial propaganda regarding the peaceful reign of Rome, propaganda that sought to distance the Julio-Claudian dynasty from its violent beginnings and establish the (illusory) notion of a peaceful empire:

> With all things at my disposal, I have been moved neither by anger nor youthful impulse to unjust punishment . . . with me *the sword is hidden*, nay, is sheathed; I am sparing thee to the utmost of even the meanest of blood; no man fails to find favour at my hands though he lack all else but the name of a man.[26]

> Unarmed, our youth can dig the fields, and the boy, trained to the slow moving plow, marvels at the sword hanging in the abode of his fathers.[27]

While providing a common, typical description of the state of Roman civic affairs, the locutionary aspect of the text meets its own ideological limit in the healthy cynicism of Romans 13:4, "the rulers do not bear the sword for no reason." In such a context where popular Roman propaganda sought to disavow the sword as a Roman tool of occupation, Paul's reminder that civic authority continues to bear the sword is a compelling ideological insight. The locutionary "state of affairs" (or Paul's ancient political realism) is complicated by the ideological notion that we all now understand—every symbolic system requires the real or implied threat of violence to be maintained. In reminding the congregation in Rome to be aware of the sword, Paul makes obvious the necessary appeal to a violence that all bids to empire must make, clarifying the illocutionary message implied by the public proclamation of imperial propaganda. Read in an intertextual manner, Romans 13:1-7 reflects *both* the locutionary message of Roman propaganda, and also its inferred illocutionary

25. Habermas, *Theory of Communicative Action*, 288.
26. Nero via Seneca, De Clementia, 1.2–4.
27. Virgil, Eclogue, II.

effect—the reification of civic authority can always and only be justified through imperial violence.

Within the cycle of political subjection outlined in Romans 13:1-7, the whole of ideology (both the locutionary and the illocutionary, the Repressive State Apparatus and the Ideological State Apparatus) is represented in its reification of civic authority. This is not to suggest that Paul read Louis Althusser, or that he was familiar with the discourse of ideological criticism, but instead he reflects an acute knowledge of power that can be found in Habermasian terms of illocutionary force and universal pragmatics. In Paul's explication of civic authority, we find both its explicit theological justification and hidden ideological content—rulers do not bear the sword for no reason (Rom. 13:4). This completes the project of ideology, as political reality can only become what it is through its inscription into the symbolic medium.[28]

In this sense, Romans 13:1-7 reflects the Althusserian notion that ideology is maintained through *both* ideological and repressive state apparatuses. Paul is prophetic in this regard, his affirmation of imperial politics contains within itself its own demise—the locutionary declaration "all authority is from God" cannot stand alone, it always requires its own violent supplement. At just the moment when ideology as ideology appears to have disappeared in the statement "there is no authority except that which God has established," Paul's appeal to the repressive state apparatus (rulers do not bear the sword for nothing) confirms the Althusserian insight "ideological state apparatuses function mainly on the level of ideology, but from time to time rely on symbolic repression."[29] The theological justification of civic authority is consistent with the

28. Slavoj Žižek, *The Indivisible Remainder: Essays on Schelling and Related Matters* (London: Verso, 1996), 226.

29. Louis Althusser, "Ideology and Ideological State Apparatuses: Notes Towards an Investigation," in *Mapping Ideology*, ed. Slavoj Žižek (New York: Verso, 1994), 112.

religious character of an ideological state apparatus, but this theological justification is never enough—its lack is revealed in its necessary appeal to the repressive state apparatus (even when this repressive apparatus is publically disavowed by popular Roman propaganda).[30]

There is a deep connection between the locutionary appeal to "a common state of affairs" in Habermas, and the proliferation of ideological state apparatuses outlined by Althusser (religious, educational, family, legal, political). Locutionary statements like "the authorities that exist have been established by God" are only possible to the degree that they are embedded in a plurality of ideological state apparatuses (ISAs), which provide an objective field to social contradictions and determine rules of good behavior.[31] Locutionary statements that provide a rational account of common conviction are never a fixed property within themselves: meaning is never immanent to the locutionary statement, but reinforced through its illocutionary (or ideological) supplement. It is the constant task of ideological state apparatuses to determine the illocutionary (even perlocutionary) effect of its own statements, embedding ideology in what appear as rational, common sense accounts of the world. "The one in authority is God's servant" (Rom. 13:4).

The goal of repeating locutionary statements like Romans 13:1–7 is to produce a subjectivity such that no appeal should be made to the repressive state apparatus (RSA), yet here Paul reveals political oppression to be a property immanent to the "state of affairs" as such, and exposes the fraudulent character of Roman propaganda. In Paul's mind, civic authority cannot exist in separation from its repressive state apparatus, contradicting Julio-Claudian propaganda of a "swordless" Roman rule, and identifying the necessary

30. Ibid.
31. Ibid., 104.

connection between repressive state authority, and its embedded character within common ideological state apparatuses. For Paul, contra Roman propaganda, there is no "outside of ideology" from which we might step—even when its violence is concealed, ideology still appears as immanent to the theological justification of civic authority, or that which is "in all and through all" (Rom. 11:36).

As mentioned previously, Romans 13:1–7 contains the cyclical whole of ideology—ideology's own theological justification (and its lack), a necessary appeal to violence, and our cynical submission to the ruling ideology (pay your taxes). It is the repetitive nature of this abusive cycle that conditions the "interpellated subject" toward seeing the ideological constellation as natural, and alienates its constituents from any rational position of dissent (as the definition of rationality is controlled by ideology).

Likewise, Paul's paraenetic advice "pay your taxes" should not be considered as "ideology, for the win"; rather it reflects a deep pragmatic assessment of the situation, given the real and imagined threat of Roman imperial violence articulated in Romans 13:4 (especially after the expulsion of the Jews in Rome by Claudius in 49 ce). Because Paul understands that "there is no outside of ideology from which we might step," he reflects the *universal pragmatism* of Habermas in the advice "continue to pay your taxes." Paul does not offer an alternative theoretical program to outduel Roman imperial ideology; rather the admonishment to pay taxes is a pragmatic, shared communitarian practice that is useful in the context of ethnic and religious persecution.[32] Here, the subversive position is not the antagonistic position; rather, because Paul fully understands the totalizing effect of Roman imperial ideology, his advice reflects a

32. McLean, *Biblical Interpretation and Philosophical Hermeneutics*, 221. For more on Habermas's Universal Pragmatics, consult Uwe Steinhoff, *The Philosophy of Jürgen Habermas: A Critical Introduction* (Oxford: Oxford University Press, 2009), 182–83.

position that is reasonable, truthful, and sensible from the perspective of the persecuted community addressed.[33] Paul understands *both* the locutionary and illocutionary effect of popular Roman propaganda, and articulates a contextually pragmatic ethic that is effective for the coordination of action (spreading the gospel) within conventionally fixed obligations.[34] Note here a more depressing feature of the text: even though Paul understands the internal mechanism of imperial ideology and its violent features, there is no alternative cognitive development or heightened consciousness that can save the Roman congregation from their mundane, public obligations to the state. At this juncture, ideology presents itself as a totalizing system of meaning, so whether you understand imperial propaganda as fiction or not—pay your taxes and spread the gospel (there is no antinomy between the two).

Application

Because modern western biblical interpretation functions within the tradition of modern western political thought, scholarly interpretation of Romans 13:1-7 continues to rehash itself through the debate between whether or not Paul was an antinomian subversive.[35] This recycling of binary categories is based on a perhaps outdated notion of political sovereignty itself, one that is perpetuated by the modern illusion that private individual political freedom is both possible and preferable. The gift that ideological criticism

33. McLean, *Biblical Interpretation and Philosophical Hermeneutics*, 221. Perhaps more could be said on this topic, such as if Paul had not yet met the congregation in Rome, and this letter is his first interaction with the Roman congregation, how might this fact affect the manner in which we understand his letter as a speech act? As speech acts "establish interpersonal relations . . . and represent states and events" between two parties, how does the unfamiliarity between Paul and the church in Rome encourage, or inhibit communitarian understanding? See Habermas, *Theory of Communicative Action*, 308.
34. Habermas, *Theory of Communicative Action*, 297.
35. This contested notion is predictably split between those who theologically benefit from Paul being anti-statist or pro-statist.

imparts to the world (or the gift that unfortunately keeps on giving) is that there is no private, interior space whereby the authentic political subject might resist the effects of ideology. Pauline biblical interpretation, and the fault lines from which it interprets Paul as "pro-law" or "against-law," subversive or not, is based on the questionable modern notion that this choice is of any great significance to Paul to begin with.

Romans 13:1-7 articulates a theologically ordered cosmos within which modern notions of political authenticity are somewhat irrelevant—Paul is neither pro-law or contra-law. The question simply reflects the concerns of some of our own, for whom modern western political liberty may have existed at some point.

Let us focus our lens even more: how should the ethical Christian fashion their disposition to the state, when the state continues to appear more and more irrelevant to the new seat of global authority, which is global capital? Modern western biblical scholarship has been fascinated by the injunction Romans 13:1-7 makes on modern notions of authentic political subjectivity, because perhaps it still believes in its own dead myths of political autonomy, freedom, and western statecraft? There is still a latent orientalism in the notion of Paul as subversive political agent, as this reinvigorates the western myth of political autonomy and critical dissent in protestant biblical interpretation. (Is this not clearly a case of fashioning Paul in our own image of western revolutionary figure?)[36]

Thus, the single most important interpretive question is no longer how should one fashion his or her disposition toward the State, but rather how should one fashion his or her disposition toward the ubiquitous universality of global capital. Contemporary biblical scholarship—as it is exists within the complex matrix of global

36. See Edward Said, *Orientalism* (New York: Vintage, 1979).

capital—has (so far) failed to offer any meaningful cognitive orientation from which to map the influence of global capital on its own interpretation of texts, and therefore continues to serve as one of global capital's chief spokespersons.[37] Some helpful attempts have recently been made to articulate the local effect of capital within niche disciplines like ecological criticism, LGBT and feminist criticism, Marxist biblical criticism, and so on, but the discourse of biblical interpretation as a whole has failed to recognize the influence of global capital as that which hermeneutically isolates *itself* from criticism.

So now, the endless proliferation of disciplinary sub-genres in biblical interpretation can continue in perpetuity, as long as it does not challenge the golden egg of all capitalist interpretation—capital.[38] This is precisely how biblical interpretation continues to function as an ideological state apparatus, confirming the Althusserian base-superstructure insight.[39] In the practice of capitalist biblical interpretation (and that is what it is), political reality becomes "itself" through its inscription into the symbolic medium of the ancient world, as these ancient texts preserve the normative, ideological utility of Pauline theological ethics like submission to authority and paying taxes. Now, only an approach that combines the universality of public use of reason (see Habermas) with an engaged subjective position can offer an adequate cognitive mapping of the discourse of biblical interpretation, and identify global capital's own inscription into the symbolic medium of the ancient world.[40]

37. Perhaps this idea is made most obvious in HarperOne and Rupert Murdoch's recent takeover of more than 50 percent of popular Christian publishing.
38. This is what Michel Foucault recognizes as the ability for relations of power to extend beyond the limits of the state, as the state cannot contain the whole field of power relations within itself. See Foucault, "Truth and Power," in *Power/Knowledge: Selected Interviews and Other Writings, 1972–1977*, ed. Colin Gordon (New York: Vintage, 1980), 122.
39. Althusser, "Ideology and Ideological State Apparatuses," 105.
40. Slavoj Žižek, *The Year of Dreaming Dangerously* (London: Verso, 2012), 5.

A rigorous recognition of the effect of global capital on biblical interpretation (particularly Rom. 13:1-7) should not be viewed as an obstacle to interpretation. It is not a false consciousness that should be rejected in favor of a more immanent reading of biblical truth—to do such a thing would only repeat the naïve modernist insight that truth remains immanent to itself, or apart from capital.[41] A lesson from Paul: there is no safe place of critical dissent from which to articulate an alternative political ethic, as language is always controlled and fashioned by its own ideological constraints. Those of us involved in the Occupy movement and other recent protest movements have learned this lesson quite acutely—the State currently exists only to confirm and secure the interests of global capital, and will continue to supplement the interest of capital through its repressive state apparatuses, "for it does not bear the sword for nothing."

The strange perlocutionary impact of Romans 13:1-7 in an age of capital is this: in your limited subjectivity, become aware of power and its theological justifications, familiarize yourself with the deceitful rhetoric of your new emperor (global capital), and be prepared to suffer under the violence necessary to maintain capital's own symbolic efficacy. Romans 13:1-7 is most helpful in this regard. Its lack of alternative ethic reminds us of the totalizing, universalizing effect of capitalist ideology, and mediates the proto-ideological insight Paul stumbles upon: theological justifications of power are always maintained by the threat of symbolic violence. In Romans 13:1-7, we see the whole of ideology represented in the perverse fact that even though Paul understands the violent mechanism of ideology (and the lies of Nero) he can do nothing but continue to pay his taxes. In this regard, the subjective position fashioned by capital as a universal, totalizing system of meaning is not an obstacle to biblical

41. Žižek, *Indivisible Remainder*, 189.

interpretation, but rather a similar subjectivity fashioned by a familiar political deadlock.

Conclusion

The historically conditioned consciousness should question a modern history of interpretation that has sought to fashion a political subjectivity based on Romans 13:1-7. This is not to suggest that we should stop doing history, but rather that the world of capital is quickly passing biblical interpretation by—the modern categories of political subjectivity (a free, rational, autonomous subject) are irrelevant in light of the ubiquity of global capitalism, and the totalizing effect of ideology both then and now. The sooner we recognize this insight, the sooner we can develop kinship between ourselves and our great brother Paul, who also suffered under the totalizing effect of repressive state violence and its theological justification.

11

Occupy Solomon's Portico

On the Community of Goods in the Longue Durée

Jonathan Bernier

Let me begin with a story. It begins with the advent of anatomically modern *Homo sapiens*, let us say about two hundred thousand years ago. They subsist on nomadic hunter-gathering for quite some time, until around about ten thousand years ago when they discover agriculture and begin to settle down. They first build villages and later cities. With urbanization comes ever-increasing industry, advancing inexorably from the simple Neolithic technology of the first farmers to the marvels of the contemporary world. Alongside this movement came religious evolution: from animism to polytheism to monotheism; some might extend this sequence to include a post-monotheistic phase known as atheism. There is also political evolution: from band to tribe to chieftain to state. Somewhere in there one must situate pastoral nomadism, perhaps after hunting and gathering and before agriculture, although it tends to remain a proverbial fly in the ointment resisting easy integration into this tale.

It is a wonderful story, a just-so story.[1] The most interesting thing about this story—aside from the fact that it is told, albeit in varying forms, both by persons on the Right and the Left[2]—is that it is a lie. Of course this lie contains half-truths—the best lies always do. No doubt there existed human persons who made a living as hunter-gatherers (and hunter-fisher-gatherers) long before there existed human persons who made a living as farmers; no doubt there was a time before the advent of the urban; no doubt there was a time before the industrial revolution; and so it goes. The lie is to be found in the implication, one made explicit throughout the period since the Enlightenment, that those who make a living primarily from hunting and gathering or from pastoral nomadism occupy a space on the evolutionary scale somewhat lower than those who make a living using the most cutting-edge technology; a sort of latter-day recasting of the Great Chain of Being. According to this lie, they are not thus understood to be our contemporaries but rather our ancestors, and when we do acknowledge their contemporaneity it is only as

1. The most definitive study of the emergence of this story is Adam Kuper, *The Reinvention of Primitive Society: Transformations of a Myth* (London: Routledge, 2005), revised edition of Adam Kuper, *The Invention of Primitive Society: Transformations of an Illusion* (London: Routledge, 1988); cf. especially his discussions of "Barbarian, savage, primitive," pp. 20–39 and Lewis Henry Morgan on pp. 59–81. For the interests of this study, see especially Kuper's discussion (pp. 79–80) on Marx and Engels's engagement with Lewis Henry Morgan, *Ancient Society* (New Brunswick, NJ: Transaction, 2000 [1877]).

2. The major difference between Right and Left appropriations of this story tends to be found within a moral judgment on the movement from primitive to civilization: for the Right this tends to represent a salutary progress towards civilization whereas for the Left it tends to represent a lamentable fall from primitive perfection. The Left's appropriation of this story is of greatest interest to this study and finds its most classic articulation in Friedrich Engels, *Der Ursprung der Familie, des Privateigentums und des Staats*, Karl Marx/Friedrich Engels Gesamtausgabe [Mega] 1.29, ed. Joachim Herrmann and Hansulrich Labuske (Berlin: Dietz, 1990 [1884]), 3–114, which constitutes in main a Marxist (or perhaps more precisely "Engelian") interpretation of Morgan, *Ancient Society*. Cf. the still-powerful leftist critique of the Left's fall narrative in Murray Bookchin, *Re-enchanting Humanity: A Defense of the Human Spirit against Anti-Humanim, Misanthropy, Mysticism and Primitivism* (London: Cassell, 1995), 120–47.

our contemporary ancestors. Cultural distance is converted as if by alchemy into temporal distance.

James C. Scott—known to biblical scholars as the man who coined the term "hidden transcripts"[3]—has recently argued that this narrative needs to be largely turned on its head. Many of the groups that we in the human sciences traditionally describe as "pre-state" are in fact "post-state."[4] What unites hunting, gathering, and fishing with pastoral nomadism as well as certain forms of agriculture is that they facilitate mobility: a group engaging in these livelihoods can more easily flee efforts at state control than a group whose livelihood depends upon permanent settlement. Thus he suggests that many of the hunter-gatherer-fisher, pastoral nomad, and swidden agriculture groups known from the historic era and presumably also the prehistoric were in fact persons seeking to elude or escape state control. This would include groups who had never lived under state regimes and also groups that had lived under state regimes and now sought to live independently of them.

Such a narrative resonates strongly with Norman Gottwald's argument that pre-monarchic Israel was the result of a "retribalization"; indeed, Gottwald's understanding of ancient Israel as emerging from a process of anti-statist retribalization could be translated with fairly minor alteration into Scott's understanding of many so-called pre-state people as in fact post-state people.[5] The highlands in which the pre-monarchic Israelites settled would then

3. Cf. James C. Scott, *Domination and the Arts of Resistance: Hidden Transcripts* (New Haven, CT: Yale University Press, 1990).

4. James C. Scott, *The Art of Not Being Governed: An Anarchist History of Southeast Asia* (New Haven, CT: Yale University Press, 2009).

5. Cf. the discussions in Norman K. Gottwald, *The Tribes of Yahweh: A Sociology of the Religion of Liberated Israel, 1250–1050 BCE* (Sheffield: Sheffield Academic, 1999 [1979]), 293–337 and 474–97; cf. also the more recent discussion in Norman K. Gottwald, *The Politics of Ancient Israel*, Library of Ancient Israel (Louisville: Westminster John Knox, 2001), 35–45, 158–72. Cf. also the important volume on Gottwald and *Tribes*, Roland Boer, ed., *Tracking The Tribes of Yahweh: On the Trail of a Classic*, JSOTSup 351 (Sheffield: Sheffield Academic, 2002).

be construed as examples of what Scott describes as zones of refuge, to which "much of the population of the hills" came "to evade the manifold afflictions of state-making projects in the valleys."[6] My particular interest in this essay is not ancient Israel, however, but rather two other moments in the history of state-evasion: the early Christian occupation of Solomon's portico and the experience, in our own time, of widespread occupation of public spaces against the will of the state.

The year 2011—what Slavoj Žižek has called "The Year of Dreaming Dangerously"[7]—will be remembered as a year of revolution, and quite likely will be spoken of in the same breath as 1848, 1871, 1917, 1968, and 1989. Such revolutionary times transform our understanding of what is humanly possible, and thus what is historically and exegetically possible. Thinking back to Scott, what is significant about 2011 is that in both the Arab Spring and the Occupy movement, people set out to carve a space—a literal space—of opposition to state regimes that sought to subordinate the needs of the human person to the demands of this or that ideology. To a certain extent this is a function of the increasing enclosure of all terrestrial space within effective sovereign state control: there is simply not as much as room to flee physically from the state as there was during Iron Age I. And whilst certainly there was still much more space to move beyond the control of the state in the first century ce than there is today, nonetheless the Roman Empire presents as a moment of significant expansion of state control over Europe and the ancient Near East; the legions and other apparatuses of Roman state control made it that much more difficult to withdraw into the desert or the hills as it might have been a millennium or a millennium and a half earlier. It is against that reality that I

6. Scott, *The Art of Not Being Governed*, 22.
7. Slavoj Žižek, *The Year of Dreaming Dangerously* (London: Verso, 2012).

aim to situate Acts 4:11 and Acts 5:12-13 and argue that, just as Tahrir Square and Zucotti Park became spaces of local resistance to universalizing power in 2011 in the Arab Spring and the Occupy movements, so too did Solomon's portico become such for the earliest Christian believers. For this we need a hermeneutics of situation.

Toward a Hermeneutics of Situation

If the postmodern entailed a "hermeneutic of suspicion" (Jean-François Lyotard's "incredulity toward metanarratives),"[8] the post-postmodern (or, as Nealon puts it, in conscious allusion to Fredric Jameson,[9] "the cultural logic of just-in-time capitalism") entails a "hermeneutic of situation,"[10] one "designed to size up and respond to contemporary capitalism."[11] Here, the situational character of the revolutions of 2011 is, perhaps, brought into proper focus. Yes, these movements and moments were intensely localized, lived out as they were in Tahrir Square or Zucotti Park and a myriad other spaces ostensibly public but long since nationalized and privatized by the insatiable desire of state and market. Yet, in these distinct locales it seemed as if the whole world was speaking as one to the cosmos of global capital.

8. Jean-François Lyotard, *The Postmodern Condition: A Report on Knowledge*, trans. Geoff Bennington and Brian Massumi (Minneapolis: University of Minnesota Press, 1984), xxiv.
9. Viz. to Fredric Jameson, *Postmodernism, or, The Cultural Logic of Late Capitalism* (Durham, NC: Duke University Press, 1991).
10. Jeffrey T. Nealon, *Post-Postmodernism, or, The Cultural Logic of Just-in-Time Capitalism* (Stanford: Stanford University Press, 2012), xii. It is interesting to consider this idea of a post-postmodern "hermeneutic of situation" alongside the "principle of analogy," articulated (in)famously by Ernst Troeltsch, *Religion in History*, trans. James Luther Adams and Walter F. Bense (Minneapolis: Fortress Press, 1991), 13–14, viz. that "[t]he observation of analogies between similar events in the past provides the possibility of imputing probability to them and of interpretation what is unkown [*sic*] about the one by reference to what is known about the other." It follows reasonably from this principle that as our situation changes—that is, as we accumulate new experiences and thus new analogies—so too do the bases, indeed the very conditions, of our historical judgments.
11. Nealon, *Post-Postmodernism*, 92.

Global capital emerges then as the situation in which we must situate all contemporary situations: the context of all contexts, the meta-context, Jameson's "totality" that is late capitalism,[12] now mutated, if we are to follow Nealon, into a just-in-time capitalism. Of this situation, Alain Badiou, writing in the midst of the revolutions of 2011, suggests,

> Under the interchangeable rubrics of "modernization," "reform," "democracy," "the West," "the international community," "human rights," "secularism," "globalization," and various others, we find nothing but an historical attempt at an unprecedented regression, intent upon creating a situation in which the development of globalized capitalism, and the action of its political servants, conforms to the norms of their births: a dyed-in-the-wool liberalism of mid-nineteenth-century vintage, the unlimited power of a financial and imperial oligarchy, and a window-dressing of parliamentary government composed (as Marx put it) of "Capital's executives." To that end, everything which the existence of the organized forms of the workers' movement, communism and genuine socialism had invented between 1860 and 1980, and imposed on a world scale, thereby putting liberal capitalism on the defensive, must be ruthlessly destroyed, and the value system of imperialism—the celebrated "values"—recreated. Such is the sole content of the "modernization" underway.[13]

What a situation, if Badiou is correct: a situation in which the modest gains that the working class (both what Marx called the *Proletariat* and the *Lumpenproletariat*) have obtained over the last two centuries—gains that include the very emergence of this thing that we often, although typically without much analytical precision, call

12. Cf. the discussion in Jameson, *Postmodernism*, 399–418.

13. Alain Badiou, *The Rebirth of History: Times of Riots and Uprisings*, trans. Gregory Elliott (London: Verso, 2012), 4–5. Although Žižek, *Year of Living Dangerously*, has offered a more comprehensive analysis of 2011—writing as he did after the Occupy movement, whereas Badiou wrote in the short interval between the Arab Spring and the Occupy movement—I find Badiou's analysis more compelling. Ultimately, this is due to an overall preference for Badiou's larger philosophical framework than for Žižek's, if only because I find the former's focus upon the situation (cf. discussion later in the paper) much more amenable to a hermeneutic of situation than the latter's Lacanian-Marxist hermeneutic of suspicion.

the "middle class" (one wonders: "middle" between what and what?)[14]—are destroyed under names that increasingly are not even cloaked by the pretense of euphemism ("modernization" might lack much in the way of content, but there can be little question what an "austerity measure" might entail). One is reminded of the words that other great cultural critic, Tacitus, attributed to Calgacus: *auferre trucidare rapere falsis nominibus imperium, atque ubi solitudinem facient, pacem appellant*, "to robbery, slaughter, plunder, they falsely give the name 'empire'; they make a desert, and call it peace."[15] Violence everywhere, not least the violence to a language used to deny the very existence of the violence: that is the situation in which the early

14. David Madland, Karla Walter, and Nick Bunker, "Unions Build the Middle Class," in *The Occupy Handbook*, ed. Janet Bryne (New York: Back Bay Books, 2012), 273–75, rightly suggest that "[u]nions make the middle class safe by ensuring that workers have a strong voice in both the market and in our democracy. . . . [Yet, a]s unions have become weaker over the last four decades, they have gradually lost their ability to perform these functions—and the middle class has withered" (275). Too true. Yet, one wonders: should not those most fully protected by organized labor be described as working class? Alongside such lines, in their introduction to a recent volume devoted fully to anarchist economics, Deric Shannon, Anthony J. Nocella II, and John Askimakopoulos, "Anarchist Economics: A Holistic View," in *The Accumulation of Freedom: Writings on Anarchist Economics*, ed. Deric Shannon, Anthony J. Nocella II, and John Askimakopoulos (Oakland, CA: AK Press, 2012), 11–39, note that anarchists typically recognize the existence of a "working class," viz. "those who have to work for a living but have no real control over that work or other major decisions that affect them, i.e. order-takers" (19), as well as a "ruling class," viz. "those who control investment decisions, determine high level policy, set the agenda for capital and state" (20); and further note that some, but not all, anarchists also recognize a "'fuzziness'" between these classes, that is a "third" or "middle" class, viz. those who, whilst perhaps technically workers, have "a high degree of social power—often directly over working people. Examples of this include high-paid lawyers, tenured professors at elite universities, and so on. This class is sometimes conceived as having their own set of material interests, in opposition to the ruling class and the working class, and sometimes conceived as having similar interests as workers, but being placed above them in capitalist society due to their social power (20). If one accepts the two-level analysis, there would of course be no middle class; and if one accepts the three-level analysis, then one would probably want to locate most unionized workers within the working class. One might suggest that rather than the movement of such laborers into a putative middle class, what we have seen over the last two centuries is an increase in the material conditions of the working class, precisely through the efforts of the labor movement; and the weakening of that movement, induced in large part by its historic collusion with state powers, can only weaken the position and condition of this working class.
15. Tacitus. *Agricola and Germany*, trans. Anthony R. Birley (Oxford: Oxford University Press, 1999).

Christians existed, and one not unlike that in which we find ourselves today.

A Tale of Two Universalisms

Continuing with Badiou's analysis of the situation, we read the suggestion that

> [t]he present moment is in fact that of the first stirrings of a global popular uprising against this regression. As yet blind, naive, scattered and lacking a powerful concept or durable organization, it naturally resembles the first working-class insurrections of the nineteenth century. I therefore propose to say that we find ourselves in a *time of riots* wherein a rebirth of History, as opposed to the pure and simple repetition of the worst, is signalled and takes shape. Our masters know this better than us: they are secretly trembling and building up their weaponry, in the form both of their judicial arsenal and the armed taskforces charges with planetary order. There is an urgent need to reconstruct or create our own.[16]

Badiou expresses well a pressing reality of our time: what we are facing today is nothing less than a cosmic struggle between competing universalisms. We have already discussed one of these universalisms, naming it "capitalism," once late, now just-in-time. The other has, at least in the Occupy movement, adopted for itself the name "99%."

This second universalism, this 99%, "[a]s yet blind, naive, scattered and lacking a powerful concept or durable organization,"[17] has not necessarily worked out in exhaustive detail a platform or a programme; rather, it stands as a signal example of Ernst Bloch's "Not-Yet-Conscious," which "as a whole is the psychological representation of the Not-Yet-Become in an age and its world, on the Front of the world."[18] Following the line of thought that Bloch

16. Badiou, *Rebirth of History*, 5–6.
17. Ibid., 5.

explores across the three volumes of his masterpiece, *The Principle of Hope*, we might suggest that the Not-Yet-Conscious of the 99% is but the current expression of that universal desire for utopia in a world quite far fallen from grace: a desire expressed over and against that false utopia that is global capitalism.

When one, as a New Testament exegete, considers the Occupy movement in terms of clash of universalisms, one cannot but be reminded of Ferdinand Baur's suggestion that

> [i]t is a consideration of real significance for the history of the world, that the epoch which saw the Roman Empire complete the union of all the nations of the world as it then was in a universal monarchy, also witnessed the beginning of the religion in which all religious particularism disappeared and gave way to universalism. Christianity thus stood, in respect of its universalism, at the stage which had already been attained by the power and genius of Rome in its world-wide monarchy.[19]

We might today be less sanguine than was Baur, the doctrinaire Hegelian, in suggesting that "[i]n fact we may say that the time had come when the human spirit was to make this momentous advance,"[20] or at the very least prefer to give to his next sentence—"As the barriers and divisions between different countries and nationalities were dissolved before the ever-advancing power of the Romans, and their general subjection to a common head caused men to be aware of the unity in which their differences disappeared, the whole spiritual consciousness was proportionately enlarged, and found itself led more and more to disregard the distinctions and exclusiveness which separated men from each other, and to lay hold

18. Ernst Bloch, *The Principle of Hope*, trans. Neville Plaice, Stephen Plaice, and Paul Knight (London: Basil Blackwell, 1986), 1:127.
19. Ferdinand Christian Baur, *The Church History of the First Three Centuries*, trans. Alan Menzies (London: Williams and Norgate, 1878), 1:2–3.
20. Ibid., 1:3.

of what was universal."[21]—a more distinctly materialist spin, a turning of Baur upon his head, just as Marx turned Hegel. Such a spin might look like what Jameson described as "the ultimate horizon of human history as a whole . . . [that is], the whole complex sequence of the modes of production"[22] Here we situate the advent of both Roman and Christian universalism within the revolutionary transition from one such mode to another. Or, to return to Scott, what was happening in the era of the empire was a universalism wherein all space became imperial space: the space of the state, made legible by the genius of the Caesars, who thus became quite rightly the gods of this universalism.

Regardless how we frame the matter, Baur's emphasis upon the universalism of early Christianity—as well as its "Other," viz. the Roman Empire—is quite apposite when one considers that on the day of Pentecost[23] "Parthians, Medes, Elamites, and residents of

21. Ibid.

22. Fredric Jameson, *The Political Unconscious: Narrative as a Socially Symbolic Act* (Ithaca, NY: Cornell University Press, 1981), 76. The theory of the modes of production—which states that the economic organization, or base, of any given society conditions fundamentally the mode of life within said society—is arguably that which most distinctly renders an interpretation as Marxist in orientation. Cf. the overview of Jameson's specific treatment of the modes of production provided by biblical scholar Roland Boer, *Jameson and Jeroboam* (Atlanta: Scholars Press, 1996), 79–97.

23. Statements about what happened on the first Christian Pentecost, or at other moments narrated by Acts, raise the spectre of historicity. There often seems a strong correlation between radical politics and what we might describe as minimalist assessments of the historicity of biblical narratives; a signal example of this in the study of the Acts of the Apostles is perhaps the work of Todd Penner, who on the one hand is sympathetic to both feminist and postcolonial concerns, as exemplified in Caroline Vander Stichele and Todd Penner, eds., *Her Master's Tools? Feminist and Postcolonial Engagements of Historical-Critical Discourse* (Atlanta: Society of Biblical Literature, 2005), whilst on the other tends towards a minimalist approach to historicity in the Acts, as exemplified by Todd Penner, *In Praise of Christian Origins: Stephen and the Hellenists in Lukan Apologetic Historiography* (New York: T&T Clark, 2004). The association of minimalism and radical politics is perhaps predicated upon the supposition that one either studies *histoire événementielle* or the *longue durée* (to borrow terms from the *Annales* school); it is not self-evident however that such an either/or option is necessary, and there is something quite attractive to the suggestion in Bernard J. F. Lonergan, *Method in Theology* (Toronto: University of Toronto Press, 1990 [1971]), 197–266, that one ought to study the former (which he designates simply "history") and the latter (which he designated "dialectic") in a sequential fashion, with the discoveries of history serving as the data for dialectic; for a fuller discussion of

Mesopotamia, Judea and Cappadocia, Pontus and Asia, Phrygia and Pamphylia, Egypt and the parts of Libya belonging to Cyrene, and visitors from Rome, both Jews and proselytes, Cretans and Arabs" (Acts 2:9–11a) all heard the word preached to them, in their own language. If Badiou is correct to describe Paul as "the foundation of universalism,"[24] then we do well to recognize that this foundation is itself built upon the universalizing that was the international focus of the Jerusalem community.[25]

The Idea of Communism

Of course, in saying that Christianity was universalizing since the beginning, one would want to avoid that tired idea that Judaism was particularistic whilst Christianity was universalistic. Baur himself fell into this trap, arguing that "Christianity is elevated above the defects and limitations, the one-sidedness and finiteness, which constitute the particularisms of other religions,"[26] "paganism" and Judaism included. Baur could not be more mistaken on this matter: Christianity itself clearly built upon its Jewish heritage in developing its universalism, for that heritage did not simply, as Baur suggested, "attach itself to outward rites and ordinances, nor identify itself with the positive authority of a purely traditional religion."[27] When the earliest

Lonergan in this regard, cf. Jonathan Bernier, *The Quest for the Historical Jesus after the Demise of Authenticity: Toward a Critical Realist Philosophy of History in Jesus Studies* (London: T&T Clark, forthcoming). Regardless, whilst space does not permit a full engagement with the matter, let it suffice that I have antecedent to this published work undertaken the work necessary to judge whether one can reasonably affirm that there was an early Christian community of goods that gathered in Solomon's portico, and indeed I do thus affirm as a necessary condition for this study.

24. Badiou, *Saint Paul*.
25. Cf. the still decisive dialectical (albeit in the Lonerganian rather than the Marxist understanding) study of the emergence of the world mission from the cradle of the Jerusalem community in Ben F. Meyer, *The Early Christians: Their World Mission and Self-discovery* (Wilmington, DE: Glazier, 1986), 53–113.
26. Baur, *Church History*, 6.
27. Ibid.

Christians sought warrant for their international mission, after all, it was to the prophets of Israel that they turned.

Nonetheless, the story of history is first and foremost the story of the nova, for a story without the new is no story at all (imagine a plot that lacks any change in the situation of its characters). More to the point, Christianity had to develop new forms of organization that would allow its new message to flourish and advance. Similarly, of the 2011 revolutions, Badiou writes that

> [l]est this moment flounder in glorious but defeated mass mobilizations, or in the interminable opportunism of "representative" organizations, whether corrupt trade unions or parliamentary parties, the rebirth of history must also be a rebirth of the Idea. The sole Idea capable of challenging the corrupt, lifeless version of "democracy," which has become the banner of the legionaries of Capital, as well as the racial and national prophecies of a petty fascism given its opportunity locally by the crisis, is the idea of Communism, revisited and nourished by what the spirited diversity of these riots, however fragile, teaches us.[28]

The Idea of Communism: lest there be no mistake, Badiou does not mean necessarily a Marxist idea of the communism. Once, "during an international conference on the idea of communism, Antonio Negri . . . publicly took [Badiou] as an example of those who claim to be communists without even being Marxists," to which Badiou replied, "that was better than claiming to be a Marxist without even being communist."[29] For Badiou, the Idea "for two centuries, *or perhaps since Plato*, has been the Idea of communism."[30] Anthropologist David Graeber, a significant intellectual figure in the development of Occupy's ethos, has suggested that Occupy Wall Street comes more out of the anarchist than the Marxist tradition.[31] Although not all

28. Ibid.
29. Ibid., 7.
30. Badiou, *The Communist Hypothesis*, trans. David Macey and Steve Corcoran (London: Verso, 2010), 254. Emphasis added.
31. David Graeber, "Occupy Wall Street's Anarchist Roots," in *The Occupy Handbook*, 141–49.

anarchists are communist, certainly the communitarian ethos adopted at the various Occupation sites, at least in theory if not always in actual practice, would place its anarchism solidly in that tradition.

One would not be far from the mark in suggesting that something much like this Idea was present among the earliest believers in the Jerusalem community. Are we not told that "the whole group of those who believed were of one heart and soul, and no claimed private ownership of any possessions, but everything they owned was held in common" (Acts 4:32)? Not for nothing have some of the more prominent thinkers on the Left seen in this a sort of communism *avant la lettre.*[32] Indeed, one might go as far as to suggest that the Idea of communism, to again use Badiou's term, was quite alive and well for the probably quite short lifetime of the so-called "community of goods."[33] This community of goods, we learn elsewhere in Acts (4:11 and 4:12), was centred spatially upon Solomon's portico.

Intensification, Contraction, and Localization

Near the end of *Rebirth of History*, Badiou offers the "Doctrinal Summary" of his "proposed definition of a political truth":[34]

> A political truth is a series of consequences, organized on the condition of an Idea, a massive popular event, in which *intensification, contraction,*

32. Among the more prominent are those that appear in Rosa Luxemburg's 1905 *Kirche und Sozialmus* and Karl Kautsky's 1908 *Der Ursprung des Christentums: Eine Historische Untersuchung*; cf. now the treatment of these classic Marxist considerations of earliest Christianity in Roland Boer, *Criticism of Religion: On Marxism and Theology II* (Leiden: Brill, 2009), 59–120.
33. I find compelling the argument that Paul converted to the Christian movement approximately eighteen months after Jesus' death; cf. the overview of the relevant data in Rainer Riesner, *Paul's Early Period: Chronology, Mission Strategy, Theology*, trans. Doug Stott (Grand Rapids, MI: Eerdmans, 1998), 64–72. If we follow the relative chronology in Acts, the *terminus ante quem* for the dissolution of the community of goods would thus be just under eighteen months from Jesus' death; when one considers that the community of goods originated some seven weeks after Jesus' death, cumulatively this means that the community had a maximum lifespan of approximately sixteen months. Conceivably, it was considerably lower, depending upon the length of time between the dissolution of the community and Paul's conversion.
34. Badiou, *Rebirth of History*, 85.

> *and localization* replace an identitarian object, and the separating names bound up with it, with a real presentation of the generic power of the multiple.[35]

Badiou then follows up with a commentary upon this sentence, amplifying each sub-statement ("A political truth is," "a series of consequences," etc.). We could here well do the same with reference to the community of goods.[36] We will instead focus mainly upon the three terms, intensification, contraction, and localization, mentioning only in addition to our previous brief discussion of the universal and the Idea the significance that Acts describes the members of the community of goods as "those who believed": a term that probably should be equated with what Badiou calls throughout his work "militants," that is, those who commit themselves fully to a political truth, to an Idea. That said, let us consider, in reverse order from Badiou's own presentation of the terms, localization, contraction, and intensification in the community of goods.

Says Badiou, quite rightly: "A political event occurring everywhere is something that does not exist. . . . A non-localized Idea is impotent."[37] In 2011, such sites were ostensibly public spaces: Tahrir Square and Zuccotti Park, two places that ought to be public but had become increasingly dominated by capital and its executives. Among

35. Ibid., emphasis added.

36. It might seem strange to suggest that the earliest believers were proclaiming a "political truth." Yet, if Alain Badiou, *Theory of the Subject*, trans. Bruno Bosteels (London: Continuum, 2009), 125, can describe Paul as the "brilliant and ill-humoured Lenin" of the "universal Church," then it seems altogether apposite to consider the early Christian movement as political, at least in Badiou's own terms. In so doing, however, one needs to register some disagreement with Badiou, *Theory of the Subject*, 125, who suggests that in universalizing the Christian message Paul was acting against Peter. Whilst it is perhaps the case that Paul more fully grasped the universalizing consequences of the Christian *kerygma* it does seem probable that Peter too recognized that gentiles were to be included in the Christian movement; the very accusation in Galatians 2 that Peter vacillated in his relationships with gentile believers suggests that he was actively engaged in determining the best and most appropriate means by which to integrate said believers into the Christian community.

37. Badiou, *Rebirth of History*, 92.

the earliest believers, it was Solomon's portico (cf. Acts 4:11; 5:12), into which none dared enter but the believers (cf. Acts 5:13). Yet, although these are localized "sites of unity and presence," nonetheless "[i]n such a site the massive event is exhibited, exists, in a universal address."[38] The local site is from whence the address goes forth, but the address's validity is not limited to the local site; indeed, it is precisely through such local unity and presence that a universality begins to emerge.

This emergent universality is a possibility only because "[t]he historical situation contracts around an active, thinking minority whose provenance is multifaceted. It produces a sort of presentation of itself, which is simultaneously pure, complete and very limited, a sample of the generic being of a people."[39] The Occupy sites presented themselves as the voice of the 99%; likewise, the early believers seem to have considered themselves the reconstitution of all Israel. In neither case does either view the broader group—the 99%, Israel—less significant for its failure to enter into the contracted minority. Rather, the contracted minority sets about to evangelize the larger group, by proclaiming its truth, its good news: people are not just resources to be used and used up by global capital; Christ Jesus is risen from the dead, and offers new life to all Israel, if not all humanity. The contraction constitutes, at least from the perspective of those on its inside, not an exclusive group, but rather the base for an active effort to transform the majority. In an apparent, but not actual, paradox, the local contraction becomes the impetus for universal proclamation, international mission the fruit of intense localization.

Such a contraction, localized at a particular site, becomes the *Sitz im Leben* for "a general subjective intensification, [during which] a

38. Ibid.
39. Ibid., 91.

violent passion for the True occurs, which Kant had already identified at the time of the French revolution under the name of 'enthusiasm.'"[40] "A violent passion for the True": one ought to recall the deaths of Ananias and Sapphira, narrated in Acts 5:1-11. One would normally not expect the death penalty for lying about a charitable donation. Yet, says Peter in 5:4, "You have not lied to men but to God," thus tempting the Spirit of the Lord (5:9): that is, you have not lied to us apostles, but to the Truth to which we, and this entire community of goods, witness. As suggested by Žižek in his speech to Occupy Wall Street, the Holy Spirit is "an egalitarian community of believers who are linked by love for each other, and who only have their own freedom and responsibility to do it."[41] Solomon's portico becomes a site for, as Badiou suggests occurs at such moments, the "intensification and radicalization of statements, taking of sides and forms of actions."[42] As per Žižek, for the early Christians such intensification is the work of the Holy Spirit.

Dissolution and Organization

Intensification also begins to help explain the dissolution of the community of goods. As Badiou suggests, "[i]ntensification explains the rapid exhaustion of this kind of moment; it explains Robespierre's bizarre withdrawal just before Thermidor; it explains why Saint-Just said 'the revolution is frozen'; it explains why at the end there are only scant detachments in the squares, on the strike and occupation pickets, on the barricades (but it is they who will be the vector of the organized moment, should it arrive)."[43] As were many Occupy sites

40. Cf. ibid., 90.
41. Slavoj Žižek, "Don't Fall in Love with Yourselves," in *Occupy! Scenes from Occupied America*, ed. Astra Taylor, Keith Cessen, and editors from *n 1*, *Dissent*, *Triple Canopy*, and *The New Inquiry* (London: Verso, 2011), 70.
42. Cf. Badiou, *Rebirth of History*, 90.
43. Cf. ibid.

ultimately dismantled by police intervention, so too does it appear that the community of goods, and the localization within Solomon's portico, were ultimately dismantled by an intervention orchestrated in part by the Pharisee Saul (later Paul) of Tarsus (cf. Acts 8:1-3), apparently acting in league with certain temple authorities (cf. Acts 9:1-2); yet, even before this, exhaustion apparently begins to afflict the apostles, at least in part, for they are no longer able to attend to the needs of all those who had joined the movement and thus must appoint others for that task (cf. Acts 6:1-6).

Exhaustion is perhaps even more evident in the apparent failure to re-establish the community of goods after the scattering. Believers return to Jerusalem, otherwise we would not have had events such as the Jerusalem council; yet it does not seem that they enter into an arrangement as radical as existed initially. One suspects that exhaustion prevented such from occurring: the community of goods was just too difficult to maintain long-term, as indeed the incident with Ananias and Sapphira demonstrates dramatically. Yet, as Badiou reminds us, those who remain on the barricades at the end will become "the vector of the organized moment," and thus it is not a surprise to find such figures as Peter and Barnabas, both members of the community of goods, becoming also major figures in the missionary expansion *and consequent organization* of churches across the Mediterranean world. Localization, contraction, and intensification thus became the basis for, even as they gave way to, the international establishment of the church; and this in turn, although it is a much bigger stronger movement, led eventually to the conversion of the Roman Empire to the organization that resulted from this early enthusiasm.

Thus we can respond to Boer's legitimate concern that by thinking the community of goods to have been an actually occurring phenomenon, any Christian effort to create such a community is a fundamentally reactionary enterprise.[44] If the community of goods represents a sort of recurring yet never enduring revolutionary moment in human history, then the effort to generate such moments becomes problematic when we expect that this moment, this one here, is the final moment, the *eschaton*, after which no more revolutionary moments will be necessary because the revolution is completed once and for all. The community of goods, the Occupy movement, represented genuine breakthroughs of the human spirit against the ever-encroaching powers of domination, and their significance in the *longue durée* is not that they constitute the new normal but rather that people achieved a glimpse of potential but yet other-than-actual normativities.

Conclusion

If we tend to forget that Christianity began with a revolutionary moment almost two millennia ago, perhaps that is because the Christian revolution was ultimately so successful. It eventually converted the very empire that killed its Lord. Yet, it seems, the road to that fateful conversion started with a handful of militants, gathered in Solomon's portico: a handful of militants following a man already killed by the state, and who would soon be scattered to the wind by further state repression. This lesson should not be forgotten: seemingly insignificant and apparently defeated movements can have impacts that are not fully registered for years, decades, even centuries. One wonders whether current struggles against rape culture or racialized police violence would have as much vitality if it were not for the energies released, the lessons learned, the hopes glimpsed, during the heady days of 2011. Perhaps we should begin to see 1200 BCE, or 30, 1848, 1871, 1917, 1968, 1989, and 2011 CE, not

44. Boer, *Criticism of Religion*, 115–16.

as separate revolutions but rather as singular (and non-exhaustive) moments within a single revolution: localized breakthroughs, each of which in their very localization had a paradoxically universalizing influence, and this precisely because the effort to enclose us all within a singular logic, the logic of power, state, and now capital, continues universally. And thus as we ask ourselves "What was Occupy?" we might do well to listen to Badiou one last time:

> [T]he difficulties of a politics are never universal, as enemy propaganda—along the lines of "your communist hypothesis is nothing more than a chimera that cannot be put into practice, a utopia that has nothing to do with the real world"—would always have us believe in order to discourage us once and for all. Its difficulties are caught up in a network in which it is possible, although often difficult, to know their place, what surrounds them, and how to approach them. We can therefore speak of a *space of possible failures*. And it is within that space that a failure invites us to seek and to theorize the point at which we are now forbidden to fail.[45]

Forbidden to fail: the hope that issued from Solomon's portico, from Tahrir Square, from Zuccotti Park—the hope for a world in which all might have their needs met, their basic humanity affirmed—that hope must be forbidden from failure, no matter what situations, what contexts, in which we find ourselves. Thus does the hermeneutics of situation begin, despite all the reasons that we might have to despair for the present let alone the future, to emerge as a hermeneutics of hope.

45. Badiou, *Communist Hypothesis*, 39–40.

12

On Trying to Praise the Mutilated World

Reading Revelation in the Midst of Ecological Crisis

Ryan L. Hansen

> Any real change implies the breakup of the world as one has always known it.
>
> –James Baldwin[1]

One of the stranger tasks of my scholarly career has been to think through how reading the Apocalypse of John might inform and equip readers interested in living through and doing something about the ecological crisis that the world currently faces.[2] Can a book whose action is dominated by scenes of global catastrophe provide resources for avoiding the same? Or does the book of Revelation consign

1. James Baldwin, *Nobody Knows My Name* (New York: Vintage, 1993), 117.
2. This title is a play on the title of the poem by David Zagajewski, "Try to Praise the Mutilated World," in *Selected Poems*, trans. Clare Cavanaugh (New York: Farrar, Straus, and Giroux, 2002), 60.

(or, worse, encourage) the world to such destruction? Certainly, the imagery of cosmic destruction that makes up the majority of the dramatic action in the Apocalypse lends itself to dangerous interpretations and destructive ethics, and more than some of John's language invites necessary critique.[3] This important point should be acknowledged up front. However, my own reflections on reading Revelation in the midst of ecological crisis will not be devoted to spelling out the dangers and leveling the critique of John's language and distortions of that language. For that discussion, one can do no better than Barbara Rossing's excellent study *The Rapture Exposed*.[4] My own reading takes a different starting point in reading John's apocalyptic imagery as critique of political economy rather than literal destruction of cosmic reality. This is not an attempt to let some of the damaging language in the Apocalypse and in its interpreters off the hook, but rather to let the Apocalypse speak to the ecological crisis on its own terms as well as letting the crisis speak back in its own terms. Responsible biblical interpretation requires this exchange and communication.

Despite its current cultural usage in the west, "apocalypse" for John did not mean disaster or ruin, but rather unveiling. Apocalypse pulls the curtain back to show not only God's determination to do something about evil—the unmaking of what is wrong and putting things right—but also unveils the truth of John's and his audience's present situation (Rev. 1:19, "Write, therefore, what you have seen, what is, and what must take place after this").[5] For John, the future is perhaps less inscrutable than the present. While the future is assured

3. See, for example, Brian K. Blount, *Revelation: A Commentary*, New Testament Library (Louisville: Westminster John Knox, 2009), 309–10; Tina Pippin, *Apocalyptic Bodies: The Biblical End of the World in Text and Image* (London: Routledge, 1999), 81–92.
4. Barbara R. Rossing, *The Rapture Exposed: The Message of Hope in the Book of Revelation* (New York: Basic Books, 2004).
5. All quotations from Scripture are the author's translation unless otherwise noted.

because God exists as Omega, the present course of action for small, slain Lamb-following communities in Roman subjugated Asia Minor is in question. What shall those who follow the slain Lamb do about a culture that worships local and Roman gods (including Caesar) and an economy that reinforces the story that those gods hold everything together? In order to convince his audience to take a particular course of action he must make the mundane monstrous. In order to draw his churches away from the sleepiness of everyday idolatry, John presents a picture of their commonplace and involves it in the cosmic (though not dualistic)[6] battle between God and the Dragon, between the Lamb and the beast, between angels and demons. In doing so, John calls his audience to abandon practices that cooperate and participate in the idolatry of Rome.

While apocalypse as revelation of future may not be able to be brought to bear on the ecological crisis—the destination human society seems to be headed for in an uninhabitable or difficultly habitable planet seems a far distance from the new heavens and new earth where human life can flourish—the concept of apocalypse as revealing "what is" may hold some promise for the task.[7] I intend to pursue this path in exploring the way John's vision calls for resisting participation in the Roman cultic-economy by revealing its present monstrosity. John does this by presenting opposing rhetorical constructions of the cosmos, one with Rome and Caesar at the center, and the other with the slain Lamb at the center with its urban corollary "New Jerusalem." As these two "rhetorical cosmologies" collide, the former falls apart and the latter emerges as given.[8] Each of

6. See Ryan Leif Hansen, *Silence and Praise: Rhetorical Cosmology and Political Theology in the Book of Revelation*, Emerging Scholars Series (Minneapolis: Fortress Press, 2014), 85 n. 7; 163.

7. It will not do to try to connect the cosmic dissolution depicted by John with the current ecological destruction and crisis on a one-to-one correlation. John did not have the destruction of our twenty-first century ecological system in mind while reporting his vision to churches in Asia Minor, and, as I will demonstrate in this paper, his vision of cosmic destruction serves very different symbolic and theological purposes.

these rhetorical discourses assumes a form of life.[9] The revelation of Christ at the center of the Roman world construction dismantles the Roman cosmological discourse and along with it its hold on John's audience—a new way of inhabiting the cosmos is opened up.

Two analogies of apocalypse may help to delineate this concept. In 2007, the city of Sao Paolo, Brazil categorized all public advertising as "visual pollution" and placed a ban on such advertising in all its visual forms: signs, billboards, "even the Goodyear Blimp."[10] Taking down some of the more sizable billboards unveiled previously unknown problems. Specifically, an entire favela, or shantytown, was hidden behind some particularly large advertisements.[11] Clearing away the visual pollution disclosed something that the billboards had hidden from view. The advertising was revealed to be something other than it was by the hidden element behind it. Ads aimed at forming desire for achieving a better life and constructing the idea of an ideal inhabitant of the city were covering over the reality that an entire neighborhood of impoverished people were being ignored. Once this reality was disclosed, it could no longer be overlooked. This is apocalyptic.

More recently, in the city of Harbin, China, daily life ground to a halt due to severe levels of air pollution.[12] Dubbed "China's airpocalypse," the problems range from not being able to see more than ten meters, to air pollution measurements at least forty times greater than what the World Health Organization deems safe, to a

8. The concept of rhetorical cosmology is explored in depth in Hansen, *Silence and Praise*.

9. Vernon K. Robbins, *The Invention of Christian Discourse*, Rhetoric of Religious Antiquity (Dorset: Deo, 2009), 1:xxvii–7. See Hansen, *Silence and Praise*, 28–30.

10. Bob Garfield, "Clearing the Air," *On the Media*, April 20, 2007, http://www.onthemedia.org/story/129390-clearing-the-air/transcript. My thanks to Channon Ross for directing my attention to this interview.

11. Vincius Galvao in Garfield, "Clearing the Air."

12. Steve Bynum, "China's 'Airpocalypse,'" *WBEZ*, October 23, 2013, http://www.wbez.org/programs/worldview/2013-10-23/chinas-airpocalypse-108989.

worry about heavy metals such as cadmium in the drinking water supply.[13] The poor air quality traces back to coal plants near the city, spewing the pollution into Harbin's air. Economic growth and progress in China depends on this coal-fueled power. In addition, Western companies and consumers bear some responsibility for this pollution, having displaced manufacturing from their own areas to cheaper locales like China. The pollution is a necessity of globalized capitalist progress and growth, but the rhetoric of technological and economic progress crashes up against the reality of unsustainable living conditions for the people of Harbin. The world of growth and progress constructed by global capital is unmasked by the untenable nature of the living conditions in places like Harbin. This, too, is apocalyptic.

Apocalypse discloses something that was previously covered over. In John's case, it was the hidden victory of the slain Lamb whose death uncovers and is the undoing of an unjust and idolatrous system of empire. In the face of the ecological crisis, what needs to be uncovered is both the need for drastic overhaul to the way our world operates and the means of living differently. The call of John to costly witness and non-participation in the face of seemingly limitless power may be able to provide resources for alternative ways of inhabiting our scarred cosmos in the face of seemingly limitless inertia.

The Ordeal: Then and Now

The central focus of John's vision is the unveiling of God enthroned at the heart of the creation. The vision of the throne in chapter 4 is a vision of the world as it should be. But already at the outset there is a sense of disturbance or dissonance in that the sea appears

13. Judith Shapiro in Bynum, "China's 'Airpocalypse.'"

before the throne (Rev. 4:6). The sea is a multivalent image that makes several other appearances throughout Revelation. It is the source of the Beast in chapter 13; it seems to be an element of ordeal and judgment when the saints who refuse the beast and its image sing the song of Moses beside it in chapter 15; and it is the means of ongoing trade for Babylon in chapters 17–18. These three references could point to the sea as a symbol of chaos or evil or, at the very least, the necessity of judgment within God's creation.[14] Therefore, the sea existing before the throne of God in heaven could signify the ongoing need for judgment in creation, the ongoing nagging presence of evil in an otherwise perfectly constructed and rightly ordered creation (Rev. 4:2-11).[15] The sea represents, following Bauckham's argument, "the destructive potential which remains to threaten the created universe."[16]

This nagging sense of destructive potential for John is the misconstrual of the world system under Roman domination. Rome places itself, rather than the One seated on the throne, at the center of the cosmos. The Roman gods and Caesar hold all things in their proper place, and this entire system is propagated through the rhetoric of cult and economy.[17] This cultic economic discourse functioned to define society, history, and indeed the whole cosmos in a way that made Roman power seemingly inevitable and unquestionably beneficial. As Steven Friesen argues, "The logic of

14. Jonathan Moo, "The Sea That Is No More: Revelation 21:1 and the Function of Sea Imagery in the Apocalypse of John," *NovT* 51 (2009): 148–67,166–67.

15. Sean M. McDonough argues that the throne room scene functions as "a kind of archetype of the eschaton." See "Revelation: The Climax of Cosmology," in *Cosmology and New Testament Theology*, LNTS 355, ed. Jonathan T. Pennington and Sean M. McDonough (London: T&T Clark, 2008), 182.

16. Richard Bauckham, *The Theology of the Book of Revelation*, New Testament Theology (Cambridge: Cambridge University Press, 1993), 53. This is the reason that, when all things are made new, John reports that, "the sea was no more" (Rev. 21:1 NRSV).

17. Steven J. Friesen, *Imperial Cults and the Apocalypse of John: Reading Revelation in the Ruins* (Oxford: Oxford University Press, 2001), 17–19.

imperial cults allowed for no termination of the world."[18] This was because the imperial cult's primary function was the building of a cosmology. The discourse of the cult defined the experience of space and time for the everyday Roman citizen, creating a "meaningful geography in which Rome was central" and a sense in which time was shaped through festivals and holidays.[19] For John, participating in the economy, which was saturated with idolatry, only served to further prop up the Roman system. To successfully navigate the economic fabric of Rome was to participate in the cultic discourse that worshiped Caesar rather than God and the Lamb.[20] It was to continue to live in and support the cosmos with Rome at the center rather than the Lamb.

The throne of God exists at the heart of reality and the Lamb exists in the midst of the throne (5:6). The majority of the action throughout the Apocalypse is centered on God's determination to do something, by means of the slain Lamb, to unmake the cosmos governed by Rome and make all things new so that the Lamb becomes the center. John envisions the dissolution of the world run by Rome occurring as the world-made-new by God and the Lamb emerges. Cosmic destruction heralds the arrival of God on the scene, shown vividly by John when the world is violently torn apart by earthquake, darkening of the sun, the moon becoming blood, the shaking loose of the stars, the vanishing of the sky and the displacement of every mountain and island. In the midst of all of this, every person flees from "the face of the one who is seated on the throne and from the wrath of the Lamb" (6:12–17). Rather than taking the cosmic destruction at the literal level, interpreters

18. Ibid., 130.
19. Ibid., 124–26.
20. See Hansen, *Silence and Praise*, 57–60. Though prevalent in Revelation, this stark contrast between Caesar and God is not assumed by every early Christian text, see perhaps Romans 13:1-7, as well as *1 Clem*. 21:6, Tertullian, *Apologeticus XXX*, 7.

should notice primarily the simultaneity of the presence of God and the undoing of the cosmos as a system. Hence, at the end of every cycle of seven in the book—cycles that depict the undoing of the cosmic acting space—instead of total dissolution, readers encounter theophanic phenomena (thunder, lightning, earthquake, hail).[21]

In the face of this, John calls for his audience to witness to the way things will be when God and the Lamb reign instead of Caesar and the Roman gods (7:16 :: 16:8–9; 7:17 :: 8:10–11; 7:9 :: 6:17).[22] This witness will of course be costly, and John recognizes this, regularly depicting the witnesses and saints as witnessing by their blood, being conquered by the beast. Their witness is a "torment" to the beastly system and will not be tolerated (11:7–10). In John's Greco-Roman context, refusing honor and worship to Caesar and the Roman gods was an insult to and rejection of those gods' governance of the world, and conjured images of a "reversed world" that threatened the stability and continuance of that governance and the state of things.[23] The refusal of participation in cult and economy that John called for, then, would inevitably bring persecution and trouble to those who took up its radical call (13:15).

John's term for all of this—the nagging sense of trouble, the clash of worlds at the entrance of God and the Lamb, the persecution of those who resist Rome—is "ordeal" (θλίψις, 1:9; 2:9, 10, 22; 7:14). John presents this ordeal in order to call his audience out of it and to call them to action. John puts his audience face to face with the catastrophic, with the loss of their world-system, with the monstrous so that they can no longer go back to the way things are, but must

21. See Hansen, *Silence and Praise*, 80 n. 37; 81, 98, 103–104, 146.

22. Ibid., 95–97.

23. Henk Jan de Jonge, "The Apocalypse of John and the Imperial Cult," in *Kykeon: Studies in Honor of H. S. Versnel*, Religions in the Graeco-Roman World 142, ed. H. F. J. Horstmanshoff et al. (Leiden: Brill, 2002), 137–40. "Pagans felt that the Christian ideology undermined and subverted their world in a way that reminded them of the lawlessness and rebellion of primeval ages" (140).

yearn for the new by living according to the new. The worship that sustains the world of Rome stops; the worship that sustains the world made new by God and the Lamb carries on. John's cosmological discourse attempts to make it problematic to live comfortably under Roman rule so that his audiences can live under the rule of God and the Lamb. These standards were difficult for his audiences to measure up to; as Friesen notes, "They were so high that to keep them would make it almost impossible to survive under Roman authority in imperial society. That was precisely John's point."[24]

The ordeal faced by current inhabitants of the earth is a different one, but one that, I will argue, can be addressed by John's Apocalypse. Today's ecological crisis is not one of emperor cult and sacrifice, but one of increasingly difficult modes of life, disappearing species, potentially irreversible ecological damage, and perhaps, ruin of life on earth as we have known it. The projected damage that may be caused by the current ecological crisis has been elevated in proportion to the attention that is paid to it. A recent intergovernmental panel on climate change found it "extremely likely" that at least half of global surface temperature increase in the last century can be attributed to anthropogenic causes, mainly greenhouse gas concentrations.[25] The amount of greenhouse gasses already released into the atmosphere have established a commitment to further warming such that even if emissions were halted today—a preposterous proposal—warming trends could persist for centuries.[26] The rise in temperature has been projected recently to increase possibly up to 7.2 degrees Fahrenheit

24. Friesen, *Imperial Cults and the Apocalypse of John*, 209.

25. IPCC 2013: *Climate Change 2013: The Physical Science Basis, Contribution of Working Group I to the Fifth Assessment Report of the Intergovernmental Panel on Climate Change*, ed. T. F. Stocker et al. (Cambridge: Cambridge University Press, 2013), 17.

26. Ibid., 1106–1107.

(4 degrees Celsius).[27] This rise would be "catastrophic rather than merely dangerous."[28]

Some of the coming effects of this crisis are extended periods of drought, more intense and lengthening monsoon seasons, reduced air quality, warming and acidifying oceans, ice sheet melt, and rising sea levels.[29] Extreme weather events have already emerged in various locations around the world, like Hurricane Katrina, Superstorm Sandy, and Super Typhoon Haiyan, producing death and damage on an alarming scale.[30] Continued warming will most likely produce continued ecological disaster. But exposure to such disaster will not be uniform, and "countries in tropical areas are more likely to be hit harder."[31] Exposure to increased natural disasters is not only geographically determined, but also relates to economic realities: "[D]eaths from natural disaster are generally linked to a nation's economic welfare and its degree of income inequality."[32]

The economic aspect of the ecological crisis may be the most pressing. It is the capitalist economy, and the way of life that it sustains for the developed and industrialized world, that drives much of the greenhouse gas emissions that are causing such harm to the

27. Steven C. Sherwood et al., "Spread in Model Climate Sensitivity Traced to Atmospheric Convective Mixing," *Nature* 505 (2014): 37–50.

28. Steven C. Sherwood, quoted in Damian Carrington, "Planet Likely to Warm by 4C by 2100, Scientists Warn," *The Guardian*, December 31, 2013, http://www.theguardian.com/environment/2013/dec/31/planet-will-warm-4c-2100-climate.

29. IPCC 2013, *Climate Change 2013*,19–29.

30. The link between extreme weather and climate change is likely, but has not garnered overwhelming scientific agreement; see John Carney, "Storm Warnings: Extreme Weather is a Product of Climate Change," *Scientific American*, June 28, 2011, http://www.scientificamerican.com/article/extreme-weather-caused-by-climate-change/ and Carney, "Global Warming and the Science of Extreme Weather," *Scientific American*, June 29, 2011, http://www.scientificamerican.com/article/global-warming-and-the-science-of-extreme-weather.

31. Robert R. M. Verchick, "Adaptation, Economics, and Justice," *Economic Thought and U.S. Climate Change Policy*, ed. David M. Driesen (Cambridge, MA: Massachusetts Institute of Technology Press, 2010), 277–95, 279.

32. Ibid., 279. See Matthew E. Kahn, "The Death Toll from Natural Disasters: The Role of Income, Geography, and Institutions," *Review of Economics and Statistics* 87, no. 2 (2005): 271.

global ecology. Consider the recent estimates the Obama administration released regarding the cost of carbon. The estimates were a way to measure the economic impact of continuing to release the current rate of carbon into the air. With the future cost estimate, a carbon tax in the present—on gasoline and carbon producing corporations—could be calculated. But differences of opinion exist about how much the present owes the future, how much of an economic claim the future damage has on the present way of doing business. The difference, according to Eduardo Porter, can be attributed to the divergence between a moral stance of keeping the global rise in temperature as low as possible, and an industrial stance that wants a profitable return on investment in the future.[33] In other words, does the present owe more in order to protect the future from calamity, or is the present only obligated to pay what can be considered fair within the current economic reality? Porter suggests that the cost of drastic change to the way things are is simply too high for the current system, not because the moral argument is wrong, but simply because the current system speeds along on its way: "Four years after committing to a 2-degree ceiling, the world's current policies will lead us, by the end of the century, to blow past 3."[34]

The economic reality of the global ecological crisis is that the current global capitalist system exists as a major cause of anthropogenic warming due to production of elevated levels of greenhouse gases like carbon dioxide, methane, and nitrous oxide.[35]

33. Much of the discussion in this paragraph is done in dialogue with Eduardo Porter, "Counting the Cost of Fixing the Future," *New York Times*, September 10, 2013, http://www.nytimes.com/2013/09/11/business/counting-the-cost-of-fixing-the-future.html.

34. Ibid. Porter reports that a 3.45 degree rise could cost the global economy nearly trillion. This kind of global temperature rise could flood significant portions of the world's major coastal cities. For an example of what it could do to US coastal cities, see Baden Copeland et al., "What Could Disappear," *New York Times*, November 24, 2012, http://www.nytimes.com/interactive/2012/11/24/opinion/sunday/what-could-disappear.html.

35. On the anthropogenic production of nitrous oxide due to agricultural practices, see S. Park et al., "Trends and Seasonal Cycles in the Isotopic Composition of Nitrous Oxide Since 1940,"

The ordeal that we face is that our way of life in the West and other developed nations changes the world. When we think of ecological crisis we tend to think of extremes: oil spills, urban smog, coal strip-mining, or large-scale deforestation, and these are all very real elements of the crisis. But standing in the shadows of those extremes is the fact that the everyday amenities of the standard of life that the developed world has adopted requires all of those elements and more.[36] The extremes that are conjured up in the mind at the mention of global warming are sustained by "the energy-saturated nature of our fossil-fueled lifestyles," exhibited by open refrigerated aisles in most American grocery stores.[37] As Elizabeth Kolbert memorably puts it, "If you want to think about why humans are so dangerous to other species, you can picture a poacher in Africa carrying an AK-47 or a logger in the Amazon gripping an ax, or, better still, you can picture yourself, holding a book on your lap."[38] It is the mundane elements of life lived within the universal system of capital, and the commitment to the prolongation of that system, that drive the extreme instances of ecological damage.

Slavoj Žižek discusses what the economic reality of globalized capital means for those facing down the ecological crisis. He writes,

> The December 2009 Copenhagen talks between the top representatives of 20 great powers about how to fight global warming failed miserably—the result was a vague compromise without any fixed deadlines or obligations, more a statement of intentions than a treaty. The lesson is bitter and clear: the state political elites serve capital,

Nature Geoscience 5 (2012): 261–65. My thanks to my friend Adam Cobb for pointing me in the direction of this report.

36. See Andrew C. Revkin, "Did 90 Companies 'Cause the Climate Crisis of the 21st Century'?" *New York Times*, November 21, 2013, http://dotearth.blogs.nytimes.com/2013/11/21/did-90-companies-cause-the-climate-crisis-of-the-21st-century.
37. Andrew C. Revkin, "Oil, Inertia, and the Energy Quest," *New York Times*, June 2, 2010, http://dotearth.blogs.nytimes.com/2010/06/02/oil-inertia-and-the-energy-quest.
38. Elizabeth Kolbert, *The Sixth Extinction: An Unnatural History* (New York: Henry Holt and Company, 2014), 266.

> they are unable and/or unwilling to control and regulate capital even when the very survival of the human race is ultimately at stake. Fredric Jameson's old quip holds today more than ever: it is easier to imagine a total catastrophe which ends all life on earth than it is to imagine a real change in capitalist relations. . . . All one has to do here is to compare the reaction to the financial meltdown of September 2008 with the Copenhagen conference of 2009: save the planet from global warming . . . all this can wait a little bit, but the call 'Save the banks!' is an unconditional imperative which demands and receives immediate action.[39]

This critique is insightful because it illustrates that even in the face of the impending catastrophe, the entrenched nature of the system in the lives of those who benefit from it produces its own inertia. There is a disinterest in taking meaningful action because meaningful action would upset the current comfortability of those who benefit from the system.[40] John's rhetoric of cosmic upheaval as a call to costly disengagement and non-participation from a system of benefit may provide some resources to navigate the current climate. Reading Revelation in the midst of ecological crisis may help us to locate a mode of resistance to a system that is damaging the earth.

On Trying to Praise the Mutilated World: A Clash of Rhetorics

It seems that the ecological crisis facing humanity and the world remains unaddressed with the moral seriousness it would require. I have suggested above that this is due to the form of life that the developed world is committed to masks the untenable nature of the arrangement. Put another way, the rhetoric of progress and growth produced by technological globalized capitalism hides the

39. Slavoj Žižek, *Living in the End Times* (London: Verso, 2010), 334.

40. See Stephen Castle, "Europe, Facing Economic Pain, May Ease Climate Rules," *New York Times*, January 22, 2014, http://www.nytimes.com/2014/01/23/business/international/european-union-lowers-ambitions-on-renewable-energy.html?.

reality of the outcome of that way of life. Perhaps this is why the two largest greenhouse gas emitters, the United States and China, have the lowest concern about climate change. In the United States, only 40 percent of people, and in China, only 39 percent will admit climate change is a serious threat.[41] Even though there is a strong sense in those surveyed in the United States that climate change is backed by solid evidence (67 percent), relatively few are willing to admit the anthropogenic nature of such change (44 percent) and even fewer that it poses a "very serious problem" (33 percent).[42] Even in the face of knowledge about the problem, the failure to enact meaningful change persists.

What can account for this failure? I suggest that the commitment to the discourse that sustains the way things are is too strong a force to allow alternative discourses and forms of life to emerge. George H. W. Bush's statement at the Rio Earth Summit in 1992 exemplifies this: while discussing the need to take action to reduce global warming he insisted, "The American Way of Life is not open to negotiation."[43] The commitment to a form of life that is comfortable is strong enough to ward off challenge from the necessity of change in the face of catastrophe.

But it may also be that scientific discourse about the crisis itself lacks the power to capture the imagination and spur action. This is not to say that the science and research is unimportant, because it

41. Cathy Barker, "U.S. Stands Out as Among the Least Concerned About Climate Change," *Pew Research Center*, September 27, 2013, http://www.pewresearch.org/fact-tank/2013/09/27/u-s-stands-out-as-among-the-least-concerned-about-climate-change.

42. Bruce Drake, "Most Americans Believe Climate Change is Real, but Fewer See it as a Threat," *Pew Research Center*, June 27, 2013, http://www.pewresearch.org/fact-tank/2013/06/27/most-americans-believe-climate-change-is-real-but-fewer-see-it-as-a-threat.

43. Quoted in David M. Driesen, introduction to *Economic Thought and U.S. Climate Change Policy*, 4. Driesen continues, "The choice of a frame linking climate mitigation to lifestyle change suggests that sophisticated political operators believed that even during an era when the American people knew that global warming was a problem, they had sufficient allegiance to free markets to make this framing ineffective" (5).

is vital to understanding the issue. However, there is certainly no lack of information about the challenges facing the global ecology, and yet inertia to change persists. One recalls the reported words of F. Sherwood Rowland, who won a Nobel Prize together with Paul Crutzen for their work examining the damage CFCs (chlorofluorocarbons) were doing to the Ozone over Antarctica. Upon returning home one night from research, he told his wife, "The work is going well, but it looks like it might be the end of the world."[44] Though their work inspired the eventual outlawing of CFC use, we continue to live in ways that do near irreparable harm to our world. It may be that the precision of scientific narration of the crisis is not sufficient to address and enact the radicality of change required in the face of the crisis.[45]

It may even be the case that the scientific discourse on the ecological crisis, as important as it is, is captured by the discourse of progress and growth in such a way that it cannot but produce the damage it seeks to help alleviate.[46] As René Descartes said, the aim of science is to make us "masters and possessors of nature."[47] This is the

44. Quoted in Elizabeth Kolbert, *Field Notes from a Catastrophe: Man, Nature, and Climate Change* (New York: Bloomsbury, 2006), 182.

45. This brings to mind Walker Percy's statement, "How it is possible for the man who designed Voyager 19, which arrived at Titania, a satellite of Uranus, three seconds off schedule and a hundred yards off course after a flight of six years, to be one of the most screwed-up creatures in California—or the Cosmos," used as a subtitle of his work, *Lost in the Cosmos: The Last Self-Help Book* (New York: Farrar, Straus, and Giroux, 1983).

46. A forthcoming NASA-funded study seems to suggest this: "Technological change can raise the efficiency of resource use, but it also tends to raise both per capita resource consumption and the scale of resource extraction, so that, absent policy effects, the increases in consumption often compensate for the increased efficiency of resource use." Quoted in Nazeef Ahmed, "Nasa-Funded Study: Industrial Civilization Headed for 'Irreversible Collapse'?," *The Guardian*, March 14, 2014, http://www.theguardian.com/environment/earth-insight/2014/mar/14/nasa-civilisation-irreversible-collapse-study-scientists.

47. René Descartes, *Discourse on Method: Of Conducting One's Reason Well and of Seeking the Truth in the Sciences*, ed. and trans. George Heffernan (Notre Dame, IN: University of Notre Dame Press, 1994), 87 (VI.2). Descartes continues, "This is to be desired not only for the invention of an infinity of artifices that would enable one to enjoy, without any effort, the fruits of the earth and all the goods that are found there, but also, principally, for the preservation of health, which is without doubt the first good and the foundation of all the other goods of this life."

same logic that produces the ability to turn fossil fuel into energy. To know scientifically is vital to understanding the crisis, but perhaps to know in this way is already to participate and produce for the system that propagates the crisis. The same scientific discourse that projects future warming can also proclaim, "The United States has 250 billion tons of recoverable coal reserves—enough to last 100 years even at double the current rate of consumption."[48] J. R. R. Tolkien observed this possibility of scientific knowledge as well, characterizing the physical science research that produced good things, but also "poisonous gasses and explosives" as "things not necessarily evil, but which being as they are, and the nature and motives of the economic masters who provide all the means for their work being as they are, are pretty certain to serve evil ends."[49] Perhaps the insufficiency of scientific discourse to redirect the crisis is that it is captured by and participates in the wider discourse that perpetuates the crisis.[50]

What is needed is a form or life, a discourse, a rhetoric, capable of producing resistance to the way things are now. Perhaps only a truly alternative discourse can produce a true alternative way of life. Joseph Sittler, the earliest ecological theologian, realized this when he wrote,

> A theological analysis can therefore omit further talk about the facts [of

Descartes's observation presciently foreshadows both the peril and promise of modern science. This idea of control and manipulation of the world is, of course, not a novum of modern science, but extends from ancient time the phenomenon of ecological destruction stemming from the idea that humans stand apart from and over their environment rather than within it; see the discussion of this in Michael Williams, *Deforesting the Earth: From Prehistory to Global Crisis* (Chicago: University of Chicago Press, 2003), 73–76, 100–101.

48. Quoted in Wendell Berry, "Faustian Economics: Hell Hath No Limits," *Harper's Magazine* (May 2008): 36.
49. J. R. R. Tolkien, "Letter to Peter Hastings," in *The Letters of J.R.R. Tolkien*, ed. Humphrey Carpenter with the assistance of Christopher Tolkien (Boston: Mariner Books, 2000), 190. See Ralph C. Wood, *The Gospel according to Tolkien: Visions of the Kingdom in Middle-earth* (Louisville: Westminster John Knox, 2003), 31.
50. Cf. John R. Turner, "The Deflating Power of Progress: A Nietzschean View of the Millennial Promise of Science," in *War in Heaven/Heaven on Earth: Theories of the Apocalyptic*, Millennialism and Society 2, ed. Stephen D. O'Leary and Glen S. McGhee (London: Equinox, 2005), 185–93.

> the crisis] because *Life* magazine can outphotograph the theologians, *Look* magazine has recently demonstrated that it can certainly outdramatize them, *Time* magazine can outinterview and propagandize the theologians, and the scientists certainly outsearch and outproduce empirical data about this matter.[51]

Sittler advocated for the development of a "rhetoric of rural values" that could resist the dominant modern rhetoric that is capable of so much ecological destruction. This is not a sentimentality or a nostalgia for a bygone golden age of rural life, but a re-telling of a former way of life that can move that way of life into practices in the present.[52] Can a rhetorical form of life be formulated that is not captured by the dominant discourse that damages the earth and resists alternative options?

John's vision of cosmological destruction may provide surprising resources for such a project. John presents a vision where the cosmic reality—purportedly held together by worship of Caesar and other Roman gods—fragments and dissolves. The sun and moon fail, the

51. Joseph Sittler, *Evocations of Grace: Writings on Ecology, Theology, and Grace*, ed. Steven Bouma-Prediger and Peter Bakken (Grand Rapids, MI: Eerdmans, 2000), 77.

52. Joseph Sittler, "Closing Address: Creating a Rhetoric of Rural Values," in *Preliminary Report: A Family Farm Action Agenda* (Madison: Wisconsin Conference of Churches, 1985), 41–43. My thanks to Peter Bakken for kindly granting me access to this publication. The reflections of Sittler, a Lutheran, resemble those of Dietrich Bonhoeffer, likewise a Lutheran, in another context facing another crisis. Bonhoeffer recognized the Nazi threat required not the sleepy old tools that had always been used, but imaginative, reinvigorated theological resources. As Edwin Robertson describes, "From the beginning Bonhoeffer's cry was 'No Rusty Swords,' and in the first section of *Ethics* he shows how inadequate the old weapons were to deal with the forces of evil let loose by Nazism. Reason, Fanaticism, Conscience, Duty, Freedom, and Integrity were all honourable weapons, but like the rusty swords described in Cervantes' *Don Quixote*, were no longer effective. The parallel with Don Quixote is an extended one. 'Here is the immortal figure of Don Quixote . . . who takes a barber's dish for a helmet and a miserable hack for a charger.' In Germany we have 'an old world venturing to take up arms against a new one' or 'a world of the past hazarding an attack against the superior forces of the commonplace and the mean.' By the time Bonhoeffer had written that, he had plenty of experience with the superior forces of the Nazis. The old weapons were helpless against their pernicious power, and all his life Bonhoeffer sought to replace the old rusty swords with new ones," Edwin H. Robertson in Dietrich Bonhoeffer, *No Rusty Swords: Letters, Lectures, and Notes, 1928–1936*, ed. Edwin H. Robertson, trans. Edwin H. Robertson and John Bowden (New York: Harper and Row, 1965), 1:13–14.

stars fall, the waters are turned to blood, the sky vanishes, earthquakes split the ground. Startlingly, this loss of the stability of the world is met by the followers of the Lamb not with dismay but with praise. Indeed, John depicts the saints as giving thanks, in modes of silence and praise, for this cosmic upheaval. But this should not be understood as *schadenfreude* at the misfortune and ruin of the churches' opponents. Rather, John depicts praise in the face of the mutilated world as a means of disengagement from the Roman system of idolatry, economic excess, and violent domination. John depicts the loss of the Roman-ordered cosmos not as a way of disentangling his readers from the world but as a way of encouraging resistance in his readers' daily existence. In silence, he encouraged non-participation and non-cooperation within the Roman system, and by praise he encouraged alternative (and costly) forms of inhabiting the world. The loss of the world in John's vision is a way of pushing against the inertia that realizes a problem, but continues on the same path—John eliminates the possibility of traversing that same path by eliminating the path.

In calling his audience away from the practices of trade that he saw as saturated with idolatry, John called them away from what he perceived as the real destructive power in the world, the wrong worship that tells the wrong story about the world and its peoples. In his depiction of the saints' praise at the unmaking of this wrongly construed world he seeks to open up alternative ways of living. This can be seen, for example, in places like Revelation 11:18, when the undoing of the reign of the world at the entrance of the reign of the Lamb is hailed as a time of "destroying the destroyers of the earth." Or again, it can be seen in the contrast between the response of the merchants, kings, and seafarers on the one hand, and the multitude in heaven on the other at the downfall of Babylon (Rev. 18:9—19:3). Indeed, there is a sense that this call even in John's day had an ecological element. A large amount of the deforestation in the Greco-Roman world was due to agriculture to feed the imperial center, fuelwood used for urbanization, and shipbuilding for trade (cf. 18:13; 8:9).[53]

Praising the mutilated world, then, for John, is a way of presenting a true alternative to participation in the idolatrous cultic economy of the Roman Empire. The cosmic destruction is not just a cautionary tale of "what *may* happen if unjust oppressors do not repent,"[54] but a way of presenting alternative forms of life for navigating a system that are not captured by the logic and outcomes of that system. Some may see in this reading and proposal a call for sectarian withdrawal. The alternative way that John spells out for his audience is not a way of disengaging from the world, but a way of being missional, of bringing about the repentance of the nations (11:13; 21:24-26; 22:2).[55] As I have sought to spell out here and elsewhere, the ethical vision John proposes is not a rival within the Babylonian system, nor does it derive its identity from being against the system, but finds its identity in being after the Lamb, a true and costly alternative.[56]

Praising our mutilated world then, when taking its cue from John the Seer, is a way of saying the American Way of Life *is* up for negotiation. It is a way of unmasking a destructive system's deceptive

53. See Williams, *Deforesting the Earth*, 73–101. It is also interesting to note that the only human-made element said to be destroyed within the images of cosmic upheaval are ships (Rev. 8:9).

54. Barbara R. Rossing, "For the Healing of the World: Reading Revelation Ecologically," in *From Every People and Nation: The Book of Revelation in Intercultural Perspective*, ed. David Rhoads (Minneapolis: Fortress Press, 2005), 175. Rossing's critique of rapture theology, especially its ecological consciousness, is excellent in *The Rapture Exposed*. I differ with Rossing's point that the plagues are warnings of possible destruction because I see the destruction not as literal ecological disaster but as John's undoing of Roman cultic cosmological discourse. Rather than an ecological consciousness, then, I see Revelation as producing a costly alternative to the Roman imperial order, and indeed every imperial world order.

55. See the discussion in Richard Bauckham, *The Climax of Prophecy: Studies on the Book of Revelation* (London: T&T Clark, 1993), 326–37; cf. Hansen, *Silence and Praise*, 8–9, 67, 89, 109–10, 117–19, 122–27.

56. See the discussion in Hansen, *Silence and Praise*, 163–64.

rhetoric and in doing so proposing a (costly) alternative. There is perhaps no better example of placing the rhetoric of ruin in contradistinction to the rhetoric of progress and economic growth than the work of Wendell Berry in telling the story of destructive strip mining for coal in his native Kentucky. Berry tells of visiting Hardburly, a mining camp in Perry County. Berry writes,

> From the town I drove on up the mine road to the top of the mountain, into the dumbfounding waste that the strip miners have left behind them. I had been there before; three years ago I watched the bulldozers making the first cut into one of the now ruined slopes above the house and garden of yet another ill-fated mountain landowner. But it is impossible to remember it as it is; memory somehow refuses to accommodate the full dimension of the ruin. And standing there in the very presence of it, one feels one's comprehension falling short of the magnitude of its immorality. One is surrounded by death and ugliness and silence as of the end of the world. . . . Standing and looking down on that mangled land, one feels aching in one's bones the sense that it will be in such a place as this—a place of titanic disorder and violence, which the rhetoric of political fantasy has obstructed from official eyesight—that the balance will finally be overcast and the world tilted irrevocably toward its death. . . . Since I left Hardburly I have been unable to escape the sense that I have been to the top of the mountain, and that I have looked over and seen, not the promised land vouchsafed to a chosen people, but a land of violence and sterility prepared and set aside for the damned.[57]

Berry's evocative prose points the way toward a rhetoric that can form a costly alternative to the way of destruction. By unmasking the rhetoric of industrial-technological progress and economic growth as destructiveness he calls for costly non-participation and imagination, costly forms of living otherwise. With Berry's hellish imagery in mind, perhaps all the recent discussion in certain ecclesial circles regarding whether "love wins"[58] and concerns about "erasing hell"[59]

57. Wendell Berry, "The Landscaping of Hell: Strip-Mine Morality in East Kentucky," in *The Long-Legged House* (New York: Harcourt, Brace, and World, 1965), 27–28.

should be construed not as discussions of the afterlife, but as calls for finding truly alternative (and costly) ways of living and inhabiting the earth. In the next two sections I want to provide some brief reflections toward this end.

Seven Letters to Seven Churches: Local Resistance in John's Churches

If a reading of John's rhetoric calls for truly alternative forms of life to those provided by free market ideology, one of those forms of life is embodied in attending to the local.[60] John's cosmic vision of upheaval and new creation begins not with a universal declaration to a universal church, but with seven letters to seven churches. While the seven stand in for the whole it is important to recognize that it is the seven particular churches that make the one. John could provide a cosmic vision of the defeat of the reign of Rome and the emergence of the reign of God and the Lamb, but that victory had to be worked out and participated in on the local level. The victory of

58. Rob Bell, *Love Wins: A Book About Heaven, Hell, and the Fate of Every Person Who Ever Lived* (New York: HarperOne, 2010).
59. Francis Chan, *Erasing Hell: What God Said About Eternity, and the Things We Made Up* (Colorado Springs: David C. Cook, 2011).
60. I am aware that my appraisal of local resistance may not be shared by all the contributors to this volume. Michael Hardt and Antonio Negri propose, perhaps, the most incisive critique of a romanticizing of the local as somehow "*outside* and protected against the global flows of capital and Empire," in their book *Empire* (Cambridge, MA: Harvard University Press, 2001), 45. I acknowledge that the "production of locality" is one of the central features of the global flow of capital and empire, and that this concept of locality is by no means "autonomous or self-determining but actually feed into and support the development of the capitalist imperial machine." Yet in regards to ecosystems, I insist, with people like Wendell Berry, that humans do not stand apart from "nature" or the earth, but are deeply a part of it. In that sense, all one has is the particularity of the place in which one is situated. This is not to fetishize the local as "preexisting" or "natural" or even particularly "authentic" and therefore beyond question, but to recognize that the exigency of one ecosystem may not directly correspond to another. Local practices within a global vision is ideal (the seven churches are addressed in a *circular* letter), but in a system where, as Bob Dylan sings, "the executioner's face is always well hidden" one may hope, on the local level, one might at least recognize the executioner's voice. Bob Dylan, "A Hard Rain's A-Gonna Fall," Ó 1963 by Warner Bros. Inc.; renewed 1991 by Special Rider Music.

the Lamb was not to remain on some abstract universal level without touching the local places of Smyrna, Laodicea, or Philadelphia. Each church had a locality that came with its own set of problems from the beast, and required its own concrete worked-out resistance. If the Lamb was going to have victory over the entire world, it would not happen apart from the Lamb's victory in the specificities of Ephesus, Pergamon, Sardis, and Thyatira.

The specificity of the letters reveals that there were different issues that John's apocalyptic vision was meant to address. Not every church was to resist the beast's influence in quite the same way. For instance, Steven Friesen makes a convincing case that the church in Pergamon was facing more intense "external hostility from mainstream society" than the other churches and that this is the referent of "Satan's throne" in 2:13.[61] The only named martyr in the work is Antipas of Pergamon, signifying that the resistance to the saints is felt more intensely there than elsewhere. For this reason they are commended for holding fast, while exhorted to not follow the teachings of those from within the community who would call for compromise with the idolatrous system (2:14–16).

In Laodicea, on the other hand, the issue wasn't external pressure but internal ineffectiveness in bearing witness to the way of the Lamb (3:15–16). John uses the specificity of Laodicea's faulty water supply, which ran tepid and emetic rather than medicinally hot or pure and cold, to call out the church for not functioning as they should in their local setting.[62] In the letter to Thyatira, Hemer suggests that John's reference to the feet of Christ as "burnished bronze" had something to do with the local patron-god of bronze workers, Apollo Tyrimnaeus, who was represented by a bronze statue in the city (2:18).[63] Perhaps

61. Steven J. Friesen, "Satan's Throne, Imperial Cults, and the Social Setting of Revelation," *JSNT* 27, no. 3 (2005): 365.

62. See the discussion in Colin J. Hemer, *The Letters to the Seven Churches of Asia in their Local Setting*, Biblical Resource Series (Grand Rapids, MI: Eerdmans, 2001), 187–91.

in using this local imagery John meant to redirect their focus and piety from the cult to the way of the Son of God whose call to costly sacrifice calls them away from the compromise taught by "Jezebel." It also could function to reframe their work as artisans; their work is for Christ not for their pagan patron.[64]

All of these localities play out in different ways in the vision, and they all contribute to and participate in the cosmic victory of God and the Lamb over the dragon and the beasts. All of the promised gifts for those who conquer appear as elements of the Lamb's victory and the New Jerusalem (2:7 → 22:2; 2:11 → 21:4, 8; 2:17 → 19:12; 2:26-27 → 19:15; 3:5 → 19:8; 3:12 → 21:9–14; 3:21 → 20:4). This suggests, again, that the cosmic victory of the new heavens and new earth is not contemplated apart from the way local bodies of followers of the Lamb live out the Lamb's way in local and particular places.[65]

In the face of the ecological crisis, a return to the local is not a sectarian flight, not an anti-urban neo-agrarian fantasy[66] (after all,

63. Ibid., 111–16.

64. Cf. ibid., 117. This reframing again suggests not a withdrawal from culture, but an engagement conceived as non-participation.

65. See Paul Minear, "The Cosmology of the Apocalypse," in *Current Issues in New Testament Interpretation: Essays in Honor of Otto F. Piper*, ed. William Klassen and Graydon F. Snyder (New York: Harper, 1962), 34: "The Lamb that was slain had actually defeated the Beast who seemed omnipotent. Wherever the two creations had met, there the Beast had readily deceived his worshipers by appealing to their reliance on the observable continuities of space and time. But there also the Lamb had revealed to his servants the purpose of God in the present *kairos*, the nearness of the heavenly Jerusalem to the streets of Smyrna, the dawning of the light at the moment of great darkness."

66. Ragan Sutterfield rejects the misconception that creation is somehow separate from human society, including the urban environment, arguing that "When we think and talk about creation, we tend to think that there are two distinct things, us and it. We go to a National Park and talk about how wonderful it is to be in creation, but we don't say that in the midst of [a] crowd on a New York City subway," *Farming as a Spiritual Discipline* (Indianapolis: Englewood Review of Books, 2009), Kindle edition, ch. 1, location 76. Related to this is the counterintuitive but myth-dispelling work by William B. Meyer, *The Environmental Advantages of Cities: Countering Commonsense Antiurbanism* (Cambridge, MA: Massachusetts Institute of Technology Press, 2013). Meyer argues that based on density, urban populations actually consume less and damage ecology less than those same populations would in other less urban configurations. While this is true, overall energy consumption and pollution have to

the eschatological goal in the Apocalypse is a city), but a way to attend to the importance of particular places. Understanding the local within the global is a way to resist the flattening out of all space and time by the commodification of the market. Once every place can be rendered as either a commodity to be extracted or a target market for those commodities, every place loses its particular identity—every place becomes no place. There is not one overarching solution to global climate change, but lots of little solutions to healing and attending to particular places, each affected in their own way by global climate change.[67] Sustainable farming practices may be coordinated on a large scale, but they can only be carried out at the local level.[68] It may be that in our hyper-globalized world, where the market determines how times and places function and what value they have, that attending to the rhythms and values of the local might be the only way to live out a true alternative.[69]

The call to localization is costly. One cannot enjoy all the benefits and mobility (upwards and otherwise) that globalized capital has to offer and expect to maintain a commitment to local place and culture.

decrease—while cities may do comparatively less damage, the fact remains that the ways we live and consume still inflicts damage.

67. For instance, local solutions will look different for the multi-island nation of Kiribati, which is facing the probable loss of their entire land area, than they will for farmers in the US Midwest. See Jeffrey Goldberg, "Drowning Kiribati," in *Bloomberg Businessweek*, November 21, 2013, http://www.businessweek.com/articles/2013-11-21/kiribati-climate-change-destroys-pacific-island-nation#p1.

68. United Nations Conference on Trade and Development, *Trade and Environment Review 2013: Wake Up Before it is Too Late: Make Agriculture Truly Sustainable Now for Food Security in a Changing Climate* (United Nations, 2013).

69. See Wendell Berry, "The Way of Ignorance," in *The Way of Ignorance* (Emeryville, CA: Shoemaker and Hoard, 2005), 62–63: "I have no large solution to offer. There is, as maybe we all have noticed, a conspicuous shortage of large-scale corrections for problems that have large-scale causes. Our damages to watersheds and ecosystems will have to be corrected one farm, one forest, one acre at a time. The aftermath of a bombing has to be dealt with one corpse, one wound at a time. And so the first temptation to avoid is the call for some sort of revolution. To imagine that destructive power might be made harmless by gathering enough power to destroy it is of course perfectly futile."

Sittler describes the loss of connection to people, places, and land in the modern, mobile world:

> Most American people have no home that is the symbol of their childhood: their unfolding memory does not gather the felt stuff of common experience about a core-place. That in life which blooms with significance—granted a material thread of continuity—is hopelessly blasted by the mores of our transient existence. A young man is born in Ohio, goes to school in Massachusetts, marries a girl from Virginia. Their first child is born in the Bronx, baptized in a church that knew them not as children and will not see them in old age. The young father goes to work in Manhattan for a corporation chartered in Delaware, writes advertisements for the consumption of people he never sees and for whom he has no immediate responsibility. And at any time he may and probably will be ordered to move in two weeks to Dallas, Texas, there to pick up certain contacts (how expressive a word, that, for the way we moderns meet one another!) that will be useful to him when after two years he is transferred to Seattle, Washington. This brutalizing rootlessness of the life of an increasing number of our citizenry produces a creeping symbolic starvation; the very matrix of small meaningfulness in life which can become the womb of profounder and vaster structures of meaning is rendered anemic, becomes sour and brittle.[70]

In a global economy where capital moves with ease, people have also gained ease of movement, but this to the detriment of our ecosystems, for we cannot live without a place.[71] John's call to work out the costly witness to the way of the Lamb on the local level may be one way to resist the dominance of the economic destruction of our global ecology. This calls for a commitment to place, a costly denial of the seductive benefits of the placeless market, and a reordering of desire.[72]

70. Sittler, *Evocations of Grace*, 22–23.

71. See Michael Rass, "A Climate Reporter Declares His Own 'No Fly Zone,'" *PRI's The World*, November 21, 2013, http://www.pri.org/stories/2013-11-21/climate-reporter-declares-his-own-no-fly-zone.

72. Wendell Berry is perhaps the most insightful writer today on the work of attending to the local; see "The Work of Local Culture," in *What Are People For?* (San Francisco: North Pointe, 1990), 166: "The loss of local culture is, in part, a practical loss and an economic one. For one thing, such a culture contains, and conveys to succeeding generations, the history of the use

The memory of the parish structure of churches may need to be recovered here, but only time will tell if churches in greenhouse gas reliant cultures are willing to "Come out of her" (Rev. 18:4).[73]

The Leaves of the Tree: The Ongoing Work of Healing

My vocation as a Christian interpreter of the book of Revelation necessitates a postscript of hope to a rather grim essay. John's eschatological vision of a renewed heaven and earth funds the resources for resistance throughout the rest of the work. It is only because the victory of the Lamb is assured at the outset that the saints can display their patient endurance of holding out for a better world. It would be beneficial to briefly look more closely at John's vision of the new creation. At first blush, the heavenly city looks to be perfect and without defect. The conspicuous absence of seven elements that mark the marred cosmos give the impression that the New Jerusalem has everything in its right place.[74] As I said earlier in the essay, this

of the place and the knowledge of how the place may be lived in and used. For another, the pattern of reminding implies affection for the place and respect for it, and so, finally, the local culture will carry the knowledge of how the place may be well and lovingly used, and also the implicit command to use it *only* well and lovingly. The only true and effective 'operator's manual for spaceship earth' is not a book that any human will ever write; it is hundreds of thousands of local cultures." Berry, "Local Knowledge in the Age of Information," in *The Way of Ignorance*, 123: "How can the best work be done? Or: How can we give the best possible care to our highly variable economic landscapes, in which no two woodlands, no two farms, and no two fields are exactly alike? If we are to ever get to the right answers to this question, then the people of the periphery will have to cultivate and cherish knowledge of their places and communities, which are always to some extent unique. This will be *placed* knowledge; out of place, it is little better than ignorance; and it is learnable only at home. To speak of it will require a *placed* language, made in reference to local names, conditions, and needs. . . . A refined, discriminating knowledge of localities by the local people is indispensible if we want the most sensitive application of intelligence to local problems, if we want the best work to be done, if we want the world to last. If we give up the old orientation of agriculture to the nature of individual farms and fields, and reorient it to industry, industrial technology, and the global economy, then the result is uniformity, oversimplification, overspecialization, and (inevitably) destruction."

73. See Allen Dwight Callahan, "Babylon Boycott: The Book of Revelation," *Interpretation* 63, no. 1 (2009): 48–54.

vision seems a far cry from the trajectory we are on as we continue to damage the environment.

And yet, upon further examination, there are strange presences of trauma in the heavenly city. At the center of the city exists the slain Lamb, still wounded and bleeding, still bearing the marks of costly counter-witness (21:22-26; 22:1-5). This implies that the blood and the vocation it entails still marks the city and its inhabitants, even after all things have been made new. Similarly, the leaves of the tree of life in the city are said to be "for the healing (θεραπείαν) of the nations" (22:2). Rather than zapping away all infirmity and damage, this image of ongoing therapy and healing in the new creation suggests that the new creation is not a replacement of the damaged world, but its remedy. In the world of the seven churches that resist the beast on the local level, the new creation makes its incursion into the wracked world and the churches live out its reality proleptically, practicing resurrection in the midst of ruin. However, even when the end is reached, and all impurity and death is stripped away, there is still, John suggests, a necessity for a healing presence, a healing process even. The end does not bring an end to the necessity of healing. Perhaps this is all the outworking of the foundational statement of the One on the Throne, "Behold, I am making all things new" (21:5). The present active indicative of ποιῶ might suggest the ongoing work of renewal rather than an instantaneous event. What is promising about these realizations is that what is damaged is not excluded from participation in the new creation.[75] The eschaton does not require perfection worked out ahead of time.

74. Moo, "The Sea That is No More," 149, 165.

75. Perhaps the wounds of creation are deep enough that they require the qualitative time of eternity to heal, not unlike Bilbo and Frodo, as ring bearers, require healing beyond their own world and time which can only be found in the Undying Lands; J.R.R. Tolkien, *The Return of the King* (New York: Ballantine Books, 1965), 328–40.

But all of this remains on the level of hope rather than certainty. From the ruins of the mutilated world springs the possibility of renewal. For John, however, this is no guarantee, but the hope of a gift. The healing of the damaged (destroyed?) earth is something that comes from the outside rather than a teleology that gets worked out within historical processes. For John, it is given to the churches to participate in the renewal, but never to produce it on their own power and initiative. Still, the work must be done because it is given. Even in the face of such alarming trends, the call of following the Lamb into costly non-participation and alternative forms of life is all one has while living in Smyrna, Laodicea, Chicago, or Beijing.[76]

76. As J. R. R. Tolkien has Gandalf say at the Council of Elrond regarding the destructive power of the One Ring and the solution to its threat, "We should seek a final end to this menace, even if we do not hope to make one," quoted in Wood, *The Gospel According to Tolkien*, 44.

13

Why Bother with Biblical Studies?

Richard Horsley

The most important effect of Occupy Wall Street may have been to bring wider recognition to the structural conflict between the 1 percent and the 99 percent. Bolstered by neoliberal ideology, the extremely wealthy have relentlessly consolidated economic power and gained political power with which they intensify their control over resources and the labor of others. With its insistence on profits and the growth of wealth and with ever more sophisticated devices, global capital siphons off more resources and impoverishes ever larger percentages of the people. It also affects the atomization of individuals through control of the media and centralized electronic communication and the disintegration of community and civil society. The disastrous crisis (crash!) of global capitalism in 2007–2008 was the shock and "wake-up" call that led some to become more critical of the system. But it was Occupy that brought discussion and protest into the public square of the extent to which global capitalism determines the lives of people around the world: not just impoverishing increasing numbers of those people, but manipulating powerful governments into bail-outs and weaker governments into cutting desperately needed services to their people, and by despoiling the earth to the tipping point of collapse.

The New World Disorder: The Effects of Global Capitalism

In the Introduction, Bruce Worthington sketches an incisive analysis of global capitalism, its drive to maximize wealth in the socially antagonistic form of exorbitant wealth for the 1 percent, its thriving on crises, and its transnational power to manipulate even the largest states. In anticipation of how a more political hermeneutics or interpretation of the Bible might address our situation, we might note briefly some of the related aspects of the effects of capitalism's development in its various stages, through industrialization, consumerism, and now financialization. Global capitalism needed to privatize the common good, starting with the enclosure of the village commons and extending through the current craze of privatizing public utilities, public works, and public education. In the process of alienating people from their land and alienating their labor, it dissolved community (and often family) in which people's lives had been embedded. Individualism was not only a key aspect of bourgeois ideology, it was also the effect on people who, without supportive community, were forced to rely on selling their labor. Advertising not only channeled people's desires into consumption of unnecessary goods, but acted as an effective solvent of communal and personal values. With the ownership of the mass media, capitalism also transformed culture in two seemingly contradictory ways. It transformed different particular cultures into commodities and thus both expropriated and marketed multiculturalism. And it effectively dissolved and replaced (all) culture(s), including people's history and cultural/religious tradition that had bound them together in community or broader society. We might say that not only are people deprived of any meaningful cognitive orientation, but also that global capital depends and thrives on disorienting people, on creating the episodic virtual reality in which people live. With the evolution of electronic media and devices, the growth of individualism and greater atomization of peoples has become more complete.

Lest we confine the discussion to how global capitalism has become the context for biblical and other interpretation (and for those who strive for political interpretation), we should at least recognize also how global capitalism, like previous empires (often thought of as "political"), displaces or destroys not just people's culture but the people themselves. For example, it relentlessly takes control of land that previously provided the means of livelihood for millions of people, making them into homeless refugees, then has states and their military suppress dissent, repress local resistance, and take larger-scale military action where deemed necessary to maintain social, political, and economic order. For example, NAFTA agribusiness and other transnational corporations made it impossible for over a million independent Mexican small farmers to make a living from their land. When many of them became refugees, the US military intensified violent control over border-crossing, while the flow of refugees and migrants provided very low-cost labor for agribusiness and other enterprises. Meanwhile, the "behind the scenes" US support of Central American states' political repression through killings and jailings further exacerbated (and continues to exacerbate) the flow of refugees.[1]

Biblical Studies

The field of biblical studies was developed on the basis of, and as an expression of Western European bourgeois culture, whose assumptions, orientation, approaches, and interpretive concepts it shares. As part of the (often tacit) agreement between church and state following the French Revolution, theology (including biblical studies) agreed not to interfere in the business of the state and the expanding capitalism that it fostered. With the increasing dominance of individualism in bourgeois culture, religion was not only relegated to the margins of societal life but increasingly reduced to individual belief.[2] Biblical studies functioned and were supported in the training of churches' clergy, who nurtured the faith of believers. Well before the proliferation of disciplines in the twentieth century (such as literature and sociology) in the academic division of labor into discrete "fields," biblical studies had developed its own methods ("criticisms") and theological schemes and conceptual apparatus. As it became further marginalized from political-economic life, it remained in its ghetto, accepting the definition of its subject matter, Scripture or sacred texts, as strictly religious.[3] What came to dominate biblical studies in many ways was the Christian theological scheme of Christian origins: beginning with revelation (in the teaching of Jesus), the spiritual and universal new religion of Christianity superseded the overly political and parochial old religion of Judaism. Much of the agenda of biblical studies, including the Program of the Annual Meeting of the Society of Biblical Literature, is still

1. For instance, the military initiative "Operation Condor", witnessed by key conflicts in Argentina, Chile, and other Central or South American nations.
2. See esp. Talal Asad, *Genealogies of Religion* (Baltimore: Johns Hopkins University Press, 1993), ch. 1, a critique of Clifford Geertz's influential definition and theory of religion.
3. Any suggestion that, for example, Jesus or the Gospels had a political dimension (as in the work of H. S. Reimarus, published anonymously in Gotthold Lessing's *Wolfenbüttel Fragmente*) was quickly refuted or explained away.

conceptually structured in terms of "(early) Judaism" and "(early) Christianity."

In the modern scientific context, the historical critical approach came to prominence, with the "objective" observer establishing the "historical" meaning of the religious text-fragment with all the philological aids available. The text-fragment and its meaning, however, remained narrowly religious and/or confined to an ancient language abstracted into lexicons. In any case, it had nothing to say to the extra-exegetical world. In reaction—or boredom—biblical studies began to diversify and splinter, in three different directions, in the 1980s and 1990s.

Some interpreters imported analysis of rhetoric and modern literature. This led to the recognition of sustained arguments and sustained narratives. But the arguments and narratives remained religious. Literary criticism at least discerned a "world"; but it was confined to the world within the (now longer) text. Others creatively adapted social science. But what they adapted was mainly the conservative structural-functional social science, concerned with social stability of the overall social system consisting of various social strata, an approach that had been abandoned by social scientists by around 1970. Some in the field moved into various kinds of literary criticism, on the one hand, others into social science criticism, on the other hand. But both of these innovations remained within the individualism of capitalist culture and its separation of religion from political-economic life.

A variety of perspectival "criticisms" that are often lumped together as "postmodern" biblical interpretation honed sharp criticism of the pretentious ideology of objectivity and established nuanced (mainly scholarly) racial, ethnic, gender, sexual, geopolitical, or postcolonial identities. These criticisms also remained largely within the confines of the dominant individualism and restriction of biblical studies to religion. As in other fields, they were the further extension of the bourgeois revolution. They limited the contextualization of the interpreters mainly to the social-cultural and eclipsed not only the historical context but also the political-economic concerns of the texts, as Christina Petterson explains. As capitalism generated additional profits from "multiculturalism," it became increasingly evident that the establishment of these diverse identities were "consistent with the goals and expectations of global capital," as Worthington (via Alan Badiou) explains.

The Challenge of These Essays

This collection of essays calls for acknowledging that global capitalism is the determining situation of biblical studies as the field has developed. This important challenge strikes directly at the most basic assumptions, concepts, and approaches of the field--although we may be preaching to a small choir. It may be doubtful that biblical interpretation can thereby become "meaningful" within the context of revolving crises on which global capital thrives. As noted, one of its primary features is the creation of a "universal system of *non*-meaning" (if I may gloss Worthington's formulation). Biblical studies' pursuit of meaning seems like a feature of modern bourgeois culture that global capitalism has displaced and made nearly impossible in its near pervasive effects. What the essays here are seeking is some sort of critical leverage on global capitalism from the memory and unfulfilled possibilities provided by non- or pre-capitalist social formations and political economic struggles, from texts that seem suggestive perhaps precisely because they derive from different historical contexts. Again as Petterson suggests, if both the interpreters and the texts were historicized, then possibly the "otherness" of biblical texts in their contexts could help to challenge the universal categories of capitalism. Biblical texts might serve as part of "a reservoir for thinking in non-capitalist terms." The assumption of Worthington, Petterson, and their associates is that while global capitalism is the determinative context of interpreters in their individualistic focus on religion, it does not determine the biblical texts in their respective contexts, which are different. This recognition, I suspect, is (at least partly) one of the results of some of many frustrations and initiatives in biblical studies during the last fifty years or so.

Earlier Steps toward More Comprehensive Interpretation

Worthington and his colleagues also recognize that well before Occupy raised wider awareness of how global capitalism now determines our lives, at least some interpreters were already engaged in "political exegesis." This is the connection in which they have asked me to respond to the essays. Partly because I wholeheartedly agree with their analysis of our situation and their interpretive agenda, I will, however inadequately, attempt to represent a handful of scholars, born roughly between 1930 and 1950, who recognized both that the capitalism that developed into global capital determines the context in which we work and that "biblical" books and texts are about political economy inseparable from religion, in different historical contexts.[4]

I should explain briefly, however, that this small group of colleagues has been striving, often working independently (though learning from each other's work), to do more than *exegesis*. What we usually mean by that term has connotations of close philological analysis of short text-fragments ("pericopes"). Clergy were trained to do exegesis in biblical studies, focused narrowly on "religion" and the

4. Most notably, in the work of Norman K. Gottwald. See Gottwald, *The Tribes of Yahweh: A Sociology of the Religion of Liberated Israel 1250 to 1050 BCE* (Maryknoll, NY: Orbis Books, 1979).

individual. Having discerned (in the 1960s) that most books of the Bible were and are concerned with all of life, politics, economics, and religion inseparably, and that our own situation was not just an already marginalized church or religion but the burgeoning political-economic-religious conflicts in the country and the world, it seemed to us necessary to strive toward more comprehensive analysis in order to generate more comprehensive interpretation. In the twentieth century, a variety of specialized fields or disciplines were developed in the university. In the last several decades, biblical studies itself splintered into different "criticisms," each with its own interests and perspective and constituency. Accepting the label "political interpretation" might facilitate gaining a place along with the various "criticisms" in the annual meeting program of the Society of Biblical Literature. It seems that specialists in one "criticism" rarely pay any attention to the work in other "criticisms."

Moving toward more comprehensive analysis and interpretation, however, requires drawing upon many of the "criticisms" and analyses into which academia in general, as well as biblical studies in particular, have splintered. In launching the work of the "Paul and Politics Group" in the SBL twenty years ago, some of us purposely invited African American, feminist, and Jewish interpreters, along with those with sociological, political, and archaeological interests and some Roman historians as well, to deal with "Paul and politics" on the interrelated levels of the assemblies, Israel, the Roman Empire, and the politics of interpretation. Understanding the climate crisis requires bringing together botany, chemistry, oceanography, meteorology, history, economics, politics, media studies, computer modeling, and a multifaceted analysis of how global capitalism works. Similarly, although surely less complex than the climate crisis, a more comprehensive understanding of "biblical" texts requires a combination of historical, anthropological, economic, political, and cultural-religious analysis—and a similarly more comprehensive analysis of our own (different) situation. So I am trying to speak for those of us who were earlier striving for more comprehensive interpretation, which is what I see this collection of essays as doing.

How did some interpreters come to recognize both that developing capitalism determined their own situation and that biblical texts are concerned with political-economic matters along with religious matters—and how did they strive for more complex interpretation? I focus on a few of the significant factors, what likely stimulated them, and the resulting adjustment in interpretation.

Recognition of developing capitalism as the context of our interpretation was surely influenced by grandparents' stories of their farms lost to the bankers, or their low-wage jobs to industrial collapse in the Great Depression, and by the United States military overthrow of the elected government of Jacobo Árbenz Guzmán in Guatemala at the behest of the United Fruit Company and the CIA overthrow of the elected government of Mohammad Mosaddegh in Iran to protect the profits of the British and US oil companies, in the early 1950s. Such events also exposed the Cold War ideology as propaganda. It became clear from development programs, manipulations by the IMF and World Bank, and trade treaties such as NAFTA, that capitalism was becoming global.[5] The highly complex analysis and argument of Michael Hardt and Antonio Negri's *Empire* (2000) helped crystallize fuller recognition of how global capitalism, in its complex expansion and intensification, had become the new form of dominating imperial power able to manipulate even the most powerful states (including the US military as its enforcer), yet with internal structural weaknesses, conflicts, and crises.

5. The IMF and World Bank were created at the end of World War II supposedly to help stabilize the world economy, but evidently in the interests of advanced capitalism.

Anti-colonial struggles led to more critical awareness of how European companies and states, followed by the North American, had invaded, enslaved, and controlled peoples, disrupting traditional ways of life and displacing people, using the Bible as handmaid. Indigenous resistance was dismissed by Western social scientists as merely religious ("Nativist," "revitalization," or "millenarian" movements, "religions of the oppressed"), which led some of us to recognize that structural-functional sociology and anthropology tended to obscure more than illuminate political-economic conflict.[6] Only when subject peoples moved into "revolt" were they recognized as political, and militarily suppressed by the Western (Northern) imperial states. We recognized many of these as peasant revolts. This led to reading some of the stories in Joshua and Judges and 1 Samuel and the books of the Maccabees and Josephus's histories with new eyes.[7] These were stories of guerrilla warfare and peasant revolts. It also led eventually, once Roman historians presented a more candid construction of Roman conquests and a more comprehensive and critical recognition of *Romanitas* and the emperor cult, to the recognition that the Roman Empire was the context of Jesus and the Gospels, Paul's mission and letters, and other NT texts. It was possible to begin shifting the focus away from Jesus, Paul, and "early Christianity" versus "early Judaism" to the broader political-economic-religious conflict between the Roman imperial order and resistance movements that began among subject people of Israelite heritage and spread among other subject peoples, and to the texts they produced.[8]

6. Alvin W. Gouldner's *Coming Crisis of Western Sociology* (New York: Basic Books, 1970), a commissioned systematic survey of the field, not only pronounced the abandonment of conservative, dehistoricing structural-functional social science, but revealed the extent to which the whole "liberal arts" education had been shaped into pro-capitalist ideology to counter the threat of communism following 1917 and during the Great Depression.

7. The Maccabean Revolt was also being studied by counter-insurgency experts at the Hoover Institute at Stanford.

So why and in what circumstances do peasants (who comprised the vast majority of people in all traditional agrarian societies) revolt? Historical and anthropological studies opened up how the fundamental forms of peasant/agrarian life tend to be village communes comprised of multigenerational families and that these disintegrate under invasion and/or pressure for taxes, rents, "modernization," and "development."[9] Such studies were suggestive for analysis of many biblical books, from stories of early Israel, opposition to the monarchy, collections of prophecies, and the stories about and teaching of Jesus in the Gospels. With analysis and insights from such studies, it was possible to discern more clearly the differences not only between the modern capitalist system and the ancient tributary system as the broad historical context in which "biblical" texts were produced, but also the differences between the ancient tributary system and (for want of another term) the communal mode of production, under pressure and even disintegrating, evident in the Gospels and in or "underneath" the texts produced by scribal circles who served the rulers.[10]

8. Among the earliest steps were Neil Elliott, *Liberating Paul: The Justice of God and the Politics of the Apostle* (Maryknoll, NY: Orbis Books, 1994); and Richard A. Horsley, ed., *Paul and Empire: Religion and Power in Roman Imperial Society* (Harrisburg, PA: Trinity Press International, 1997), which included abridgements of Paul Zanker, *The Power of Images in the Age of Augustus* (Ann Arbor: University of Michigan Press, 1990) and Simon Price, *Rituals and Power* (Cambridge: Cambridge University Press, 1985).
9. For example: Eric Hobsbawm, *Primitive Rebels* (New York: Norton, 1965); James C. Scott, *The Moral Economy of the Peasant* (New Haven, CT: Yale University Press, 1976). The works of Karl Marx were excluded from "liberal education" in the United States. Thus probably very few of us read *Precapitalist Economic Formations* when it became available in translation by David Cohen (New York: International Publications, 1964), which distinguishes the different formations that Gerhard E. Lenski would fuse in his synthetic model of agrarian societies (*Power and Privilege: A Theory of Social Stratification* [Chapel Hill: University of North Carolina Press, 1969]).
10. The most comprehensive treatment was, again, Norman Gottwald's *Tribes of Yahweh* (1979), whose subtitle "The *Sociology of the Religion of Israel*" probably reflects what Neil Elliott's essay above calls the "constraints" of publishing in biblical studies. For early Palestine and Jesus, see my essays (starting in 1979) published in *Bandits, Prophets, and Messiahs: Popular Movements in the Time of Jesus* (Harrisburg, PA: Trinity Press International, 1985), and *Jesus and the Spiral of Violence: Popular Jewish Resistance in Roman Palestine* (San Francisco: Harper and Row, 1987).

It is difficult to assess the influence of the civil rights movement, the anti-Vietnam War movement, and Latin American liberation theology on biblical interpretation. The civil rights movement, in which some of us were intensively involved, included political-*economic* organizing, extending primarily religious communities into alternative economic communities. It also brought to wider awareness the deep and rich tradition of biblical interpretation of enslaved and impoverished people. In this collection, Willie Baptist and Liz Theoharis insist that the biblical interpretation and leadership of the poor can become an important source of resistance to capitalist domination. The intensive involvement of clergy, laity, and theological students in the anti-war movement as well as the civil rights movement led to greater difficulty for biblical studies in maintaining the separation of religion from political-economic affairs. Latin American liberation theology—more influential in the field of theology, at least in the United States—while dependent on conventional European biblical scholarship, opened up the fuller political-economic-religious concerns of biblical texts along with political-economic analysis.[11]

The documentation and analysis is worked out more fully in *Galilee: History, Politics, People* (Harrisburg, PA: Trinity Press International, 1995).

11. In this connection we might reflect on the political-economic-religious implications of a theme/ term that is central in a range of biblical texts. Clearly interrelated (in the Hebrew) are that YHWH *shaphat* (liberated/ effected justice for) the Israelites from hard labor in Egypt, that leaders of the people's resistance to the kings of fortified cities in Palestine were *shophetim* (liberators), and that the customs, rulings, and measures in which the people applied the Mosaic covenantal commandments to social-economic life were *mishpatim* (customs/rules of justice). In the continuation of the theme in Greek texts, Jesus implements a renewal of covenantal *dikaiosynē* (justice) in the Gospels, and Paul proclaims that the *dikaiosynē* (justice/ liberation) of God has again been revealed and that the assemblies of loyalists are to practice/ embody *dikaiosynē* (justice).

Particular Texts and Issues

The very suggestive essays in this collection find significant analogies, parallels, or other connections between certain Bible texts and the issues protested by Occupy. It is all the more pertinent to examine those texts-in-contexts as comprehensively as possible since many of them also involve some of the same issues in the texts discussed in the other essays. Genesis 41 and 47, for example, focus on the control and expropriation of food production and control of produce, which also entails the impoverishment of the producers and the rulers' taking control of their land. The story of Naboth's vineyard, focused on seizure of land (entailing manipulation and murder), belongs in a longer narrative about rulers taking control of land and food production and impoverishing people. The Gospel of Matthew tells the story of a prophet generating a movement among people who are in debt, like the earlier Israelite peasants whose wealthy creditors were condemned by earlier prophets for manipulating them into debts in order to seize their lands. Since the historical situations and the particular structure and dynamics of political-economic power relations addressed in biblical texts were significantly different from those under global capitalism, however, we should discern those differences (drawing on critical historical investigation and analysis, inside and outside the field) as we inquire how biblical texts and history may be relevant.

The Production of Food

Gregory Fewster criticizes recent ecological hermeneutics as "surfacy" and ineffective because of its failure to recognize that what is driving the climate crisis is global capitalism. This should not be surprising since, as noted above, the field of biblical studies is a development of bourgeois culture and has acquiesced in the reduction of religion to individual belief and its relegation to insignificance for the "*real*" world of politics and the economy. Biblical interpreters paid virtually no attention to the incisive analysis of how the climate crisis is driven by capitalism by Joel Kovel, although some seem to be aware of Naomi Klein's more wide-reaching, if less theoretically profound, recent bestseller that makes the case again.[12] Given the extensive recent attention to food in widely-read books, TV cooking shows, pronouncements from the health-care industry, and new government warnings (all embedded in global capitalism), however, it is suggestive to focus on food as a possible area in which at least some people might be able to gain some leverage on one aspect of global capital's control.

Because food, along with water and air, is what sustains human life, its production (or gathering) is the basis of any economy, from household and village commune to temple-state or city-state to agrarian empire or global capitalism. Agrarian food production by Egyptian and Israelite peasants, a portion of which was expropriated by the rulers as the economic base in ancient Egypt, is simply assumed in the "Joseph story" that Fewster explores. The section (chs. 37–47) about Joseph's interpretation of the Pharaoh's dream becomes the legend by which the Genesis narrative explains how Pharaoh's regime manipulated the peasants into yielding up a greater portion of their crops—a fifth, not just a tenth (Genesis 41; 47)—and ratcheted up its control of the overall production process. Joseph collected a heavy levy of grain during years of plentiful harvests into the regime's storehouses ostensibly as a surplus from which the whole land could be fed during years of bad harvests. When such years came, however, he extorted the peasants' livestock (including draft animals), all their

12. Joel Kovel, *The End of Nature: The End of Capitalism or the End of the World?* (New York: Zed, 2007); Naomi Klein, *This Changes Everything: Capitalism vs. the Climate* (New York: Simon and Schuster, 2014).

other goods, and eventually their land and labor as the price of supplying them some grain. This is how Pharaoh's Egypt became a land of hard labor.

The predatory practices of the Monsanto corporation that Fewster summarizes provide an instructive window onto the manipulative devices by which capitalism has taken ever more extensive control over the production of food. In today's far more complex industrialized and globalized economy, of course, food production is just one among many interrelated industries, all now manipulated from the top by finance capital. Monsanto figured out how to make immense profits by combining genetic engineering, political influence, and gangs of intimidators and lawyers to coerce small and large farmers into buying GMO seed (rather than use their own seed saved over from previous years' crops). Monsanto's use of genetic science and its extortion and intimidation of farmers is reminiscent of Joseph's use of occult knowledge (dream interpretation) and ancient royal-religious forms of extortion. More broadly, what corresponds to Joseph's use of knowledge and coercion are the many devices by which global capitalism manipulates people into debt (credit cards, home equity loans, sub-prime mortgages, developmental loans) in order to extort an ever "growing" share of people's income and resources into centralized control (corporations, banks, the 1 percent).

Land-Grabs and Debt

Both in "biblical" texts and under capitalism, the wealthy and powerful (rulers) take control of peoples' land (or other bases of livelihood) by forcible seizure and by manipulation of people into debt. Far more often than not, biblical texts condemn both practices (although there are egregious examples of land seizure) and the Bible includes many short and sustained narratives and prophetic statements of the people's resistance and outright revolts.

Robert Wafawanaka writes of how African peoples were killed and their land taken by Europeans under flag of the European imperial Bible, specifically its claim that Israel, as the "chosen people," conquered the "promised land" and slaughtered "the inhabitants" (literally "those who sit [in one or another fortified city]," hence better translated as "the rulers"). Wafawanaka finds in the Naboth's vineyard story a narrative that condemns those who gained centralized political-economic power and used it to take away people's land. As he points out, the story has many links with its immediate narrative context, the Elijah-Elisha cycle of stories. The historical situation of the ancient Israelites, of course, is different from that of Africans during and following European colonization. Whether or not the Elijah-Elisha cycle reflects historical events, the Israelites in the narrative were struggling against the consolidation of power by a nascent monarchic state. Africans were colonized and conquered by expanding capitalist companies backed by highly developed states. More recently, under global capitalism, the IMF, the World Bank, and other banks have induced African (and other) countries to take development loans at interest, then when they are unable to repay on schedule, force them to cut back on services to their people.

Partly as a response to the economic crash in 2008, with the ensuing millions of foreclosures on sub-prime mortgages and others left "underwater" from plummeting housing values and similar impoverishing effects everywhere, a few of us set up a session at the Annual SBL Meeting on "Debt and the Generation of Wealth and Poverty." Debt as the means of generating wealth by impoverishing people had long seemed evident both in capitalist society and in "biblical" texts and the situations they addressed. It is impossible to read very far into the prophecies of Amos, Isaiah, or Micah before finding sharp indictments of the powerful for generating their wealth by getting the poor into debt and taking control of their land, the basis of their livelihood.[13] In our own context, the largely "working-class" students in my seminars on "Christmas and Consumer Capitalism" spoke bluntly about how credit card debt, set up by advertising, effectively pulled their families deeper into debt with every successive holiday season.[14] Finance capital, already having a vice-grip on many African countries, devised ever more predatory ways of manipulating people into debt, such as "home equity loans" on top of mortgages and those "sub-prime" mortgages in North America.

In dealing with the situation in the monarchies of Judah and Israel in the eighth century BCE that prophets such as Amos, Micah, and Isaiah were addressing, however, biblical scholars generally write as if economic development just happened, naturally: A region's economic goals "evolve"; economic advances "unfold." Biblical texts, however, tell a different story. During a period of Assyrian imperial withdrawal in the early to mid eighth century, (the regime of) King Uzziah deliberately and systematically expanded cattle raising into the Negev, with fortresses and cisterns, and expanded oil and wine production in the Shephelah and hill country, with "farmers and vinedressers" (2 Chron. 26:9-10). As indicted in many a prophecy,

13. Some of us were dealing with the problem of people in debt and exploitation by their wealthy creditors in prophetic and Gospel texts in our courses and first publications. See especially the articles of Marvin L. Chaney, such as "Bitter Bounty: The Dynamics of Political Economy Critiqued by the Eighth-Century Prophets," in *The Bible and Liberation: Political and Social Hermeneutics*, eds. Norman Gottwald and Richard Horsley, rev. ed. (Maryknoll, NY: Orbis Books, 1993), 250–63. Concise summary treatment for Jesus and the Gospels in Horsley, *Sociology and the Jesus Movement* (New York: Crossroad, 1989), 88–90.

14. When production of commodities for sale supplanted production of goods for their use value, advertising and marketing were built into capitalism, with firms on "Madison Avenue" and then "marketing divisions" of expanding conglomerates. That people might fall into debt by pursuing the American Dream glosses over the production of images and the channeling of desire.

the Judean monarchy (king and officers), like their counterparts in the kingdom of Israel (under Jeroboam II), were also manipulating villagers into debts, on the basis of which they would take control of their land. Archaeological and other evidence suggests that they were then trading the oil and wine produced to the Phoenicians for luxury goods and material for monumental construction and military equipment.[15] Matthew Coomber makes clear that the "Judean rulers" were not only the beneficiaries but also the agents of further economic development in the late eighth century through manipulation of debts. By then, in addition to expropriating produce to trade for luxury items, they had come under pressure for tribute from the Assyrians—or were building up their military fortresses and armaments to rebel against or resist the Assyrians.

Both the Naboth's vineyard story (in the larger Elijah-Elisha narrative) and the prophecies of Micah and Isaiah address a conflict between the people's communally based relation to the land (in which each household had use of a family inheritance) and the monarchy's overriding claims on the people's land and labor (and utter disdain for the communal customs).

Ahab's consolidation of political-economic power went hand in hand with the sacralizing ideology and rituals already developed in the Canaanite/Phoenician city-states. The monarchy's claim to general authority over people and land, including its claim on a portion of the people's produce, was mystified as part of the people's obligation to appease the divinized personified natural-civilizational forces that determined the productivity of the land (Ba'al, Lord Storm, and Asherah, Mother Earth). This sacred monarchic economy came into direct conflict with what looks like the ancient Israelite equivalent of what James C. Scott calls "the moral economy" of peasant village communities (based on historical and anthropological

15. Chaney, "Bitter Bounty."

studies of various societies).[16] Naboth refuses Ahab's demand to yield up his vineyard by appealing to the traditional Israelite understanding of the land as parceled out as (unalienable) family inheritance (not the same as private ownership). But Jezebel, representing the newly established sacred centralizing monarchic economy, uses monarchic power to subvert the customary village self-governance that would otherwise help enforce the village "moral economy." As Wafawanaka comments, the manipulation violates the Mosaic covenantal commandments against coveting and false witness, as well as murder and theft, which had been instituted to protect people's relation to the land, the basis of their livelihood, against the centralization of power by a would-be monarch. The prophet Elijah's pronouncement of judgment against Ahab and Jezebel is an appeal to the God of Israel as the transcendent guarantor of the household and communal relation to the land. The rest of the Elijah-Elisha cycle tells of the people's persistent resistance: Yahweh commissions Elijah to foment revolt (anointing a people's king) and his protégé Elisha finally carries out the anointing of Jehu as God's agent, who leads a bloody revolt.

The prophecies in Isaiah 5:8-10 and Micah 2:1-4 on which Coomber focuses condemn the powerful and wealthy living in the "great" or "beautiful houses" who have the leisure to "lie on their beds," scheming" (the meaning of "covet") how to "steal" people's "houses and fields." As Marvin Chaney explained, the scheme was to get people into debt and, when they could not pay up, to seize their houses (households) and lands. But these houses and fields were understood in the Mosaic covenant and the "moral economy" in

16. Historians and anthropologists of comparative material (for example, medieval English; the "articles" of southwest German peasants in 1524–25; modern southeast Asian peoples) have found that many, perhaps most, peasant peoples have measures by which the villagers attempt to keep each village family/ lineage viable economically. The concept is laid out in James C. Scott, *Moral Economy of the Peasant* (New Haven, CT: Yale University Press, 1976) and applied to the covenantal ideals of Israelite village communities in Horsley, *Covenantal Economics* (Louisville: Westminster John Knox, 2009), chs. 2–3.

which it was rooted as inheritance of the component lineages of the village commune. The wealthy and powerful seizing land for debts was blatant violation of the commandments against coveting (scheming to take control) and stealing (seizure) that were meant to protect the economic viability of households in their village community.[17] With the people no longer able to generate effective collective revolt, as Elijah-Elisha had touched off, individual prophets now appealed to the divine court of justice, whose condemnation they pronounced against the wealthy in their "great houses."

In his magisterial anthropological and historical survey of *Debt: The First Five Thousand Years,* David Graeber (an eager academic participant in Occupy) suggested that a blanket cancellation of debts would go far toward alleviating the global crisis of widespread debt, in imitation of the Jubilee cancellation of debts and return to the ancestral lands in the Holiness Code (Leviticus 25).[18] Critical biblical scholars are suspicious that this was a utopian ideal, no such practice having even been seriously entertained. This ideal was probably a Judean scribal adaptation of an ancient Near Eastern royal ideology. According to some inscriptions, Assyrian kings (emperors) promised cancellation of debts in royal decrees that evidently appealed for popular support against officers of the previous regime or local "bigmen" who had manipulated villagers into debt. Whether or not any such Jubilee was ever implemented historically, there does not appear on the horizon any global agency that could pronounce and

17. The constraints, customary laws and measures against exploitation of the poor in the (early) Israelite village commune also included encouragement of loans at no interest and cancellation of debts and release of debt slaves, as noted above. While not confident that they can distinguish village customs and practices from the form of laws and measures as adapted in the legal collections in the Torah/ Pentateuch (Covenant Code; Deuteronomy; Holiness Code), some scholars nevertheless conclude that just such measures were observed in Israelite village economic life. See Douglas A. Knight, *Law, Power, and Justice in Ancient Israel* (Louisville: Westminster John Knox, 2011).
18. David Graeber, *Debt: The First 5000 Years* (New York: Melville House, 2014), 390–91.

implement a global cancellation of debts--which would lead to the complete collapse of global capitalism.

A more likely scenario for drawing on the stories of the people's resistance to exploitation led by Elijah and Elisha and later prophecies that condemn exploitation and debt mechanisms, along with the communal values and customs in which they are rooted, lies in the active cultivation of collective memory by communities of people, however subordinated and exploited. At the very least these prophecies and the customs they defend offer an almost diametrically different model from global capitalism for the use of the basis of people's livelihood. As global capital thrives from crisis to crisis, the cracks in the system appear ever more evident and the steady resistance seems more evident, at least locally. Some of the pockets of that resistance have previously cultivated and could again cultivate memory of the Israelites' collective resistance to, and the prophets' condemnation of, exploitation by monarchic power, in Africa, in Latin America, and in certain communities in North America, and these communities might well draw on these memories in their own collective action and communal solidarity in resistance. And it is conceivable that others could draw upon the memory of communal-based social-economic forms among indigenous peoples in Africa or Asia in generation of collective local resistance.

A Local-Community Renewal Movement

A shared assumption in these essays is that neoliberal ideology has become a hegemonic discourse in the culture of global capitalism. The ground for neoliberalism was well prepared by the culture of bourgeois capitalism. Individual freedom was central to bourgeois culture and individualism became central in Western culture generally (particularly in North American culture). Biblical studies as a subfield of theology, developed on the basis of this culture, fully shares its individualism. And nowhere has this individualism been more persistent than in recent American liberal interpretation of Jesus.

Although its motivating concerns were often social discontent, the development of sociology and of the social sciences generally in Western Europe and North America served to support and protect individualism. What was called structural-functionalism in particular was developed as a way of avoiding issues of power-relations (who had power over whom), especially with regard to the control of resources. People understood as individuals were found to belong to particular strata in society, social complexity being mainly a matter of "social stratification."[19] Whatever deviance, dissidence, or social conflict might emerge was explained as somehow functional for the overall social system. As social and political conflict became more widespread and intense in the 1960s, however, social scientists began abandoning structural-functionalism.

Ironically, when some biblical scholars began to ask social questions in the 1970s, they borrowed the structural-functional social science that had just been abandoned by social scientists. One of the most influential efforts was Gerd Theissen's "sociology of literature" applied to the early tradition of Jesus' teaching. Focusing on selected individual sayings of Jesus (still standard procedure especially in study of Jesus), taken out of literary context and taken more or less literally, he constructed Jesus and his "first followers" as "wandering charismatics" who had purposely abandoned their homes and families for an itinerant lifestyle as vagabonds. This itinerant radicalism was functional for the larger social system, of course, since it siphoned off discontent into harmless individual asceticism. Despite sharp criticism of Theissen's construction as conservative sociology that explained

19. Americans in particular took pride in the social mobility available to individuals. But there is less mobility today in the United States than in other well-developed countries.

away serious social conflict,[20] the burgeoning enterprise of liberal interpretation of Jesus (e.g., on the part of the Jesus Seminar) seized upon itinerant radicalism. Fusing Jesus' aphorisms with fragments from the ancient Cynic philosophers who reject the dominant Greco-Roman culture, the Seminar reduced Jesus' sayings about "the kingdom of God" to an individual "kingdom." Liberal scholarly interpreters could thus relish some of the pithy "countercultural" aphorisms of Jesus, while avoiding taking too seriously "the hard sayings" of Jesus, which were safely pushed to the margins as having pertained only to the radical itinerants, and the judgmental prophetic sayings, which were dismissed as secondary.

Despite the trenchant criticism of the hypothesis, along with the assumptions and method that led to it, and the critical dismantling of the Cynic parallel, this individualistic liberal interpretation of the individual sayings of Jesus persists and has spilled over into readings of the Gospels. Robert Myles rightly discerns that this romanticization of Jesus' itinerant ministry in Gospel interpretation reinforces the dominant neoliberal ideology that views homelessness today as an individual choice, and not a result of unemployment, housing shortage, and other effects of global capitalism run amok. In an exegesis of a particular pericope (Matt. 4:12-25) that moves mainly from one key Greek word to another, as defined in NT handbooks, Myles argues that in the Gospel of Matthew Jesus' "itinerant ministry" is rather a response to "the intrusion of external political realities."[21] Jesus and his disciples withdrew from their "already marginal social statuses," places that secured their social identity in "normalized" "first

20. John H. Elliott, "Social-Scientific Criticism of the New Testament and its Social World," *Semeia* 35 (1986): 1–33; Horsley, *Sociology and the Jesus Movement*, ch. 2.

21. In countering the anachronistic scholarly projection that Jesus and his fisherman followers had voluntarily left a secure "comfortable middle class" life of artisans and small (fishing) businesses for a life of homelessness, he reaches outside the pericope of Matthew 4:12-25 for K. C. Hanson's illuminating historical reconstruction of the rise of the "fishing industry" under Herod Antipas.

century Palestinian society" (with "full participation in the reigning ideological-political order"), to a "deviant" place further to the margins. Correspondingly, in Jesus' alternative vision of reality, the kingdom of heaven, the "expendable homeless population . . . at the very bottom of first century society," is heralded a central place. While Jesus had enjoined "*entire political systems*" of city-states and "the entire ideological-political constellation" to "repent," his withdrawal earned him fame (only) among masses of others "located on the margins of Palestinian society."

In sharp contrast with the depoliticizing, individualistic interpretation of Jesus as a wandering itinerant, the Gospel of Matthew as a whole story presents him as a prophet engaged in a renewal of Israel in its village communities in opposition to and by the rulers. After the summary statement of his teaching in the local village assemblies (*synagōgai*) throughout Galilee and a summary of his extensive healings (4:23-25), Jesus delivers a renewal of the Mosaic covenant as a charter for community life in the renewal of Israel (chs. 5–7). Jesus and the disciples are engaged in a renewal of the people in their village communities, which were disintegrating from the economic drain of their resources by the rulers, leaving them hungry and in debt (addressed in the Lord's Prayer).[22] The political conflict portrayed in the story is all the more striking when read in the historical contexts of Jesus' mission and of the communities addressed by the Gospel.

Expansion of the Movement among Peoples Subjected to Empire

The book of Acts picks up where the Gospel story, at least that of Luke, leaves off. And Jonathan Bernier's "Occupy Solomon's Portico"

22. On the renewal of covenantal community in Matthew and the mission of Jesus, see further Horsley, *Covenant Economics*, chs. 7, 8, 10.

sets the history narrated in the book of Acts in stark political relief as the site in which an eclectic bunch of "militants" and "commune-ists" both proclaimed and embodied an alternative society in continuing opposition to the very institutional center, symbolic as well as concrete, of an increasingly exploitative political-economy (see the discussion of the temple above). Perhaps the recognition of Peter and the other disciples as "militants" will catch the attention of readers accustomed to misunderstanding the story of the "first Christians" as merely a shift from one religion to another. In the context of the Roman Empire, *pistis/fides* meant (exclusive) *loyalty*, more specifically to a particular figure (usually Caesar). The standard translation as "faith" or "belief in" depoliticizes the narratives in Acts and the references by Paul to people who had become loyal to Jesus Christ. Peter's proclamation in the temple courtyard and Solomon's Portico that the long-anticipated prophet of the renewal of Israel had come in Jesus, who had been killed by the Romans but vindicated by God as the Messiah who would complete the restoration of Israel, was inducing Judean pilgrims from the Diaspora as well as local Judeans to become loyal to the vindicated prophet/messiah. And the high priestly rulers charged with maintaining the Roman imperial order in Judea as the heads of the central political-economic institution of the temple recognized that increasing numbers of people becoming loyal to Jesus was a threat to the fragile social order in Palestine that periodically erupted into overt conflict.

Bernier borrows Badiou's concept of "localization" to draw an analogy between Occupy and the "militants" gathered in Solomon's Portico. While Occupy became a crystallizing moment for already widespread opposition to global capitalism (by the "multitude"),[23]

23. While the beginning of Occupy Wall Street was local in its locale, it was directed against the financial center of global capital and was also located not far from what had been the towers of the World Trade Center.

however, the Jerusalem commune was a key step in what began as a local movement among one people subjected to the empire and then expanded steadily outwards among other subject peoples. While there was resistance to Roman conquest and domination elsewhere by other peoples, the resistance by Galileans and Judeans was sustained, from 63 BCE, with widespread revolt in 4 BCE and 66–70 and 132–35 CE, and many scribal protests and popular movements in between.[24] It is only when we read the extended (historical) narrative of Acts as sequel of the story of Luke, that we begin to get a sense of how it fits into the deeply conflicting politics and political-economy of Roman Palestine and how the local Jesus-movement and its first local expansion, and then wider expansion, began to have implications for the Roman imperial order and the subsequent history of the Roman Empire. The people who produced the historical narrative of Luke-Acts had the sense that they and the leaders of the movement in which they stood (the heroes of the story) were involved in events that constituted the turning point of world history. The Roman Empire was the broader context in which the decisive events were occurring. But history was moving not through (the history of) Rome, as the imperial ideology had it, but through (the history of) Israel, one of the peoples who had been subjugated by Rome, and now more particularly through the movement of fulfillment that had finally reached Rome (by the end of Acts).

The Christ-loyalists gathered in the temple courtyard and Solomon's Portico were indeed a protest movement. But this was a function of their drive to expand the movement generated in Jesus' mission, followed by his vindication by God after his ignominious execution, all in fulfillment of Israelite tradition/ history. The scope of the movement only gradually became international—or since nation

24. Discussion with references in Horsley with Hanson, *Bandits, Prophets, and Messiahs,* and Horsley, *Jesus and the Spiral of Violence*, chs. 3–4.

and nationalism are modern developments, we should say interpeople—as the participants became aware in retrospect (the programmatic "to the ends of the earth," 1:8). But in Luke-Acts, its expansion started in Jerusalem, where the disciples' first act was to reconstitute the symbolic twelve representatives of Israel. After being empowered, at Pentecost, to expand the movement, including speech in diverse languages, the disciples who had come with Jesus to "occupy" the temple at the Passover festival used its courtyard and porticoes as the principal "public space" in which to recruit local and Diaspora Judeans into the movement.

As Galilean country people now ninety miles from their home villages, however, in an expanding community that included Diaspora Judeans much further from their hometowns, they had to arrange for their subsistence. Having come from Israelite village communities with covenantal traditions of cooperation and mutual aid and recent stays in other villages to heal and teach where local families had shared their food, they establish a "commune" in which goods are shared in common. Lest we miss the symbolism as well as the concrete economic alternative, this is a telling juxtaposition: Herod's Temple, one of the great wonders of the Roman imperial world, that took taxes, tithes, and offerings from the villagers, headed by the wealthy priestly families who made high interest loans to poor families in order to take even further control of their land and labor; and in its shadow, somewhere in the alleyways of Jerusalem, the fledgling commune of Galileans and others in which goods were shared in common but who were aggressively recruiting Judeans into their movement of renewal of Israel as an alternative society.

In the continuing narrative, the movement does not become merely religious or a new religion. Recent interpreters have noted that in Acts the movement makes its peace with Roman officials, while repeatedly blaming Diaspora Judeans for their hostility. As the movement expands among other peoples through Asia Minor and into Greece and, by the end of the story, to the very center of the empire in Rome, it does not become any less political or any less an alternative society to the Roman Empire. And as the movement expanded beyond its base, the Jerusalem community, while experiencing repression, did not exhaust itself, but continued as the center of the movement, partly by receiving a "collection for the poor among the saints in Jerusalem" that Paul had contracted to organize (Gal. 2). The interpeople, intercity association of "assemblies" thus also retained an economic dimension while persisting "in, but not of" the Roman imperial order. Despite its confidence about being the vanguard of history, however, the movement that the Acts narrative portrays was still small and insignificant. It had not yet expanded to the point that it would become "successful" as a new religion, that is, co-opted as the official religion of the empire under Constantine.

Ideology and Sustainability

Like Gregory Fewster, Ryan Hansen hopes to find illumination from the Bible on the deeper roots of the current climate crisis, now from the Apocalypse to John. The trouble is that the Apocalypse may lend itself to dangerous interpretations and destructive ethics.[25] However, as critical scholarly interpreters have come to understand texts more critically on their own terms and in their historical political context, some have recognized that "the imagery of cosmic destruction" does

25. This is not just by preachers of the "Christian Right" who regularly use texts from the Apocalypse to calculate and prove that the world is coming to an end by a particular date. "Dangerous" interpretations of texts understood as "apocalyptic" are also perpetuated by biblical scholars themselves. Through most of the twentieth century, mainline biblical/NT scholarship believed that "(early) Judaism" and "(early) Christianity," including Jesus and Paul, were caught up in "apocalypticism," as articulated not only in "apocalyptic" texts but also in the Gospels and Paul's letters, focused supposedly on the imminent end of the world in what Rudolf Bultmann called "cosmic catastrophe." See further my criticism of this view in Horsley, *The Prophet Jesus and the Renewal of Israel* (Grand Rapids, MI: Eerdmans, 2012), chs.1–5.

not "make up the majority of the dramatic visionary action in the Apocalypse." This elaborate vision was addressed to assemblies of Christ-loyalists in the province of Asia in the late first century CE, encouraging them to persist in their resistance to the Roman imperial order despite sharp repression. It may not be appropriate to expect the Apocalypse to speak on its own terms to the current destruction of the environment by the global capitalism, the new form that empire has taken in recent decades. Yet a critical rereading may be suggestive for some readers interested in doing something about the worsening ecological crisis, as Hansen suggests.

The Apocalypse confronts modern interpreters with a visionary text that they do not understand. The vision unfolds in a series of (seven) sevens ("and I saw"). Key is to figure out the relationship of the visionary imagery to the general political-religious situation of the seer and addressees and to historical events (then, not now). The Apocalypse to John draws on a rich Judean scribal tradition of visions in which sages sought to understand violent imperial domination in visions of disruption in the divine/heavenly governance of earthly events (evident particularly in the Book of Watchers and Animal Vision included in *1 Enoch*). Despite appearances that historical events are utterly out of control, as imperial forces attack and even kill those loyal to God (or Christ, the Lamb that was slain), God remains ultimately in control, as the transcendent heavenly emperor on the glorious divine throne. But particularly powerful heavenly forces (the dragon) have rebelled against the divine governance, been cast out of heaven, and are wreaking violence in earthly affairs.

The central fourth step in the unfolding revelation (chs. 12–14) is transparent in its reference to the general historical situation of those addressed in what appear to be the climactic events of history. The Roman Empire (first beast) to which the dragon has given his power is seeking to devour the messiah (child) born from the people of Israel (the woman). And the second beast has devised the elaborate imperial cult in which people are forced to do obeisance in loyalty to the first beast (Rome/Caesar; 13:11–17). But with the enthronement of the Son of Man, the time of judgment has come. Other heavenly and/or earthly events flow into or out of or respond to the imperial domination of the beast(s), with regular reassurance that Christ/the Lamb and the martyrs have been vindicated by God, that is, saved in heaven.

After the seven letters to the seven assemblies, the seer "in the spirit" is called up to the very height of heaven where God is enthroned in splendor across a "sea of glass." The latter is the sea of waters above held back by the firmament of the heaven (as in Gen. 1) across which the Creator is enthroned. The opening of the seals prefigure what is about to be revealed about the current situation of those who are loyally serving God and resisting repressive imperial rule. Conquest, war, famine, and death plague those who are being martyred for the word of God, but God appears in judgment, which is an utterly awesome "earth-shaking" event (symbolized by the sun darkening, etc.), as the sky (firmament of heaven) rolls up so that the kings and magnates and warlords and wealthy have nothing to shelter them from the terrifying divine day of wrath (6:1–16). As Hansen notes, this visionary imagery is rooted in an Israelite prophetic tradition of theophany (see, e.g., God's coming in judgment in Isa. 13). But earthly life is not to be damaged until the servants of God are sealed (7:1–17).

Two passages in the Apocalypse may be particularly suggestive to those who recognize that global capitalism, including the worsening climate crisis, in the context of biblical interpretation today are the visionary description of the "second beast" and the description of "Babylon the Great" and "the kings of the earth."

The "second beast" is a symbol of the Roman emperor cult. The revelation does not offer much about its scale and workings, but it required far more than mere ("sleepy") idolatry, the "worship" of lifeless works of human hands, something that biblical scholars could not discern insofar they were working with a narrow, reductionist view of religion as individual faith. Starting about thirty years ago, Roman historians began to explain just how elaborate were the honors to Caesar and Rome institutionalized in the built environment of temples, shrines, rebuilt city-centers, and annual games/ festivals in nearly every city of the empire.[26] The presence of the emperor came to pervade public space; the built environment surrounded people with images and rituals of the divine power that determined their lives. They built up their wealth, of course, by draining resources and labor from their slaves and other dependents in the cities and on rural estates (all displaced people).

This constantly "in-your-face" imperial presence in the built environment that replaced what had been the "civic center" of ancient "civil" society might well suggest a critical investigation of the much more massive and complex built environment and media environment of images and rituals of global capitalism that has replaced modern civil society. In the cities of the Roman Empire, the images and rituals of Caesar, the divine power that had come to control their life, were constantly and everywhere explicitly "in your face." In global capitalist society the images and rituals are also pervasively "in your face" (and ears, etc.) but serve to veil and mystify the superhuman power that has come to control our life. Despite this contrast, it is conceivable that we might discern in the ubiquitous mystifying images and rituals of capitalism (not just of "marketing") the religious dimension of controlling power that corresponds to

26. See the abridgments of the analyses of Simon Price and Paul Zanker in Horsley, *Paul and Empire*.

emperor cult (the "second beast") in the cities into which Christ-loyalists formed alternative communities.

The description of Babylon the Great and the kings of the earth in Revelation may be suggestive for those trying to get a critical handle on how the climate crisis is driven—and exploited—by global capitalism. Babylon and the kings of the earth live in luxury shipped by merchants who have grown rich from the cargoes of luxury goods: fancy foods, spices, clothing, military equipment, and slaves and other victims of trafficking. The broad analogy seems fairly obvious; only now the scale of consumption and wealth is incomparable. With globalized consumer capitalism, not just the .1 percent or even the 1 percent, but a high percentage of people are living far above a level that is sustainable, as the resources of the earth are being exhausted (double sense intended). And it is no longer just luxury goods and humans being trafficked. Even food is grown by agribusiness on one continent (where people's land was seized) and trucked, then flown, then trucked again by burning oil to other continents, and clothes and computers and cell phones are manufactured in megacorporation-controlled sweatshops in Asia powered by burning coal, and shipped and trucked to other continents by burning oil. It is a messenger from heaven whom the seer hears declare, "Fallen is Babylon the Great." Today it is scientists who have concluded that the earth, the climate, is about to be destroyed—unless of course capitalist growth can be stopped and reversed and people in the "developed" world move drastically toward a sustainable level of consumption.[27]

27. It would thus be no mystery what in the situation of the crisis of the climate under global capitalism would correspond both to refusal to submit to the Caesar cult and to the command to "Come out of her (Babylon/Rome)." The utopian vision of the New Jerusalem coming down earth is problematic, despite some compelling aspects. As in earlier "revelations" amidst violent imperial repression, the people are to be renewed, empowered, and illuminated by the divine presence, with no need of a temple. And there will be healing for the people. But the New

The Violent Exercise of Power and Forming Alternative Communities

As Bruce Worthington points out, popular interpretation of Romans 13:1-7 has been shaped by and even remained within modern Western political thought. The issue has thus been the legitimacy of the modern state (whether rulers have their authority from God, and whether Christians must [therefore] be obedient to them), the text being read as an abstract statement by the great apostle. Worthington also supplies a concise summary of the principal recent interpretations. But we are now living in and under the power of global capitalism. In this new situation, Worthington argues, the state is no longer relevant and the old debates divert attention from the dominance of global capital. The interpretive question is no longer "how does Romans 13 fashion my disposition towards the state?" but "how does Romans 13 fashion my disposition towards the true seat of authority in the world, that of global capital?" With Worthington's indulgence, however, I would suggest a certain reformulation. This includes a critical assessment of the relation between global capitalism and the state (their interrelated power and [lack of] authority) and of Paul's stance toward Roman imperial rule.

It may help the analysis to make a distinction between (political-economic) power and authority. Authority is political power that enjoys legitimacy among the people over or among whom it is exercised. The legitimacy of the state might come from religion, propaganda, ideology, democratic election, some social contract or constitution, some recognized service or benefit to the people, or any combination of these. Too much exercise of arbitrary power or the people's perception that power is being exercised against them

Jerusalem is imagined as full of luxury and as yet another imperial center to which pilgrims will bring the glory and honor of other peoples (also prominent in late prophetic books).

or their interests might erode legitimacy. The capitalist economic system received some legitimacy through "liberal education" of professionals and the "middle class." But it is not clear that *global* capitalism ever had much legitimacy. And it is difficult to see any authority left in global capital after the crash of in 2008 and the "bail-out" of banks whose use of power ruined so many people's lives (they were "too big to fail"). The states that bailed them out against the perceived interest of their people also lost legitimacy.

The state is not irrelevant but instrumental to global capitalism's expansion, consolidation, and exercise of economic power. Global(izing) capitalism's manipulation and control of states in North America became clear in NAFTA and, before that, in the manipulation of loans to smaller states by the IMF and the World Bank. The US military, with assists from NATO, maintains sufficient international stability for investment and extraction and is global capitalism's military enforcer. States also deregulated corporate action, giving them free reign, in keeping with neoliberal ideology, and further enabled global capital's manipulation of the political processes. As Worthington points out, the pretense of democracy is a key component in the ideology of global capitalism. Moreover, the media coverage of the (illusory) democratic political process, which forms part of the "entertainment" offered in the capital-owned and operated media, provides a veil or (smoke)screen that effectively diverts the public's attention from the actions and effects of capital. States, or the parties "in power," still have considerable power (but less and less authority), and they exercise power on behalf of and for the benefit of capital.

Just as the situation in which we interpret is no longer the modern state but global capitalism, to which the state is subordinate, as Worthington insists, so Roman imperial domination, under which Paul was catalyzing communities and communicating with them, was not comparable to the modern state. If anything, while different in form, it was comparable to global capitalism insofar as it exercised power over subject peoples, but had no authority. Classical historians have been far more candid in recent decades about how the Roman warlords at the head of the legions destroyed villages and cities and slaughtered or enslaved people as a way of terrorizing the remaining populations into submission and payment of tribute. They imposed the rulers of their own client states that had no authority. Not just the Gospel of Mark, but Josephus as well, indicates that the high priestly "authorities" and their scribal representatives had no authority among the people. The imperial order was maintained in the cities by the local oligarchy (often politely termed "aristocracy") as clients of the emperor, who had long since consolidated political-economic power.

As for Paul's own stance toward the Roman imperial order with its rulers, he was convinced it stood under God's condemnation and was "passing away," yet still wielding power and not well-disposed to the communities that were loyal to their own alternative "Lord." In his "revelation" he became convinced that the violence and domination of "the rulers of this era/time" had been exposed in the crucifixion of Jesus (Gal. 1:15–16; 1 Cor. 2:6–8). In his vindication by God, Jesus had displaced Caesar as the Lord and Savior who was reigning in heaven; at the imminent "day of the Lord," he would establish God's direct rule on earth, having subjected every (Roman imperial) ruler and power (1 Cor. 15:24–25). Meanwhile, Paul had been commissioned not just to proclaim the "gospel" but to catalyze assemblies of loyalists whose politics were in (that is, derived from) heaven, as they awaited the final step in the fulfillment of history that had begun with the crucifixion (Phil. 3:20–21). This may sound delusional to us. But this is what he said in letter after letter. In ad hoc letters to somewhat different local situations in Philippi, Thessalonike, and Corinth, he urges the communities of Christ-loyalists to avoid attracting attention, even to avoid interaction with outsiders, while also recruiting others into the movement, as they awaited the judgment (destruction) of the elite who boasted in the "Peace and Security" (or Prosperity) of the Roman imperial order (1 Cor. 7:29-31; 1 Thess. 5:1-11). Precisely while he was building an interpeople alternative society based in local communities of peoples subjected to the Roman Empire, he wanted to avoid evoking reaction and repression.

Worthington's answer to the question he poses, "how does Romans 13 fashion my disposition towards the true seat of authority in the world, that of global capital?" is in effect that we recognize the often veiled connection between certain types of political power. We have already come to recognize that global capitalism is doing violence against both people and the planet. It has no authority, but exercises power, both subtly and not at all subtly. As biblical scholars, however, we can both learn from analyses of our own situation under global capital and do our own historical homework. Worthington has sharpened his insights into both our current situation and the text with the help of Louis Althusser and others. This enables him to discern what Paul is saying in the text addressed to the assembly of Christ-loyalists in Rome because he knows the historical context as Neil Elliott and others have laid it out. Knowing that Nero's claim to have sheathed the sword was merely propaganda ("deceitful rhetoric"), he can see in Romans 13:1-7 that Paul is in fact (carefully) criticizing the violence of the Roman Empire. This insight into the text then leads us to further analysis and insight into our own situation. Worthington even draws an analogy. Rome's or the emperor's violence is like the violence of global capital. This enables us to see that global capitalism is the new form of empire (Hardt and Negri), capital the new form of the emperor (and we could add, similarly divine or sacred and beyond or above criticism).

Far from doing nothing but continue to pay his taxes, however, Paul and his co-workers had devoted their lives to catalyzing fledgling local communities in an expanding movement in which they embodied an alternative society. Our situation under global capital is far more complex than the cities of the Roman Empire, including the ways in which our lives are embedded in society dominated by global capital, from our food and clothing to our mortgages, health care, and pensions. That Paul and his co-workers were driven to form communities that were at least semi-independent, "in but not of" the Roman imperial order, is at least suggestive--on which more just below.

Alternative Communities in, but not of, the New Form of Empire

I have waited to comment on Roland Boer's explanation of the feasibility of subsistence economics because several of the biblical texts discussed in other essays are also suggestive for local responses to the domination of global capitalism. He focuses on evidence of subsistence agrarian communes in the ancient southern Levant, the area marginal to the dominant empires, where Israel arose. Exploited as the economic base of agrarian empires, these communes made a comeback when imperial regimes succumbed to the perpetual crises in which they operated. Communities of subsistence economics persisted in various modes of production, with different functions in each. As noted above, James C. Scott found that the village communities he studied in southeast Asia and those examined in historical and anthropological studies of different eras and areas shared some of the same features that Boer finds in subsistence communities in the ancient (and more recent) southern Levant. In addition to biodiversity of crops and herds that reduce risk to food production, village communities have traditional customs and cooperative measures by which they keep component households, and thus the whole community, economically viable (e.g., reallocation of land, gleaning, common pasturage, woodland, streams).

As mentioned above, something similar appears evident in the covenantal commandments and the traditional customs and measures of mutual aid that were adapted in the legal collections of the Pentateuch, mentioned in stories such as Naboth's vineyard, and for the violation of which the prophets indicted the wealthy and powerful. That these had become sufficiently strong as Israelite tradition seems evident in the measures Nehemiah takes (cancellation of debts, release of debt-slaves) to keep the subsistence communities viable as the economic base of the Persian regime. I have argued that the Gospels portray Jesus' mission as focused on the renewal of covenantal community in the villages of Galilee. The sharing of goods in the Jerusalem commune in Acts appears to be derived from the Israelite tradition of subsistence economics and the experience of the disciples on mission in village communities. One might argue that the idea of the collection for the poor among the saints in Jerusalem derives from this tradition and even that Paul and his co-workers' formation of new communities has similar derivation. These were not "churches," but *ekklēsiai*, synonym (in Greek as well as Semitic derivation) of *synagōgai*, that is, the local assemblies of semi-autonomous village communities.

It is important to emphasize, over against individualist biblical studies amidst an individualist culture and individualist neoliberal ideology, that these texts are about communities, their subsistence and/or renewal or establishment, and that collective responsibility and action are involved. Also collective action, including innovative action, is rooted in and draws (often quite creatively) on Israelite cultural tradition (social memory), including customs that had proven their importance in generations of experience while being adapted to circumstances. As Boer points out, local self-governance was usually dominated by the male elders. In crises, however, women or marginal figures such as shepherds or bandits might emerge as leaders of collective action. It may be important to attend to these features of the rich tradition of (alternative) communities and collective action in "biblical" texts and history as suggestive for people seeking ways to resist or carve out some alternative forms of life while under the domination of global capital.

Many, mostly younger, people in my limited circle of acquaintance are becoming engaged collectively and often communally in initiatives aimed at fundamental social transformation. Most of them have little or no acquaintance with biblical texts, much less biblical studies. But I can imagine that there could be some suggestive conversations if biblical studies opened up in the way pioneered by this collection of essays. Let me summarize some of the initiatives of which I am aware, proceeding roughly according to their focus and/or breadth.

Most daring perhaps would be the move to subsistence that Boer explains is feasible. Indeed it would require desiring little, and many of those who are dedicating much or most of their time to political action against global warming and climate change have made exactly that move. Because the anti-culture of global capitalism has dissolved most historical memory of alternative forms of social-economic life, few are even aware of traditional subsistence community life, much less that it is feasible. Biblical studies can contribute by helping revive historical social memory that has previously informed community renewal and collective action.

Many recent initiatives are focused mainly on food production. Short of a group of people moving to establish a subsistence economic community, there are several initiatives of local food production in the United States and Canada. These may not be motivated explicitly as resistance to domination by global capital, but have that effect by reducing the market for agribusiness. Individual families and small groups have moved back into farming, making a modest income supplying some or most of the needs of various numbers of people in nearby towns or small cities. They have also purposely trained others interested in moving back into farming. The flip side of this is local consumers, breaking their dependence on agribusiness, buying food from local farmers, keeping them economically viable. Farmers who produce sustainably also form cooperatives that sell locally and regionally, competing successfully with agribusiness. Individuals and small groups, sometimes cooperatives, have initiated urban gardening, in front or back yards, on vacant lots or other city-land, and even on rooftops. In the Community Supported Agriculture movement (CSA), groups usually in cities buy shares in the annual crop as an advance to the farmer(s) who can thus avoid borrowing from (now mega-) banks. In recent years the organization of farmers' markets has expanded, some including city subsidies to low-income people (often in urban "food deserts") so that they can afford fresh produce. Such farmers' markets also become centers of community socializing that would otherwise not happen. All of these initiatives practice sustainable agriculture and reduce the burning of fossil fuels.

In addition to alternative food production, we see a number of moves toward local community cooperation motivated precisely by opposition to control by global capital. One is community solidarity in keeping fast-food chains or the Wal-Mart's out. Another is to support local banks and to revive or start credit unions in order to take at least some money back from the mega-banks and to harbor local resources. (Some Catholic churches in US cities also served as credit unions for largely immigrant worker members. Covenantal measures of local communal support included liberal lending at no interest to needy neighbors, as in Exod. 22:24–25.) An older initiative, now expanding, is workers forming cooperatives to continue local production where transnational corporations close factories or to generate local production of goods or services. Associations of such cooperatives have persuaded non-profit or civic institutions such as museums or symphony orchestras to contract for goods and services with them rather than with (subsidiaries of) large corporations.

In another form of community-based economic subsistence (and resistance), people with highly diversified training and skills are cooperating to form informal non-monetized networks of barter (a good old village custom), with either a local form of currency or a local form of credit (for hours of services or produce contributed), which strengthens the local community network and keeps scarce resources from being sucked up by transnational chains, megacorporations, agribusiness, and big banks. In the area of Boston where I live, a wider community network of considerable ethnic and educational diversity, led by young families, are beginning to implement a "community transitional economy" that includes urban agriculture, CSA shares, farmers' markets, a network of barter, support of small local businesses, and withdrawal from global capitalist corporations and keeping these out of neighborhoods. Many of the participants are also engaged in collective action, organizing blockage of foreclosures on homes or stopping the continuing generation of energy from fossil fuels, and insisting that the city use whatever leverage it has to reestablish affordable housing. They have not yet figured out how to organize in sufficient numbers to gain minimal leverage on global capital, such as to negotiate with insurance companies or to get the "Commonwealth" to divest pension funds of state employees in fossil fuel companies.

It is difficult to know just how much the fissures and cracks in the global capitalist system are widening, as collective initiatives emerge from the multitude toward a transitional community economy, including some experiments with subsistence economics. There are many movements of renewal of local social-economic community in resistance to different forms of empire in "biblical" texts, movements that were partly motivated and informed by a strong cultural tradition of cooperative communal economics. Through more comprehensive analysis of the texts, biblical interpreters can open access to these movements and the cultural tradition on which they drew, while also discerning the form of political-economic-religious domination that they were resisting.

There are of course also many problematic texts and aspects of texts that have been easily used in support of forms of domination. These can be exposed, criticized, and critically learned from. Perhaps biblical interpreters can bring such resources into current political-economic-religious discussions wider than but including classrooms and churches. One of the principal things that biblical interpreters can bring into the public discourse is greater historical awareness, including historical alternatives to thinking in capitalist terms. Integral to global capitalism's power is its dissolution or suppression of history and its commodification of people's culture, taking its edges off as it is transformed into mere entertainment that sells additional unneeded mass-produced commodities to be consumed for a price. One way to resist the global capitalist culture of ahistorical non-meaning consumed by atomized individuals would be for communities to cultivate and share and draw upon historical traditions, cultivating recognition of unfulfilled historical potential.[28] Individualism is simply impotent. How to do this is yet another problem that biblical interpreters must face, as explored by Neil Elliott's incisive analysis of the interlocking constraints on

28. Taking seriously one of Alain Badiou's titles, *The Rebirth of History: Times of Riots and Uprising* (London: Verso, 2012).

professional academics that are becoming ever tighter in our current situation. Since the technology of communications has passed me by, I must utterly defer to a younger generation adept in how to use the communications technology but also how to counter its atomizing and non-meaning effects. Certainly one matter that seems clear from the atomization that global capitalism has effected is that biblical interpreters, like other academics and intellectuals, must find ways of mutual support and of working cooperatively, even collectively. And that would also enable the attempt toward more comprehensive critical analysis and interpretation of biblical texts, tradition, and history.

Index

Africa, 17, 18, 28, 33, 34, 57, 164, 171-90, 320, 328-33
Ahmad, Aijaz, 93-94
al-Gaddafi, Muammar, 153
Allison, Dale, 233
Althusser, Louis, 77, 104, 257-58, 262, 348
Arab Spring 268-69

Badiou, Alain 13, 19, 270-82
Baldwin, James, 285
Baptist, Willie, 15, 21, 26, 324
Barrett, C.K., 248,
Barton, Stephen C., 220,
Bauckham, Richard, 191n1, 290
Baur, Ferdinand Christian, 273-75
Beck, Glenn, 74
Begg, Christopher, 182
Bellah, Robert N., 73
Bernier, Jonathan, 19, 54, 265, 336-37
Berry, Wendell, 304-310
Bhabha, Homi, 97
Black Power, 56, 75
Bloch, Ernst, 272
Boer, Roland, 16-17, 91, 93-96, 103, 109, 281, 349-51
Boone, Raymond H., 165
Bourguiba, Habib, 151-57
Bretton Woods, 145-46
Brookman, W.R., 170
Brown, Michael, 183
Brown, Robert McAfee, 169
Brueggemann, Walter, 103-104
Bucko, Adam, 168-70
Bush, George H.W., 79, 252, 298

Capitalism, 4-9, 16, 17, 20, 57, 59-62, 65, 70, 73, 103-104, 111, 120, 136, 138, 144-45,149-50, 153, 155, 160, 170, 195, 221, 239, 245-47, 261-64, 269-70, 272-73, 276, 278-79, 283, 313-21, 323-28,

333, 335, 337, 341, 343, 345-49, 351-55; and Post-Colonial Biblical Studies, 86, 91, 95, 98-99; and Debt, 131, 133-35, 329, 333; and Ecology, 289, 294-97, 308-09, 342, 344
Carbon footprint, 192
Carter, T.L., 250
Carter, Warren, 3, 224-25, 236
Chaney, Marvin, 114, 331
Chomsky, Noam, 60, 65
Christianity, 75, 79, 175-77, 192, 195, 272-76, 282, 316-17, 322
Civil Religion, 73-77, 79
Cochran, Clarke, 210
Collins, John, 175
Communism, 4, 19, 111, 270, 275-77
Community of goods, 265, 277-282
Conditionality loans, 147-50, 160
Coomber, Matthew, 17, 131, 330-31
Credit, 5-6, 131, 134, 138, 171, 327, 329, 352-53
Crossley, James, 217
Crutzen, Paul, 299
Cultural-evolutionary theory, 139, 141, 161
Cynics, 220, 335
Davies, W.D., 233, 236
Debt, 5-6, 14, 17, 25, 45, 69, 126-27, 131-61, 163-64, 171-74, 186, 190; and remission, 102
Descartes, Rene, 299
Dimon, Jamie, 135, 160
Dirlik, Arif, 93
Douglass, Frederick, 39
Dube, Musa, 94, 172, 174
Duling, Dennis, 236

Eagleton, Terry, 70, 72, 78
Ecological, 7-8, 18-19, 163, 191-99, 202, 204, 211, 212, 262, 285-87, 293-303, 307, 325, 341
Ecology, 14, 204, 294, 299, 309
Elliott, Neil, 15, 53, 249, 348, 354
Enlightenment, 11, 266
Environmental, 7, 11, 116, 121, 127, 129, 191-92, 196, 203, 212
Evangelical, 14, 71,

Farisani, Elewani, 184
Farming, 16-17, 113, 139-40, 143, 148, 157, 159, 161, 193, 197, 201-202, 204, 212, 308, 352
Fewster, Gregory, 18, 191, 325-27, 340

Food, 16-18, 30, 32, 46, 117-20, 124, 140, 151, 154, 157, 191, 193, 198-212, 325-27, 344, 349, 351-52
Foucault, Michel, 9
Fox, Matthew, 169-70
France, R.T., 220
Friedman, Milton, 4
Friesen, Steven, 72, 80, 290
Fritz, Volkmar, 188

Gadamer, Hans-Georg, 18, 247-48, 251-55
Garner, Eric, 183
Genetic engineering, 197, 327
Giroux, Henri A., 68
Gottwald, Norman, 20, 267
Gray, Freddie, 183

Habel, Norman, 187
Habermas, Jurgen, 18, 247, 255, 257-59, 262
Hamilton, Clive, 196
Hanson, K.C., 238-39
Hardt, Michael, 96, 177, 321, 348
Harrington, Daniel, 238
Harvey, David, 217
Hawkins, R.M., 250
Hedges, Chris, 196, 211
Hemer, Colin, 306,
Herman, Edward S., 60
Hermeneutical, 9, 11, 13, 192, 218, 247-48, 252, 262
Hinkelammert, Franz, 62
Historically effected consciousness, 251-55
Homelessness, 7, 18, 163, 217-22, 230-32, 235, 335
Horrell, David, 196
Horsley, Richard, 20, 24, 313

Ideological, 9-10, 16, 20, 59, 66-72, 77-83, 102, 110, 121, 184, 197, 217-18, 225-26, 230 232, 236, 239, 240, 242, 255-63, 336
Ideology, 11, 18, 70, 73, 77-78, 137, 163-64, 180, 186, 189, 236, 243, 257-64
International Monetary Fund, 7, 146
Itinerancy, 220-21, 227, 240,

Jameson, Fredric, 98, 101, 104, 269-70, 274, 297
Jensen, Hans, 204, 212
Jewett, Robert, 249,
Jobling, David, 93, 98, 102

Kallas, James, 250
Keener, Craig, 235, 238

King Jr., Martin Luther King, 28-29, 34, 37, 166
Kitzberger, Ingrid Rosa, 88, 90
Klein, Naomi, 4-5, 59, 326
Kolbert, Elizabeth, 296
Kovel, Joel, 326
Kyoto Accord, 192

Latifundialization, 141
Lawrence, Louise, 235
Lebacqz, Karen, 188
Lefebvre, Henri, 230
Leif Hansen, Ryan, 19, 285, 340
Levinas, Emmanuel, 255
Liberation Theology, 26, 33-34, 66-67, 74, 106, 324
Locke, John, 246
Lundblad, Barbara, 50
Luz, Ulrich, 222-24

Malchow, Bruce, 186
Martin, Trayvon, 183
Marxist, 62-63, 72, 91, 199, 218, 229, 262, 276
Mbuwayesango, Dora, 176
McKinlay, Judith, 94
Meiksins-Wood, Ellen, 101
Meltzer, Allen, 148
Monsanto, 18, 191, 193, 197-203, 206-07, 210-11, 327
Moo, Douglas, 248
Moorcraft, Paul L., 174
Moore, Stephen, 87, 89-92, 94, 98-100
Moxnes, Halvor, 230-31, 240
Munro, Winsome, 250
Myles, Robert, 18, 217, 335

Nealon, Jeffrey T., 269-70
Negri, Antonio, 96, 177, 276, 321, 348
Neirynck, Frans, 223
Nelson, Richard, 186
Neoliberal, 18, 59, 65, 68, 74, 217-20, 224, 231, 233, 235, 237, 243, 313, 333, 335, 346, 350
New Jerusalem, 287, 307, 310
Ngũgĩ wa Thiong'o, 179

O'Brien, William, 203
O'Hanlon, Rosalind, 92-93
Obama, Barack, 295
Occupy, 19, 53-55, 59, 62, 65, 136, 163-65, 168-70, 177, 247, 263, 268-69, 272-73, 276, 279-80, 282-83, 313-315, 319, 325, 332, 337, 339

Palin, Sarah, 53
Payer, Cheryl, 147
Pennington, Jonathan, 229-30

Petras, James, 7
Petrella, Ivan, 66-67, 83
Petterson, Christina, 16, 85, 318-19
Political, 3-4, 7, 10, 12, 18-20, 25, 39, 42, 44, 45, 48-49, 60, 63-65, 77, 98, 106, 109-111, 132-34, 140, 143, 146-48, 151, 158, 163-64, 166-68, 171, 173, 179-80, 184-87, 189, 193-94, 199, 201, 203-05, 218-19, 221-26, 228-34, 236, 238-40, 242-43, 245-48, 250-58, 260-65, 270, 277-78, 286, 296, 304, 313-22, 324-25, 327, 328, 330, 334-38, 340-41, 345-48, 351, 354
Poor People Campaign, 166
Porter, Eduardo, 295
Postcolonial, 16, 43, 86, 92-98, 100-102, 106, 163-64, 172, 174, 179-80, 203, 317,
Postmodern, 11-13, 16, 95, 97-98, 194, 269, 317
Poverty, 7, 15, 21-22, 24-35, 37, 39-42, 44-47, 50-51, 66, 72-73, 146, 150, 163-64, 166, 170-73, 187, 220, 328
Pringle, Thomas, 174
Production, 5, 8, 16, 18, 71, 95-96, 101-102, 109, 116, 119-21, 123, 141-42, 144, 151, 155-56, 193, 198-200, 202-03, 210-12, 274, 295, 323, 325-27, 329, 349, 351-53
Publishing, 15, 53, 55, 68, 80
Pui-lan, Kwok, 164-66

Rationality, 5, 11, 111, 253-54, 259
Religion, 16, 27, 34-35, 44, 55, 66, 68, 73-74, 77, 79, 82-83, 111, 166, 186, 273, 275, 316-320, 322, 324, 326, 337, 339-340, 343, 345
Rennstich, Joachim, 144
Resistance, 4, 19-20, 44, 46, 79, 82, 98-99, 112, 127, 154, 196, 199, 201, 206, 211, 269, 297, 300, 302, 305-06, 310, 315, 322, 324, 328, 331, 333, 338, 341, 352-54
Rieger, Joerg, 164-66
Robin, Mari-Monique, 200-201
Rohrbaugh, Richard, 90
Roman Empire, 10, 19, 22, 44, 48, 49, 98, 178, 268, 273-74, 281, 303, 320, 322, 337-338, 340-41, 343, 348-49
Ronald, Pamela, 197-199
Ross, Jerome C., 166-67
Rossing, Barbara, 286

Rousseau, J.J., 246

Sahlins, Marshall, 127
Saldarini, Anthony J., 231
Samkange, Stanlake, 179
Schiffrin, Andre, 80
Schüssler Fiorenza, Elisabeth, 67
Scott, James C., 46, 267-68, 274, 330, 349
Scramble for Africa, 172, 176-177
Secular, 71, 73, 120, 270
Segovia, Fernando, 87, 89-90, 92-4, 99
Seow, C.L., 183
Sherwood Rowland, Frank, 299
Sinclair, Upton, 76
Sittler, Joseph, 300-301, 309
Smit, Peter-Ben, 90
Smith, Adam, 104, 110, 123
Soja, Edward, 230
Staley, Jeffrey, 88, 90, 94
Starbucks, 195
Stott, John, 248
Stringfellow, William, 77
Subsistence, 16, 17, 109-10, 112, 116, 118, 120-28, 139-41, 143, 150-54, 158, 339, 349-51, 353-54
Sugirtharajah, R.S., 94, 97

Tahrir Square, 269, 278, 283
Tat-siong Benny Liew, 94
Tea Party, 247
Thain, John, 134
The Poverty Initiative, 15, 27, 34, 40
Theissen, Gerd, 219, 334
Theoharis, Liz, 15, 21, 26, 324
Theology, 22-24, 26, 33-34, 37, 55, 66-67, 71, 74, 106, 121, 165, 230, 316, 324, 333
Therborn, Goran, 63-64
Thompson, E.P., 101
Thurow, Lester, 149
Tolbert, Mary Ann, 177
Tolkien, J.R.R., 300
Tunisia, 17, 150-59, 161

Universal pragmatism, 259
Universality, 4, 102, 261-62, 279

VanZanten Gallagher, Susan, 97
Veltmeyer, Henry, 7
Violence, 188, 221, 225-26, 231-32, 234, 242, 256-257, 259, 263-264, 271, 282, 304, 341, 347-48

Wafawanaka, Robert, 17-18, 163, 328, 331
Wallerstein, Immanuel, 63-64
Wallis, Jim, 31

Walsh, Jerome, 182
War on Poverty, 166
Warrior, Robert Allen, 175, 188
Washbrook, David, 92-93
Wealth, 5, 7, 22-23, 31, 42, 44, 46, 50, 58-59, 64, 77, 82, 98, 103-104, 122, 125, 135, 139, 144, 146, 148-160, 164-165, 170, 176, 239, 313-314, 325, 327-339, 342-344, 350
White, Lynn, 193-194
World Bank, 7, 146-47, 321, 328, 346
Worthington, Bruce, 3, 54, 62, 245, 314, 318-19, 345-46, 348

Zilonka, Paul, 227
Žižek, Slavoj, 8, 105, 195, 221, 225-26, 268, 280, 296
Zuccotti Park, 19, 269